UTOPIA LIMITED

POST-CONTEMPORARY INTERVENTIONS

Series Editors: Stanley Fish and Fredric Jameson

UTOPIA LIMITED

The Sixties and the Emergence of the Postmodern

Marianne DeKoven

DUKE UNIVERSITY PRESS *Durham and London 2004*

© 2004 Duke University Press
All rights reserved
Printed in the United States of America on acid-free paper ∞
Designed by Rebecca Giménez
Typeset in Sabon by Keystone Typesetting, Inc.
Library of Congress Cataloging-in-Publication Data appear
on the last printed page of this book.

for Maggie, Dan, Julien and Annabel

CONTENTS

I have wanted to write about the sixties for twenty years. When I finished my first book in 1982 (on Gertrude Stein), I began working on a book about the sixties. I spent a year reading American radical history. At the end of that year I felt that the long perspective my reading had given me did not, as I had hoped it would, alter my sense that my experience of the sixties was too close to allow me to develop a meaningful intellectual perspective, a thesis, or an argument. I wrote instead an article on John Sayles's novel *Union Dues*,[1] arguing (couched in literary-critical language about the usefulness of realist fiction in articulating explanatory myths) that he got it right: sixties radicalism had been destroyed by its own internal divisions, by the narcissistic machismo of its leader-heroes, and by the ludicrous detachment from reality of the jargon-spouting, anti-democratic Marxist-Leninist faction of SDS that called itself the Progressive Labor Party. I also argued, extrapolating from Sayles, that feminism was the only hope for the survival and perpetuation of the ideals of the movement (these analyses were not new at the time, and have been repeated many times since). After I wrote that essay, I turned my focus back to the earlier twentieth century, to modernism, for the next fifteen years.

During that time I was thinking about postmodernism as well as about modernism. I began to teach courses that incorporated postmodernist theories, and to include postmodern ideas and ideas about postmodernism in my critical work. My view of postmodernism underwent a long evolution, from an initial embrace of it as a continuation of the earlier twentieth-century and sixties avant-gardes, to a rejection of some of its most vocal proponents' simplistic, monolithic, reductive repudiation and often demonization of modernism, to a wary respect for some of its formulations, to my current sense of it as a complex, multivalent, non-self-consistent "cultural dominant."

When the desire to write about the sixties reasserted itself, sometime in the mid-nineties, I found I was motivated primarily by two clusters of ideas; when they came together, I felt I could write a book that, I hoped, would not repeat what had already been said, and that would not be one more testimony, either pro or con, from a former "sixties person." The first cluster of ideas revolved around the question of the emergence of the postmodern. When and how did it happen? What exactly was involved; what was at stake? Although many theorists of postmodernity and postmodernism have discussed this question (and many have not, either not finding it interesting or not considering postmodernism a discretely historical phenomenon), I still had unanswered questions about the relationship between the emergence of the postmodern and mid- to late-twentieth-century cultural and political history.

The second cluster of ideas revolved around the confusing simultaneity, in the immediate and also later aftermath of the sixties, of a sense of continuity and also a contradictory sense of rapid change in relation to the sixties radical and countercultural movements. Elements of the sixties movements were still visible. Some of their meanings and implications seemed to remain more or less as they were, and yet, for the most part, those meanings and implications had changed. I began to look at the texts that had been most important to me in the sixties with these two clusters of ideas in mind. I found in those texts the pivot from the modern to the postmodern that became the subject of this book. That pivot explained to me both how and when the postmodern emerged, and why I had that confusing sense of the sixties as at once still present and also utterly gone.

In retrospect, I can see that I had felt "rewired" in the aftermath of the sixties. I continued to feel and live as if sixties values and commitments persisted in my life and in the world, although "the movement" itself had been defeated and had simultaneously self-destructed. I believed that as a feminist scholar and teacher, I was the same person who had been part of the sixties political and countercultural movements, and in some sense I was (and am). Nonetheless, the social-political-cultural-psychic context for those values and commitments — the lifeworld or structure of feeling within which they now found their home — had changed materially: we had entered postmodernity.[2] Within that contextual shift, the values and commitments themselves, historically contingent as they are, inevitably changed.

I had originally thought I would integrate memoir segments into the textual analyses of this book. However, they came to seem a distraction from rather than an addition to those analyses. I also felt that I had another, very different agenda for those life experiences that could be realized best in fiction rather than in memoir. I wrote a novel based on the connections, disconnections, and attempted reconnections between my sixties and post-sixties lives, *Short Time There*, at the same time I was writing *Utopia Limited*.

Another factor leading to my decision not to include memoir segments in this book was the unremarkable ordinariness, at least in terms of my participation in the various political and countercultural movements, of my sixties experience. I was never a leader of any group; I never really "put my body on the line." I never dropped out, went to jail, or went back to the land. I stayed in college, graduated, and, after a two-year hippie interval (during which I went to school abroad and worked as a receptionist as well as being part of a very temporary, shoestring alternative theater group), went to graduate school. I fervently supported the Civil Rights movement but I was a bit young — I graduated from high school in 1965, at the age of sixteen, so I did not sit in or go south, nor was I present in Washington in the summer of 1963. I did not join SDS until 1967, and I did it then, with reservations about their loudmouth profile, because they were the most visible (as well as audible) and committed antiwar group on campus. Having been a "Young Citizen for Johnson" in high school, I did not even oppose the war until early 1966. I was part of the initial occupation of University Hall at Harvard in 1969 but I left before the bust because I was directing a play and had to go to my own rehearsal; when I tried, I could not get back into the building, but others tried and did get back in. I participated in the Harvard strike of 1969 but went to enough classes, wrote enough papers, and took enough exams to do well; I wrote my senior honors thesis during that time. I went to many marches and demonstrations but not the enormous, famous ones, and was never clubbed over the head, gassed, or arrested. I was in Chicago during the

1968 Democratic Convention but stayed home and watched it on television — my mother begged me not to go to the demonstrations, and I did not go. I was at the disastrous 1969 SDS Convention in Chicago, when Weatherman emerged and SDS splintered fatally; I was part of an "alternative New Left caucus" but we were utterly powerless and irrelevant. I did not become a feminist until 1972, when I joined a consciousness-raising group in graduate school. I considered myself a hippie, or freak as we called ourselves then, and I lived in communal situations, but I was never part of a rural commune, and I never rejected, or freed myself of, bourgeois values and ways of life as extensively as many others in the counterculture at least tried to do, nor did I go as far with drugs as many did. I went to a large (though not famous) outdoor rock festival in England in 1970, but I was not at Monterey, Woodstock, the Isle of Wight, or, fortunately, Altamont. Characteristic of my self-protective belatedness as a sixties person, I went to San Francisco in the summer of 1968, not 1967, and only stayed for a couple of weeks. Nonetheless, my involvement in and commitment to radical politics and the counterculture, like the involvement and commitment of many others with sixties histories similar to mine, were genuine and passionate, and seemed more important than anything else at the time.

Just before I went to graduate school in 1971 I met the man I married in 1975 and am still married to; we live in a house we bought in 1979; we have two children and two dogs; we are both tenured university professors; we are registered Democrats who voted for McGovern (for whom we campaigned), Carter, Mondale, Dukakis, Clinton, and Gore; we live an extremely bourgeois life. Sometime in late 1971 or early 1972, when a demonstration or protest on the Stanford campus (where I was in graduate school) failed to materialize, a friend said to me, "the sixties are over." I thought at the time, surely not; look at all the still massive antiwar protest going on; look at all the radical groups still active, in fact increasingly militant and violent (which frightened and repelled me but did not make me feel that the sixties were over); look at all of us freaks; look at all the communes. But he was right. Both of us, and the rest of our graduate school cohort, some "sixties people" like us and some not, were doing our best to excel in our graduate course work. I was living in a communal house then but it was a disaster — various people were not speaking to one another; one potentially violent man had a gun. I began living mostly in my car; shortly after that I moved in permanently with my future husband. For most of the seventies I was increasingly caught up in the dramas of my personal life: marriage, Ph.D., baby, job. At the same time, I reorganized my life, psyche, politics, expectations, and intellectual commitments around feminism, in the context of which one's personal life *was* political, and which felt to me like, and in many ways was (is), a continuation of the sixties.

It was really late-seventies disco, and the attitudes and styles associated with it, that made me feel in a deep and profound way that the sixties were gone. What could be more utterly different from sixties rock and hippie mores than disco? The music was shallow, banal — bubblegum top 40. The guys with slicked-back pompadours and three-piece suits, and, even more, the women with evening gowns, high heels, stockings, heavy makeup, and stiff, stylized hair, seemed to me to come from some sickening parodic time warp. We lived in Brooklyn, and I commuted to Rutgers University over the Verrazano Bridge (and still do). *Saturday Night Fever* cut very close to the bone. What's more, I loved it — John Travolta was irresistible. The music was eminently danceable. Where was I? What was going on?

Many — perhaps too many — narratives and analyses have been written and filmed about what happened to the sixties and to sixties people: how they lost and/or recovered the sixties, how they and the world changed or did not change, how they did or did not change the world and were or were not changed by it, how they sold out or refused to sell out. I have no desire to write another of those narratives. I took stock in the early eighties, when I thought I was writing a book on the sixties, of my relation to the sixties movements, and found that I had rejected both the deluded, self-destructive violence and narrow factionalism of late-sixties radicalism and also the inward-turned, self-righteous self-involvement and hypocrisy, or the empty-minded vapidness, of what remained of the counterculture, epitomized to me by a hippie friend who scorned the matching set of (very cheap) dishes my husband and I had, without much thought, acquired, insisting instead on having, at significant effort, each dish, mug, and glass different from all the others (she was also living with someone at the time, with, as far as I could see, all the trappings of bourgeois life but without acknowledging them). At the same time, I found it impossible to protect our young child, as I had originally planned to do, from what I still considered the corrupt, evil capitalist culture around us. I had intended that he would never watch television other than PBS, that he would never eat any artificial food, especially with sugar in it, he would never have plastic toys or be tainted by American mass consumer culture in any way. But there I was loving *Saturday Night Fever*, *Star Wars*, and various other popular movies and television shows. Once he had a regular babysitter and went to daycare and preschool, it was all over. GI Joe, some years later, was my last holdout. The sight of a toy Vietnam soldier in my home was unbearable to me. But after my absolute refusal to let him have any GI Joe toys came to seem pointless when all his friends had them and brought them over, I insisted that he at least buy them with his own money, but even that got to be too much trouble.

My husband and I were very involved in advancing our careers and trying to make more money so we could buy a house, take vacations, save for our son's (and possible other child's) college education, and have a life. Getting tenure became an enormous, pressing, and immediate goal. It seemed a means to an end, like all the rest of it, but finally, there we were, this was our life. We were in the culture as it was, part of its ineluctable new postmodern dominant for better and for worse: clichés from *The Big Chill*. I refused the *Big Chill* nostalgia, though, or tried to (not easy, in fact impossible, during the movie, but affirmed immediately afterward in reaction against the movie's cloying, manipulative simplemindedness). I did not feel that the sixties had been snatched away from me, leaving me "helpless, helpless, helpless."[3] I had deliberately rejected what had become dead-end ways of life from the sixties, and knowingly embraced a different, more apparently bourgeois and conventional sort of life, voting for Democrats (almost all of them as the lesser evil, but vote I did); immersed in and enjoying consumer and popular cultures, even though at the same time feeling that the sixties had changed the nature and experience of these ways of life enormously; and also believing that my work as a feminist was the best way to uphold and to project into the future what really mattered most about the sixties: the egalitarian vision of social justice and meaningful life for those heretofore disenfranchised. By the mid-nineties, armed with the intellectual project of cultural studies and with decades of feminist, poststructuralist, and postmodern theory, I was ready to try to understand how these changes had come about, not in the aftermath of the sixties, but in the sixties.

In the immediate wake of September 11, the sixties seemed to me at once to have receded into a more distant past, and also to have become more present than they had been since the height of the culture wars. The antiwar movement that defined so much of what we think of as "the sixties," and the Vietnam War that produced it, seemed to belong to a different world.[4] The violence of much late-sixties radicalism seemed no longer just naive, misguided, and embarrassing, but shameful — an ugly look in the mirror — even for those of us (or at least for me) who did not participate in it but justified it up to a point and felt some of its motivating rage.[5] The utopian passions that inspired the sixties political and countercultural movements, assuming the necessity and inevitability of total social, political, and cultural transformation, seemed to me not just deluded and superseded but also retroactively contaminated by the all-or-nothing fanaticism of contemporary fundamentalisms.

The sense of massive mobilization, however — the camaraderie of strangers — was reminiscent of the sixties: people setting aside the exigencies of their daily lives and giving themselves to one another, in the context of the overwhelming urgency, displacing all other concerns, of the historical moment. The horror of September 11, and one's own deep, unavoidable implication in it, also resonated in a raw, primal way with the daily horror of Vietnam. As in the U.S. sixties, the necessity of changing American "foreign policy" — America's relation to the rest of the world, and therefore, inevitably, to itself — had become unavoidably clear. Generally, the sixties' sense of standing at a historical crossroads, where the fate of the world is at stake and the political, having attained momentous significance, must be reimagined, had also returned in the wake of September 11.

Aside from this preface, all but the final revisions of this book were completed before September 11. Postmodernism/postmodernity as the defining paradigm of the contemporary cultural-political moment — my assumption in this book — may seem to have receded, or even to have lost relevance, in the face of what is now perceived as the challenge to modernity represented by the September 11 attacks. Western culture, and American culture and society in particular, have become, in this view, the prime location and driving force not of postmodernity but of modernity. However, I argue in this book that postmodernity remains in continuity with the key elements of modernity that figure most prominently in our sense of modernity not just as the September 11 target, but also as the most salient paradigm for understanding the current global situation.[6] Postmodernity, as both the "cultural logic of late capitalism" (Fredric Jameson's crucial theorization) and also as the engine of egalitarian populism and of the politics of subjectivity (my central concerns in this project), is in many ways the culmination of the modernity so closely identified with American-dominated globalism. Further, the primarily Jamesonian idea of postmodernity on which many of my arguments in this book are based encompasses the antinomy of a homogenized consumer-capitalist globalism and fragmented local particularisms; of a pervasive market secularism and an equally pervasive, frequently fundamentalist return or rise of spirituality and the religious.[7] Postmodernity, therefore, encompasses both the late-industrial, contemporary evolution of Western-style "modernity" and also the anti-Western, sometimes progressive, sometimes fundamentalist reactions against modernity, which, like all cultural-political phenomena in postmodernity, are at once local and global.

Postmodernity, as many have argued, assumes and incorporates modernity, taking it beyond itself to some of its "logical conclusions." In discussing the culmination of modernity and the inception of postmodernity in the sixties, therefore, I am discussing not the emergence of a social-cultural-psychic-political order that has nothing to do with modernity, or repudiates it in favor of some entirely unrelated order. Rather, I am discussing, specifically, the end of the grandly synthesizing utopian master narratives of modernity, and of their inevitably attendant hierarchies, that marked the emergence of postmodernity. I see postmodernity as a post-utopian, multiply diffuse ("diverse"), egalitarian-populist, thoroughly commercial order, which is precisely *post*-modernity, not nonmodernity. It is defined by modernity's own democratizing individualism; defined, as Jürgen Habermas argues, by modernity's incomplete projects of democracy and justice, coupled, in its decentralized diffusion, with a multiplicity of local, particularist, progressive resistances and antimodern, passionate fundamentalisms. In this book, I do not focus on the antimodern fundamentalisms, or on the massive engine of globalization (or "empire," in Hardt and Negri's analysis — see bibliography, part I) that so concern us now. Rather, I analyze the emergence of the postmodern in the sixties understood as both the end of modernity's totalizing, grandly synthesizing utopianism, which achieved its culmination and final flowering in the radical and countercultural movements of the sixties, and the shift of modernity's democratizing, capitalist, and individualist impulses to a commercial, popular, populist, subjectivist, multiple and diffuse, unevenly critical or resistant, egalitarianism. This emphasis may sound overly optimistic in light of the multiply frightening and dangerous current political situation throughout the world in the Bush II era. Nonetheless, I think the sites of complicit, local, popular, populist postmodern resistance and utopian desire I discuss here remain in place, along with the destructive global capitalist hegemony, and those together continue to constitute the current conjuncture, despite worldwide violence and oppression and the ominously growing power and terrifying agendas of a disastrous U.S. regime.

ACKNOWLEDGMENTS

The two readers for Duke University Press must come first in these ac-knowledgments, along with Christine Froula, who also read the entire manuscript. Their readings were brilliant and penetrating; their sugges-tions for improvement were extremely helpful.

Richard Poirier's editorial suggestions strengthened an earlier version of chapter 2 that appeared in *Raritan* while he was editor in chief. Anne Janowitz and Cora Kaplan made incisive suggestions about a still earlier version of chapter 2 that were useful to me not only in revising that chapter but also in writing the rest of the book. William Galperin made intriguing interventions into, and amplifications of, the argument of chap-ter 3. Ana Douglass introduced me to *Learning from Las Vegas*, which became a central, defining text not just for part 2 but for the entire book. Anthony Alessandrini, a fellow participant in the Center for Critical Anal-ysis of Contemporary Culture at Rutgers University's seminar on "The Aesthetic," 1997–98, asked, in his capacity as respondent to my presenta-tion to the seminar, helpful and pointed questions about the arguments of an earlier version of chapter 8. Linda Zerilli's responses to chapter 14 were thought-provoking and inspiring. Patrick O'Donnell provided useful editorial advice about an earlier version of chapter 15 that appeared in

Modern Fiction Studies when he was its editor. Bruce Robbins encouraged me to stay with the idea of "structure of feeling," crucial to my central arguments, despite its lack of critical cachet.

My fellowship at the Center for Critical Analysis of Contemporary Culture (CCACC) was very important to the development of this book. I particularly want to thank the Director of CCACC, George Levine, and the Associate Director, Carolyn Williams, for their great generosity, both intellectual and personal, and for providing the kind of community in which creative critical thought can flourish unhampered.

Semesters of released time, in 1998 and 2002, provided by Rutgers University's Faculty Sabbatical Leave Program, have been crucial to my ability to write, and to finish writing, this book.

I presented versions of several of this book's chapters at various conferences, colloquia, and lectures, and received useful responses from the audiences at all of them. I particularly want to thank the Institute for Research on Women at Rutgers University (IRW), its Associate Director, Beth Hutchison, its office manager, Marlene Importico, and its former administrative assistant, Arlene Nora. I was Director of IRW from 1995 to 1998, when I began writing this book in earnest. The support I received from the staff of IRW in particular, and from the extraordinary women's community at Rutgers in general, was immeasurably helpful, and their example was inspiring. I would like to thank Bonnie Smith, the Director of IRW from 1998 to 2001, for inviting me to present a version of chapter 14 as an IRW lecture. Her response, along with other responses from that audience of brilliant women scholars, was enlightening; the confidence and support I derive from being part of that community have been invaluable.

Other organizations have provided welcoming venues for presentation of versions of various chapters: the Association for the Psychoanalysis of Culture and Society, particularly Marcia Ian and Carolyn Williams, organizers of its 2001 Conference at Rutgers, for sections of chapters 1 and 11, the Department of English at Rutgers University for chapter 3, the Society for the Study of Narrative Literature for chapter 2, the Northwestern University Women's Studies Lecture Series, convened by Linda Zerilli, for chapter 14, the Feminist Futures Seminar in New York for selected excerpts from the entire book.

I have received unstinting, rock-solid support from the former Chair of the Rutgers University English Department, Cheryl Wall, and from the Associate Dean for the Humanities in the Faculty of Arts and Sciences at Rutgers University, Barry Qualls. When he was Chair of the English Department, Barry granted me a semester of research leave in 1999, without which this book would certainly not be appearing now or any time soon. Barry's advice has also been particularly helpful in the final stages of preparation of the manuscript for publication. I would like to thank Myra Jehlen, Director of the Graduate Program in Literatures in English at Rutgers, for similarly helpful advice about preparation for publication.

I have taught a course called "The Sixties and the Emergence of the Postmodern" to graduate students and undergraduates at Rutgers a number of times while writing this book. My students' often surprising and enlightening responses and insights are woven into the choices and arguments I have made throughout. There have been too many students in these classes for me to be able to thank them all individually here, so I will have to acknowledge them en masse. Thank you all.

My adored family and friends (especially, Linda Bamber, Marjorie Berger, Marcia Ian, Jonathan Strong, and Carolyn Williams) are most crucial to anything I do. My husband, Julien Hennefeld, my children, Maggie and Daniel Hennefeld, my mother, Annabel DeKoven, and my father-in-law, Edmund Hennefeld, make all aspects of my life both possible and extremely rich (our dogs, Zoe and Phoebe, keep us all saner and happier). I would particularly like to thank Julien, on whom I rely utterly in every possible way, for countless hours of patient listening and thoughtful, deeply intelligent, invariably correct advice. My children, Maggie and Daniel, are my life. I have acquired that relation to my children from my mother, who has always supported me in everything I do. I would also like to acknowledge my mother-in-law, Lillian Hennefeld, who died in 2001. She felt no generation gap whatsoever with the radicals and counterculturalists of the sixties—her life was dedicated to precisely the same values and commitments. I miss her greatly.

Ken Wissoker and Christine Dahlin of Duke University Press have been remarkably helpful, insightful, and superbly professional. Ken Wissoker is one of the best editors I have worked with. I would also like to thank Pam Morrison and Lynn Walterick for their fine editorial work.

PART ONE

Modern to Postmodern

INTRODUCTION

Modern, Sixties, Postmodern

The postmodern emerged in what I would call the long sixties, extending from the late fifties to the early seventies; from the heyday of the Beat movement and the rise of popular youth culture to Watergate. The thesis of this book is that certain aspects of sixties radical politics and counter-cultures, visible in representative texts, embodied simultaneously the full, final flowering of the modern and the emergence of the postmodern. My purpose is to understand, by means of textual analysis, the connection of specific aspects of sixties radical and countercultural movements to the rapid emergence of the postmodern from the dominant modernity of the sixties. These characteristic sixties radical movements include the Civil Rights and Black Power movements, the New Left, antiwar and student movements, second-wave feminism, and gay liberation. Countercultural movements include alternative hippie and communal ways of life, consciousness-expanding use of drugs, nontraditional and non-Western-oriented spiritual practices, as well as a range of avant-garde, underground, and popular cultural production and practices, in all the arts.

I do not argue that radicalism and the counterculture *were* postmodern, or were in some direct way the beginning of postmodernism/post-modernity, an argument that has been made for various manifestations of sixties culture and politics.[1] Rather, I argue that these sixties political and cultural movements and their texts were in fact primarily, dominantly, in some ways quintessentially modern; concomitantly with their full realization and extension of their modern projects, they moved into the post-modern. Contradictory modern and postmodern textual elements are interwoven in a seamless mesh, their difference invisible at the time. Frequently, the very aspects of the representative texts I analyze (I will discuss what I mean by "representative texts") that mark them as modern and modernist are the pivots on which the cultural-political shift to the post-modern occurred. I make this pivot clear in my analyses of the texts.

Books on the sixties are generally political or cultural histories, or some mixture of the two. This book is neither, both because I have a different project, and also because I assume that the large number, variety, and ready availability of cultural and political histories of the sixties and its various radical and countercultural movements make it unnecessary to reproduce those histories here. I assume those histories in the textual analyses that follow. (Major cultural and political histories and analyses of the sixties are annotated in part II of the selected bibliography; part I is devoted to key works on postmodern/postmodernity.) Books on the six-ties are also generally, to some degree, polemical. Even when they claim to be dispassionate or even-handed, these books, many of them arising from the debate over the significances of the sixties that formed the core of the culture wars, are often written from an underlying point of view either primarily in sympathy with or in condemnation of all or some of the political and countercultural movements of the sixties (often arguing for some and against others) and their variegated political-cultural after-maths. I participated in those sixties movements, and, though I now have many kinds of distance from that time and from myself as I was then, my primary feeling in relation to the sixties leans much more heavily toward sympathy than disapproval. I am also, however, strongly in sympathy with many of the post-sixties, postmodern progressive, egalitarian, di-verse political and cultural movements and cultural productions that have emerged from the sixties but have also rejected the totalizing, hierarchical master narratives of sixties modern utopianism. Nonetheless, this project is no more a polemic for the postmodern than it is a polemic for the modern or for the sixties. I am neither yearning for a lost, modernist, utopian sixties, destroyed by postmodern global consumer capitalism or identitarian sectarianism, nor arguing for an egalitarian, popular, diverse postmodern as the progressive alternative to a totalizing, hierarchical, Eurocentric sixties modernity. To make such massive, generalized judgments would be, it seems to me, to ignore the nuanced specificity and complexity of sixties and post-sixties politics and culture. Neither praise nor blame of the sixties, the modern, or the postmodern is my purpose here. My purpose is rather to understand what was at stake in the sixties shift from the modern to the postmodern, in order to assess as clearly as possible the progressive potentialities of our present moment. Projects of praise and blame, advocacy and condemnation; narratives of rise and fall or progress and regress, or of emergence from benightedness — from error to redemption — are so numerous and widespread as to seem perhaps obligatory. Nonetheless, or perhaps for that very reason, I find it most meaningful to move beyond praise and blame, advocacy and condemnation, and moralized narratives in order to engage in a dispassionate analysis of the relations among the modern, the sixties, and the postmodern.

The project of dispassionate analysis, however, as we have learned so well from postmodern theory, cannot evade the question of judgment, and that question, marked and situated as it is, and deeply invested as it is with hope and regret, is of course always vexed. While it may sometimes appear, particularly because of the extent to which I enter into the ethos of these sixties texts as I analyze them, that I have an underlying, even concealed position that I articulate only sporadically, or that I am reluctant to articulate — either a belief that all social-political-cultural hope and possibility were lost with the demise of the utopian sixties, or that postmodernism vitiates the greatness of modernism — that is, again, most emphatically not the case. Although I sometimes identify with those utopian elements of the sixties or the modernist conjunctures that postmodernity left behind, I am in fact also strongly invested in the progressive aspects of postmodernity. I believe that some extremely valuable aspirations of sixties utopian modernity were lost, but I also believe that they were in many ways deluded and were also linked to repressive formations. At the same time, I believe that postmodernity, along with its fractured politics and destructive globalizing capitalism, holds out a powerful hope of egalitarian diversity. The egalitarian and diverse thrust of the emergence of the postmodern is a central preoccupation of this book. I do indeed have an underlying commitment, which informs this project, to progressive, egalitarian, diverse cultural and political movements and productions. I do not, however, think either the modern or the postmodern, the sixties or the post-sixties, is the exclusive or even primary location of such progressive movements or cultural work. I think the modern, the sixties, and the postmodern all contain positive as well as negative significances and implications in relation to progressive agendas; specifically, the progressive agendas of egalitarianism and diversity that concern me centrally here. I believe, and this belief is reflected in this book's arguments, that the political and cultural valences of modernity, postmodernity, and the sixties as pivot between the two, are extremely complex and ambiguous. Judgment therefore must be made very carefully, in close, detailed relation to particular cultural productions and political formations. But, again, judgment, though it cannot be avoided or disavowed, and it must be careful and local, is not my concern or purpose here. I have many attachments and disattachments in relation to the issues I raise throughout this book, and these are at times apparent in my analyses, but they are not the point. The point is to say as clearly as I can what I see in these texts, in order to understand how certain characteristic sixties cultural and political formations represented in these texts served as the pivot from the modern to the postmodern, and therefore to understand where we are now and how we got here.

There is no critical consensus about the postmodern, and therefore some basic clarifying remarks are necessary. As David Harvey says, "Is postmodernism a style (in which case we can reasonably trace its precursors back to Dada, Nietzsche, or even, as Kroker and Cook [1986] prefer, to St. Augustine's *Confessions* in the fourth century) or should we view it strictly as a periodizing concept (in which case we debate whether it originated in the 1950s, 1960s, or 1970s)?"[2] Many theorists, critics, and analysts of the postmodern indeed reject periodization altogether, seeing postmodernism as a set of aesthetic practices that has been deployed since the emergence of the late-nineteenth- and early-twentieth-century avant-gardes, or since the eighteenth-century novel (*Tristram Shandy* as well as the sixteenth-century essayist Montaigne are, following Lyotard, often cited), or throughout the history of culture. They find what are generally considered postmodern aesthetic practices in many earlier art forms, including the modernism that postmodernism is generally seen as superseding or defining itself against (particular modernist, late modernist, or earlier twentieth-century avant-garde artists and movements are often cited and analyzed as fully or partly postmodernist, or at least practicing postmodern aesthetics; alternately, as deploying modern and postmodern aesthetic practices simultaneously). For those who hold this point of view, the idea of "postmodernity," which names a cultural-historical period, is irrelevant. Similarly, some critics believe that the simultaneous presence of some apparently modern and postmodern aesthetic practices or other textual elements in earlier works means that these works can just as readily represent the shift from the modern to the postmodern in earlier periods. Such analyses of simultaneous modern and postmodern elements in earlier work, however, depend on dehistoricized abstractions: for example, "the general" or "the universal" as modern and "the particular" or "the specific" as postmodern; or, "unity" as modern and "fragmentation" as postmodern. In this deracinated form, where "general," "universal," and "unity" are separated from their historical meanings within the master narratives of Enlightenment modernity, and "specific," "particular," and "fragmentation" from their historical meanings in the decenterings of postmodernity, these textual elements can be found, separately and together, throughout the history of writing. My argument is not merely that some modern and postmodern characteristics are simultaneously present in sixties texts, but that the cultural-political formations of sixties radicalisms and countercultures, as visible in representative texts, constituted the pivot from modern to postmodern in relation to shifts in the status of the central Enlightenment master narratives, particularly utopianism.

It seems necessary to me, in order to understand the massive social-cultural change that occurred during and in the wake of the sixties, to have a periodizing concept of a shift in structure of feeling. "Postmodernity" and "postmodernism" together constitute the best explanatory assemblage of concepts I have encountered for understanding this shift. The fact that aesthetic, stylistic practices commonly associated with postmodernism can be found — meaningfully, even foundationally deployed — in earlier modes of cultural production, whether or not they are in tandem with modernist stylistic practices, does not, I would argue, undercut this periodization, since stylistic, aesthetic practices need not be, and generally are not, exclusive to the cultural-historical periods of which they are nonetheless characteristic. Arguments have also been made against the periodization of modernism, for example, by showing that characteristic modernist style (as well as intellectual, social, and psychic formations) can be found in works from earlier, and also later, cultural moments; or, again, that postmodernist and/or realist or other earlier aesthetic practices can be found in modernism. Nonetheless, the periodization of modernism from the late-nineteenth to the mid-twentieth century remains a vibrant, meaningful, fruitful analytical tool.

Some theorists, critics, and analysts, who do find the periodization of the postmodern useful and relevant, subscribe, as Harvey indicates, to a different periodization, locating the emergence of the postmodern either earlier in the twentieth century (Hassan), in the wake of World War II (McHale), or later, in the seventies or even the eighties (Hutcheon). But many theorists, critics, and analysts of the postmodern who accept post-modernity as a periodizing concept — Banes, Docherty, Harvey, Huyssen, Jameson, among others — hold that it began either during or in the wake of the sixties, particularly if the period of the sixties is defined, as I define it here, as beginning in the late fifties and ending in the early seventies. It is not my purpose to make the argument for this postmodern periodization yet again — it has been made persuasively by many theorists and critics (see bibliography, part I). My argument rather is that the sixties encompassed the shift in structure of feeling from dominant modernity to dominant postmodernity — postmodernity was emergent in the sixties (I will discuss the particular significance of these terms — "structure of feeling," "dominant" and "emergent" — later in this introduction). Characteristic sixties preoccupations served as the pivot from the modern to the postmodern. In all the diverse sixties texts I discuss in this book, key textual elements associated with sixties political and countercultural formations existed simultaneously within dominant modern and emergent postmodern paradigms, serving as the pivot from modern to postmodern configurations.

What is the difference between saying, as many have said, that the postmodern began in or around the sixties, and arguing, as I do here, that the postmodern was emergent in the sixties? It may sound as if those statements are more or less equivalent. As Linda Hutcheon says, the "critique" she argues is inherent in postmodernism as she defines it "is part of what some see as the unfinished project of the 1960s" (*Politics*, 10). The crucial difference has to do with the status of the modern in the sixties. Those who argue that the postmodern began in the sixties consider the sixties preponderantly or essentially postmodern: literally, the beginning of postmodernism/postmodernity. In this view, the oppositional, radical, innovative aesthetics and politics of the sixties were projected, without significant alteration, directly into postmodernism. My argument is opposed to that position. I argue not that the sixties were postmodern but that they represented the final, full flowering of modernism/modernity, particularly of its utopian master narratives. In the full realization and extension of the popular, egalitarian, subjectivist trajectories of the modern, but in rejection or curtailment of the totalizing, utopian master narratives associated with those trajectories in modernity, the sixties political and countercultural movements were transformed into something in continuity with, but radically different from, those modern master narratives; transformed into the "utopia limited" of the postmodern.

In the interest of making my meanings in this book as clear as possible, and informing the reader about which of the many available definitions of these terms I will deploy throughout this text, I will summarize briefly what I mean by "modernism" and "modernity," "postmodernism" and "postmodernity" ("modern" and "postmodern" can refer either to "modernism" or "modernity," "postmodernism" or "postmodernity"). Before I offer those summaries, I want to situate them, and the act of producing them, within certain critical contexts. First, I do not claim to be producing exhaustive or consensual accounts of these terms here, because there are none. These terms have always been highly contested, though this contest, with postmodernity so well established, is no longer a focus of critical attention. In fact, because postmodernity is so well established as a cultural dominant or structure of feeling that it has become difficult to see, discussing postmodernity and postmodernism can mark one as failing to follow current trends in literary and cultural studies rather than as attempting to understand recent and current cultural history; as being caught in an eighties, rather than a sixties, time warp.

I frequently encounter the assumption that we do not discuss postmodernity or postmodernism any more because those terms and ideas are dated or superseded. Someone I know recently described a project focusing on Fredric Jameson's work as "tired eighties postmodern poststructuralist theory." I think, again, that discussions of postmodernism and postmodernity are considered passé not just because literary and cultural studies have moved on to other concerns, and not because there is no need for further work on these issues or nothing more to say about them. Note for example the recent renaissance in modernist studies, which had seemed moribund. Rather, because postmodernity is now so well established as a cultural dominant, we are so entirely defined by it, it has become invisible. We no longer "see" it as a phenomenon.

There are many divergent, frequently mutually exclusive, theorizations and versions of postmodernism and postmodernity, and of their relations to modernism and modernity. These diverse versions are often ideologically at odds with one another, sometimes so much so that it might seem impossible or irresponsible to synthesize their apparently opposing views, as I do here. Most notably, I synthesize the generally anti-postmodern, anticapitalist analysis by Fredric Jameson of postmodernism as the cultural dominant of a triumphant consumer capitalism with the generally pro-postmodern analysis by Linda Hutcheon of postmodernism as the locus of a progressive cultural politics of the "minoritarian and ex-centric," of "complicitous critique" and "resistance from within." Despite or beyond their ideological differences, I do not see their analyses as incompatible; rather, I see them as complementary. The thoroughly commodified cultural scene of consumer capitalism's pervasive simulacra and flattened affect analyzed so powerfully by Jameson is roughly the same as the consumer-oriented, unevenly hegemonic cultural situation Hutcheon argues is congenial, in its populism, to the "minoritarian" and "ex-centric," to the subaltern Other of modernity who can resist this incomplete hegemony "complicitously," from "within." Their emphases, and attendant polemics, diverge; their analyses converge.[3]

Many of the concepts, theories, and lexicons I draw on to discuss the modern and the postmodern in this book come prefreighted with judgmental connotation: negative (for example, Jameson's "flattening of affect") and positive (for example, Hutcheon's "minoritarian" and "ex-centric"). I am aware of these variable judgmental connotations and do not avoid them; rather, I mix them deliberately, without separating or aligning them into dualisms of pro and con, in order to represent precisely the intermingled complexity of the political-cultural valences of all the modern/sixties/postmodern formations I discuss (for the same reason, I am not interested in separating a progressive from a co-opted, conservative, or hegemonic strain of the postmodern, as some have done). Generally, I prefer to synthesize the useful elements from a diverse range of theorists and analysts of the postmodern in order to produce a comprehensive, syncretic understanding of the postmodern phenomenon rather than to enter into the postmodernism debates that are, moreover, no longer critically urgent, having peaked a decade ago. Again, as with the question of the judgment pro or con of the sixties, I find it no longer relevant or compelling to enter these debates—to advocate any particular theorist or school, or to judge positively or negatively either modernism/modernity or postmodernism/postmodernity (I would also argue that it is at best anachronistic to try to enter a debate that is no longer actively engaged by current critical discourses).

The postmodernism debates produced strong, enduring allegiances with particular theorists or schools for many critics, who assume that these debates, with their substantive and fully elaborated critical history, establish the parameters within which all subsequent discourse on these issues should operate. Some may also believe that it is the responsibility of those who work in this field not only to enter these debates on one side or another but to engage fully with the specificities of the arguments of various key theorists within them. I disagree with this position. I am not, as a result of some unseemly or lax reluctance, fear, or circumspection, avoiding detailed analysis of or engagement with the central articulations of these debates, but rather am trying to move beyond the framework of debate altogether. I am taking the content and elaborations of these debates as read, and engaging in the project of moving into their aftermath without discarding the entire question of the modern and the postmodern, as so many have done, as dated or passé.

I have found it necessary to glean insights from a diverse range and large number of thinkers in order to understand as fully as I can what is at stake in the emergence of postmodernity/postmodernism from modernity/modernism in the sixties. Given, again, that the critical moment of the great modernism/postmodernism debates that flourished in the late seventies, eighties, and early nineties is past, but that we still live utterly in postmodernity, a synthesis of key insights from a wide range of thinkers, which moves beyond the debates that they were directly engaged in, is not only a legitimate but perhaps an urgent project.[4] I have therefore adopted various key insights from a diverse array of major theorists, analysts, and critics — in fact, from the texts in part I of the bibliography — and synthesized them in a way that I hope provides as comprehensive, syncretic, and at the same time specific an understanding of postmodernism and postmodernity as I can glean from these powerful, diverse works, in order to provide the groundwork for my project here: the project of understanding the present in relation to the formative recent past.

It has also seemed unnecessary to me, either in the bibliography or in the book itself, to account for the disagreements among these thinkers; to discuss how their polemical positions are at odds with one another, or how they constitute various schools or sides in those debates that sprang from the controversy between the anti-postmodern Habermas and the pro-postmodern Lyotard and burgeoned into a substantial critical enterprise in the late-twentieth-century American academy. I have taken the same approach to the equally polemical array of books on the sixties on which I have drawn, most of them oriented either toward the debates around the success or failure of the sixties movements, or the issues and arguments engaged by the culture wars. My critical bibliography is therefore neutral in that regard, uninterested in either conflicting versions of, pessimism or optimism about, approval or disapproval of, arguments for or against, postmodernism/postmodernity, or about the successes or failures, strengths or weaknesses, positive or negative impacts, or competing versions of the histories of the sixties movements. This neutrality may seem not only to avoid controversy (again, that is not my purpose; rather, it is to move beyond controversies that no longer seem relevant, pressing, or analytically useful) but to undercut the authors' polemical intent. However, the richness and currency of these texts lies, as I see it, in their relevance beyond their polemics. The pro- or anti-postmodern, pro- or anti-sixties polemics of these texts seem to me their least interesting aspects. These texts actually converge and complement one another theoretically and analytically in useful ways that inform my synthesis of what constitutes postmodernism/postmodernity, and of what is most historically salient in the political and countercultural movements of the sixties.

While the syntheses I have made here of key elements of modernism/modernity and postmodernism/postmodernity are my own, their elements themselves are actually by now standard and familiar.[5] I am defining my terms in a basic way, in order to make clear which of the diverse, often contradictory definitions currently in circulation this book assumes (readers for whom the next few pages contain extremely familiar material: please bear with me; it is important to stake out the particular modern/postmodern terrain this book will occupy). I take "modernity" to refer to the period roughly beginning in the Enlightenment and continuing until the emergence of postmodernity in the course of the sixties. I do not fundamentally disagree with Jürgen Habermas, however, that the "project of modernity"—the movement toward democracy, equality, and justice based on reciprocity of communication—is unfinished rather than defeated or superseded by postmodernity (I also agree with those who see the current moment as still dominated by global technological, economic, cultural, and political modernization). The implication of this position for the periodization of modernity is that we are still within the period of "modernity": it continues to the present moment (this argument is particularly relevant in the wake of September 11). I agree with Habermas's periodization to the same extent that I see postmodernity as in continuity with, as well as transformation of, modernity. As has often been noted, the words "postmodernity" and "postmodernism" reveal and encode the postmodern continuity with modernity. The nature of this continuity is complex and multifaceted; its specific elements will be embedded in the textual analyses and arguments in this study. Certainly the Habermasian project of democracy, equality, and justice is central to it, as is the Jamesonian "cultural dominant" of the "triumph of ("late" or "consumer") capitalism," the massive proliferation of the new technologies, globalism, and globalization in general, and the persistence, despite repudiation of its totalized forms, and although displaced, refunctioned, and "limited," of the utopian impulse of modernity.

In modernity, democracy, equality, and justice are allied with as well as opposed to hegemonic bourgeois capitalist individualism. They are allied through individualist discourses of rights and freedom. They are opposed through hegemonic imperialism, class, racial and ethnic stratification, and male dominance. These hegemonies make the white, bourgeois Western man the Self of modernity, defined in opposition to its oppressed, suppressed Others of race, gender, class, nation, and location (this analysis is so familiar that it does not, I hope, require further explanation). Bourgeois modernity is also at once allied with and opposed to ideals of community: allied with democratic "fraternity" and civil society, opposed to socialist communalism. Socialism and communism are also prime formations of modernity, despite their basis in a repudiation of capitalism and bourgeois hegemony, since they are premised on technological modernity, and on modern utopian totalizing master narratives of equality and justice.[6] Political organization in modernity is dominated by the centralized state, economic organization either by the state (in the name of the proletariat) or by bourgeois capitalism in its various historical phases. These simultaneous but historically shifting alliances and oppositions constitute the dynamic contradictions of modernity.

In modernity's teleological master narrative of Enlightenment, superstition will give way to reason and science, which have the potential to solve all human problems, to produce steady, unidirectional upward progress, and ultimately to lead to utopia. Reason and science become in their turn a force of domination, when allied with modernity's dominant bourgeois capitalist class, in the form of the Cartesian cogito, or the separation of the knowing self from, and mastery of, the objectified, reified Other (these ideas will be developed in detail in the chapter on Marcuse). This Other encompasses body, psyche, nature, and materiality, which are in turn allied with modernity's others of race, gender, class, sexuality, and geographical location.

Modernity's cultures are characterized by metanarratives or master narratives of large synthesis, unity, and coherence. These metanarratives encompass all areas of human social, cultural, political, and psychic life: subjectivity as well as culture and society. They are characterized by truth-quests — believing in the knowability and determinacy of truth — for depth, reality, and knowledge beneath deceptive, illusory surface (or, in Brian McHale's terminology, the epistemological dominant). They emphasize new aesthetic forms consonant with modernity's reinventions of human life. They develop individualist aesthetic ideologies of uniqueness, aura, and authenticity. Their intellectual paradigms are structured by the hierarchical self-other binary, generally resolved in a synthetic third term. Their aesthetics are based on an autonomous, critical high culture and, in late modernity, the advocacy of resistant aesthetic avant-gardes, though this critical autonomy is always in dialectic with bourgeois domination and cooptation, or "affirmative" culture, in Frankfurt School terms.

I see modernism, the dominant aesthetic movement of the first half of the twentieth century (emerging in the late nineteenth century), as the crisis of modernity, where the above attributes of modernity are at once asserted and contradicted, called into question, deeply problematized (the two world wars, with all their attendant ideologies and atrocities, epitomize this contradiction). Reason, science, technology, progress contend against the encroaching abyss of unreason and distintegration, at the levels of the subject, culture and society, psyche and polis. The subject becomes at once the locus and limit as well as the instrument of knowledge. The Other of modernity rises, pushes toward audibility, visibility, subjectivity, and agency, in global movements against imperialism, Eurocentrism, racism, male dominance, and class stratification, shaking and dislodging dominant aesthetic forms as well as politics and ideologies. But this rising-up and shaking are strongly resisted by modernity's hegemonies. The result is a powerful, unevenly ironized tension of domination and subversion, with "the new" at once the aesthetic, cultural, and technological credo, and also profoundly distrusted as chaotic and destructive, this distrust linked to a yearning for imagined orders of the past. The utopian impulse of modernity is powerfully expressed in modernism, with aesthetic form, in ideologies of the ability and responsibility of form to reinvent culture and consciousness entirely, becoming one of its primary locations.

In postmodernity, emerging in the course of the sixties and continuing to the present moment, the contradictions of modernity have sundered into what Fredric Jameson calls, in *The Seeds of Time*, antinomies: contradictions that no longer have the character of mutual reciprocity, hierarchical or otherwise, or potential dynamic resolution in a synthetic third term, but rather have parted into irreconcilable, incommensurable separateness. One set of terms in this structure of antinomy involve global, multinational consumer capitalism, with its flattering and massification of the image, the surface, the simulacrum, the spectacle, the populist/popular, the consumer commodity; its flows of information through cybertechnologies, and its intensifications of global economic inequality, environmental destruction, and reactive fundamentalisms. Located on the other side of the Jamesonian postmodern antinomy are all the forms of egalitarian, local, embodied, marked, partial, complicitous, subjectivist, historicist, resistant, or subversive particularism that characterize contemporary subaltern, minoritarian, postcolonial, identity-focused, ecological, spiritual, grassroots culture and politics (Donna Haraway's work develops these aspects of the postmodern). The democratic project of modernity has become in postmodernity at once (in its historical link with capitalism) a project of capitalist globalization, and also, at the same time, a project of egalitarian populism. In this populism, the separation of "high" and "mass" culture on which modernism depended, both for the maintenance of class structure and for the critical, resistant oppositionality of the aesthetic, has broken down, and various forms of high and popular culture intermingle freely in the dominant aesthetic mode of pastiche or formal freedom/opportunism.[7] Master narratives or metanarratives of modernity are rejected or at least problematized in postmodernity, most notably those of objective science, determinate reason, technological progress, human progress, attainable psychic-social utopia, and such key intellectual metanarratives of modernity, dependent on surface/depth structures, as Marxism and Freudianism.

The binary structure of dominance and oppression, tyranny and revolution, is replaced in postmodernity by an unevenly, porously hegemonic global consumer capitalism in antinomy with, on one side, a wide proliferation of localist fundamentalisms, and, on the other, a diffuse, multidirectional, fluid, oscillating proliferation of power and resistance throughout society and culture (this differentiation is theorized, of course, most notably by Foucault and by Deleuze and Guattari). In this shift, modernity's notions of aesthetic autonomy and the critical function of art are transformed into what Hutcheon calls "complicitous critique" or "resistance from within." There is always complicity: we are always within the given of global, multinational, corporate consumer capitalism. There can be no position outside this culture — outside the existing social, political, psychic configurations; no position from which any agent can enact, either politically or aesthetically, what Marcuse calls the "Great Refusal," despite the compensatory totalizing fantasies provided by the wide proliferation of localist fundamentalisms.[8] There can instead be moves (de Certeau's "tactics") to ironize, distance, critique, subvert, resist those configurations from within them. In egalitarian, popular, subjectivist postmodernity, the general Other of modernity — of race, ethnicity, gender, class, sexuality, geographical location — everywhere emerges into subjectivity, audibility, agency, if not yet, or unevenly, actual political, social, or cultural power (these issues have been of central concern to, and are most fully and importantly articulated by, feminist, critical race, queer, and postcolonial theories of, or in relation to, postmodernism and postmodernity).[9]

Postmodernism, constituting the dominant cultural forms of postmodernity, is not a unified movement or clearly defined set of aesthetic practices — like modernism, but even more so, it is diverse, heterogeneous, full of internal contradiction. (Like modernism, it is characteristic of its historical moment but not inclusive of all cultural production in that moment.) Despite the heterogeneity of postmodernism, I use a working sense here of some common generalizations about it. Where modernism represented fragmentation but yearned, in the light of its master narratives, for unity, wholeness, and synthesis, postmodernism, in its decentering and diffusion of dualistic structures of domination, generally embraces fragmentation. Where modernism was lodged in a powerful desire for utopian transcendence, postmodernism is suspicious of the failed, oppressive utopias of modernity, and represents its persistent utopian desire in displaced, limited, post-utopian or anti-utopian terms. Where modernism embraced meta- or master narratives — universal syntheses premised on hierarchical self-other dualisms — postmodernism rejects them, emphasizing the diffuse, antihierarchical, antidualistic, local, particular, partial, temporary. Contemporary capitalist globalism and religious fundamentalism, powerfully totalizing, universalizing formations, seem to contradict this axis of differentiation of the postmodern from the modern. However, postmodern capitalist globalism is anything but unified, or premised on any idea of the universal: it is diffuse, fractured, diverse, quintessentially mobile and shifting, marked and defined both by its own internal diversifications and fluid post-national proliferations, and also by the local-particular, popular, culturally specific refunctionings of postmodern consumerism. Fundamentalisms, universal in beliefs and projected aims but highly local and particular in actual cultural, political, and ideological manifestations, are not only a reaction against the Western cultural hegemony postmodernity has instantiated, they are also part of the postmodern rejection of the dominance of reason and science.

The totalizing reason, science, technological and human progress of modernity, challenged but still in force in modernism, have been profoundly undercut in postmodernism, supplanted by various manifestations of embodiment, belief, affect, and open-ended, egalitarian, popular, multidirectional change. The sincerity, originality, authenticity, aura, depth, reality, and directionality of modernity, in tension with irony and commodification in modernism, are supplanted in postmodernism by a pervasive irony, a pervasive culture of the commodity, the image, and the simulacrum; by flatness, and by limitless, open-ended free play, themselves in antinomous conjunction with various modes of intensified affect, fundamentalist belief, and free-floating passionate enthusiasm (modes of McHale's "ontological dominant"). The high culture and avant-gardes of modernity and modernism have been not so much supplanted by as absorbed into postmodern egalitarian, popular indifferentiation, "sampling," "versioning" pastiche: the open-ended, free mixing of previously distinct modes of cultural practice and form. This egalitarian mixing also of course includes previously denigrated cultural forms, so that a "literary" novel, for example, can be comprised, in varying degrees and mixtures, of modernist, traditional, subgeneric, and graphic fictional forms, and a "genre" novel can contain many "literary" or "high literary" elements. Popular culture, vehicle and expression of postmodern egalitarianism, is no longer meaningfully distinct either from high culture or from consumer culture. The political has come to be lodged primarily in questions of subjectivity. The subject is no longer clearly demarcated or even putatively or potentially unified, but rather is fluid, permeable, fragmented, shifting, nomadic, nonessential, non-self-identical, hybrid, and no longer clearly separable from any "other." Unity and homogeneity, in general, give way to diversity and heterogeneity, directionality to flux, hybridity, and boundary-crossing. Mappable space, in Jameson's terms, has given way to postmodern hyperspace — mobile, decentered, nomadic, fragmented, border-crossing, shape-shifting, unencompassable by self-consistent, centered reason.

Despite these profound differences between modern and postmodern, the elements of continuity, particularly in the projects of egalitarian democratization, and of what in modernity is generally called individualism, and in postmodernity is called subjectivity, are crucial in the shift from the modern to the postmodern.[10] It is on the pivot of these elements of continuity (democratic egalitarianism and political subjectivity), I argue, that the shift took place in the sixties. My analysis of characteristic sixties texts will focus on these pivotal elements. The texts I have chosen to discuss were all important in the sixties, both in themselves and as representative of a substantial body of similar texts — widely read by radical countercultures, and influential in sixties ideologies, affects, and cultural-political practices.[11] Many of the texts that were most influential and widely read in the sixties have now largely fallen off the intellectual, cultural map, as we will see. The texts I discuss in this book mark very clearly the areas of continuity between sixties modernity and post-sixties postmodernity: the postmodern emergence from sixties radical and countercultural movements of subversive subcultural production and reception, of postcolonialism, of racial and ethnic studies, of cultural studies, of feminist and queer studies, and, in the postmodern fiction by Morrison and Doctorow discussed in chapter 15, of a renaissance in fiction informed by the new social movements of the sixties.

The terms "emergent," "dominant," and "residual," which I use to describe the shift or pivot to the postmodern in the course of the sixties (the modern was dominant in the sixties, then became residual; the postmodern was emergent in the sixties, then became dominant), come from Raymond Williams's groundbreaking, highly influential theories of politics and culture, particularly in *Marxism and Literature*, a book that could have been included in this study.[12] I use "dominant," "emergent," and "residual" as markers of the specific dynamics of historical change, without the implications of progress from capitalism to socialism (or of any teleology) that inhere in Williams's Marxist development of these terms. "Dominant," "emergent," and "residual" can seem too schematically periodizing, and also too teleological, bounded by precisely the phenomena of modernity, particularly the ideology of progress at the heart of the Marxist dialectic, these terms attempt to analyze. Nonetheless, no terms work better to help understand the profound historical shift in culture, politics, and psyche that is my topic here.

I also use Williams's notion of "structure of feeling" as the best designation for the modern and the postmodern social-cultural-political-intellectual-psychic orders I am discussing. "Structure of feeling," like "dominant," "emergent," and "residual," has come under various kinds of critique, from Marxists as well as anti- and non-Marxists. It can seem too vague a concept, and also too monolithic in its implications for historical periodization of extremely complex ideological, psychic, and cultural phenomena. "Structure of feeling" is useful, however, because it suggests the experiential emphasis — the combination of powerful social, political, cultural, ideological structure and the fleeting, inchoate experience of it — of my discussion of the shift from the modern to the postmodern. Williams developed the concept of "structure of feeling" to counteract the pervasive problem in political-cultural analysis of the "separation of the social from the personal" (128). The relation of the social to the personal is at the crux of the shift from modern to postmodern in the sixties: "the personal is political," a slogan of the New Left, became the defining idea of second-wave feminism. Further, in discussing structure of feeling, "we are defining a particular quality of social experience and relationship, historically distinct from other particular qualities, which gives the sense of a generation or of a period" (131). The structure of feeling of the sixties, as reflected in and constructed by its texts, is, again, characterized by the simultaneity of a final flowering of a dominant modernity and the emergence of the key elements of postmodernity.

Williams's work was crucial in the sixties but is no longer generally current, at least in U.S. academia, though it has had a profound influence on contemporary cultural studies. That fading off the intellectual-cultural map, a slipping out of consensual bibliographies of important, influential texts that must be read and studied now, is also the case for most of the texts I discuss in this book.[13] These are precisely the texts that, constituted by the dominant modern/emergent postmodern structure characteristic of the sixties, have been eclipsed and superseded by the shift in structure of feeling they reveal. It is the dominance of their modern paradigms, in such close proximity to incipient postmodern paradigms, that make them seem dated: they would have to be either more postmodern or more exclusively modern, and therefore of a different time, to remain current. Therefore, their near-disappearance off the intellectual-cultural map is part of what makes them interesting to me. The few works I discuss that remain widely read — Roland Barthes's *Mythologies*, Hunter Thompson's *Fear and Loathing in Las Vegas*, William Burroughs's *Naked Lunch*, and James Baldwin's *The Fire Next Time* — have survived into postmodernity because of their embeddedness in popular culture, cultural studies, drug and rock subcultures, and, for *The Fire Next Time*, the great literary tradition established by post-sixties African American studies.

When I chose texts to focus on, I was thinking about addressing the issues that seem to me most important, about representing the major sixties movements, and about including texts that were profoundly influential at the time but are no longer so. I was not thinking particularly about genre, except in choosing *Paradise Now*, which represents the coincidence of a genre (drama) and a movement (sixties experimental theater), and in discussing the crucial role of the genre of the new journalism (to the extent that it is a genre) in the emergence of the postmodern in the sixties. Nor was I thinking about the distinct or indistinct roles or locations of the literary and the nonliterary in the sixties; surprising, perhaps, for someone who has made an effort to think about these questions otherwise. The result is a book which is more or less evenly divided between literary and nonliterary texts. I focus on the political as well as the cultural movements of the sixties. The former are best represented, of course, by nonliterary texts, and the latter include theory as well as practice — intellectual texts as well as cultural productions. Further, I discuss only texts — I do not address in any detail the enormous, compelling range and variety of non-written cultural production that characterized the sixties. I do not, in any way, think nonliterary texts were more important in the sixties than literary writing and the other modes of cultural production. Nothing was more important in the sixties than rock music, for example, or avant-garde film and animation, underground comics, the underground, alternative press, psychedelic graphics, pop art, experimental theater (including guerrilla and street theater, and the happening). Poetry, fiction, and drama were vital, pervasive, and at the heart of the cultural work of the sixties. However, the question of the shift of structure of feeling from modern to postmodern seemed to me best investigated, at least by me, in texts — including literary texts — that treat culture and politics directly, through either theory or representation.

Most of the texts I focus on here were written by white men. This is again surprising for someone committed to sustained attention to multiple structure of difference and exclusion. I address issues of race, gender, sexuality, class, and geographical location directly in the chapters called "Endnotes," and of course in the chapters on Vietnam, on Civil Rights, Black Power, and postcolonial third world liberation movements, on second-wave feminism, and on postmodern, post-sixties, post-utopian fiction. These issues are central to my assumptions about the nature of cultural and political change in the sixties. But in many of the extended textual analyses, these issues appear only sporadically. My choice of texts, again, was motivated primarily by my understanding of where best to look for the most visible evidence of the dynamic of shift in structure of feeling in the sixties The political and cultural movements of the sixties, despite the profound changes underway, except in movements of people of color and in the women's and gay liberation movements, were dominated by straight white men. In many ways, as endpoint manifestations of the modern, the New Left and the counterculture were extraordinarily, sometimes virulently male-dominated and misogynist, normatively heterosexual, and also overwhelmingly white. I assumed that my choice of texts should reflect these facts.

Those texts I discuss at some length here are also mostly American, with some key exceptions, such as Barthes's *Mythologies*, Marcuse's *One-Dimensional Man*, and Laing's *The Politics of Experience* (Marcuse is a liminal case: his exile/expatriation to America was enormously important to his work). All the texts I discuss were widely influential in the United States, however, even if not produced here. Culture and politics in the sixties were preeminently international, incipiently global — that is a key component of their position in the shift from the modern to the postmodern. Nonetheless, the United States was a crucial location of sixties phenomena. Also, many have argued that it was in the United States that postmodernism most visibly emerged, and that U.S. culture and politics have dominated postmodernity. While it is by no means necessary to focus on American culture and politics in the sixties, neither is it misleading to do so. I am most familiar with the American sixties, and that familiarity has informed this study.

The first chapter of *Utopia Limited*, "Modern to Postmodern in Herbert Marcuse," uses Marcuse's *One-Dimensional Man*, one of the most important texts of the sixties, to raise and pursue a number of key issues in the emergence of the postmodern in the sixties. Marcuse's text is remarkable in the breadth of its reach, in its modern-to-postmodern liminality, in the extent of its imbrication in all the central concerns of this study, and also in the extent to which it has disappeared from intellectual, cultural, and political discourses. The virtual disappearance of this landmark sixties text marks the shift in structure of feeling that is my subject here. Taking off from Marcuse's altered status, this section also addresses, briefly, the phenomenon of "continental theory," or just "theory," and its role in the emergence of postmodernity in the sixties.

The second part of *Utopia Limited*, "Culture Industry to Popular Culture," focuses on one of the most widely, almost consensually accepted versions of the shift from modern to postmodern: what Andreas Huyssen has called the breakdown of the "great divide" between high culture and popular culture. I begin by discussing Roland Barthes's *Mythologies*, considered by many a founding text of postmodern cultural studies. I argue that *Mythologies* is a clear marker of the simultaneity of "culture industry," with its negative connotations, as dominant modern formation, and "popular culture," with its positive connotations, as emergent postmodern formation, in the sixties (my periodization of the sixties, again, extends from the late fifties through the early seventies).

Chapters 3 and 4, the second and third chapters of part 2, discuss three exemplary Las Vegas texts from the sixties, beginning with Tom Wolfe's piece "Las Vegas (What?) Las Vegas (Can't Hear You! Too Noisy) Las Vegas!!!!," the first essay in *Kandy-Kolored Tangerine-Flake Streamline Baby*, in chapter 3, then moving on to "Loathing and Learning," in Hunter Thompson's *Fear and Loathing in Las Vegas*, a sixties text lodged primarily in modernity, and the postmodern classic *Learning from Las Vegas*, by Robert Venturi, Denise Scott Brown, and Steven Izenour. Las Vegas becomes a paradigmatic location of postmodernity in these texts. Their differing treatment of this location is highly instructive in revealing the contours of the shift from modern to postmodern.

Part 2 concludes with an overview of movements in sixties avant-garde film and rock music, focusing on questions of race, gender, and violence as well as of the shift in the meanings of popular culture. I have titled this concluding chapter, and that of part 3, "Endnotes," because the discussions in these sections are highly abbreviated. Each addresses large areas of sixties cultural production, without extended or detailed analysis. The modes of cultural production discussed in these sections are too important to omit entirely from this study. I originally intended to devote major sections of this book to various representative works from these movements. However, for the purposes of my central arguments, I decided to limit my analyses to the complexities of the kinds of written texts I am most experienced in discussing. Further, the kind of detailed textual analysis I undertake in the rest of the book came to seem unproductive for many of these works, perhaps even superfluous. Such analysis would rapidly become repetitive and obvious. Each text I spend some extended time with in this book opens out a different set of issues in the emergence of postmodernity in the sixties. The brief survey overviews in the two "Endnotes" chapters, particularly in part 2, indicate in large, comprehensive terms the status and role of crucial modes of sixties cultural production, not discussed in detail in the book, in the emergence of postmodernity.[14]

Part 3, "Participatory Democracy to Postmodern Populism," developing issues of the popular raised in part 2, uses a key nexus of sixties political ideologies and cultural practices, that come under the rubric of "participatory democracy," to analyze the shift from totalizing modern utopian ideals of community to postmodern, post-utopian modes of commodified, complicit populism. Chapter 6 focuses on *The Port Huron Statement*, where the New Left originally formulated its ideology of participatory democracy, and where incipient movements toward postmodern populism, as well as toward the "subject politics" discussed in part 4, are also evident. Chapter 7, the second chapter of this section, uses The Living Theatre's landmark late-sixties performance piece *Paradise Now* to discuss the postmodern elements inherent in one of the most overtly modern-utopian cultural productions of the sixties. Chapter 8 discusses William Burroughs's work of the sixties as a paradigmatic instance of modernist writing shifting on the pivot of egalitarian populism toward modes of postmodernity. Part 3 ends with a very brief overview of avant-garde and postmodern fiction, with an emphasis on issues of gender, race, location, and cultural capital.

Part 4, "Subject Politics," develops issues of modern and postmodern modes of political subjectivity introduced in part 3, focusing particularly on the postmodern shift in the relation between subjectivity and politics. This section opens with a discussion of Richard Poirer's *The Performing Self*, particularly his essay "Learning from the Beatles," which makes clear what is at stake culturally and politically in the sixties and in postmodernity in the new ideologies of politicized subjectivity. The second chapter, chapter 11, analyzes R. D. Laing's *The Politics of Experience*, a text almost equaling Marcuse's in iconic status in the sixties as well as in near-total subsequent disappearance, along with brief discussions of Castañeda, Reich, McLuhan, Fromm, and N. O. Brown, to make clear the pivot from modern to postmodern notions of subjectivity in key sixties texts.

Part 4 then shifts to more overtly political texts, in three chapters on the major political movements of the sixties: Frances FitzGerald's *Fire in the Lake* and the Vietnam War; James Baldwin's early nonfiction work (with briefer discussions as well of Fanon's *The Wretched of the Earth* and of several other political works by African Americans) and the Civil Rights and Black Power movements; and works by Robin Morgan, Shulamith

Firestone, and some other theoretical and literary writers, in relation to second-wave feminism, where the guiding ideologies condensed by the slogan "the personal is political" led directly to postmodern politics of subjectivity, or "subject politics."

The last chapter, "Utopia Limited," focuses on two works of contemporary postmodern fiction by Toni Morrison and E. L. Doctorow, both emerging from the sixties and located in displaced historical settings referring to the sixties. I use these works rather than novels set directly in the sixties and post-sixties (of which there are, of course, many) because they address the question of utopia and post-utopia, the central concern of this book, in starker, more general terms, not distracted by the particular, specific histories of sixties movements and personalities. These works establish the defeat and repudiation of utopia in the wake of the sixties at the same time that they assert the persistence in postmodernity of utopian desire. The book's brief conclusion, "Post-Utopian Promise," reiterates a refusal of defeatism as well as triumphalism concerning the sixties, arguing that, although the shifted ground of the postmodern structure of feeling is undecidable in its relation to emancipatory possibility, understanding the connection of the present moment to the sixties can enable us to register the persistence in postmodernity of modes of sixties utopian desire.

The question of utopia has seemed to me to be at the center of the sixties movements, of the difference between the modern and the postmodern, and of the continuities between the two. In *Postmodernism*, Fredric Jameson has a chapter titled "Space: Utopianism after the End of Utopia." Jameson argues that postmodern spatialization is the replacement of modern temporality, attendant on the replacement of modernist depth by postmodern surface. He argues that postmodern spatial (antitemporal) and surface (antidepth) structures militate against, and seem to negate, the utopian, but that certain forms of aesthetic practice, particularly some nature-related installation art, inhabit postmodern spatialization in ways that keep modernist utopianism alive: "Spatialization, then, whatever it may take away in the capacity to think time and History, also opens a door onto a whole new domain for libidinal investment of the Utopian and even the protopolitical type" (160). He imagines or hypothesizes, among some artists and writers, "something like an unacknowledged 'party of Utopia': an underground party whose numbers are difficult to determine, whose program remains unannounced and perhaps even unformulated, whose existence is unknown to the citizenry at large and to the authorities, but whose members seem to recognize one another by means of secret Masonic signals" (180). I would argue that this is Jameson's compensatory fantasy of the persistence, however unlikely and invisible, of one of the primary formations of the modern: an unaltered, unconstrained, totally revolutionary utopianism, which is in fact repudiated by the postmodern. Nonetheless, I agree with him that, as I argue in this book, the modern utopian impulse does persist in postmodernism/postmodernity. It is neither underground nor invisible; rather, it is both visible and also pervasive, though no longer revolutionary, and very much altered and constrained. It is still critical, still a motivating force for progressive change, but it has become "limited": muted, partial, local, diffuse, multiple, skeptical, complicit, displaced, and significantly refunctioned.

Jameson also says that "one wants to insist very strongly on the necessity of the reinvention of the Utopian vision in any contemporary politics: this lesson, which Marcuse first taught us, is part of the legacy of the sixties which must never be abandoned in any reevaluation of that period and our relationship to it" (159).[15] That injunction is at the heart of the project of this book.

CHAPTER ONE

Modern to Postmodern in Herbert Marcuse

No sixties writer or thinker of Herbert Marcuse's stature and significance has fallen more dramatically than he off the current intellectual map. His Frankfurt School colleagues Walter Benjamin and Theodor Adorno, by contrast, remain major presences. Benjamin, in particular, is enjoying growing prominence, as an issue of *Critical Inquiry* devoted entirely to his work attests.[1] Theodor Adorno is also widely read. Earlier in the history of postmodernist studies, he was frequently used as an exemplum of modernist elitism in his condemnation of the "culture industry" and his attack on jazz. More recently, and more appreciatively, current theorists turn to his crucial work on aesthetics, and, with Max Horkheimer, on the *Dialectic of Enlightenment*. Yet Marcuse's *One-Dimensional Man* (ODM), one of the few most influential books of the sixties though now maintaining only a marginal critical-theoretical presence, is indebted to, and makes essentially the same central argument as, *Dialectic of Enlightenment*. Adorno's "negativity" is always implicated in (bourgeois-identified) "affirmative" culture, just as all resistance is subsumed by Marcuse's one-dimensional society. Adorno assumes the impossibility of the achievement of the goals of enlightenment just as Marcuse argues that instrumental reason always adheres to domination.[2]

Marcuse's oeuvre has been attacked on many grounds; it has also been cited and defended, over the years and up to the present—kept alive, though fairly minimally, in critical discussion.[3] It is not my purpose here to agree or disagree with either attackers or defenders, or, for that matter, to make a case for or against Marcuse's work. I will however offer some speculation concerning reasons for his near disappearance, in the course of discussing *One-Dimensional Man* as a key representative sixties text.

Like *Dialectic of Enlightenment*, *One-Dimensional Man* is a critique of instrumental, technological, scientific rationality (Marcuse calls it Reason, Horkheimer and Adorno, Enlightenment). Reason or Enlightenment is the regime of domination that has produced not just fascism (Horkheimer and Adorno's emphasis, writing as they did in the mid-forties) but also—Marcuse's emphasis as he writes in the late fifties and early sixties—the all-encompassing, enveloping bureaucracies, the totally administered societies, of both late capitalism and also Soviet-style communism. For these Frankfurt School theorists, Reason or Enlightenment is a highly complex phenomenon, with a long history, explicable only as a conjunction of philosophical, social, political, cultural, aesthetic, psychic, as well as historical problematics (Frankfurt School Critical Theory saw itself as a synthesis of the distinct disciplines relevant to these problematics, and in fact as a critique of the compartmentalized splintering of those disciplines as a symptom and effect of Reason/Enlightenment).

As a characteristic and profoundly influential sixties text, *One-Dimensional Man*, though it does not use the word "revolution," is committed to total utopian political-social-cultural-psychic transformation. Contemporary society, culture, thought, and life, in Marcuse's analysis, are so thoroughly alienated that only an entirely different order of existence offers meaningful hope. All resistance or subversion short of total transformation is not only ineffective, it is impossible, because it is immediately absorbed by "one-dimensional" society's uncanny powers of cooptation—in Marcuse's terms, its power to unite opposites and cancel the dialectic. This underlying utopian orientation toward total revolutionary change as the only alternative to total domination marks *One-Dimensional Man* as a text of modernity, and, particularly, as a text of sixties utopian modernity.[4] However, many of Marcuse's arguments and analyses are at the same time situated within emergent paradigms of postmodernity.

The book is divided into three sections: "One-Dimensional Society," "One-Dimensional Thought," and "The Chance of the Alternatives." Not given its own section, but underlying the entire text and evident in the book's subtitle, "Studies in the Ideology of Advanced Industrial Society," which virtually equates "society" with "man," is a commitment to the free individual, living an unalienated life, liberated from one-dimensional society and thought. This fully liberated existence would be possible only under the aegis of a new reality principle, to use the terms of *Eros and Civilization* (E&C), which would evolve beyond totalized domination. E&C argues that the reality principle theorized by Freud, which Marcuse diagnoses as premised on domination, is no longer necessary in the imminent world of a technology so advanced that it has the potential to liberate human beings from all alienated toil. This utopian view of technology's capability to end the struggle for existence underlies much sixties utopian revolutionary ideology (and modernity's utopian vision in general).[5] Technology, a key element of Reason's domination, therefore, contains the dialectical seeds of human liberation from that domination. The Marxist paradigm is evident here, with the great social and economic power developed by capitalism (here generalized to include Soviet-style communism) accorded the capability of transcending its own structures of oppression. Revolutionary agency, in this analysis, has shifted from the proletariat — no longer a revolutionary class, according to Marcuse, having been co-opted by the gratifications of administered society — to those whom he saw as having the least stake in the paralyzing benefits of the system: the students, African Americans, third world revolutionaries, and, later, feminists, who were beginning to rise up around him as he wrote. He retained until his death in 1979 his commitment to the "new social movements" he did so much to foster and inspire. In theorizing the total revolution of modernity, and at the same time seeing the disparate, "single-issue" political movements of postmodernity as its only possible agents, Marcuse powerfully inhabited, marked, and perhaps helped to bring about the sixties transition from the modern to the postmodern.

Often in ODM, the difference between a modern and a postmodern stance involves a slight shift of perspective, but one that is premised on utterly incompatible sets of underlying assumptions. The introduction, titled "The Paralysis of Criticism: Society without Opposition," establishes the key central arguments of the text. "One-dimensional" does not indicate flatness, sameness, or lack of depth. On the contrary, one-dimensional society is full of variegated pleasures and gratifications. What

it lacks is the second dimension of antithesis – of criticism and opposition, as the title of the introduction makes clear. It lacks the other-
dimensionality Marcuse ascribes to the dialectic, where terms (ideas, social and political formations, structures of feeling, lifeworlds) opposed
and in contradiction to those that exist have a palpable reality. In one-
dimensional society (society of domination without opposition) and one-
dimensional (nondialectical) thought, only what exists has any reality.
Yet, as I have indicated, the force of this book for sixties radicals depended
on the contradictory view that one-dimensional society and thought do
indeed harbor the potential for their own revolutionary overthrow. As
Marcuse says in the introduction:

> *One-Dimensional Man* will vacillate throughout between two contra-
> dictory hypotheses: (1) that advanced industrial society is capable of
> containing qualitative change for the foreseeable future; (2) that forces
> and tendencies exist which may break this containment and explode
> the society. I do not think that a clear answer can be given. Both tenden-
> cies are there, side by side — and even the one in the other. The first
> tendency is dominant, and whatever preconditions for a reversal may
> exist are being used to prevent it. Perhaps an accident may alter the
> situation, but unless the recognition of what is being done and what is
> being prevented subverts the consciousness and the behavior of man,
> not even a catastrophe will bring about the change. (xlvii)

The "vacillation" Marcuse acknowledges, and which does indeed characterize the shifting stance of his argument, can be seen as precisely the
dominant modern/emergent postmodern location of the text. Modernity's
belief in the meaningful possibility of utopian revolution is still a powerful
force for Marcuse, despite his evident pessimism concerning any realistic
prospect for bringing it about. Only in utter, explosive, even catastrophic
change does there lie any hope of redemption from the "containment" of
one-dimensional society: hope of meaningful, rather than empty and repressive, human liberation. But in his analysis of the almost uncanny
effectiveness of one-dimensional society and one-dimensional thought not
just in producing and reproducing the one-dimensional human but also in
making him/her more than superficially content — in substituting powerful gratifications for totally liberated fulfillment — Marcuse describes the
indifferentiated social/cultural field of postmodernity. The substitution of
limitless noncontradictory difference for massive dialectical blocks of
thesis, antithesis, and synthesis, a substitution which characterizes Mar-

cuse's one-dimensional society in its elimination of both domination and revolutionary negation or Great Refusal, is a prime marker of postmodernity. Foucauldian flows of power, encompassing continual movement back and forth of incomplete, continually contested and reconstituted hegemony alongside local, partial, continually reformulated resistance, where there is no monolithic domination or total revolution, constitute a neutral or positive view of what Marcuse damns as one-dimensional society, culture, and thought.

Throughout the text, Marcuse's analyses of one-dimensionality can be characterized as denunciation of what many postmodern theories affirm as the end of oppressive master narratives and dualisms. His analysis of the ways in which one-dimensional society, culture, and thought coopt, absorb, neutralize, and render ineffective all opposition also often describes what has come to be positively valued in some postmodern theories as complicitous critique or resistance from within (Hutcheon). This complicitous critique eschews oppressive master narratives of revolution, narratives which really always favor only one or a few oppositional group(s), in favor of broader, more egalitarian, and more realistic notions of everyday tactics (de Certeau).[6] These tactics involve partial, local refunctioning and subversion, not of a totalized domination but of an incomplete, malleable, shifting, continually redefined, recontested, and reinstituted hegemony. This notion of limitless social flexibility, and therefore of potential for (partial, incomplete, local, complicitous) resistance, refunctioning, subversion from within—postmodernism's theory of progressive politics—is precisely what Marcuse describes with great precision and in illuminating detail but sees as one-dimensional, advanced industrial society's ability to contain all qualitative change. What appears to a postmodern view as society's and culture's malleability, mutability, and therefore potential for progressive change is, from modernity's point of view, inevitably futile and illusory, because coopted and recontained. But postmodernity's point of view in some ways involves only a slight shift in emphasis, from a negative focus on the recontainment postmodernism acknowledges as both inevitable and contestable to a positive emphasis on potentialities for resistance.

In defining in the introduction what he means by transcendence of the given, Marcuse provides a remarkable instance of the at once subtle and massive distance between the dominant modern and the emergent postmodern paradigms in this text. Revolutionary transcendence, for Marcusean/Marxist dialectical materialist theory, must be both a total negation of the existing social order and also a real potentiality within that order. As Marcuse says, "the terms 'transcend' and 'transcendence' are used throughout in the empirical, critical sense: they designate tendencies in theory and practice which, in a given society, 'overshoot' the established universe of discourse and action toward its historical alternatives (real possibilities)" (xliii). Revolutionary transcendence is therefore "opposed to all metaphysics by virtue of the rigorously historical character of the transcendence" (xliii). In insisting that he is concerned only with revolutionary potentialities that actually inhere in the historical materiality of the given social order, Marcuse makes a remarkable statement: "social theory is concerned with the historical alternatives which haunt the established society as subversive tendencies and forces" (xliv). Marcuse goes on from here to argue in forceful, uncompromising terms that "contemporary society seems to be capable of containing social change — qualitative change which would establish essentially different institutions, a new direction of the productive process, new modes of human existence" (xliv). All aspects of contemporary society attest to its successful "integration of opposites" (xliv), most notably the opposite of transcendent opposition. Yet the phrase "alternatives which haunt the established society as subversive tendencies and forces" haunts this denunciation of the ineluctable containment (hence neutralization) of resistance and integration of opposites. This shadowy yet powerful, uncanny presence of subversive tendencies and forces points more toward a postmodern view of hegemony always in dynamic relation to resistance than toward a modern view of inherent contradictions in relations of production inevitably generating revolution through the agency of the self-consciousness of the exploited class. Marcuse retains the modern paradigm of the necessity for total revolutionary transcendence — what he calls the Great Refusal — at the same time that his most realistic hope lodges in a view, strongly inflected toward postmodernism, of a vulnerable, if not incomplete hegemony riddled with ("haunted by") potentialities of resistance.

In the key passage in which Marcuse enumerates his two "contradictory hypotheses," several other moments warrant attention. First, Marcuse says that "both tendencies are there, side by side — and even the one in the other." He does not expand on this notion, but if meaningful change were somehow to inhabit total containment, and containment were to inhabit meaningful change, that would produce precisely the postmodern field of simultaneous, continuous, mutually imbricated hegemony and resistance.

The closing sentence of the "two contradictory hypotheses" passage also contains some notable formulations. That sentence, again, reads as follows: "Perhaps an accident may alter the situation, but unless the recognition of what is being done and what is being prevented subverts the consciousness and the behavior of man, not even a catastrophe will bring about the change." By substituting "catastrophe" for "accident" at the end of the sentence, Marcuse shifts the meaning of the first term, which could encompass any unforeseen event, to connote violent historical upheaval. Given the emphasis on the normalization of the threat of nuclear war as a key symptom of one-dimensional society's integration of opposites elsewhere in the book, Marcuse can be seen as having it in mind in the range of catastrophes that might "alter the situation," enabling meaningful change. This possible reading (only suggested, perhaps not even fully conscious to Marcuse as he writes) gives a sense of the dire pessimism Marcuse feels concerning the possibility for revolutionary change.

Further, even such a catastrophe will be helpless to "bring about the change" unless "the recognition of what is being done and what is being prevented subverts the consciousness and the behavior of man." This sentence makes clear the supreme agency Marcuse accords to intellect and consciousness — to critical thought. The hope and responsibility for revolutionary change rests ultimately not on the predictable ("determinate") historical workings of a materialist dialectic but on human intellectual capacity. This capacity, formulated by Marcuse as more or less independent of class location in the relations of production, would enable the radical intellectual to use the lever of the dialectic to inhabit a critical oppositionality in order to see beyond the limitations of present existence and envision a utopian alternative. Here we have the faith of modernity in dialectical thought's ability to construct an alternative antithesis entirely outside its thesis, something postmodernity rejects as naive. In postmodernity, there is no Archimedean lever, no position outside ideology or social construction. On the preceding pages, Marcuse makes this modern faith explicit: "the fact that the vast majority of the population accepts, and is made to accept, this society does not render it less irrational and less reprehensible. The distinction between true and false consciousness, real and immediate interest still is meaningful. But this distinction itself must be validated. Men must come to see it and to find their way from false to true consciousness, from their immediate to their real interest. They can do so only if they live in the necessity of changing their way of life, of denying the positive, of refusing" (xlv–xlvi). Yet at the same time, we see here, in "men must come to see," in "changing their way of life," in "recognition . . . subverts the consciousness and the behavior of man," postmodernity's valorization of and emphasis on what in the sixties was called consciousness, which came to be called subjectivity or the subject as the exemplary postmodern site of the political. In this valorization of consciousness as primary agent of social change, Marcuse joins other sixties luminaries who have also more or less vanished off the intellectual (though not popular-cultural) map, such as Norman O. Brown, R. D. Laing, and Erich Fromm.

The preponderance of argument and analysis throughout the book is situated clearly within Marcuse's modernity: his loathing of what he considers the ersatz gratifications of mass consumer culture, and his conviction that no meaningful resistance is available in a society that "contains" all potential opposition. Marcuse characterizes contemporary society as marked by "the suppression of individuality" and the elimination of the critical, oppositional function of "freedom of thought, speech and conscience" by "a society which seems increasingly capable of satisfying the needs of the individuals through the way in which it is organized" (1). In this society marked by technological gratification of needs, "under the condition of a rising standard of living, non-conformity with the system itself appears to be socially useless" (2). More tellingly for postmodernity, as Marcuse, and Jameson after him, will also argue, "non-conformity with the system" is easily integrated by the infinitely flexible "system" as yet another variation on the limitlessly malleable models of conformity, generated by the infinite fluidity of late consumer capitalism.

Yet at the same time, Marcuse argues that precisely the advanced technology that, in satisfying needs and raising the standard of living, eliminates meaningful opposition also carries the potential for revolutionary change in its capability of bringing about true human freedom by eliminating alienated toil: "to the extent to which the work world is conceived of as a machine and mechanized accordingly, it becomes the *potential* basis of a new freedom for man" (3). This, again, is modernity's last utopian hope: the (now discredited) faith in the liberatory potential of cybernation that underlies many revolutionary sixties ideologies (see the discussion of Shulamith Firestone's *The Dialectic of Sex* in chapter 14).

The elimination of the struggle for existence that cybernation has the potential to bring about is the necessary condition for revolutionary change. This change, though Marcuse insists the potential for it inheres in the historical materiality of the existing system as a meaningful alternative to it, would encompass entirely new social, political, cultural, and psychic systems, completely different from and uncontaminated by any existing order of being. Here we see the Great Refusal that materialized in the sixties as "dropping out" in order to constitute communal spaces, both urban and rural, both political and countercultural, where all manifestations of "the system" were subject to continual and painful critique and (ultimately futile) attempts at elimination and replacement by unalienated, liberated modes of life, thought, feeling, and politics, uncontaminated by the competitive individualism of conformist capitalism. These alternative spaces of the radicals and the counterculture, however, were produced only by the change in consciousness Marcuse argued was the ultimate precondition of revolutionary change, not by the advent of cybernation eliminating the necessity for the struggle for existence. This change in consciousness, never as totally oppositional and uncontaminated by "the system" as its practitioners firmly believed it must and could be, proved by itself insufficient for revolutionary change — it was ultimately absorbed and recontained as Marcuse also argued it would be. But the material, meaningful, though not revolutionary or thoroughgoing change in the "system" marked and produced by this change in consciousness also marked and partly constituted the emergence of postmodernity.

Marcuse's scathing analysis of the cooptation of resistance in one-dimensional society inspired the radical left and the counterculture to attempt to throw off society's chains. The power of this analysis lies not just in the passionate clarity of its denunciations but also in the dispassionate clarity of its admiration for the efficacy of late capitalism in producing a human lifeworld and psyche — a structure of feeling — too effectively content with itself to want to undo or even become conscious of its own alienation. Again, the shift between Marcuse's modern vision of total alienation and the postmodern vision of complicitous critique he points to is at once slight and monumental.

Marcuse's attack on one-dimensional society dominates the book. The "new modes of realization" that constitute the only hope for change, based though they are on "the new capabilities of society" (for the end of the struggle for existence), would entail total liberation from, and transformation of, every aspect of this society: "economic freedom would mean freedom *from* the economy. . . . Political freedom would mean liberation of the individuals *from* politics over which they have no effective control . . . intellectual freedom would mean the restoration of individual thought now absorbed by mass communication and indoctrination, abolition of 'public opinion' together with its makers" (4). Here as elsewhere, ODM resonates powerfully with *The Port Huron Statement* (see chapter 6); here in particular, as well, Marcuse incorporates his analysis in E&C of human oppression under the reality principle defined as domination:

> We may distinguish both true and false needs. "False" are those which are superimposed upon the individual by particular social interests in his repression: the needs which perpetuate toil, aggressiveness, misery, and injustice. Their satisfaction might be most gratifying to the individual, but this happiness is not a condition which has to be maintained and protected if it serves to arrest the development of the ability (his own and others) to recognize the disease of the whole and grasp the chances of curing the disease. The result then is euphoria in unhappiness. Most of the prevailing needs to relax, to have fun, to behave and consume in accordance with the advertisements, to love and hate what others love and hate, belong to this category of false needs. . . . The prevalence of repressive needs is an accomplished fact, accepted in ignorance and defeat, but a fact that must be undone in the interest of the happy individual as well as all those whose misery is the price of his satisfaction. (4–5)

It is difficult to imagine a more unequivocal denunciation of the global system produced by late capitalism. Yet Marcuse's overall analysis of the structure of feeling produced by late capitalism is anything but unequivocal.

The argument concerning the substitution of alienated consumer gratifications for real happiness, linked to the argument that technology contains the potential for true liberation, and to the key argument concerning the flattening of the dialectic, together constitute the pivot in Marcuse to postmodernity. His most scathing condemnation of "advanced industrial society" shifts subtly to a recognition, if not an appreciation, of its complex mix of total domination with a real egalitarianism under a rising standard of living, in which false "needs and satisfactions . . . have become the individual's own" (7).

It is the collapse of the dialectic that Marcuse sees as immobilizing opposition to this oppressive state of affairs in the current conjuncture: "the people enter this stage as preconditioned receptacles of long standing; the decisive difference is in the flattening out of the contrast (or conflict) between the given and the possible, between the satisfied and the unsatisfied needs" (8). "In the political sphere, this trend manifests itself in a marked unification or convergence of opposites. Bipartisanship in foreign policy overrides competitive group interests . . . the programs of the big parties become ever more indistinguishable" (19). This flattening is based not just on the unifying force of totalized corporate-technological domination, but also on "the so-called equalization of class distinctions," in which "the worker and his boss enjoy the same television program and visit the same resort places" (8). He denounces the "ideological function" of this flattening, which he sees as betokening "not the disappearance of classes," implied by workers sharing culture and leisure with bosses, "but the extent to which the needs and satisfactions that serve the preservation of the Establishment are shared by the underlying population" (8).

This sharing of needs and satisfactions, however, needs which are satisfied for the "underlying population" to an unprecedented degree, produces a new formation, in which "the transplantation of social into individual needs is so effective that the difference between them seems to be purely theoretical" (8). Marcuse calls this "the rational character of its [society's] irrationality" (9). In a passage remarkable for its indeterminate tone poised between denunciation and grudging admiration, Marcuse describes what is in fact postmodernity: "its [advanced industrial civilization's] productivity and efficiency, its capacity to increase and spread comforts, to turn waste into need, and destruction into construction, the extent to which this civilization transforms the object world into an extension of man's mind and body makes the very notion of alienation questionable. The people recognize themselves in the commodities; they find their soul in their automobile, hi-fi set, split-level home, kitchen equipment. The very mechanism which ties the individual to his society has changed, and social control is anchored in the new needs which it has produced" (9). Marcuse comes very close here to defining the postmodern structure of feeling, where the classical alienation produced by earlier versions of capitalism, in which a reified state of existence is fully opposed by the potential for a genuine, unalienated state of existence, no longer obtains.

This state of affairs is marked by "the passing of the historical forces which, at the preceding stage of industrial society, seemed to represent the possibility of new forms of existence" (10). In this preceding stage, "the external controls exercised by his society" were reproduced in the individual by the psychic process of "introjection," in which "a variety of relatively spontaneous processes . . . transpos[e] the 'outer' into the 'inner,'" implying "the existence of an inner dimension distinguished from and even antagonistic to the external exigencies — an individual consciousness and an individual unconscious *apart from* public opinion and behavior. The idea of 'inner freedom' here has its reality. It designates the private space in which man may become and remain 'himself' " (10). It is this "private space" that the sixties counterculture, and sometimes Marcuse himself, believed could be retrieved or reinvented as oppositional consciousness, out of which a new society could be built. But in contemporary society, Marcuse argues here, where "there is no reason to insist on self-determination if the administered life is the comfortable and even the 'good' life" (49), this private, inner dimension of oppositional critical freedom has disappeared. In its place is what Marcuse calls "*mimesis*: an immediate identification of the individual with *his* society, and, through it, with the society as a whole" (10). This identification undermines the concept of alienation, Marcuse argues, on which his own analysis also depends. Marcuse deals with this contradiction by means of what amounts to more, and irreducible, contradiction: "I have just suggested that the concept of alienation seems to become questionable when the individuals identify themselves with the existence which is imposed upon them. . . . This identification is not illusion but reality. However, the reality constitutes a more progressive stage of alienation. The latter has become entirely objective; the subject which is alienated is swallowed up by its alienated existence. There is only one dimension, and it is everywhere and in all forms. The achievements of progress defy ideological indictment as well as justification; before their tribunal, the 'false consciousness' of their rationality becomes the true consciousness" (11). This "one-dimensional" Möbius strip of "alienation" and "identification," of "illusion" and "reality," of "indictment" and "justification," is, again, the undecidable postmodern universe. Marcuse sustains throughout his analyses of one-dimensional culture and thought this mixture of denunciation, fatalism, powerful critique, and hope for an alternative grounded in the ameliorative potential of the technology that has so far been synonymous with total domination.

Marcuse extends his discussion to culture, beginning in the chapter titled "The Conquest of the Unhappy Consciousness: Repressive Desublimation." Here he focuses on the one-dimensional condition of culture in the totally administered society. Marcuse makes arguments quite similar to those Horkheimer and Adorno make in "The Culture Industry: Enlightenment as Mass Deception," positing, as Horkheimer and Adorno do, the affirmative, hegemonic, counteroppositional character of popular ("mass") culture in late capitalism. But while Horkheimer and Adorno focus primarily on the ways in which the culture industry reproduces, through "escape," precisely the alienated labor from which it claims to provide release, Marcuse focuses on "repressive desublimation," or the absorption of heretofore blocked and transcended needs, desires, and energies by the totalized, dominant, dominating, one-dimensional culture (see p. 56). Marcuse's condemnations of one-dimensional culture, like his denunciations of one-dimensional society, are shot through with recognition of that culture's basis in progressive democratization and in the successful productivity which is the necessary precursor of, and condition for, total revolutionary change. And again, the culture he dissects is postmodern culture, seen primarily from the vantage point of modernity, with erratic glimpses of a vision pointing toward a postmodern view of postmodernity.

Marcuse argues that what he calls "higher culture" is not so much defeated as it is superseded by (what is still for him) mass culture. Social reality has "refuted" higher culture by gratifying many of the thwarted needs and desires formerly sublimated in higher culture. This real material progress, along with the democratization in which the "ideal" is "brought down from the sublimated realm of the soul or the spirit or the inner man, and translated into operational terms and problems," constitute the "progressive elements of mass culture" (58). Yet, insofar as "higher culture becomes part of the material culture," it "loses the greater part of its truth" (58). Despite its "progressive elements," popular culture is primarily as affirmative (in the sense of hegemony-supporting) for Marcuse as it is for Horkheimer and Adorno: "in the realm of culture, the new totalitarianism manifests itself precisely in a harmonizing pluralism, where the most contradictory works and truths peacefully coexist in indifference" (61). For Marcuse this is precisely the flattening of opposition it is his largest project in this book to condemn. Yet in his discussions of the flattening of opposition in the integration of opposites — the end of the dialectic — what he describes is actually the condition of postmodernity, the "indifference" celebrated by its advocates as the end of the oppressive, elitist, hierarchical stratification of the high culture/popular culture dualism, and of hierarchical dualisms in general.

For Adorno in *Aesthetic Theory*, high culture, or "the aesthetic," though opposed to the fully instrumentalized culture industry, is never purely oppositional — its capacity for oppositionality always exists in complex relation to its inevitable affirmativeness in and of bourgeois-dominated culture. Art for Adorno is never fully autonomous; rather, autonomy exists in or as a negation (a keyword for Adorno) of its own affirmativeness. Nonetheless, this negativity - the partial oppositionality of avant-garde art — is the best hope for culture in a late-capitalist society. Despite his intermittent pessimism, Marcuse is on the whole, as we will see, more sanguine than Adorno concerning what Marcuse calls the "aesthetic dimension," which he also, like Adorno, allies with the avant-garde, and which he sees as the last, best hope for developing and promulgating a truly oppositional, incipiently revolutionary consciousness. I would argue that it is this difference between the two — Adorno's complex skepticism, and his acknowledgment of the always-already coopted status of all art in bourgeois culture, formulations very close to postmodernism's "complicitous critique" and "resistance from within," as opposed to Marcuse's fitful but passionate hopefulness concerning total, utopian revolution achieved through avant-garde art and its changed consciousness — that has been responsible for Adorno's persistence and growing cachet in intellectual discourse, despite his ostensible "elitism," and for Marcuse's near-disappearance.

Marcuse's denunciation of repressive desublimation, rotated 180 degrees, would be a postmodern theorist's encomium. "Higher culture" had offered "the appearance of the realm of freedom: the refusal to behave. Such refusal cannot be blocked [as it is in one-dimensional culture] without a compensation which seems more satisfying than the refusal. The conquest and unification of opposites, which finds its ideological glory in the transformation of higher into popular culture, takes place on a material ground of increased satisfaction. This is also the ground which allows a sweeping *desublimation*" (70–71).

In repressive desublimation (a formulation similar to Marcuse's subsequent formulation of "repressive tolerance"), which, again, undoes the foundation of higher culture, a foundation that resides in sublimation of thwarted desire, "the Pleasure Principle absorbs the Reality Principle; sexuality is liberated (or rather liberalized) in socially constructive forms" (72). This argument, first developed in E&C, sounds to postmodern ears like a description of a desirable state of liberation, but it is the kernel of Marcuse's condemnation of popular culture: "socially constructive" means affirmative, nonoppositional. Meaningful resistance is being blocked, in repressive desublimation, by a substitute sexual libertarianism that merely buttresses the status quo without fulfilling the higher aims of eros for true, fulfilled, unalienated liberation. Defined down merely as sexuality, eros finds its potentiality for real human liberation and total fulfillment — the potentiality Marcuse argues for in E&C — betrayed.

Culture itself, according to Marcuse — not just "higher culture" — had, in two-dimensional society, been constituted in antithetical opposition to the thesis of a repressive social reality, in fact as a real alternative to that oppression. In totally administered society, "the novel feature is the flattening out of the antagonism between culture and social reality through the obliteration of the oppositional, alien, and transcendent elements in the higher culture by virtue of which it constituted *another dimension* of reality. This liquidation of *two-dimensional* culture takes place not through the denial and rejection of the 'cultural values,' but through their wholesale incorporation in the established order, through their reproduction and display on a massive scale. In fact, they serve as instruments of social cohesion" (57). Social cohesion, in Marcuse's one-dimensional society, is tantamount of course to domination, in which "the Great Refusal is in turn refused; . . . the works of alienation [the great works of 'higher culture,' superseded in their oppositionality] are themselves incorporated into this society and circulate as part and parcel of the equipment which adorns and psychoanalyzes the prevailing state of affairs. Thus they become commercials — they sell, comfort or excite" (64); the lineaments of postmodern culture are evident in this description.[7] The progressive effects of cultural democratization are thus canceled by one-dimensional culture's ineluctable affirmation of hegemony, or, for Marcuse, domination. In summary of this position, and of its ambivalent equivocations (the compensation at least "seems more satisfying than the refusal"), Marcuse asserts that one-dimensional society is

> a rational universe which, by the mere weight and capabilities of its apparatus, blocks all escape. In its relation to the reality of daily life, the high culture of the past was many things — opposition and adornment, outcry and resignation. But it was also the appearance of the realm of freedom: the refusal to behave. Such refusal cannot be blocked without a compensation which seems more satisfying than the refusal. The conquest and unification of opposites, which finds its ideological glory in the transformation of higher into popular culture, takes place on a material ground of increased satisfaction. This is also the ground which allows a sweeping [and "repressive"] *desublimation*. (71–72)

Like Adorno, Marcuse allows an exception to this ineluctable blocking of refusal. Refusal, or "contradiction," he argues, "must have a medium of communication. The struggle for this medium, or rather the struggle against its absorption into the predominant one-dimensionality, shows forth in the avant-garde efforts to create an entrangement which would make the artistic truth again communicable" (66). He cites Brecht as having "sketched the theoretical foundations for these efforts" (66) in his "alienation effect." Adorno, as we have seen, also accords a "negativity," or partial but meaningful refusal of the hegemonic affirmation with which it is also inevitably complicit, to various forms of avant-garde art. For Marcuse, however, the avant-garde is more fully imbued with resistant negativity. Only the avant-garde can occupy this position of refusal be- cause it must entail the communication of "the break with communica- tion" (68): "the word [in avant-garde literature] refuses the unifying, sen- sible rule of the sentence. It explodes the pre-established structure of meaning and, becoming an 'absolute object' itself, designates an intoler- able, self-defeating universe — a discontinuum" (68–69).

Marcuse intersperses this discussion with quotations from Roland Bar- thes's *Writing Degree Zero*, a theoretical text produced, like other struc- turalist and then poststructuralist theoretical texts, within the context of the sixties renaissance of the avant-gardes. Marcuse's endorsement of the avant-garde here — his sense that only in the avant-garde did the possibility for true cultural oppositionality, producing and enabling revolutionary change, lie — was extremely influential on, and also representative of, the sixties revolutionary avant-garde (counter)cultural sensibility. A great deal of countercultural aesthetic activity in the sixties was located within vari- ous continuities with and renewals of early-twentieth-century avant-garde traditions. This radical avant-gardeism, like radical and countercultural "two-dimensional" oppositionality in general, has been discredited in postmodernity; linked both to the naïveté of a belief in the possibility of an Archimedean lever, a utopian position at least potentially outside ideology and social construction, and to modernist hierarchical elitism in its total and Great Refusal of existing, particularly popular, cultural forms. At the same time, concomitant cultural movements of the sixties, that appeared at the time to be continuous with avant-garde cultural forms in their rejection of what was then called "bourgeois" (generally middlebrow, derivative high-cultural) aesthetic convention, movements such as pop art, happenings, street theater, underground comics, animation, and, perhaps most important, rock music, provided a pivot to postmodernity in their ambiguous, ironic, unevenly critical habitation within the general aes- thetic terms of popular culture (see chapter 5).

Marcuse ends his discussion of "repressive desublimation" with what to him is a scathing, sardonic denunciation, but which, again, with a shift

of tone at once slight and monumental, could be a neutral or even laudatory description of postmodern culture, society, and subjectivity. "This
society," he asserts, "turns everything it touches into a potential source of
progress *and* exploitation, of drudgery *and* satisfaction, of freedom *and*
oppression" (78). "Turns everything it touches" signals Marcuse's sarcasm. But the rest of the sentence, with the terms reversed — placing the
positive after rather than before the negative term — is characteristic of
postmodern analyses of complicitous critique and resistance from within,
in which both the hierarchical oppressiveness and also the naive, hope-
lessly "utopian" impossibility of total revolution are replaced by a more
hopefully feasible and egalitarian field of diverse, multiple, local, partial
subversions and resistances, existing in dynamic, fluid relation to contested hegemony.

In much of his closing attack on what Marcuse ironically, even bitterly
calls the "happy consciousness," barely any shift of tone or formulation
would be required to produce a neutral or laudatory description of postmodernity. Following a discussion of the rampant, generalized "aggres-
siveness" produced by desublimation, a discussion which critics of contemporary culture now, on both the right and the left, could use verbatim
to argue their cases either for the deleterious effects of the sixties in the
breakdown of traditional social and moral restraints and obligations, or
for the effects of the triumph of global capitalism in destroying community and social responsibility, Marcuse discusses what he calls the "Happy
Consciousness." This manifestation of the "conquest of transcendence . . .
reflects the belief that the real is rational, and that the established system,
in spite of everything, delivers the goods." Negative language then appears, describing the necessary "surrender" of "personal thought and action" to "the productive apparatus" that "delivers the goods" (79). In this
surrender, "conscience is absolved by reification, by the general necessity
of things" (79). But in the following, generally damning discussion of
guilt, linking the desublimated end of guilt to "happy" participation in
murder and mass destruction, Marcuse names a central tenet of many
postmodern ideologies: in the Happy Consciousness of the postmodern
psyche, which "has no limits" (80), "guilt has no place" (79). To Marcuse
this absence of guilt signals the defeat of the moral consciousness that is
appalled by genocidal violence, and that could be capable of the Great
Refusal. In postmodern ideology, however, the end of guilt signals the
defeat of debilitating self-limitation, self-blame, self-hatred, and thwart-
ing of human potential for self-actualization. Precisely the total liberation

Marcuse advocated, that he argued must be lodged and perhaps originated in individual consciousness, became linked, in the postmodern aftermath of the sixties, to personal growth and self-actualization, unshadowed by alienation, uninhibited by guilt (in contemporary ethical discourses, "guilt" and "morality" are replaced by "the call of the other").

Marcuse also attacks the flattening of meaningful oppositionality in language and in the social sense of history. This attack is quite familiar now in denunciations of the permeation of advertising throughout, in fact the coextensiveness of advertising with, postmodern culture, and in critiques such as Jameson's of the flattening or indifferentiation of history in postmodernity. Marcuse denounces the way in which the "Happy Consciousness" reflects the "new conformism," a very familiar notion by the early sixties. The language of this conformism integrates opposites in a way that cancels all material, potentially critical contradiction: "total commercialization joins formerly antagonistic spheres of life, and this union expresses itself in the smooth linguistic conjunction of conflicting parts of speech" (89). Marcuse gives the examples "Labor is Seeking Missile Harmony,' and . . . 'Luxury Fall-Out Shelter'" (89) to demonstrate this phenomenon. Marcuse posits a one-directional, top-down relationship between the dominant producers of this language and the passive, entirely nonagential victims (consumers) of it, a relationship characteristic of the dominant modern stance of the text, one that is repudiated by postmodern theories such as de Certeau's of the refunctioning tactics of the everyday. Characteristically, Marcuse asserts the diametric opposite of de Certeau's analysis of subversive refunctioning. Marcuse argues that "the reader or listener is expected to associate (and does associate) with them [manipulative 'impact lines' and 'audience rousers'] a fixated structure of institutions, attitudes, aspirations, and he is expected to react in a fixated, specific manner" (91).

This "anti-critical and anti-dialectical language" participates in the "*suppression of history*." For Marcuse, a genuine historical memory "may give rise to dangerous insights, and the established society seems to be apprehensive of the subversive contents of memory" (98). However, "this does not mean that history, private or general, disappears from the universe of discourse. The past is evoked often enough: be it the Founding Fathers, or Marx-Engels-Lenin, or as the humble origins of a presidential candidate. However, these too are ritualized invocations which do not allow development of the content recalled; frequently, the mere invocation serves to block such development, which would show its historical impropriety" (98 n.18). Marcuse points here to a much-contested issue in postmodern theory and social-cultural analysis. Jameson makes essentially the same argument: that history is flattened in postmodernity, indifferentiated so that all past moments become equally accessible, equally present, and their meaningful, critical, dialectical historicity is eviscerated. Linda Hutcheon, and other postmodern advocates, make the contradictory argument that postmodernism turns continually to history in order to understand the narrativity not just of all history but of all social formations, and the arbitrary, malleable constructedness of all our historical and social narratives. This malleability implies and comprehends the possibility of resistance and subversion; literally, of "rewriting" history, from the subaltern rather than the hegemonic point of view.

The question of history leads Marcuse to the question, at the heart of postmodern theorization, and crucial to this study, of the particular and the universal. Marcuse uses two contrasting statements to make his case that one-dimensional discourse, in substituting the particular for the universal, suppresses or eliminates the critical force of the universal: " 'Wages are too low,' " and " 'B's present earnings, due to his wife's illness, are insufficient to meet his current obligations' " (112–13). The divergent implications of these two formulations are clear. The first statement implies an amelioration that must be significantly socially transformative, because it "transcends [the] individual experience" of the worker who utters it and "refers to universal conditions for which no particular case can be substituted" (112). The second statement, on the other hand, has as its subject only a single worker, "B," whose particular case does not transcend its immediate circumstances: "the 'transitiveness' of meaning has been abolished; the grouping 'wage-earners' has disappeared together with the subject 'wages,' and what remains is a particular case which, stripped of its transitive meaning, becomes susceptible to the accepted standards of treatment by the company whose case it is" (113). This failure to transcend the particular toward the universal deprives particularity of all critical, oppositional potentiality. Given the sometimes fierce valorization of particularity as location of disenfranchised positionalities, over against a rejection of the oppressive hegemonic master narratives of the dominant universal in many postmodern theorizations, Marcuse's position here appears as quintessentially modern.

One moment of this argument, however, moves away from this dominant modern paradigm. In contrasting the language of dialectical contradiction to the one-dimensional, "Orwellian" language of "hypnotic nouns

which evoke endlessly the same frozen predicates" (Marcuse also quotes
Barthes's *Writing Degree Zero* as an ally in analyzing what Marcuse calls
the "magic-authoritarian features of this language"), Marcuse offers the
Communist Manifesto as "a classical example" of the dialectic: "here the
two key terms, Bourgeoisie and Proletariat, each 'govern' contrary predicates. The 'bourgeoisie' is the subject of technical progress, liberation,
conquest of nature, creation of social wealth, *and* of the perversion and
destruction of these achievements. Similarly, the 'proletariat' carries the
attributes of total oppression *and* of the total defeat of oppression. Such
dialectical relation of opposites in and by the proposition is rendered
possible by the recognition of the subject as an historical agent whose
identity continues itself in *and against* its historical practice, in *and against*
its social reality" (100). If the reader were not already aware of the opposition between dialectical and one-dimensional society, thought, culture,
and language developed throughout the book, this passage, taken out of
context, could read as a neutral or admiring analysis of postmodern complicitous critique or resistance from within. Without the element of negation, refusal, contradiction, opposition, and without the human agency
capable of using that element as a lever for total revolutionary change,
Marcuse's analysis describes precisely the condition of unresolved simultaneity of progressive and reactionary components of dominant social-
cultural formations that characterizes postmodernity. What is most striking in this passage is Marcuse's use of the copula "and" alongside the
formulation "in and against," instead of such formulations as "in contradiction with" or "over against." Marcuse's formulations, though we know
they refer to modern contradiction, point at the same time toward postmodern simultaneity, precisely the simultaneity his overt project condemns as one-dimensional.

We find a similar simultaneity in "One-Dimensional Thought," the
second part of the book. It develops Marcuse's powerful attack, informed
by his years of pioneering philosophical work along with the other critical
theorists of the Frankfurt School, on scientific, technological, instrumental rationality, or what he calls Reason, as the ideology — at once reflection
and precondition — of domination. Technological rationality is "the triumph of the one-dimensional reality over all contradiction," the obverse
of dialectical thought: "the closed operational universe of advanced industrial civilization with its terrifying harmony of freedom and oppression,
productivity and destruction, growth and regression is pre-designed in
this idea of Reason as a specific historical project" (124). Eliminate the key

word "terrifying," the word that invokes the universe of the dialectic, from the formulation "terrifying harmony," and, again, the universe of neutral or progressive postmodern simultaneity can be glimpsed.

The two-dimensional universe, "a world antagonistic in itself," which Marcuse argues has existed from the beginning of civilization up to the (his) present moment, derives its two-dimensionality from the fact that it is "a world afflicted with want and negativity, constantly threatened with destruction" (125). It is the unprecedented satisfaction of want by technology that eliminates both the agon and the inherent potential for criticism and oppositionality of the two-dimensional universe. In two-dimensionality, the contrast between the painful existence of want and alienated toil and the apprehension of a life free of those, corresponding to the contradiction between the oppressed, exploited laborers and the ruling class, produces a contrast between "is" and "ought," between oppressed reality and potential liberated reality. In classical philosophical terms, this is the contrast between the real and the ideal. As philosophy progresses, beginning with the progression from Plato to Aristotle, Marcuse argues, the ideal becomes detached from its basis in real material alternative possibility, and becomes instead the realm of the *merely* ideal—of a metaphysics that no longer contains the force of oppositional potentiality it originally represented (this is of course a radically abridged, simplified summary of Marcuse's argument). The entire history of Western philosophy for Marcuse, up to the Marxist resituation of the dialectic in historical materiality, is a history of debilitated, dematerialized metaphysics.[8]

Marcuse argues that logical, technological, mathematical, scientific rationality is the ultimate form of this sterile, dematerialized universality. What strikes me, in terms of my argument here (and beyond the obvious connections to Derrida's attack on Western metaphysical logocentrism), is Marcuse's condemnation of Reason as the ultimate manifestation of the departicularized universal, whose "abstraction from their particular 'substance' . . . is the precondition of law and order—in logic as well as in society—the price of universal control" (136). This is one of the key arguments in the postmodern repudiation of the universal as the mode of (white, male, European, bourgeois) domination, and of the concomitant postmodern valorization of the particular as the privileged site of resistance to that hegemonic universality. "By virtue of the universal concept, thought attains mastery over the particular cases" (137). Marcuse's argument against the disembodied, instrumental, self-consistent Reason that produces and maintains the one-dimensionality of domination is also an argument against the universality that transcends particulars — the universality that, as he argued earlier, the dialectic requires.

Marcuse does go on to reassert the necessity of the universal: "indeed, without universality, thought would be a private, non-committal affair, incapable of understanding the smallest sector of existence. Thought is always more and other than individual thinking; . . . all objects of thought are universals. But it is equally true that the supra-individual meaning, the universality of a concept, is never merely a formal one; it is constituted in the interrelationship between the (thinking and acting) subjects and their world" (138–39). This formulation, however, far from giving absolute priority to the universal over the particular, conceives the universal as meaningful only in dynamic co-constitution with particular, historically located subjectivity, precisely the sort of phenomenological hermeneutic that replaces the absolute transcendent universal in some postmodern, particularly feminist, philosophy. This universal is quite different from the universal implied by the contrast between "wages are too low" and "B's present earnings, due to his wife's illness, are insufficient to meet his current obligations." "Wages are too low" is indeed "constituted in the interrelationship between the (thinking and acting) subjects and their world." However, the particularity of those thinking and acting subjects is submerged in the universality of "wages are too low": "in the form he gives his statement [wages are too low], he transcends this individual experience" (112). The inconsistency in Marcuse's treatment of the crucial question of the universal marks this text's location at one of the most important points of the emergence of postmodernity.

Marcuse proceeds to focus particularly on the link between modern scientific thought and one-dimensional modes of domination. He develops a critique of the Cartesian subject-object dualism as ideology of domination that is very familiar, in its essentials, in much postmodern, poststructuralist theory. Marcuse argues that the "Cartesian division of the world" (153) into subject and object, as manifestation of the development of the scientific method, is a prerequisite for the human domination of nature.[9] Here, Marcuse's attack on disembodied Reason as, literally, a "logic" of domination brings the text as close as it comes to postmodern thought. However, the complex argument in which this critique is embedded contains at least as much analysis that attacks what has emerged as postmodern thought as it does analysis that supports it.

In *Dialectic of Enlightenment*, Horkheimer and Adorno, also attacking the "total integration" that Marcuse calls one-dimensional society, make a related attack on scientific reason as fully instrumental and as prime engine of domination in the bourgeois period (ix). However, their emphasis is on the "self-destructiveness of enlightenment" (xi) — a version of the return of the repressed: enlightenment's obliteration as "superstition" of all phenomena that do not conform to its narrow definition of scientific rationalism, its "disenchantment" of the world, the "identification of intellect and that which is inimical to the spirit" (x) — results in the haunting of enlightenment rationalism by monstrous versions of mythologized "unreason," culminating in the barbarities of the Holocaust. Reason, for Horkheimer and Adorno, is always attached to unreason, its dialectic twin; in the Enlightenment, this attachment is repressed, resulting in a return whose brutality is overwhelming. Again, the Adornian view of inevitable mutual imbrication of reason and unreason, like his analysis of bourgeois aesthetic affirmativity always inhabiting and defining avant-garde negativity, is more congenial to postmodern ideas of complicity and mutual constitutiveness than is Marcuse's view of total affirmative domination countered only by total negating liberation.

Without following the detailed development of this discussion, which, though fascinating, is not germane to my argument, I will just say that the key factors in Marcuse's positioning in relation to modernity/postmodernity concerning this issue revolve around the question, crucial to my project here, of subjectivity; specifically, the status of the subject in scientific rationality. Marcuse cites the constitutive power of the subject, in contemporary scientific thought such as Heisenberg's, in constructing scientific reality: "now 'events,' 'relations,' 'projections,' 'possibilities' can be meaningfully objective only for a subject — not only in terms of observability and measurability, but in terms of the very structure of the event or relationship. In other words, the subject here involved is a *constituting* one" (150). But for Marcuse, the nonabsolute, nondeterminate status of observable reality in contemporary scientific thought, its reliance on a constituting subject, has neither the positive valence accorded it in postmodern thought, nor the negative valence accorded it in anti-postmodern thought. In postmodern thought, the constitutive subject represents the inherent historical locatedness and interestedness (rather than the vaunted disinterestedness) of scientific thought, its social construction and therefore its susceptibility to political critique and progressive intervention. In anti-postmodern thought, the constitutive subject represents a benighted attack on the scientific method, on objectivity, on the independent reality and knowability of the physical universe, and on reason itself. It is there-

fore susceptible to reactionary, irrational, prescientific modes of super-
stititon that could plunge society back into the pre-Enlightenment dark
ages, or that in fact are not the harbinger but rather the marker of a new
contemporary dark age of ignorance, prejudice, fear, illogic, magical
thinking, and myriad consequent forms of irrational oppression. For Marcuse, the constituting role of the subject in scientific knowledge serves
rather to dematerialize nature—to transform it from a resistant historical
actuality, capable of supporting revolutionary opposition, into an abstraction that is endlessly manipulable and therefore is inevitably manipulated
in the interests of the agents of domination.

Marcuse's argument here constitutes a characteristic sixties position, in
its totalized view of the all-encompassing pervasiveness of domination,
and its fear of a solipsism that, in locating all knowledge in the subject,
abjures the possibility of politics itself. It is also a characteristic sixties
position in its undecidable relation to dominant modern and emergent
postmodern intellectual paradigms. As in postmodern thought, Marcuse
decries Cartesian dualism, which is at the heart of enlightenment modernity's rationality, as a marker and enforcer of domination. Like postmodern thinkers, he also understands the evolution of contemporary notions
of the subject as constitutive of observable, measurable reality as continuous with, rather than in repudiation of, scientific thought. But unlike
postmodern thinkers, he considers this evolution a culmination of Reason
as domination rather than, at least potentially, as a disruption of scientific
rationality's participation in structures of hegemony. At the same time, his
condemnation of the functionalist science in which the subject is constitutive of observable reality assumes, as does modernity, that unless science is
measuring an external reality that has its own independent existence and
integrity, the material world becomes fully manipulable by domination.[10]
This purely instrumental functionalism makes scientific thought, again,
subject to its usefulness to the agents of domination. In attacking postmodern thought, Marcuse has arrived, on the modern/postmodern Möbius strip of his argument in this book, at a postmodern conclusion: the
ostensible objectivity and "neutrality" of instrumental, technological scientific rationality in fact serves the purposes, if not of domination, then of
hegemony. For Marcuse, however, this fact is attributable to the detachment of scientific thought from its link to historical materiality by means
of its reconstitution within the primary agency of the subject. For postmodern thought, science's claim to objective neutrality is merely false—an
ideology covering its particular location in a hegemony masquerading as

universal but in fact constituted by the historical supremacy of white, male, bourgeois, European subjects.

Marcuse extends his attack on Reason-as-domination to the affirmative (in the sense of hegemonic) nature and function of positivist, nondialectical, noncritical philosophy, particularly linguistic philosophy, exemplified most notably for Marcuse by Austin and Wittgenstein: a philosophy that takes language as a neutral, independent given whose rules it is philosophy's job to elucidate. Linguistic empiricism, according to Marcuse, eschews modes of thought that aim at critique and transcendence of the given. This affirmative philosophy, according to Marcuse, serves as the uncritical supportive ideology for the instrumental technological rationality of domination. One manifestation of this uncritical support of the status quo is linguistic functionalism's self-limitation to the "ordinary language" that Marcuse snidely ascribes to the disingenuous stance of "familiarity with the chap on the street" (174). "The chumminess of speech is essential [to linguistic functionalism] inasmuch as it excludes from the beginning the high-brow vocabulary of 'metaphysics'; it militates against intelligent non-conformity; it ridicules the egghead" (174). Where postmodernism sees a democratizing egalitarianism in this emphasis on ordinary rather than elite language as it actually exists in contemporary usage, Marcuse sees a disavowal of the dialectic, of the power of negation inherent in the great philosophical traditions of transcendence of the given. Further, he considers this ordinary language in fact a pseudo-language that exists not "on the street," in the living language of actual human beings, but only in the sterile, disembodied environment of functionalist linguistic discourse. Marcuse believes in the transcendent, critical potentiality inherent in ordinary discourse, "haunting" it to use an earlier formulation, but which functionalist linguistic analysis carefully eliminates from its object of study. Just as Marcuse sees the constitutiveness of the subject in relativist physics as an attack on resistant, potentially transformative historical materiality, he sees the ordinary language analysis of functionalist linguistics as an attack on the potentialities for transcendence lodged within, "haunting," the ordinary and the given. While postmodern theory has seen the arbitrariness of language, derived in part from functionalist linguistics, as another measure of full social constructedness, and therefore potentially amenable to progressive intervention and reconstruction away from hegemony, Marcuse sees it as another attack on the dialectic — on potentialities for opposition that inhere within the system itself, rather than alternatives along a limitless range of difference as in the postmodern view.

The two views partially converge, however, in de Certeau's notion of the refunctioning tactics of the everyday. Here, the potentialities for resistance Marcuse finds purged from functionalist linguistics' version of the ordinary are at once discovered and (re)invented by nonhegemonic constituencies, not for the total overthrow of domination Marcuse posits as the only possible meaningful change (at this point the two analyses widely diverge again), but for a postmodern fluid, partial refunctioning by means of resistance from within. Further, Marcuse's denunciation of functionalism constructs a fully alienated universe of the everyday: "the mutilated, 'abstract' individual who experiences (and expresses) only that which is *given* to him (given in a literal sense), who has only the facts and not the factors, whose behavior is one-dimensional and manipulated. . . . the experienced world is the result of a restricted experience, and the positivist cleaning of the mind brings the mind in line with the restricted experience" (182). This restricted, totally controlled experiential universe is diametrically opposed to the Foucauldian, de Certeauvian universe of partial, incomplete, contested hegemony, with resistance available to ordinary people at every point of the shifting, dynamic field of power flows.

However, in another turn of the modern/postmodern Möbius strip in this argument, Marcuse attacks arcane philosophical language, just as ordinary language linguistics does, though Marcuse's attack has quite a different form and object: "but if this metalanguage [a language other than ordinary language, capable of criticizing the latter's support of domination] is really to break through the totalitarian scope of the established universe of discourse, in which the different dimensions of language are integrated and assimilated, it must be capable of denoting the societal processes which have determined and 'closed' the established universe of discourse. Consequently, it cannot be a technical metalanguage, constructed mainly with a view of semantic or logical clarity" (195). The issue of a technical philosophical metalanguage is most germane to poststructuralist philosophy, where an arcane specialist language was constructed not so much with a view toward semantic or logical clarity, but quite the opposite — with a view toward developing a language capable of housing, registering, and constituting the multiplicity, complexity, and indeterminacy of poststructuralist thought. Marcuse's attack on a specialist philosophical metalanguage, divorced from ordinary usage, resonates with a certain postmodern view of poststructuralism, which I share. This view sees poststructuralism not as postmodern but rather as the epitome of modernist thought and language, whose aim is to transcend the limitations of the bourgeois ordinary by revealing the multiplicity and complexity of the realities bourgeois ideologies are constructed in order to conceal.[11] The arcane difficulty of poststructuralist writing, in this view, corresponds to the difficulty and complexity of modernist and avantgarde writing, participating as well in modernism's truth-questing project, despite its denials of the possibility or desirability of a unitary "truth." In this view, which, again, I hold, the great works of continental poststructuralist theory, mostly written in, and profoundly participating in, the sixties, are part of modernism, and mark its endpoint. At the same time, these works play a key role in initiating postmodernism (sometimes explicitly, as in the project of Lyotard, and crucially, as in the oeuvre of Foucault) by theorizing its multiplicities and indeterminancies, and by critiquing the governing hierarchical dualisms of modernity.

At the same time, Marcuse's argument also resonates with de Certeau himself. The passage in which Marcuse asserts that "consequently, it cannot be a technical metalanguage, constructed mainly with a view of semantic or logical clarity," continues as follows: "the desideratum is rather to make the established language itself speak what it conceals or excludes, for what is to be revealed and denounced is operative *within* the universe of ordinary discourse and action, and the prevailing language *contains* the metalanguage" (195). While Marcuse refers here to the existence within the dominant order of the potentiality for its own dialectical negation, his formulation comes very close to de Certeau's of everyday refunctioning that takes place precisely "*within* the universe of ordinary discourse and action," by using tactics contained in, and implied by, hegemonic formations.

Marcuse chooses to conclude the book, because of his Marxist belief in the necessity of optimism, on an almost forced hopeful note, "The Chance of the Alternatives." Again, here, he recapitulates the central arguments of the book. Marcuse does make clearer here than he had in the first two sections the extent to which the Great Refusal — the total transcendence of the existing order necessary to effect any meaningful change — must come from the utterly disenfranchised margins of society, since one-dimensionality's egalitarian affluence otherwise absorbs all resistance so thoroughly. He also makes clearer the extent to which the Great Refusal is linked to avant-garde aesthetic consciousness. Marcuse emphasizes in this section what he calls, with jarring, unintended significance in the wake of the later stages of the Vietnam War, the "pacification of existence," by which he means the end of scarcity, want, and alienated toil, made possible, as it appeared then, by the promise of technology. The "pacification of existence" would allow, if accompanied by the Great Refusal, the pursuit of the "art of living" (Whitehead).

These arguments are entirely lodged within the utopian vision of modernity. In some of their particulars, they also resonate profoundly with the radical and countercultural ideologies of the sixties: "today, in the prosperous warfare and welfare state, the human qualities of a pacified existence seem asocial and unpatriotic — qualities such as the refusal of all toughness, togetherness [by which Marcuse means enforced conformity rather than communal living], and brutality; disobedience to the tyranny of the majority; profession of fear and weakness (the most rational reaction to this society!); a sensitive intelligence sickened by that which is being perpetrated; the commitment to the feeble and ridiculed actions of protest and refusal" (242–43). I am particularly struck by the feminization of masculinity implied throughout this passage, a phenomenon, discussed elsewhere (see chapter 5), which characterizes crucial aspects of sixties cultural and political formations. This feminization was one sixties pivot to postmodernity's multiplied, fluid gender constructions.

In his culminating denunciation of one-dimensional society, focused on its cooptation of the aesthetic, Marcuse makes perhaps the strongest statement in the book of one-dimensionality's nearly invincible power and efficacy:

> Setting the pace and style of politics, the power of imagination far exceeds Alice in Wonderland in the manipulation of words, turning sense into nonsense and nonsense into sense. The formerly antagonistic realms merge on technical and political grounds — magic and science, life and death, joy and misery. Beauty reveals its terror. . . . The obscene merger of aesthetics and reality refutes the philosophies which oppose "poetic" imagination to scientific and empirical Reason. Technological progress is accompanied by a progressive rationalization and even realization of the imaginary. The archetypes of horror as well as of joy, of war as well as of peace lose their catastrophic character. . . . In reducing and even canceling the romantic space of imagination, society has forced the imagination to prove itself on new grounds, on which the images are translated into historical capabilities and projects. (248–49)

These "new grounds" are the liberated aesthetic consciousness of the avant-garde Great Refusers, and of the "substratum of the outcasts and outsiders, the exploited and persecuted of other races and other colors, the unemployed and the unemployable" who "exist outside the democratic process" (256). Marcuse specifies the Civil Rights movement as the location of these outsiders — "the fact that they start refusing to play the game may be the fact which marks the beginning of the end of a period" (257). A broad spectrum of sixties counterculturalist radicals attempted to occupy the outsider position of Great Refusal Marcuse delineates here as the only hope for ending one-dimensionality.

Ultimately, Marcuse's pessimism concerning the total revolutionary change he advocated, a pessimism overriding his more ideological optimism, was justified. This pessimism was based on his understanding of the real material gains, the real egalitarian rise in the standard of living, the real end, for better and/or worse, of the two-dimensional universe of the dialectic and of oppressive hierarchical dualism. The one-dimensionality he delineated so powerfully lost the character of total alienation he ascribed to it, and became postmodernity.

PART TWO

Culture Industry to Popular Culture

CHAPTER TWO

Culture Industry to Popular Culture in *Mythologies*

One of the defining components of the sixties shift from modern to post-modern involved a sea change in the status of what we now commonly refer to as popular culture. It has become a truism that in postmodernity, the modernist distinction between high culture and popular culture has been eroded, if not fully erased.[1] Further, practitioners of cultural studies, which is quintessentially postmodern, not only take popular culture as their primary object of inquiry but also find there the most important politically progressive modes of contemporary cultural expression.[2] The status of popular culture in modernism was far more variegated and complex than cursory analysis of the "great divide" allows (Huyssen's own analysis is much more nuanced and complex than brief summaries of his central argument often imply). Most of the great modernists were enthusiasts of one form or another of popular culture, finding inspiration in, and incorporating into their aesthetic practices, a range of popular forms such as film, circus, comic strip, music hall, jazz and blues, traditional folk music, and various modes of genre fiction. But popular forms did not remain intact in modernist art — they were assimilated to and transformed by the modernists' revolutionary aesthetic practices. Further, mass (rather than popular) culture, the negatively connotative term used to indict the "culture industry," was repudiated by the modernists as both aesthetically and politically impoverished, the left seeing it as supporting dominant bourgeois ideologies, and the right seeing it as the degraded culture of the hoi poloi. This contempt for mass culture, expressed most scathingly, as we have seen, by Marcuse, and most powerfully and influentially by Horkheimer and Adorno in "The Culture Industry," has become a standard object of attack for postmodern cultural studies. In this attack, a negative view of mass culture is seen as defining modernist elitism.

Roland Barthes's *Mythologies* of 1957 is a classic and germinal textual instantiation of the sixties simultaneity of the dominant modernist contempt for mass culture and the emergent postmodernist valorization of popular culture.[3] Modernist loathing of mass culture cohabits uneasily with postmodernist fascination with popular culture in *Mythologies*. The text enacts in itself the historical moment, in the sixties, of the coexistence, of a dominant (soon to be residual) modern with an emergent postmodern paradigm.

Cultural studies, with its emphasis on popular culture, is, again, a characteristic intellectual institution and practice of postmodernism. *Mythologies*, according to several key theorist-historians and practitioners of the movement, is an initiatory and paradigmatic text of cultural studies.[4] *Mythologies*, then, to follow the syllogism, is a founding text of postmodernism. In *Mythologies*, Barthes does in fact focus on popular culture, extending the methods of literary reading to a wide range of cultural productions in a way that enacts and endorses the cultural-studies analysis of popular culture as locus of resistance. Many of *Mythologies*'s short pieces are characterized by a tone of intense interest bordering on fascination. This tone, however, must be understood in light of Barthes's primary purpose in this collection, a purpose derived from modernism's agendas, which is to demystify, denounce, and undercut the culture of the bourgeoisie.

By "bourgeoisie," Barthes generally means the petite-bourgeoisie: the lower-middle and middle-middle class fractions. He does not mean the haute-bourgeoisie of the literary elite, the high-culture class in opposition to which postmodern cultural studies is positioned. In terms of class politics, Barthes is denouncing, even waging war against, one of cultural studies' prime constituencies: the "ordinary" consumers of popular culture, the non- or anti-elite classes invoked by populism. This constituency is not generally identified with Kafka, Brecht, Beckett, or Robbe Grillet—the writers who are, in this period (as for example in *Critical Essays* and *Writing Degree Zero*), Barthes's culture heros. The figure of war comes from Barthes himself: he refers to "the bourgeois norm" as "the essential enemy" (9). This antibourgeois war is squarely within the political tradition of twentieth-century modernism and what are now known as the "historical avant-gardes."[5]

The cultural studies analysis of *Mythologies* is premised on the centrality of Barthes's unmasking and critique of bourgeois culture. This attack on bourgeois culture as ideology has in fact become a central tenet of cultural studies, and of postmodern ideologies in general. Barthes argues that modernity's ascendant bourgeoisie has made culture the site of history's enforced masquerade as immutable, timeless truth or nature. Barthes describes his purpose as to "account *in detail* for the mystification which transforms petit-bourgeois culture into a universal nature" (9). This insight is crucial to the class-inflected historicization of cultural formations at the center of postmodern social critiques in general, and of work done in cultural studies in particular. Yet cultural studies' reading of *Mythologies* subtly shifts the political significance of Barthes's critique.

As we will see, Barthes in the late fifties occupied a revolutionary utopian countercultural position, the position to be taken up by the radical youth movements that culminated in May '68. These movements aligned themselves culturally with the sixties renaissance of the avant-gardes. From within this position, the popular-cultural artifacts Barthes analyzes in *Mythologies* were seen as primarily reactionary. Barthes, like sixties countercultural radicals, believed that unmasking bourgeois culture as mythology would lead to its repudiation and transcendence in the utopian cultural and political revolutions that must soon follow.[6] These transformative revolutions would obliterate the alienated capitalist-consumerist culture of Marcuse's "one-dimensional society," or the Situationist Guy Debord's "society of the spectacle," and replace it with genuine revolutionary culture, which was to be ushered in by the avant-gardes.[7]

Simon During understands this position when he labels *Mythologies* "finally of a piece with Adorno and Horkheimer's thought"; in other words, in tune with their attack on mass culture in "The Culture Industry." During, however, redeems Barthes's text because, in pieces such as "The New Citroën," "the young Barthes expressed his belief that mass-produced commodities can be beautiful. One cannot imagine Theodor Adorno, in particular, conceding that" (44–45). Yet Barthes aligned himself fully with the Adornian advocacy of the avant-garde as oppositional aesthetic practice. He saw it as the only mode of cultural production capable of resisting, and providing an alternative to, not so much the aesthetic degradation of mass culture but rather its function as guarantor of bourgeois hegemony. It is precisely this understanding of the political meanings of popular culture that cultural studies, as exemplary intellectual institution of postmodernism, contests. For cultural studies, certain productions of popular culture constitute the prime site of nonelite, populist (including stratifications of race, gender, sexuality, and location as well as of class) resistance to high-cultural hegemony. In this postmodern paradigm, the "enemy," to use Barthes's term, has become the entrenched, exclusionary, conservative canonicity of high culture, particularly of high modernism, as institutionalized in the mid-century universities. In that high culture, as viewed from the vantage point of postmodern cultural studies, the very modernism/avant-garde celebrated in the sixties as harbinger of a utopian egalitarian revolution has become part of the forces that guarantee elite hegemony and its hold on cultural capital. Yet the sixties, of which *Mythologies* is representative and characteristic, was, at the same time, the site of the initiation of postmodernity, including the breakdown of the "great divide" (of high and popular culture) and the emergence of an egalitarian, newly revitalized and diverse, refunctioned, ironized commercial popular culture. We can see these contradictory structures seamlessly meshed together in sixties texts such as *Mythologies*.

Barthes did not write *Mythologies*, even the pieces where his erotic investment in popular culture is most apparent, to celebrate the beauty of the new Citroën. In fact, I would argue that in such pieces he is just as much ventriloquizing as he is occupying the position of the infatuated consumer, in order to understand, demystify, and repudiate that position. Yet, in doing so, he opens up the space of postmodernism's valorization and reinvigoration of the popular. Postmodernism adopts his fascination, or rather the fascination flooding unevenly through his text, and jettisons the revolutionary utopian politics that led Barthes to explore such fascination in order to work free of it. Postmodernity substitutes for Barthes's sixties radical utopian politics an anti- or post-utopian politics of local, particular, limited, partial resistance or subversion-from-within. Barthes mostly loathes (to anticipate Hunter Thompson's term; see chapter 4) the objects of his demythologizing study even as he legitimates them intellectually. He must legitimate them because he knows that they are the crucial locus of what we must learn in order to "make the revolution."

The loathing of what must be called mass culture in *Mythologies* —
Barthes's view of it as both prime representation and also direct enforcer
of the repressive social-political institutions of the bourgeoisie — is clearest in the short piece "Operation Margarine." This piece describes a narrative process that initiates a critique of oppressive institutions such as the
army or the church, only to recuperate or reinstate those institutions all
the more forcefully at the end, either in spite of, or by means of, the initial
critique: "to instil into the Established Order the complacent portrayal of
its drawbacks has nowadays become a paradoxical but incontrovertible
means of exalting it. Here is the pattern of this new-style demonstration:
take the established value which you want to restore or develop, and first
lavishly display its pettiness, the injustices which it produces, the vexations to which it gives rise, and plunge it into its natural imperfection;
then, at the last moment, save it *in spite of*, or rather *by* the heavy curse of
its blemishes" (41).

Barthes considers this process characteristic of mainstream bourgeois
fictional narratives — he cites as typical examples the treatment of the army
in James Jones's *From Here to Eternity* and Jules Roy's *Les Cyclones*, and
of the church in Graham Greene's *The Living Room*. The treatment of the
army in the first "show[s] without disguise its chiefs as martinets, its
discipline as narrow-minded and unfair," and, in the second, demonstrates
"the scientific fanaticism of its engineers, and their blindness"; its "pitiless
rigor." Yet at the end both "turn over the magical hat, and pull out of it the
image of an army, flags flying, triumphant . . . bring out the flag, save
the army in the name of progress, hitch the greatness of the former to the
triumph of the latter" (41). Crucially, *From Here to Eternity* accomplishes
this redemption by inserting "into this stupid tyranny . . . an average
human being, fallible but likeable, the archetype of the spectator" (41).
This spectatorial stand-in, the figure of bourgeois identification, is allowed
to vent resentment of, even resistance to these dominant institutions only
so that their power and authority can be fully recuperated. (This recupera-
tive structure is now generally considered to characterize middlebrow
culture — resolving tensions rather than leaving questions open — but no
negative judgment of recuperation is involved in the current analysis of the
middlebrow, as it is in Barthes's "Operation Margarine.")

Barthes's analysis of critique-as-recuperation in Greene's novel, in relation to the church, is even more sharply focused: "finally, the Church: speak
with burning zeal about its self-righteousness, the narrow-mindedness of
its bigots, indicate that all this can be murderous, hide none of the weak-

nesses of the faith. And then, *in extremis*, hint that the letter of the law, however unattractive, is a way to salvation for its very victims, and so justify moral austerity by the saintliness of those whom it crushes" (41). The church is recuperated not in spite of but by means of its oppressiveness. In the closing word "crushes," Barthes's sarcastic mockery takes on an edge of bitterness.

In "Operation Margarine" Barthes is unmasking, and attacking, a manipulative orchestration of narrative in the service of the workings of hegemonic ideology: an initial critique is made only in order to pave the way for a reinstitution of authority — "Established Order" — all the more firmly entrenched. Barthes's tone in this piece is, as I have noted, mocking, sarcastic, just as it is throughout most of *Mythologies*. He is showing us that, to the extent we allow ourselves to occupy the position of that "average human being, fallible but likeable, the archetype of the spectator," we are dupes of bourgeois ideology. For postmodernism, on the other hand, it is precisely this "average human being" through whose subjectivity points of resistance can be articulated in the reception and refunctioning of popular culture. For Barthes, to understand how we are manipulated is to begin to free ourselves from the manipulation, and therefore, by implication, from the controlling cultural force of these mythologies in general: free ourselves to participate instead in an alternative revolutionary avant-garde culture. In this Marcusean rather than Althusserian analysis, the intellectual *can* open up a space at least potentially free of bourgeois capitalist ideology.

In postmodern analyses of popular culture, this narrative of critique followed by, or engendering, recuperation has taken on an entirely different valence. Mockery, sarcasm, and attack have come to be considered at once elitist and naive, as has any self-positioning (at least potentially) apart from that "average human being, fallible but likeable" — self-positioning outside the power of dominant culture and its ideologies. In postmodernity, none of us, however analytically sharp, escapes culture and its constructions; there is no outside, no Archimedean lever, no utopian space beyond ideology.

Further, the political emphasis of the analysis has shifted significantly. Recuperation and reinstatement of authority are no longer now the focus of the analysis. They have come to be seen as almost an afterthought, an inconsequential narrative lip-service, as it were, to hegemony. They are allied with the conventional forms, resurgent in postmodernity, that enable access to a wide, popular audience, while avant-garde/high culture is seen to appeal only to a narrow elite. It is from within this popular convention, and against it, that postmodern resistance and refunctioning work, generally ironically. In postmodern analysis, and in postmodern cultural production, critique coexists with recuperation, it is not obliterated by it. Further, it is the critique that matters — that is where the politically meaningful, progressive aspects of popular culture reside.[8] To attack or mock the regressive, hegemony-supporting functions of popular culture is to show that one aligns oneself with Adorno-Horkheimer's elitist attack on the culture industry, and with the cultural elite's use of hierarchies of taste (as analyzed most tellingly by Bourdieu) to mark and guarantee its superiority.

Barthes does not distinguish in this piece between what we might call middlebrow fiction, such as the three narratives of army and church discussed so far, which is squarely within the category of the literary, and the advertising campaign for margarine that gives the piece its title and central focus.[9] One of Barthes's central structuralist theses in *Mythologies* is that bourgeois culture is unified ("one-dimensional" in the Marcusean sense), having absorbed into itself in modernity all classes and all their cultural productions. Barthes argues that all culture, except the avant-gardes, which themselves depend on the bourgeoisie, is bourgeois culture: "in a bourgeois culture, there is neither proletarian culture nor proletarian morality, there is no proletarian art; ideologically, all that is not bourgeois is obliged to *borrow* from the bourgeoisie. Bourgeois ideology can therefore spread over everything and in so doing lose its name without risk . . . there are revolts against bourgeois ideology. This is what one generally calls the avant-garde" (139).

This indifferentiation of cultural production, despite its claim that bourgeois culture entirely coopts proletarian culture, is one of the aspects of *Mythologies* most useful to postmodern cultural studies, which is far less interested in differentiating among modes of cultural production than in treating all cultural texts as social texts. But this indifferentiation also works against the distinction in cultural studies between elitist, canonical high-literary modes and progressive popular culture. Barthes, in a crucial and characteristic sixties gesture, is refusing the distinction between elitist and popular culture that cultural studies, and postmodernism in general, assume.

An advertising campaign for a particular brand of margarine reveals most clearly for Barthes the pattern he is analyzing, a pattern in which, again, "one inoculates the public with a contingent evil to prevent or cure an essential one" (42). The advertisement begins by imagining the scandalized response of cooks in the classical French tradition of butter-based cuisine to the very thought of margarine:

> One can trace in advertising a narrative pattern which clearly shows the working of this new vaccine. It is found in the publicity for *Astra* margarine. The episode always begins with a cry of indignation against margarine: "A mousse? Made with margarine? Unthinkable!" "Margarine? Your uncle will be furious!" And then one's eyes are opened, one's conscience becomes more pliable, and margarine is a delicious food, tasty, digestible, economical, useful in all circumstances. The moral at the end is well known: "Here you are, rid of a prejudice which cost you dearly!" It is in the same way that the Established Order relieves you of your progressive prejudices. . . . What does it matter, *after all*, if margarine is just fat, when it goes further than butter, and costs less? What does it matter, *after all*, if Order is a little brutal or a little blind, when it allows us to live cheaply? Here we are, in our turn, rid of a prejudice which cost us dearly, too dearly, which cost us too much in scruples, in revolt, in fights and in solitude. (42)

Just as fat is transformed by the manipulative lies of advertising into a general social good, the brutality and blindness of the Established Order (army, church, bourgeois capitalism itself) — once we have been inoculated by a bad-faith critique — are transformed by the manipulative lies of bourgeois literature into "the transcendent good of religion, fatherland, the Church, etc." (42).

The mythographer, the sixties cultural-political radical, is left with his scruples, revolt, fights, and solitude: his rage, his will to resist and discredit operation margarine in all its variegated manifestations, and his self-positioning outside its reach, in an alternative revolutionary utopian cultural space. Where the cultural products that participate in operation margarine begin with an ostensible critique that is then neutralized ("contained," in Marcuse's term) by its deployment in the service of a full reinstatement of Order at the end, Barthes's initially detached, even admiring interest and amusement in the workings of advertising give way to an impassioned, scathing final revolt, a jeremiad of loathing — the characteristic stance, tone, narrative mode of the sixties radical: "the Army, an absolute value? It is unthinkable: look at its vexations, its strictness, the always possible blindness of its chiefs. The Church, infallible? Alas, it is very doubtful: look at its bigots, its powerless priests, its murderous conformism. And then common sense makes its reckoning: what is this trifling dross of Order, compared to its advantages? It is well worth the price of an immunization. . . . What does it matter, *after all*, if Order is a little brutal or a little blind, when it allows us to live cheaply?" (42).

In the body of *Mythologies*, the narrative strategy Barthes uses in "Operation Margarine" reappears frequently: amused dismissiveness, drawing the reader into a superior conspiracy of mocking condescension, edges steadily toward anger, and culminates in scathing denunciation, where the political stakes are enormously raised. The loathing at first expressed in a tone of distanced mockery, of haughtily amused dismissiveness, becomes at the end of the piece a full-blown denunciation.

A number of other pieces in *Mythologies*, in addition to "Operation Margarine," analyze the hegemonic workings of various mainstream bourgeois literary institutions and discourses, including criticism. In an exemplary instance of a revisionary rereading of Barthes as fully, rather than contradictorily and incipiently, postmodernist, Simon During reprints "Dominici, or the Triumph of Literature" in his *Cultural Studies Reader*, citing it as an attack on literature in general, rather than, as Barthes describes it, an attack specifically on "the Literature of the bourgeois Establishment" (43). Gaston Dominici, whom Barthes evidently believes was unfairly convicted in a widely publicized trial, was "the 80-year-old owner of the Grand 'Terre farm in Provence . . . convicted in 1952 of murdering Sir Jack Drummond, his wife and daughter, whom he found camping near his land" (translator's note in text, 43). Dominici claimed self-defense: Drummond had attacked him first. His bourgeois judges could not believe that any *Sir* Jack Drummond would do such a thing.

"Dominici" is, in fact, in many ways an ideal instance of a postmodern populism suspicious of the literary. It demonstrates very clearly the alliance of literary discourse with the ruling class, the power elite — the way in which hegemonic power, specifically power over a culturally marginal rustic, is constructed and enforced by and through literary discourse. But while During establishes this reading of "Dominici" in a very lucid, concise manner, his Editor's Introduction nonetheless revises the meaning of Barthes's discussion of literature:

> Here Barthes shows that "literature" is not separate from everyday life and its power flows. On the contrary, he analyses a case in which an inarticulate rural labourer [Dominici is in fact a landowner] is condemned in terms of a discourse which is profoundly literary: the judges

describe Dominici's motives in terms borrowed from literary clichés; they gain their sense of superiority because they speak "better" French than he — where "better" means more like written prose. And, in reporting the trial, the journalists turn it into more literature — where "literature" does not just mean the literary canon but the conventional system of writing and representation in which the canon remains uncontested. . . . this remains a classic account of how hegemony is produced through interactions between various institutions and discourses — in this case, literature, the law, and journalism — over the body of those who can hardly talk back. (44)

Note how Barthes's "Literature of the bourgeois Establishment," by which he means conventional, mainstream, bourgeois, and "classical" literature as taught in "the schools of the Third Republic" (43) at the time, is here collapsed into the general, unqualified category "literature," which for During is a monolithically hegemonic discourse on a par with "the law and journalism." For Barthes, however, modernist/avant-garde literature actually stands in opposition to the bourgeois literary discourses — "Literature" — deployed against Dominici: "descending from the charming empyrean of *bourgeois* novels and *essentialist* psychology, Literature has just condemned a man to the guillotine" (43, emphasis added). Barthes cites Camus and Kafka, in fact, on Dominici's side of the ethical equation (for political ethics are at the center of this piece), over against the bourgeois M. Genevoix, the classical Corneille, and the official language of school essays:

This [the Public Prosecutor's version of events] is credible like the temple of Sesostris, like the Literature of M. Genevoix. Only, to base archaeology or the novel on a "Why not?" does not harm anybody. But Justice? Periodically, some trial, and not necessarily fictitious like the one in Camus's *The Outsider*, comes to remind you that the Law is always prepared to lend you a spare brain in order to condemn you without remorse, and that, like Corneille, it depicts you as you should be, and not as you are. . . . Their [the journalists'] remarks show that there is no need to imagine mysterious barriers, Kafka-like misunderstandings. No: syntax, vocabulary, most of the elementary, analytical materials of language grope blindly without ever touching, but no one has any qualms about it. . . . And yet, this language of the president is just as peculiar, laden as it is with unreal clichés; it is a language for school essays. (44–45)

Modernist/avant-garde literary practice, for Barthes, is the champion, ally, voice of the disenfranchised Dominici, not the tool of his oppressor. Camus and Kafka speak with Barthes, to reveal and condemn the power of hegemonic discourse over its victims. Evidently, Camus and Kafka, modernism and the avant-garde, oppose the "language for school essays," "laden . . . with unreal clichés," deployed against Dominici. Again, for Barthes as sixties radical, literature is not a monolithic institution of hegemony; in fact, it is precisely modernist/avant-garde sensibility and aesthetic practice that resist bourgeois hegemony.

"Dominici" attacks the role of bourgeois discourses in enforcing class inequality. Barthes also concerns himself with questions of race and gender in *Mythologies*, not centrally, but visibly. This visible interest has been an important factor, I think, in *Mythologies*' importance to practitioners of postmodern cultural studies. In a much-cited sequence, for example, Barthes offers, as a seemingly random instance of the workings of "mythology," a powerful deconstruction of the cultural promulgation of imperialist ideology: "and here is now another example [of the structure of signification in "myth"]: I am at the barber's, and a copy of *Paris-Match* is offered to me. On the cover, a young Negro in a French uniform is saluting, with his eyes uplifted, probably fixed on a fold of the tricolour. All this is the *meaning* of the picture. But, whether naively or not, I see very well what it signifies to me: that France is a great Empire, that all her sons, without any colour discrimination, faithfully serve under her flag, and that there is no better answer to the detractors of an alleged colonialism than the zeal shown by this Negro in serving his so-called oppressors" (116).

This is clearly no random, neutral example of the workings of mythology, any more than is "Dominici": Barthes is centrally concerned with imperialism and racism, as he is with class stratification. Yet the political meaning that led Barthes to choose this particular *Paris-Match* cover as an exemplary cultural text is made subsidiary, in his argument, to its demonstration of the workings of signifier and signified in the semiological structure of myth. The conclusion of the above analysis — the sentence that follows immediately after "in serving his so-called oppressors" reads: "I am therefore again faced with a greater semiological system: there is a signifier, itself already formed with a previous system (*a black soldier giving the French salute*); there is a signified (it is here a purposeful mixture of Frenchness and militariness); finally, there is a presence of the signified through the signifier" (116). The political meaning of the photo is firmly reinserted in parentheses: made subordinate to, just one among many instances of, the structural-linguistic analysis that is Barthes's primary project here. While analysis of racism, imperialism, and class inequality is central to the practice of postmodern cultural studies criticism in its readings of popular culture, for Barthes in this sixties text it is a central but quasi-repressed, only obliquely acknowledged agenda.

Barthes's critique of hegemonic gender constructions is similarly, perhaps even more, repressed, only very obliquely acknowledged. It emerges most clearly in "The Lady of the Camellias," which is the last piece in the book before the closing section, "Myth Today." "The Lady of the Camellias" opens with a feminist statement remarkably strong and clear for a male intellectual in the mid-fifties:[10] "They still perform, in some part of the world or other, *The Lady of the Camellias* (it had in fact another run in Paris some time ago). This success must alert us to a mythology of Love which probably still exists, for the alienation of Marguerite Gautier in relation to the class of her masters is not fundamentally different from that of today's petit-bourgeois women in a world which is just as stratified" (103). Yet the argument immediately shifts from an analysis that makes gender equal to class as codeterminants of Marguerite's subordination to an attack on bourgeois love in which gender has slipped out of sight: "we do not deal here with one passion divided against itself but with two passions of different natures, because they come from different situations in society. Armand's passion, which is bourgeois in type, and appropriative, is by definition a murder of the other; and that of Marguerite can only crown her effort to achieve recognition by a sacrifice which will in its turn constitute an indirect murder of Armand's passion" (104). The question of gender is not dropped; rather, it is subsumed under the question of "the mythological content of [bourgeois] love, which is the archetype of petit-bourgeois sentimentality" (104). Again, Barthes's central purpose is to attack the petite-bourgeoisie, while in postmodernist ideologies such attacks have become discredited as naive and elitist. The specific critiques of racism, sexism, and classicism that are subsidiary points for Barthes have become central to postmodern analyses of, and investment in, the local-particular constructions of the new social movements.

If one accepts some version of the equation of popular culture with the feminine,[11] however, it is possible to argue that *Mythologies*, in making popular culture its object of study, also brings the feminine into the sphere of intellectual legitimacy. All those trivial objects of feminine domestic consumption, heretofore beneath serious notice, are redefined by Barthes as carriers of the largest cultural meanings. This move is at the heart of the postmodern/cultural studies valorization of the popular, and *Mythologies* is therefore indeed one of its initiating texts.

Barthes's characteristic sixties concatenation of loathing and fascination in relation to popular culture is clearest in the juxtaposition of two essays, one in the middle of the book and the other toward the end: "Toys" and "Plastic." "Toys" is an attack on modern bourgeois acculturation of children very familiar from sixties countercultural and subsequent New Age alternative education and parenting discourses, and also characteristic of Barthes's own project of reclaiming agency for the modern subject constructed as passive consumer. Barthes rues the absence of opportunity for creativity in children's toys: "invented forms are very rare: a few sets of blocks, which appeal to the spirit of do-it-yourself, are the only ones which offer dynamic forms" (53). Bourgeois toys are designed rather to indoctrinate children into "the myths or the techniques of modern adult life: the Army, Broadcasting, the Post Office, Medicine . . . School, Hair-Styling . . . the Air Force . . . Transport . . . Science" (53). Barthes uses this distinction between open-ended or creative and literally imitative toys to articulate his central modernist/countercultural ideology:

> . . . faced with this world of faithful and complicated objects, the child can only identify himself as owner, as user, never as creator; he does not invent the world, he uses it: there are, prepared for him, actions without adventure, without wonder, without joy. . . . The merest set of blocks, provided it is not too refined, implies a very different learning of the world: then . . . the actions he performs are not those of a user but those of a demiurge. He creates forms which walk, which roll, he creates life, not property: objects now act by themselves, they are no longer an inert and complicated material in the palm of his hand. But such toys are rather rare: French toys are usually based on imitation, they are meant to produce children who are users, not creators. (53–54)

The parallel with Barthes's later articulations of the writerly as opposed to the readerly text, or the text as opposed to the work, is very clear. All of these formulations are characteristic expressions of the sixties modernist/avant-garde, neoromantic belief in creativity as a source of meaningful agency over against the construction of passive, instrumental subjectivity in bourgeois capitalist modernity.

The final section of "Toys" moves on to discuss the materials characteristically used in the construction of these loathsome instruments of bourgeois acculturation to passive consumerism. Not surprisingly, Barthes does not like plastic:

> The bourgeois status of toys can be recognized not only in their forms, which are all functional, but also in their substances. Current toys are made of a graceless material, the product of chemistry, not of nature. Many are now moulded from complicated mixtures; the plastic material of which they are made has an appearance at once gross and hygienic, it destroys all the pleasure, the sweetness, the humanity of touch. A sign which fills one with consternation is the gradual disappearance of wood, in spite of its being an ideal material because of its firmness and its softness, and the natural warmth of its touch. . . . It is a familiar and poetic substance, which does not sever the child from close contact with the tree. . . . Wood makes essential objects, objects for all time. . . . Henceforth, toys are chemical in substance and colour; their very material introduces one to a coenaesthesis of use, not pleasure. (54–55)

We are firmly within modernist ideology here, with its valorization of "nature" over "chemistry," "poetry" and "pleasure" over "use," the "essential" over the contingent, the timeless over the ephemeral.

The essay "Plastic" is just as firmly lodged within the postmodern intellectual paradigm as "Toys" is within the modern. The coexistence of the two essays within the same volume is characteristic of sixties texts. In the later essay, plastic has become not the dead offensive matter of antinatural, anticreative bourgeois utilitarianism but rather "the stuff of alchemy," product of "the magical operation par excellence: the transmutation of matter" (97).[12] As Barthes develops his theme, his language becomes predictive of his later poststructuralist writing: "so, more than a substance, plastic is the very idea of its infinite transformation; as its everyday name indicates, it is ubiquity made visible. And it is this, in fact, which makes it a miraculous substance: a miracle is always a sudden transformation of nature. Plastic remains impregnated throughout with this wonder: it is less a thing than the trace of a movement. . . . plastic is, all told, a spectacle to be deciphered. . . . Hence a perpetual amazement, the reverie of man at the sight of the proliferating forms of matter. . . . And this amazement is a pleasurable one . . . since the very itinerary of plastic gives him the euphoria of a prestigious free-wheeling through Nature" (97–98). Barthes initiates a number of characteristic postmodern motifs here: the valorization of transformation, of pure movement and of objects as unstable traces of movement, of spectacle and its attendant amazement, and of "prestigious free-wheeling through Nature," where nature is no longer a revered, inspiring other, and the nature/culture divide has blurred.

His near-ecstatic fascination here, a clear instance of the "postmodern sublime," could not be further removed from his loathing of plastic in "Toys." This ecstatic fascination, again, encompasses precisely the breaching of the nature/culture dualism he deplores in "Toys": "The hierarchy of substances is abolished: a single one replaces them all: the whole world *can* be plasticized, and even life itself since, we are told, they are beginning to make plastic aortas" (99). Loathing is not extirpated — it echoes clearly in "the whole world *can* be plasticized," and in the middle of the essay Barthes repeats elements of his attack on plastic in "Toys": "In the hierarchy of the major poetic substances, it [plastic] figures as a disgraced material . . . whatever its final state, plastic keeps a flocculent appearance, something opaque, creamy and curdled, something powerless ever to achieve the triumphant smoothness of Nature" (98). Yet, in the essay's final move from the modern to the postmodern, it is precisely this "hierarchy" that Barthes then accords plastic the miraculous power of abolishing.

Mythologies inscribes — early as it comes in the sixties, we might better say that it helps to announce — the sixties as the moment of historical simultaneity of the dominant modern and the emergent postmodern. In the dominant paradigm of modernity, as we have seen in Marcuse as well, mass culture is considered the home and enforcer of the reactionary bourgeois status quo, to be replaced through revolution by a culture based on utopian avant-garde consciousness. In the emergent paradigm of postmodernity, popular culture is seen as the privileged site of resistance to the oppressive Enlightenment master narratives, and modernist/avant-garde aesthetic practices are seen as a cultural expression of the white, Western, imperialist, masculinist, bourgeois hegemony that characterizes modernity. As I argue throughout this book, it is important to remember the utopian range of *Mythologies* and other sixties texts, their loathing of repressive bourgeois cultural forms as well as their egalitarian embrace of the popular, not in order to revert to that superseded structure of feeling, but in order to remember fully the intellectual dynamics of its viability in its historical moment, retaining the ability to hold contradictory ideas in our minds, so as, by refusing to erase its recent history, to be able to see the present more clearly.

CHAPTER THREE

Las Vegas Signs Taken for Wonders

Las Vegas is a key location, both literally and symbolically, of postmodern American culture.[1] Tom Wolfe's position in relation to Las Vegas in his essay "Las Vegas (What?) Las Vegas (Can't Hear You! Too Noisy) Las Vegas!!!!," in *The Kandy-Kolored Tangerine-Flake Streamline Baby*, is in many ways similar to Barthes's position in relation to popular culture in *Mythologies*, as we saw it most clearly in "Operation Margarine": initially neutrally descriptive, amused, and also somewhat fascinated and conde-scendingly admiring; by the end increasingly judgmental, repudiating, ap-proaching full-blown loathing (though Wolfe's position, in a single essay, of course does not display the same complex range as Barthes's — rather it is vacillating and ambiguous, although the general development in the essay is from neutral enjoyment to judgmental repudiation).[2] Since the issues around which Wolfe constructs his essay recur in both Thompson's and Venturi et al.'s treatments of Las Vegas, which I discuss in chapter 4, I will discuss Wolfe's essay with reference to those two texts.[3]

Wolfe wrote extensively, and mainly admiringly, about popular culture in this period. He introduces the title essay of this volume, which is about customized cars, by saying, "you have to reach the conclusion that these customized cars *are* art objects, at least if you use the standards applied in a civilized society" (76). He compares customized cars to the work of Picasso and Miró; he says of one car, "if Brancusi is any good, then this thing belongs on a pedestal, too" (83). The use of the word "pedestal" is a characteristic Wolfean, and sixties, move: high art and popular culture are one.[4] The culture industry, or corporate culture, is not the problem for the customized car artist; rather, the problem is the advanced age of the industrialists and their alienation from the sixties youth culture Wolfe celebrates: "the customizers don't think of corporate bureaucracy quite the way your conventional artist does . . . namely, as a lot of small-minded Babbitts, venal enemies of culture, etc. They just think of the big companies as part of that vast mass of *adult* America, sclerotic from years of just being too old, whose rules and ideas weigh down upon Youth like a vast, bloated sac" (98). Wolfe is in sympathy alternatingly, simultaneously, ambivalently, with the customizers and with "your conventional artist."

As its title indicates, "Las Vegas (What?) Las Vegas (Can't hear you! Too noisy) Las Vegas!!!!" has as a central motif the postmodern phenomenon of sensory bombardment, saturation, overload: "noise" (Don DeLillo's echt-postmodern novel *White Noise* uses this notion as an organizing trope). The term "motif" is an important indicator of the structure of this essay, which is seemingly casual, associative, unstructured, loosely repetitive, but in fact carefully interweaves a set of recurring motifs established at the beginning, with tonal emphasis generally shifting, again, as in Barthes, from distanced, mildly fascinated amusement to something that approaches condemnation.

Wolfe begins with "Raymond" (one thinks of the Las Vegas sequence in *Rain Man*, and wonders if there is any Wolfe influence in that choice of names), or rather he begins with an incomprehensible, jarringly arresting paragraph, nine lines of print, consisting of almost nothing but the word "hernia," without quotation marks, intermittently printed "*HERN*ia," punctuated with commas or semicolons after each repetition of the word and interspersed only with "eight is the point the point is eight," "all right," and "hard eight." Wolfe uses this disorienting opening paragraph to immerse us in the sensory, linguistic, semiotic dislocations of Las Vegas — literally, hernias, both ruptures and apertures, opened in the body, the psyche, the culture, the social, and discourse.

Our bafflement and curiosity are immediately relieved in paragraph two. The word "hernia" is being repeated in this mechanical way by someone named Raymond, "who is thirty-four years old and works as an engineer in Phoenix." "Eight is the point the point is eight" is the recurring line of "the wavy-haired fellow with the stick, the dealer, at the craps table about 3:45 Sunday morning" (4). "Hernia" is Raymond's version of the crap dealer's croon, and as soon as the latter starts it up — "All right, a new shooter . . . eight is the point, the point is eight" — Raymond immediately "dron[es] along with him in exactly the same tone of voice, "Hernia, hernia, hernia; hernia, HERNiA, HERNiA, hernia; hernia, hernia, hernia" (4). Raymond is "a good example of the marvelous impact Las Vegas has on the senses," an impact Wolfe summarizes as "toxic schizophrenia" (6). Wolfe's readers participate to some extent in this toxic schizophrenia, because we are made to see the essential similarity of the crap dealer's chant to Raymond's. We see that, despite what turns out to be a psychotic break induced in Raymond by an extended binge of drugs, alcohol, and sleeplessness (also itself a characteristic Las Vegas phenomenon), he is not far off in his mimicry — because he has become psychotic, he is in tune with a deep-structural Las Vegas herniation: "he was quite right about this *hernia hernia* stuff" (6). Though the narrator describes him as "psyche-dilic" [*sic*], and "enjoying what the prophets of hallucinogen call 'consciousness expansion'" (6), Raymond is not the sixties neoromantic, modernist archetype of the stoned/schizophrenic seer we see in R. D. Laing or Carlos Castañeda, or for that matter Allen Ginsberg or Timothy Leary. He has in no way chosen this visionary truth quest. He is an engineer from Phoenix who has come to Vegas for a good time; his is the involuntary cultural schizophrenia of postmodernity. Thompson will merge these two figures in his protagonist, who *is* on a self-conscious, volitional, though always ironic truth quest, yet is also produced by, and as, Las Vegas toxic schizophrenia. In Venturi et al., there is no seer. Knowledge has become partial, collaborative; the narrative voice is neutral, nonjudgmental, there to learn.

Wolfe introduces most of the other central recurring motifs of this essay within the first few pages. The crap dealer's response to Raymond is to give him "that patient arch of the eyebrows known as a Red Hook brushoff" (4). In its reference to what used to be a tough Brooklyn waterfront Mafia neighborhood, this is Wolfe's signal that one does not have to scratch the surface of Vegas very hard in order for the Mob to become visible in this theme park of American power and money ("How's your old Cosa Nostra?" [5], Raymond asks the craps dealer). Thompson also emphasizes the underlying Vegas power structure of the domination of ruthless extralegal big money. This power structure is central to Thompson's vision, but in Venturi et al. the violent money-power that built and controls Las Vegas is not the issue, and Vegas is just any contemporary locus of the postmodern commercial culture from which we must learn, extraordinarily instructive only because it is extraordinarily commercial.[5] This shift of emphasis away from violent power and domination is prophetic for postmodern self-imagining, where binary hierarchical domination is revisioned as more open-ended, multiple, multidirectional power flows and reciprocal movements of hegemony and resistance.

Around the craps table where Raymond's standoff with the dealer is in progress, Wolfe finds most of the rest of his cast of archetypal Vegas characters: "The gold-lame odalisques of Los Angeles were staring. The Western sports, fifty-eight-year-old men who wear Texas string ties, were staring. The old babes at the slot machines, holding Dixie Cups full of nickels, were staring at the craps tables, but cranking away the whole time" (4). Despite his characteristic sixties sexism, of which more later, Wolfe understands that the greatest damage done by the thoroughly pervasive commodification Las Vegas represents is the commodification of women. The women in this essay are commodified either as sex—the "gold-lame odalisques" owned by powerful older men—or as "old babes at the slot machines," mechanistically reliable producers of Mob profit (they "crank away the whole time"). The former recur in the essay as ludicrously commodified show girls, as deeply damaged prostitutes, and, most troublingly, as "little high-school buds . . . wearing buttocks de-colletage step-ins" (11), ogled, surveilled, and lusted after by the Wolfean narrator himself as sexual predator.

The "old babes at the slot machines," with their "old hummocky shanks" (6), are abjected as physically repulsive embodiments of Vegas absurd: "Abby and Clara have both entered old babehood. They have that fleshy, humped-over shape across the back of the shoulders. Their torsos are hunched up into fat little loaves supported by bony, atrophied leg stems sticking up into their hummocky hips. Their hair has been fried and dyed into improbable designs. . . . eight o'clock Sunday morning, and—marvelous!—there is no one around to snigger at what an old babe with decaying haunches looks like in Capri pants with her heels jacked up on decorated wedgies" (19). There is no one around to snigger except our narrator. We become the privileged spectators of this insider's condescending, superior, debunking view of Las Vegas.[6] Thompson mixes this view with that of the helpless victim of Vegas — a version of Raymond. In Venturi, that superior condescension — the oppositional, loathing refusal of the modernist seer — is precisely what will be renounced.

Despite Wolfe's avid narrative participation in most of this sexual commodification and (as we will see) pathologization of women, he manages to produce a set of gender representations that have very little distance to go to become feminist arguments. These gender representations are similar, in their extreme alienation from, and reification of, the feminine, to those in *Fear and Loathing in Las Vegas*, where women are at once objects of prey and sexual commodification and also De Kooningesque monsters of violent, devouring sexuality. Both texts enact the complex, agon-ridden gender configurations at work in the sixties shift from modernity to postmodernity. In Venturi's Las Vegas, gender, like the violent money-power of the Mob, is both ignored and profoundly constitutive, as we will see, both of what we are told and also of what we are shown.

Wolfe has a great deal more to say about the Las Vegas sensory bombardment that has, along with drugs, alcohol, and sleeplessness, driven Raymond into characteristic Vegas "toxic schizophrenia." Auditory bombardment consists first of slot-machine noise, which is "much like the sound a cash register makes before the bell rings" (Wolfe does not allow us to forget how much money is being made here). "The whole sound keeps churning up over and over again in eccentric series all over the place, like one of those random-sound radio symphonies by John Cage" (7). The essay is filled with such references and comparisons of Vegas to high modernism and the avant-garde; these allusions both remind us of the simultaneity or cohabitation of dominant modernist and emergent postmodern paradigms in the sixties conjuncture, and predict the "breakdown of the high-low divide": the self-conscious, ironic mixing of high culture with commercial culture that has increasingly come to characterize Las Vegas.[7]

The other element of auditory bombardment Wolfe catalogues is Muzak: the juxtaposition of Muzak with slot-machine noise as a Cage symphony constitutes, again, an objective correlative of this boundary-crossing shift to postmodernity. Wolfe uses Muzak to introduce the postmodern Las Vegas we will find in Venturi: he emphasizes Muzak's pervasiveness, marking a "communal fear that someone, somewhere in Las Vegas, was going to be left with a totally vacant minute on his hands" (7). He moves seamlessly from the pervasiveness of Muzak to the symbolic fact that the radio in his rental car could not be turned off, feeding him continually and indiscriminately with pop music, advertising "for the Frontier Bank and the Fremont Hotel," and "Action Checkpoint News." This flattened, indifferentiated world of continuous postmodern radio sound, where "news" has no more or less significance than random electronic noise, is represented by Wolfe with a characteristic mixture of appreciative amusement and satirical edge: "the newscast, as it is called, begins with a series of electronic wheeps out on that far edge of sound where only quadrupeds can hear. A voice then announces that this is Action Checkpoint News. 'The news — all the news — flows first through Action Checkpoint! — then reaches You! at the speed of Sound!' More electronic wheeps, beeps and lulus, and then an item: 'Cuban Premier Fidel Castro nearly drowned yesterday.' Urp! Wheep! Lulu! No news a KORK announcer has ever brought to Las Vegas at the speed of sound, or could possibly bring, short of word of the annihilation of Los Angeles, could conceivably compete within the brain with the giddiness of this electronic jollification" (14).

From this "happy burble" of questionable tabloid misinformation, which also looks forward to DeLillo's *White Noise*, Wolfe considers it no distance at all to the skyline of signs that is Venturi's central focus: "Las Vegas is the only town in the world whose skyline is made up neither of buildings, like New York, nor of trees, like Wilbraham, Massachusetts, but signs. One can look at Las Vegas from a mile away on Route 91 and see no buildings, no trees, only signs. But such signs! They tower. They revolve, they oscillate, they soar in shapes before which the existing vocabulary of art history is helpless" (8). Wolfe goes on to produce a tongue-in-cheek list of sign styles, in tune with the light irony of this section of the essay: "Boomerang Modern, Palette Curvilinear, Flash Gordon Ming-Alert Spiral, McDonald's Hamburger Parabola, Mint Casino Elliptical, Miami Beach Kidney" (8). Venturi et al. quote this list verbatim as accurate description, with tongue in a highly ambiguous relation to cheek. Again, in Venturi's postmodernity we are to learn, accept, and admire; not to judge. Neon signmakers are the art heros of *Learning from Las Vegas*. Venturi et al. will reconceive as affirmation what Wolfe perceives ironically: "Men [of the Young Electric Sign Co.] like Boernge, Kermit Wayne, Ben Mitchem and Jack Larsen, formerly an artist for Walt Disney, are the designer-sculptor geniuses of Las Vegas, but their motifs have been carried faithfully throughout the town by lesser men, for gasoline stations, motels, funeral parlors, churches, public buildings, flophouses and sauna baths" (9). Wolfe's architectural-historical context, however, will be totally rewritten rather than adapted by Venturi et al. Wolfe introduces these Young Electric Sign Co. geniuses with one of his characteristic high-modernist allusions: "In the Young Electric Sign Co. era signs have become the architecture of Las Vegas, and the most whimsical, Yale-seminar-frenzied devices of the two late geniuses of Baroque Modern, Frank Lloyd Wright and Eero Saarinen, seem rather stuffy business, like a jest at a faculty meeting, compared to it" (9).

For Wolfe, there is a continuity between the whimsical, imaginative, excessive, erudite, academic architecture of the scions of high modernism and the postmodern populist imaginative excessive whimsy of Las Vegas signs. Wolfe both asserts that continuity and mocks it, as he does in his comparison of slot-machine noise to a Cage symphony, by pointing to the absurdity of this juxtaposition of high art with the commercial vernacular at the same time that he invokes the universe of postmodern pastiche — the indifferentiated mixing, sampling, versioning of high and popular culture. Again, Wolfe is at the undecidable sixties cusp of modern and postmodern, where Las Vegas has at once nothing and also everything in common with a high modernist Yale architecture seminar. Venturi et al., at least in professed ideology, break completely with high modernism, establishing an almost Manichean dualism of vilified modernism and lionized postmodernism, where the Yale seminar has literally been wrested away from Wright and Saarinen, their continuity with Las Vegas signs erased, and the critique of those signs, always clearly visible to Wolfe at the same time that he celebrates them, erased in the same stroke. Thompson repeats Wolfe's simultaneously appalled and amused description of the Vegas skyline as made of signs. For Wolfe and Thompson, solid denizens of dominant sixties terminal modernity, the postmodernity of the Vegas skyline of signs — neither the premodernity of "trees in Wilbraham, Massachusetts" nor the urban modernity of "buildings in New York" — is alluring and exciting, but it is also an unnatural, bewildering monstrosity slapped down on American nature, producing "toxic schizophrenia."

Wolfe continues to remind us that the Mob, in the person of Bugsy Siegel, created this monstrosity out of his prophetic vision of the "new American frontier" (10). Wolfe's account of Siegel's role in the early history of Las Vegas — his rise and fall and the ultimate triumph of his vision — develops the essay's central motifs. Wolfe begins this section with more of the mockingly hyperbolic language about Las Vegas style that he so clearly enjoys producing:

Siegel put up a hotel-casino such as Las Vegas had never seen and called it the Flamingo—all Miami Modern . . . Such shapes! Boomerang Modern supports, Palette Curvilinear bars, Hot Shoppe Cantilever roofs . . . Such colors! All the new electrochemical pastels of the Florida littoral: tangerine, broiling magenta, livid pink, incarnadine, fuchsia demure, Congo ruby, methyl green, viridine, aquamarine, phenosafranine, incandescent orange, scarlet-fever purple, cyanic blue, tessellated bronze, hospital-fruit-basket orange. And such signs! Two cylinders rose at either end of the Flamingo—eight stories high and covered from top to bottom with neon rings in the shape of bubbles that fizzed all eight stories up into the desert sky all night long like an illuminated whisky-soda tumbler filled to the brim with pink champagne. (11)

Wolfe develops several important themes here. First, he tells us again that the neon, plastic, violently colored style of the Florida littoral is deracinated and imposed gratuitously, irrelevantly, upon the desert, where it has no organic or "natural" place, in quintessential postmodern pastiche. Then, in the list of colors, Wolfe reminds us of the toxicity of Las Vegas schizophrenia. Many of the descriptive adjectives and color names themselves refer comically, self-mockingly to chemicals, violence, disease, or, as in "cyanic" blue, literally to poison: "electrochemical," "broiling," "livid," "methyl," "viridine," "phenosafranine," "scarlet-fever," "hospital-fruit-basket."

With "incarnadine," which is repeated two pages later, interestingly linked to the abjection of the feminine, in "inevitable buttocks decolletage pressed out against black, beige and incarnadine stretch pants" (13), Wolfe perhaps makes an oblique reference to *Macbeth* in the general theme of sleeplessness, or deliberately "murdered sleep," as part of Las Vegas toxic schizophrenia ("Macbeth does murder sleep," 2.2.35; "incarnadine" is of course a reference to the grotesquely red, blood-soaked world produced in Macbeth's distraught, guilty imagination by his crime). With this *Macbeth* reference, Wolfe is again reminding us not only of toxic schizophrenia, and of "high culture," but also of the violent, criminal ambition that produced, maintains, and is maintained by this unnatural world of Las Vegas.

A similarly toxic, dangerous, violent, drug- and alcohol-saturated sleeplessness is also a central motif of *Fear and Loathing in Las Vegas*. Venturi et al., however, present the deliberate destruction of diurnal patterns in Vegas neutrally, nonjudgmentally, as a feature of the way Vegas architecture is geared toward how people actually use the space, in post-modern opposition to modernism's coercive, top-down utopian ideals of architectural form.

Wolfe ends the Flamingo passage with a description of its eight-story-high neon sign, "an illuminated whisky-soda tumbler filled to the brim with pink champagne," lighting up the desert sky "all night long." The light, bubbly, comic-amazed tone of this description—comparable, again, to Barthes's tone in the early sections of the *Mythologies* essays—reminds us that Wolfe is genuinely fascinated and amused by Las Vegas, impressed by its postmodern freedom from historical and "natural" constraints, just as Barthes is fascinated and impressed by the alchemical virtuosity of plastic or by the beauty of the new Citroën. But the simultaneous, sickening associations of the mixture of "whisky-soda" with "pink champagne," and the association of that mixture with alcoholic schizophrenic toxicity, along with the reminder, in "all night long," that Vegas never sleeps or allows its denizens to sleep, reiterates the motif of loathing in Las Vegas.

The description of the "newscast" on KORK (like the cork of the popping bottle of pink champagne)—the "happy burble" of postmodern sound—is embedded in a sequence of fairly unmitigated loathing, opening with the Vegas history of Bugsy Siegel's vision. Despite his personal failure, due to criminal overreaching of Hollywood-heroic proportion, just as in Warren Beatty's subsequent film, "Siegel's aesthetic, psychological and cultural insights, like Cezanne's, Freud's and Max Weber's, could not die. The Siegel vision and the Siegel aesthetic were already sweeping Las Vegas like gold fever. . . . All over Las Vegas the incredible electric pastels were repeated. Overnight the Baroque Modern forms made Las Vegas one of the few architecturally unified cities of the world—the style was Late American Rich—and without the bother and bad humor of a City Council ordinance" (11–12). Wolfe's invocation of modernist heros Cézanne, Freud, and Weber is heavily ironic, even mock-heroic. The Siegel aesthetic and the Siegel vision, imposing unity from above in a totalizing sweep just as postmodern manifestos like Venturi's accuse modernism of doing, in fact have nothing in common with (what imagined itself as) pure, disinterested, anticapitalist modernism that repudiates and replaces a "Baroque" derivative corruption or bastardization, motivated only by "gold fever." The unity and grand sweep of the Siegel vision—ludicrously but aptly called his "aesthetic [Cézanne], psychological [Freud] and cultural [Weber] insights"—come not from an aesthetic or intellectual but from a purely venal motive. Las Vegas postmodern has nothing to do, for Wolfe, with the populism of the "ugly and ordinary" that Venturi et al. discover there. It has to do not with the repudiation but with the corruption of modernism — its cooptation by big violent money for "Late American Rich," the ideological opposite (but is it really the dialectical twin, or the repressed political unconscious) of the postmodern demotic everyday Venturi et al. espouse. "Without the bother and bad humor of a City Council ordinance": neither democracy nor populism, for Wolfe, is the name of this game.

The references to Cézanne, Freud, and Weber, seemingly casual, are in fact metonyms for central motifs of the essay. We have already seen the aesthetic vision of Siegel-as-Cézanne: the transplanted Florida littoral, the "incredible electric pastels," the skyline of neon signs. That the Las Vegas aesthetic has no referent but money, that it is a direct corruption by big money of heroic modernism, and that it is quintessentially or even terminally "toxic," as in nuclear annihilation, is hammered home in a hilarious interview with "Major A. Riddle — Major is his name — the president of the Dunes Hotel. He combs his hair straight back and wears a heavy gold band on his little finger with a diamond sunk into it" (16). In other words, he is a Mob stereotype. Major Riddle (?!) is describing a new Dunes floor show he has in the works that the narrator says will "be beyond art, beyond dance, beyond spectacle, even beyond the titillations of the winking crotch" (16). Riddle's description opens with money — "this machine [producing a revolving, exploding *Gesamtkunstwerk*] will cost us $250,000," an impressive sum in the pre-inflation early sixties. Riddle proceeds to focus on the fact that the machine's designer "used to work with this fellow Frank Lloyd Wright," and that the machine "uses the same mechanism that's in the Skybolt Missile" (18). The narrator then fantasizes the show as "one vast Project Climax for our times, Sean Kenny, who used to work with this fellow Frank Lloyd Wright, presses the red button and the whole yahooing harem, shrieking ooh-la-la [it's a "Casino de Paris" girlie show] amid the din, exits in a mushroom cloud" (18). Wright is not invoked undecidably here, as at once guiding genius and ironic antinomy, the way Cage was, or the way he and Saarinen were, earlier in the essay. "Frank Lloyd Wright" has become, as we move closer to Wolfe's sixties modernist position, a metonym of all that Vegas has corrupted and destroyed.

As Wolfe's essay progresses, he shows us with increasing clarity and emphasis the significance of the human casualties of Vegas toxic schizophrenia, derived not only from the Siegel aesthetic but also from the Siegel psychological and cultural vision—the casualties Wolfe opens with "Raymond" in order to establish as his primary focus.[8] "Finally, the casualties start piling up" (22), and the human casualties who elicit the narrator's and reader's sympathy are the "breaking up," and broken down, prostitutes who people the psychiatric ward of the County Hospital, victims of the Siegel psychological vision of extreme exploitation. It is not clear whether Wolfe recognizes the complicity of his narrative lechery toward the "young buds" and their "Vegas decolletage" in the psychic havoc wrought by objectification and abjection of women he witnesses, and finds pathetic, at the County Hospital. But it is clear that, unlike Venturi et al., and like Thompson, Wolfe wants us to see both the violent power-money that rules Vegas and also its helpless victims—the Raymonds, or Hornette Reilly (the name is pathetically ironic), a prostitute whose Vegas life causes her to "break up": " 'Look' she says, 'I'm breaking up. I can't tell you how much I've drunk. About a bottle of brandy since four o'clock, I'm not kidding. . . . this slob is lying here like an animal. He's all fat and his skin looks like oatmeal—what's happening to me? I'm going to take some more pills. I'm not kidding, I'm breaking up. I'm going to kill myself. . . . I'm breaking up, and I don't even know what's happening to me' " (24).

The doctor she's talking to refuses to put her in the pleasanter private sanatorium; she will have to go to the County Hospital, where "three-fourths of the 640 patients who clustered into the [psychiatric] ward last year were casualties of the Strip or the Strip milieu of Las Vegas, the psychiatrist tells me" (25). The narrator takes us to that psychiatric ward, where we meet women who are not breaking, but have broken, up, like a cell phone transmission: like the postmodern image-world of waves and particles Wolfe announces here. "I'm not even her doctor . . . I don't know her case. There's nothing I can do for her," the psychiatrist says of a "girl, probably a looker in more favorable moments," who "puts her face in her hands, convulsing but not making a sound. She retreats to her room, and then the sounds come shrieking out" (26). Is this girl one of the young buds in their buttocks decolletage? Is this a moment of unconscious or semiconscious narrative self-criticism? That question is unanswerable from the information the text provides. Yet it is clear that these shrieks of private torment and despair, unlike the electronic squeaks of the happy public postmodern burble of KORK, of the slots and the crap dealer's croon, are entirely differentiated and full of meaning.[9] They come from an earlier, modernist narrative — the narrative of the psychic havoc wrought on the individual by the deformations of modernity. The point here is that, as the ultimate realization of capitalist modernity, Vegas postmodernity inevitably produces an extreme form of that psychic havoc — again, what Wolfe dubs toxic schizophrenia.

Raymond is here too, in the psychiatric ward. He is one of the lucky ones. He "might pull out of the toxic reaction in two or three days, or eight or ten. Others have conflicts to add to the chemical wackiness" (26). Wolfe now, in the penultimate section of the essay, uses his strongest language of loathing, of ethical condemnation, to describe how the core processes of Vegas put people in the psychiatric ward. The ward's characteristic denizens, in addition to the broken prostitutes, the nameless, lost women, and Raymond are "a man who has thrown all his cash to the flabby homunculus who sits at every craps table stuffing the take down an almost hidden chute so it won't pile up in front of the customers' eyes; a man who has sold the family car for next to nothing at a car lot advertising 'Cash for your car — *right now*' and then thrown that to the homunculus, too, but also still has the family waiting guiltlessly, guilelessly back home; well, he has troubles" (26).

Wolfe does not, however, end the essay with this damning sequence. The psychiatric ward had been his last narrative stop on his way out of town. He gets in his "big white car," an ironic Vegas echo of Moby-Dick that we will see again, with the allusion made more explicit, in Thompson, and heads straight for the airport. On the way he reprises first the happy postmodern auditory milieu — the "wheeps, beeps, freeps, electronic lulus," the "giddiness of this electronic jollification" (14) of "Action Checkpoint News, 'Monkey No. 9,' Donna, Donna, the Prima Donna,' and friendly picking and swinging for the Fremont Hotel and Frontier Federal" — and then the resplendent postmodern visual milieu of "the Strip," where "the Boomerang Modern, Palette Curvilinear, Flash Gordon Ming-Alert Spiral, McDonald's Hamburger Parabola, Mint Casino Elliptical and Miami Beach Kidney sunbursts are exploding in the Young Electric Sign Company's Grand Gallery for all the sun kings" (27). Unlike Barthes, Wolfe closes not with loathing but with amused, though heavily ironic, admiration (the irony deepened by the casualties in the psychiatric ward). On his way to the airport to catch his plane, he "sense[s] that something is missing" (28). He then "remembers" a conversation he had had with a group of Vegas entrepreneurs about

the sign they are building for the Dunes to put up at the airport. It will
be five thousand square feet of free-standing sign, done in flaming-lake
red [incarnadine?] on burning-desert gold. The d — the D — alone in the
word Dunes, written in Cyrillic modern, will be practically two stories
high. . . . [hyperbolic description of the sign's wonders] "You'll be able
to see it from an airplane fifteen miles away," says Jack Heskett. "Fifty
miles," says Lee Fisher. And it will be sixty-five feet up in the air —
because the thing was, somebody was out at the airport and they noticed there was only one display to be topped. That was that shaft
about sixty feet high with the lit-up globe and the beacon lights, which
is to say, the control tower. Hell, you can only see that forty miles away.
But exactly! (28)

The essay ends on an ironic-prophetic note: as we saw on KORK and in Las
Vegas in general, nothing in postmodernity is exempt from the pervasiveness of late-capitalist consumer culture, of signs taken for wonders.

Just before his conversation with Major Riddle about the "Casino de
Paris," the Project Climax of Wright's disciple, Wolfe sets the stage for the
positive postmodern reading of Las Vegas: Venturian Vegas demotic, the
populist Vegas of the "ugly and ordinary" everyday, of American postmodern popular culture as of and for the people. He does this by contrasting democratic Las Vegas to elitist Monte Carlo, most explicitly by means
of contrasting American popular to European modernist high culture:

Las Vegas has become, just as Bugsy Siegel dreamed, the American
Monte Carlo — without any of the inevitable upper-class baggage of the
Riviera casinos. . . . Thousands of Europeans from the lower orders
now have the money to go to the Riviera, but they remain under the
century-old status pall of the aristocracy. At Monte Carlo there are still
Wrong Forks, Deficient Accents, Poor Tailoring, Gauche Displays,
Nouveau Richness, Cultural Aridity — concepts unknown in Las Vegas.
For the grand debut of Monte Carlo as a resort in 1879 the architect
Charles Garnier designed an opera house for the Place du Casino; and
Sarah Bernhardt read a symbolic poem. For the debut of Las Vegas as a
resort in 1946 Bugsy Siegel hired Abbott and Costello, and there, in a
way, you have it all. (16)

For Venturi et al., you indeed there have it all. For Wolfe, and for Thompson, with at least one foot still in that modernism, if not of the aristocracy
and the culture of the Wrong Fork (though that culture has enormous

appeal to Wolfe), at least of the heroic artist (Sarah Bernhardt) and of art as anticapitalist, oppositional, utopian way of life (the symbolic poem), you only have it all "in a way": only when looking forward into emergent postmodernity, ignoring the soon-to-be residual modernity that is still dominant in the sixties.[10]

CHAPTER FOUR

Loathing and Learning in Las Vegas

Hunter Thompson's *Fear and Loathing in Las Vegas* is, self-consciously, and by critical consensus, an epitaph for the sixties.[1] It is intended to make us feel "the brutish realities of this foul year of Our Lord 1971" (23): the sixties have imploded in a self-destructive orgy of drugs and violence of which Altamont is merely a symptom and objective correlative. Thompson makes Las Vegas the graveyard of the sixties. Las Vegas begins in the book as the antithesis of all that the sixties counterculture stands for, and this repudiation of Las Vegas — the primary meaning of "fear and loathing in" — persists in Thompson's overt narrative accounts of Vegas culture. Thompson's most apparent, overt narrative self-positioning is in alignment with a countercultural, anti-Vegas, sixties sensibility, ethos, and aesthetic.

This primary allegiance is most (literally) visible in the wonderful illustrations by Ralph Steadman, a longtime friend of Thompson's, which have played a key role in the continuing viability of this book.[2] Steadman's drawings are characteristic of sixties underground graphic style: comic-absurd, hypersatirical, and self-mocking; excessive, unbuttoned, and raw, but carefully stylized and witty in their outrageousness. Nonetheless, like the book as a whole, and like underground comics as a genre, Steadman's drawings are at once modern in their use of stylization in the service of the most profound truth-telling, and also postmodern in their deployment of popular culture form, at once ironically and in good faith, in the service of resistance-from-within. The ink splats that Steadman drips randomly throughout the book are also on the modern/postmodern cusp: modernist in their foregrounding of their own medium and therefore of their status as art; postmodern in their insistence on surface and on casual, easily destroyed imperfection and ephemerality.

Even as Thompson insists on the status of Las Vegas as anathema to and graveyard of the sixties and object of fear and loathing, Las Vegas is also depicted in *Fear and Loathing*, particularly in part 2, as the most appropriate setting for, and even reflection of, the destruction and self-immolation of the radical counterculture in the late sixties. The fear and loathing, increasingly, are not *of* Las Vegas itself but of the countercultural self *as* Las Vegas, reflected precisely *in* Las Vegas, rather than as stranded, outcast, or alien there. As it is for Conrad's Kurtz, (frequently alluded to by Thompson), the heart of darkness, conceived initially as alien and other, home of the most barbarous atavism, is finally lodged in the enlightened self. Las Vegas, as visible and outward form of the inner rot of the sixties, is merely the most appropriate setting for the self-destruction of the counterculture, where the death orgy can proceed with the greatest ease, rapidity, and absence of friction.

LOATHING

This sense of Vegas as the most fitting and appropriate milieu for the self-loathing survivors of the trashed sixties underlies the narrative sequence and affect of *Fear and Loathing*, but it stops short of being made explicit. Thompson's ostensible view of Vegas remains alienated, separated, rejecting, horrified (determined by fear and loathing). He insists repeatedly that he does not belong there and must get out as soon as he can. In an important sequence, he marks Las Vegas as precisely the place most separate from and external to the sixties — the Archimedean vantage point entirely outside the observed phenomena of the sixties, from which one can see the historical and geographical contours of its rise, fall, and demise:

> Strange memories on this nervous night in Las Vegas. Five years later?·
> Six? It seems like a lifetime, or at least a Main Era — the kind of peak

that never comes again. San Francisco in the middle sixties was a very special time and place to be a part of. Maybe it *meant something*. Maybe not, in the long run . . . but no explanation, no mix of words or music or memories can touch that sense of knowing that you were there and alive in that corner of time and the world. Whatever it meant. . . . You could strike sparks anywhere. There was a fantastic universal sense that whatever we were doing was *right*, that we were winning. . . .

And that, I think, was the handle — that sense of inevitable victory over the forces of Old and Evil. Not in any mean or military sense; we didn't need that. Our energy would simply *prevail*. There was no point in fighting — on our side or theirs. We had all the momentum; we were riding the crest of a high and beautiful wave. . . .

So now, less than five years later, you can go up on a steep hill in Las Vegas and look West, and with the right kind of eyes you can almost *see* the high-water mark — that place where the wave finally broke and rolled back. (66–68)

Las Vegas is certainly not the place or time where/when the sixties happened. Thompson continually describes Las Vegas as replete with pre-, post-, and antisixties cultural phenomena, from Sinatra, Dean Martin, and Debbie Reynolds to Nixon and Agnew. It is decisively removed from and antithetical to that quintessential sixties place and time in Thompson's life and consciousness, and in the life and consciousness of the country, which, for him, and emblematically for the culture at large, is the San Francisco Bay Area in the mid-sixties. But it is from a hill in Las Vegas that Thompson can now see and contemplate the history and location, and perhaps the meaning (or lack thereof), of the sixties. Las Vegas is represented not just as the antithesis to, or in the death of, but also, contradictorily, as the intellectual, cultural, political, emotional, and literary legacy of the sixties: "in a town full of bedrock crazies, nobody even *notices* an acid freak" (24). It is from the vantage point of Las Vegas that Thompson can not only act out the violent end of the sixties but can also, literally, look back on, see, and feel the loss of its utopian promise. But perhaps elements of that promise survive in postmodern Las Vegas. As the book's subtitle announces, and as the narrator tells the hitchhiker in the opening sequence, "we're on our way to Las Vegas to find the American Dream" (6). This seems, and is, absurdly ironic, here and throughout the book. If they find anything at all, it is a corrupted, absurd, betrayed, and/or dead American Dream. But at the same time, in the complex representational layering of this book, the statement that they are "on [their] way to Las Vegas to find the American Dream" is also true.[3]

Despite the tone and narrative content of comic, ludicrous, amoral excess that dominates the book, Thompson's more somber, ambitious, and ethical intentions, as has frequently been noted, are revealed in his epigraph from Dr. Johnson: "He who makes a beast of himself gets rid of the pain of being a man." I would argue that the pain of being a man derives for Thompson not merely from drug excess, or even from the corruption of the initially idealistic drug culture Duke's and Gonzo's exploits represent, but, at a deeper, more comprehensive level, from the defeat of the sixties. The book's extended orgy of drugs, alcohol, and violence, while based on the excessive actuality of Thompson's own life (though not, apparently, of his life while he was actually in Las Vegas, or writing the book; see *Fear and Loathing in America*, 405–06), is more discontinuous than continuous with the sixties in its extremity of excessiveness: it is the fulfillment of the right wing's paranoid fantasies about the counterculture, enacted in ironic, self-obliterating anguish. The hitchhiker whom the narrator informs that they are on their "way to Las Vegas to find the American dream" is an avatar of the fear and loathing the narrator and his enormous Samoan "attorney" (alias Dr. Gonzo, based on Thompson's friend, the Chicano attorney Oscar Acosta, the person of color alter ego of classic American fiction) will inspire, as well as feel, in Las Vegas. The hitchhiker's fear and horror at the drugged, frenzied, manic behavior of the narrator and Dr. Gonzo—the hitchhiker gets out of the car as quickly as he can and runs off into the desert—foreshadows the reaction of almost everyone they have dealings with in Las Vegas. It is as if the underlying sincerity of their mission, their search for the American Dream, rather than the excessiveness of their drugged behavior alone, inspires this fear and loathing. This search is not just absurd, as it is most clearly and primarily, but also at once tragic and ironic because, as the narrator says, in its utopian sixties incarnation, its object is lost, just as the object of the same search was to Gatsby. The excess of their behavior is itself produced by the futility of their mission, a futility that matters as much as it does only because of the depth of their sincerity.

The simultaneity of overt alienation from and muted identification with Las Vegas—the simultaneity of loathing and, in Venturi et al.'s term, learning—persists throughout the book, steadily escalating until Las Vegas seems to become the narrator's (un)natural habitat. The book establishes itself from the opening sentence as a nightmarish trip: "we were somewhere around Barstow on the edge of the desert when the drugs began to take hold" (3). The narrator and his "attorney," the cartoonish heros Duke and Gonzo (as in the coinage "gonzo journalism," invented to describe Thompson's work by Boston Globe writer Bill Cardoso), have acquired their ludicrously excessive supply of drugs in California, proper home of the sixties, but these drugs do not "take hold" until they are out of the orbit of California and in the desert on which Las Vegas sits. "The trunk of the car looked like a mobile police narcotics lab. We had two bags of grass, seventy-five pellets of mescaline, five sheets of high-powered blotter acid, a salt shaker half full of cocaine, and a whole galaxy of multi-colored uppers, downers, screamers, laughers . . . and also a quart of tequila, a quart of rum, a case of Budweiser, a pint of raw ether and two dozen amyls (4). "Screamers, laughers" cues the reader to view this extraordinary assemblage of drugs as a self-mocking joke, while the comparison of this absurd cache to "a mobile police narcotics lab" establishes the narrative identification with "the enemy," foreshadowing our heroes' sojourn at the District Attorneys' Convention, at which they are at once alienated and, uncannily, completely at home.

The narrator immediately establishes his alienation from himself, a characteristic sixties motif: the alienation essential to maintaining the official narrative of his fear and loathing *of* Las Vegas while the evidence mounts that Las Vegas is precisely where he, as embodiment of fear and loathing, belongs. They are driving in a rented Chevy convertible the narrator calls the "Great Red Shark," a joke avatar of the car, a white Cadillac convertible, in which, in part 2, they become integrated into Las Vegas, which of course the narrator calls the "Great White Whale." The narrator focuses first on the initial effects of the acid he has just taken, the drugs that "take hold" once they are "on the edge of the desert." He has told Gonzo that he feels "a bit lightheaded," and asks him to drive. "And suddenly there was a terrible roar all around us and the sky was full of what looked like huge bats, all swooping and screeching and diving around the car . . . And a voice was screaming: 'Holy Jesus! What are these goddamn animals?' " (3). Of course the screaming voice is his own.

This disconnection from his own voice is necessary to the disjunction between his acknowledged, ostensible horror at Las Vegas, which is the only reaction to Vegas he expresses directly, and the extent to which he is actually at home there. Even perhaps more important, this disconnection is also central to his status as a journalist. *Fear and Loathing*, beginning as a piece on the Mint 400 motorcycle race commissioned by *Sports Illus-*

trated, was ultimately commissioned by, and originally appeared in, *Rolling Stone*, under the pen name Raoul Duke, the name Thompson's narrator uses in the book. Along with Tom Wolfe, Norman Mailer in his political works, Truman Capote, Michael Herr, Joan Didion, and others, Thompson is part of "the new journalism," a characteristic sixties phenomenon.[4] The new journalism broke down the practice it considered a myth of distance and detachment in the stance of journalistic "objectivity," acknowledging instead the partiality and embodiedness of the journalist's subjectivity, and the particularity of the point of view from which s/he inevitably writes. The new journalist incorporates him/herself into the writing, making the self a narrator/actor, as in fiction. Mailer's *Armies of the Night* is a quintessential instance of this practice, where "fiction" and "history" are systematically broken down as distinct categories, and remixed, with the character (as in fictional character) of the narrator/actor/author presiding over, centered in, and central to the hybrid narrative.

The new journalism is strongly linked to the sixties evolution of the politics of subjectivity/subjectivity of politics, as the example of Mailer again most clearly demonstrates. The author-as-narrator-as-journalist-as-character is evidently a highly complex, multiple, self-reflexive, self-conscious literary construct. The often rueful, hapless, self-mocking disconnection of the journalist from his/her professional role is a convention of the genre. The journalist is one of us, given greater access than we have to events by his or her professional credentials, but no more knowledgeable, expert, insightful, masterful, or authoritative than we are. The phenomenon of the new journalist as narrator, and of new journalism in general, is a characteristically transitional, modern/postmodern textual phenomenon of the sixties. In its democratic, egalitarian self-positioning as no more authoritative than the reader, its self-conscious, ironic narrative hybridity, its repudiation of "objectivity," its insistence on the partiality (in both senses of the term) and locatedness of the subject, and on the subjectivity of politics/politics of subjectivity, it is postmodern. *Fear and Loathing*, in particular, has defied classification; it is a quintessentially postmodern hybrid of journalism, "personal narrative," social-historical analysis, and fiction, with the latter comprised of multiply allusive modes of pastiche.

Like other sixties writing, however, it is at the same time profoundly lodged in modernity. The new journalism still believes in both truth and authenticity. The new journalist rejects the authority and claims to objectivity of the profession of journalism not in order to give up on access to truth but in order to acquire it more legitimately and profoundly. The partiality and locatedness of the new journalist's point of view does not imply renunciation of the notion of an underlying truth, or of an authentic subjective self-positioning in relation to the quest for this truth. On the contrary, as in modernism, this acknowledgment of the epistemological force of subjectivity is a means toward realizing truth more authentically and profoundly than the "objectivity" of realism can, as in Virginia Woolf's "luminous halo or envelope" replacing the "series of gig lamps symmetrically arranged," in her landmark essay "Modern Fiction." Just as Mailer believes he penetrates and articulates the essence of American-ness — the nightmare the American Dream has become — in *Armies of the Night*, so Thompson does as well, through his elaborately constructed narrative persona Raoul Duke, in *Fear and Loathing*. Again, his quest for the American Dream in Las Vegas is primarily, overtly ironic and absurd, but also, at what must be called a deeper level, profound and tragic. This structure of ironic surface and profound, disturbing depth is characteristically modern. The emotional power of the book, I would argue, is primarily produced by this classic American sense of the betrayal and loss of the dream and promise embodied in America; in particular, of the utopian dream and promise of the American sixties. The book makes this claim for itself partly by its numerous allusions to not just to *Heart of Darkness* but to *The Great Gatsby* and *Moby-Dick*.

At the same time, however, the structure of surface and depth exists alongside or cohabits in the book with a different, in fact opposed structure, in which the postmodern lesson learned in Las Vegas is that surface is all. The betrayal of the American Dream — the death of the sixties — as embodied in Las Vegas is itself a truth: that America has moved on from the sixties, and Las Vegas is the space into which it has moved. In this narrative structure, the ironic surface of the book is not a delusion or veil through which we are meant to look at the deeper, tragic truth. The pervasive irony and self-mocking, comic excess of the book, like the absurd excess of Las Vegas, utterly ironic in its way, is itself the truth of post-sixties, postmodern America. The persistent utopian desire associated with the sixties is transmuted into, or grafted onto, the utopian aspects of Las Vegas, attached now to egalitarian postmodern commercial culture, as expounded by Venturi et al., rather than to modernity's agenda of anticapitalist social and cultural transformation.

This complex, partly contradictory set of narrative structures is established by Thompson with great economy. Duke feels he must explain himself to the terrified, bewildered hitchhiker, who is a comic stand-in for the reader, innocently picked up by this narrative and carried, unwilling and increasingly appalled, into the absurd, grotesque, ludicrous, violent nightmare of Duke's and Gonzo's quest. As we have seen, the first thing Duke tells the hitchhiker is that "we're on our way to Las Vegas to find the American Dream" (6). In the face of the hitchhiker's persistent bewilderment and mounting fear, Duke insists: "our vibrations were getting nasty — but why? I was puzzled, frustrated. Was there no communication in this car? Had we deteriorated to the level of *dumb beasts*? Because my story *was* true. I was certain of that. And it was extremely important, I felt, for the *meaning* of our journey to be made absolutely clear" (8). "Dumb beasts," of course, echoes Thompson's epigraph from Dr. Johnson. Duke is struggling against his self-imposed bestial condition, produced by drugs, alcohol, and sleeplessness, just as in Wolfe's essay, in order to make absolutely clear the meaning of his true story. In addition to the mobile narcotics lab array of drugs he and Gonzo purchase, and the guns, they also buy "a super-sensitive tape recorder, for the sake of a permanent record" (9). This tape recorder appears, comically, later in the book, to narrate a sequence that has supposedly gotten beyond Duke's narrative control (the final version of the manuscript is, however, as Thompson acknowledges in his letters, the carefully produced result of revision; see *Fear and Loathing in America* 347–460). At one level, the book's quest for the American Dream in Las Vegas is a true story, the meaning of which must be made absolutely clear. The super-sensitive tape recorder is a figure for the professional commitment of the journalist to the truth of his story. The quest for truth is, indeed, an underlying, deep structure of the book — a truth in which the utopian Northern Californian sixties are replaced by the grotesque Las Vegas seventies. But at the same time, from the point of view of the hitchhiker, and in Thompson's own narration of Duke's and Gonzo's terrifying, ludicrous, comic-grotesque, absurd excesses, no tape recorder, no matter how supersensitive, can communicate the truth as experienced by two such cartoonish characters, whose postmodern embodied partiality is thoroughly ironic, at cross-purposes with truth, sincerity, deeper meaning, and any master narrative as portentous as that of the American Dream. Duke is no modernist holy fool, privileged with profound insight into a deeper truth beyond the superficial perceptions of the well-adjusted and conventional. Thompson goes out of his way to make Duke's excesses (while comic and appealing, in their insouciant defiance of Authority) of such a carefully documented enormity that they carry him well beyond privileged eccentricity or marginality and fully into pathology, at the same time that he makes these excesses, this pathology, seem at home, appropriate, even inevitable in Las Vegas; again, as Wolfe does.

At the end of this sequence, a flashback in which Duke and Gonzo are in LA preparing for this journey, they decide that, in order to cover the Mint 400 off-the-road motorcycle race (their official assignment) properly, they need their own motorcycle — not just any motorcycle but an extraordinary one, a Vincent Black Shadow, that is, as Duke says, " 'pure hell on the straightaway. It'll outrun the F-111 until takeoff.' 'Takeoff?' he [Gonzo] said. 'Can we handle that much torque?' 'Absolutely,' I said. 'I'll call New York for some cash' " (9). Apart from the comedy of this sequence, which is its primary effect, the need for a motorcycle that would outdo all the others at the race contradicts the need for a supersensitive tape recorder: Duke's purpose is not to be the classical unobtrusive reporter, the mere recording instrument of the truth, but rather to be as visible as possible in the event he is covering, and to participate in it spectacularly rather than merely to observe it. At the same time, the hopeless ludicrousness of his ambition, and the delusional state of both men, is figured in the interchange about outrunning the F-111 "until takeoff." Thompson here mocks the grandiose militaristic machismo of events like the Mint 400 and uses Duke and Gonzo as the primary vehicles of this mockery (Thompson is also, of course, a genuine motorcycle afficionado; see most notably *Hell's Angels*). The reader will not be surprised that Duke and Gonzo fail to acquire a Vincent Black Shadow, or any motorcycle at all, and essentially fail to cover the race, though they are present, in their drugged insanity, participating in this event in their absurd disconnection from it in a way that Thompson wants us to understand as characteristically Vegas.

Thompson uses the faux-naive, self-mocking Gatsby motif to establish the LA inception of their quest. When Dr. Gonzo is skeptical about the extent of their credit, Duke reassures him:

> "This won't make the nut," he said, "unless we have unlimited credit." I assured him we would. "You Samoans are all the same," I told him. "You have no faith in the white man's culture. Jesus, just one hour ago we were sitting over there in that stinking baginio, stone broke and paralyzed for the weekend, when a call comes through from some total

stranger in New York, telling me to go to Las Vegas and expenses be
damned — and then he sends me over to some office in Beverly Hills
where another total stranger gives me $300 raw cash for no reason at
all . . . I tell you, my man, this is the American Dream in action! We'd be
fools not to ride this strange torpedo all the way out to the end." (11)

Duke continues: "The only way to prepare for a trip like this, I felt, was to
dress up like human peacocks and get crazy, then screech off across the
desert and *cover the story*. Never lose sight of the primary responsibility.
But what *was* the story? Nobody had bothered to say. So we would have
to drum it up on our own. Free Enterprise. The American Dream. Horatio
Alger gone mad on drugs in Las Vegas. Do it *now*: pure Gonzo journalism" (12; Gonzo journalism is a chemically enhanced, souped-up version
of the new journalism). The irony here is too heavy and stressed to require
comment. What is less evident, and perhaps warrants notice, is the contradiction between the imperative to *"cover the story,"* which is "the primary
responsibility" of the good journalist, and the simultaneous imperative to
invent the story, reinterpreted as the American Dream itself. Covering and
inventing the story are evidently at odds (though not necessarily entirely
contradictory: it is possible to report a story one creates; however, at this
point in the text they are at odds) — here we see precisely the simultaneity
in this text of old and new journalism, of modernity's truth-quest and
postmodernity's ironic, located subjective performativity. The American
Dream is implicated for Thompson in both modes of journalism: he considers the pursuit of the story, powered by limitless credit from a total
stranger in New York, the American Dream in action; at the same time, he
says that the invention of the story, Free Enterprise and Horatio Alger's
self-reliant resourcefulness, is also the American Dream. The connection
between the two versions of the American Dream comes from Thompson's ironic vision of Las Vegas: limitless credit in order to lose everything;
Horatio Alger "gone mad on drugs."

The book takes this Horatio Alger gone mad on drugs — Thompson's
ironic narrative persona — and drags him through the ostensible disillusionment of a "doctor of journalism," as he repeatedly calls himself, failing in his mission to "cover the story," or even to invent the story, in the
face of Las Vegas's multiple absurdities. At the same time, again, Duke
seems, both despite his fear and loathing and because of it, to fit in quite
well. Violent machismo, linked to a fear and loathing of women, is a
recurring motif, an integral part of this ironic search for the American

Dream. This machismo is a legacy of one mode of sixties masculinity, that of the Hell's Angels Thompson was so deeply involved with, and of the violent, hard-line Marxist-Leninist wing of New Left radicalism. The emergence of this machismo as a primary mode of postmodern masculinity largely defeated the gentle, androgynous, long-haired, gender-utopian male mode that was one dominant style of sixties masculinity, as I discuss in chapter 5.

Duke reiterates his Gatsbyesque mission as they approach Vegas: " 'we're on our way to Las Vegas to cover the main story of our generation' " (19), he tells the hitchhiker; "old Americans go out to the highway and drive themselves to death with huge cars. But our trip was different. It was a classic affirmation of everything right and true and decent in the national character. It was a gross, physical salute to the fantastic *possibilities* of life in this country—but only for those with true grit. And we were chock full of that" (18). Dr. Gonzo elaborates on this "true grit": " 'Volume! Clarity! Bass! We must have bass!' [the sound on the car stereo is already deafening] He flailed his naked arms at the sky. 'What's *wrong* with us? Are we goddamn *old ladies?*' " (18). In *Fear and Loathing*, the violent machismo and accompanying contempt for women of both Duke and Gonzo, of which this remark is a mild example, seem just as comfortable and appropriate in Las Vegas as their drug and alcohol orgy and their "limitless credit." This mode of masculinity is at once moribund, as antithesis to emergent feminism, and also the basis for the extreme forms of violent masculinity and backlash against feminism that are pervasive in post-sixties global cultures (see chapter 5).[5]

In narrating Duke's arrival in Las Vegas, Thompson insists on the emotional distance of fear and loathing. Vegas first appears as "the strip/hotel skyline looming up through the blue desert ground-haze. The Sahara, the landmark, the Americana and the ominous Thunderbird—a cluster of grey rectangles in the distance, rising out of the cactus. . . . We would have to run the gauntlet, and acid be damned. Go through all the official gibberish . . . sign in for the press passes—all of it bogus, totally illegal, a fraud on its face, but of course it would have to be done" (22). Immediately following this burst of alienation, Duke has a related eruption of horror at a "line" that "appears in his notebook, for some reason": "KILL THE BODY AND THE HEAD WILL DIE." He associates this with "some connection with Joe Frazier," whose victory over Muhammad Ali he considers a proper end to the sixties: Tim Leary a prisoner of Eldridge Cleaver in Algeria, Bob Dylan clipping coupons in Greenwich Village, both Kennedys murdered by mutants, Owsley folding napkins on Terminal Island, and finally Cassius/Ali belted incredibly off his pedestal by a human hamburger, a man on the verge of death. Joe Frazier, like Nixon, had finally prevailed for reasons that people like me refused to understand — at least not out loud. . . . But that was some other era, burned out and long gone from the brutish realities of this foul year of Our Lord, 1971. A lot of things had changed in those years. And now I was in Las Vegas as the motor sports editor of this fine slick magazine. (22–23)

Duke, as unreliable, limited narrator, is puzzled by the appearance of this line in his notebook, but the reader can connect it, again, to Thompson's epigraph from Dr. Johnson: in their depraved assault on their human bodies, making beasts of themselves, they get rid of the pain of being human; the head dies. Or, in their depraved assault on their heads and bodies, with the weapon of drugs, they become beasts, relieving themselves of the pain of being human. The book's official fear and loathing of Las Vegas is associated with the tone of the above passage — the tone of horror at the "proper end to the sixties." Las Vegas appears as the culmination of this horror, the place where Duke as hippie manqué is forced into the role, "bogus, totally illegal, a fraud on its face," of "motor sports editor of this fine slick magazine." However, it is in this role that Duke is pursuing the American Dream, in all its Gatsbyesque splendor. The American Dream, for better or worse, has come to reside in Las Vegas. Duke and Gonzo are just as much part of, implicated in, produced by the "proper end to the sixties" as they are alienated from and horrified by it. "There is no way to explain the terror I felt when I finally lunged up to the clerk and began babbling. All my well-rehearsed lines fell apart under that woman's stoney glare. 'Hi there,' I said. 'My name is . . . ah, Raoul Duke . . . yes, *on the list*, that's for sure. Free lunch, final wisdom, total coverage. . . . why not?'" (23). Duke presents himself here as utterly disconnected from the Gatsbyesque quest for the American Dream as "free lunch, final wisdom, total coverage." The "stoney glare" of the desk clerk is one of dozens of avatars in the book of varyingly hostile, murderous, hideous, potentially engulfing femininity, always to be handled from a violent distance of contempt, fear, and loathing.

This drama with the desk clerk is protracted: she tells Duke his room is not ready, and also that someone is looking for him. This inspires in Duke a lurid paranoid acid fantasy in which the desk clerk figures as a moray eel: "the woman's face was *changing*: swelling, pulsing . . . horrible green jowls and fangs jutting out, the face of a Moray Eel! Deadly poison!" (23–24). However, the terrible difficulties he imagines do not materialize. The man looking for him is merely Lacerda, the photographer he is assigned to work with, who casually gets Duke's room while Duke checks in at the press table. Again, Duke fits right in: "in a town full of crazies, nobody even *notices* an acid freak" (24). The misogynistic sexual fear and (self-)loathing violently abjected and projected onto women is part of the fear and loathing *in* (rather than of) Las Vegas that connects Vegas to the feared and loathed post-sixties self.

Duke's acid hallucinations, which produced bats on the desert and reptiles in the hotel lobby, fade as they reach their room: "I was no longer seeing huge pterodactyls lumbering around the corridors in pools of fresh blood. The only problem now was a gigantic neon sign outside the window, blocking our view of the mountains — millions of colored balls running around a very complicated track, strange symbols & filigree, giving off a loud hum" (27). Duke describes this to Gonzo as "a big . . . machine in the sky, . . . some kind of electric snake . . . coming straight at us" (27). Gonzo tells him to "shoot it," but Duke says "not yet" because "I want to study its habits" (27). The "gigantic neon sign" at once invokes the standard view of Vegas as unnatural neon monstrosity, a perversion of and alienation from nature — "blocking our view of the mountains" — and also merges with Duke's paranoid acid hallucinations of murderous reptiles: "some kind of electric snake . . . coming straight at us." These are figures, of course, for Las Vegas as modern fear and loathing. But Duke's desire to study the habits of this monstrous electronic snake before he shoots it — a desire that at the moment seems, like so much else in the book, merely comic and absurd — also bespeaks the book's postmodern agenda of learning from Las Vegas, a necessity because Vegas embodies the truth of the book's post-sixties present.

This motif is clarified, as Duke and Gonzo load up on drugs again in their room and turn on the television: "The TV news was about the Laos Invasion — a series of horrifying disasters: explosions and twisted wreckage, men fleeing in terror, Pentagon generals babbling insane lies. 'Turn that shit off!' screamed my attorney 'Let's get *out* of here!'" (29). As throughout the book, our heros see themselves as the antithesis of all that Nixon and the Laos invasion represent, but their insane, violent, aggressive, drugged behavior reflects and enacts rather than repudiates the "horrifying disasters" of the death of the sixties and the endgame of the Vietnam War. Out on the road, after they have fled the TV news, Gonzo goes "into a drug coma"; Duke, in a state of extreme paranoia, imagines that everyone he sees is talking about him, and wants to "drive down Main Street aiming a black bazooka-looking instrument [one of their weapons] at people," but decides "Las Vegas is not the kind of town" where one can do that (29). Turning up the music in the car, rolling down the windows, and feeling "this is what it's all about," "total control now," he is horrified to hear "The Battle Hymn of Lieutenant Calley" on his own tape deck (29). Thompson's irony is so heavy here that his narrative conceit of Duke's delusional denial of his complicity in the death of the sixties, and in Vegas culture, is extremely thin. Duke and Gonzo arrive at their destination, the sponsor of the Mint 400 motorcycle race they are covering, which turns out to be "Of course. The Mint *Gun Club*! These lunatics weren't letting *anything* interfere with their target practice" (32). Again, Duke and Gonzo, feeling utterly alienated and alien, in fact fit right in.

At the Mint Gun Club, in the chapter narrating Duke's attempt to do his journalistic job at the motorcycle race, Thompson abandons the ostensible narrative belief, however ironic, in the possibility of covering the story. This chapter is titled "Covering the Story . . . A Glimpse of the Press in Action . . . Ugliness & Failure." "Ugliness and failure" of course echoes and corresponds to "fear and loathing." (All the chapter titles express a comic-ironic fear and loathing. Chapters 2–4 are titled "The Seizure of $300 from a Pig Woman in Beverly Hills," "Strange Medicine on the Desert . . . a Crisis of Confidence," and "Hideous Music and the Sound of Many Shotguns . . . Rude Vibes on a Saturday Evening in Vegas.") The motorcycle race becomes invisible as the dust kicked up gathers and hangs in the air until it is impenetrable, and observer reporting is an absurd impossibility. Only a participant in the race could "cover the story," as in the new journalism, and, despite his fantasies of a Vincent Black Shadow, and his strident, unconvincing assertion that "we were gathered here in Las Vegas for a very special assignment: to cover the Fourth Annual 'Mint 400' . . . and when it comes to things like this, you don't fool around" (37) the race is not the story in which this new journalist is actually participating. Duke, as (ironic) questing hero, is learning from Las Vegas about the limits and location of his search for the American Dream: "the idea of trying to 'cover this race' in any conventional press-sense was absurd. . . . It was time, I felt, for an Agonizing Reappraisal of the whole scene" (38). "Agonizing Reappraisal," of course, is a Vietnam cover-up euphemism for

American defeat. Duke's final act at the race, as he makes a last tour in the press vehicle without finding any actual race participants, comes in an encounter with a group of maniacal armed patriots, in dune buggies "covered with ominous symbols: Screaming Eagles carrying American Flags in their claws, a slant-eyed snake being chopped to bits by a buzz-saw made of stars & stripes, and one of the vehicles had what looked like a machine-gun mount on the passenger side" (39). Duke surmises that they are "retired petty-officers from San Diego" (38). When they challenge Duke in an aggressive way — "what *outfit* you fellas with?" — he says " 'the sporting press . . . we're friendlies — hired geeks. . . . If you want a good chase,' I shouted, 'you should get after that skunk from CBS News up ahead in the big black jeep. He's the man responsible for *The Selling of the Pentagon*" (39–40). Again, Duke identifies, no matter whether ironically or in self-defense, with the reactionary armed violence of Las Vegas, against the antiwar commitments of his own (former) sixties self.

After this "Agonizing Reappraisal of the whole scene," Duke and Gonzo spend "A Night on the Town . . . Confrontation at the Desert Inn . . . Drug Frenzy at the Circus-Circus" (the chapter title of this episode). Thompson establishes Vegas, again, this time embodied in the Desert Inn, as utterly alien cultural territory, the anti-sixties: "this was Bob Hope's turf. Frank Sinatra's. Spiro Agnew's. The lobby fairly reeked of high-grade formica and plastic palm trees . . . Debbie Reynolds was yukking across the stage in a silver Afro wig . . . to the tune of 'Sergeant Pepper,' from the golden trumpet of Harry James" (44). Debbie Reynolds singing Sergeant Pepper in a silver Afro wig, in the land of high-grade formica and plastic, and of Hope, Sinatra, and, most egregiously, Agnew, is not just the absurd negation but also the ironic postmodern assimilation of the sixties, not really different in kind from the pervasive use of great sixties rock songs in television commercials, so common by now as to have become unremarkable and barely noticeable.

This chapter begins with a stipulation of the breakdown of journalistic distance, a claim for experiential immediacy and accuracy: "Saturday midnight . . . Memories of this night are extremely hazy. All I have, for guide-pegs, is a pocketful of keno cards and cocktail napkins, all covered with scribbled notes" (41). The implication is that, in the Desert Inn and at the Circus-Circus, we have arrived at last at the story Duke is really covering, where his participation becomes most directly, unmediatedly reported. At the Circus-Circus, a casino whose own name incorporates a self-mocking, ironic acknowledgment of its status as postmodern simulacrum, Duke and Gonzo are right at home since they are on ether now, and "ether is the perfect drug for Las Vegas. In this town they love a drunk. Fresh meat. So they put us through the turnstiles and turned us loose inside" (46). Duke implies that they are only simulating drunkenness, and are therefore spies in the house of the postmodern commercial simulacrum — since they are really on drugs rather than alcohol, they are still of the sixties and alien in Las Vegas. However, in fact, again, their alienation is invisible in their surroundings and therefore deeply in question. Ostensibly, they are a comic fifth column in enemy territory; in fact, the unquestioned ease with which they move through, and blend into, this territory is an objective correlative of the sixties transition to postmodernity: Duke and Gonzo, the sixties holdovers, are doing just fine in a postmodern universe they think is utterly alien but in which, in fact, they are actually in large part at home, since it has emerged so seamlessly from sixties culture itself.

Thompson hints at this insight with characeristic obliqueness, in his development of the Circus-Circus episode. Immediately following his statement that "ether is the perfect drug for Las Vegas," Duke says "the Circus-Circus is what the whole hep world would be doing on Saturday night if the Nazis had won the war. This is the Sixth Reich" (46). Again, Las Vegas is the epitome of hyperfascist culture, the Third Reich doubled, but at the same time, it is the place where "the whole hep world," the world of sixties people, would be found on Saturday night. In his ensuing jeremiad against the absurdities of the Circus-Circus, which offers "every conceivable kind of bizarre shuck" (46) — his elaboration of the ways in which it epitomizes Vegas as the "Sixth Reich" — Duke's emphasis falls heavily on an entertainment device that provides megalomaniacal aggrandizement of the self: "Stand in front of this fantastic machine, my friend, and for just 99¢ your likeness will appear, two hundred feet tall, on a screen above downtown Las Vegas. Ninety-nine ¢ more for a voice message. 'Say whatever you want, fella. They'll hear you, don't worry about that. Remember you'll be two hundred feet tall' " (47). Duke then has a horrific vision: "Jesus Christ. I could see myself lying in bed in the Mint Hotel, half-asleep and staring idly out the window, when suddenly a vicious nazi drunkard appears two hundred feet tall in the midnight sky, screaming gibberish at the world: '*Woodstock Über Alles!*' " (47). This vicious nazi drunkard is of course Duke's comic nightmare double; Circus-

Circus, heart of the Last Vegas fascist simulacrum, "vortex" of the "American Dream" (47), is the comic-horrific new home and destination of the failed, belated hippie.

The book's push-pull drama of loathing and learning to love, of "humping the American Dream," is played out more clearly, more starkly, through Gonzo's acting-out than through Duke's ambivalent vacillations. The "dark double," as in classic American and international modernist literature, literalizes in his actions—he acts out—the disavowed, repressed impulses of the white male self: the suicidal and predatory violence of the death of the sixties and of the emergence of postmodernity. The self-mocking self-consciousness of this use of the "dark double" in *Fear and Loathing* is in fact an aspect of its postmodernity. In one of the great comic scenes of the book, Gonzo takes a bath, in an acid frenzy, with Jefferson Airplane's classic drug anthem "White Rabbit," sung memorably by Grace Slick, from their landmark sixties album *Surrealistic Pillow*, playing over and over at deafening top volume, never quite loud enough for Gonzo. Duke says, "the volume was so far up that it was hard to know what was playing unless you knew *Surrealistic Pillow* almost note for note . . . which I did" (59). Gonzo wants Duke to assist in his suicide by acid rock: " 'Let it roll!' he screamed. 'Just as high as the fucker can go! And when it comes to that fantastic note where the rabbit bites its own head off, I want you to throw that fuckin radio into the tub with me' " (60). Duke throws a grapefruit at Gonzo instead, Gonzo threatens Duke with a knife, and Duke eventually defuses the situation by threatening Gonzo with a can of mace, one of the weapons of choice of riot police at sixties demonstrations. Duke tells himself to "ignore that nightmare in the bathroom. Just another ugly refugee from the Love Generation" (63). Immediately following this ironic death-of-sixties episode comes Duke's earnest meditation on the life and death of the sixties that I have already quoted, in which he describes the essence of the sixties as "a fantastic universal sense that whatever we were doing was *right*, that we were winning," a "sense of inevitable victory over the forces of Old and Evil . . . riding the crest of a high and beautiful wave," and then says "now, less than five years later, you can go up on a steep hill in Las Vegas and look West, and with the right kind of eyes you can almost see the high-water mark—that place where the wave finally broke and rolled back" (68). Ludicrous satire and bitter earnestness coexist undecidably here perhaps more clearly than anywhere else in the book.

The last four chapters of part 1 confirm the inevitability of Duke's and Gonzo's defeated, but potentially liberating, identification with Las Vegas.

With the Mint 400 race over, and disaster looming, Gonzo catches "the next plane to L.A." (69), and Duke elaborately carries out an unimpeded escape (no one tries in the least to stop him) from Vegas as if it were a high-security prison, though not before having gone "back to the airport souvenir counter and spent all the rest of my cash on garbage — complete shit, souvenirs of Las Vegas, plastic fake-Zippo-lighters with a built-in roulette wheel for $6.95, JFK half-dollar money clips for $5 each, tin apes that shook dice for $7.50" (69). At the time of *Europe on Five Dollars a Day*, these are rip-off prices. But more important, each item reflects ironically on Duke's and Gonzo's post-sixties identification with Las Vegas. They are the "tin apes that shook dice."

In this chapter — chapter 9, titled "No Sympathy for the Devil . . . Newsmen Tortured? . . . Flight into Madness" — Duke imagines himself as the beleaguered devil of the Rolling Stones song, persecuted by the militaristic might of Las Vegas: "rum will be absolutely necessary to get through this night — to polish these notes, this shameful diary . . . keep the tape machine screaming all night long at top volume: 'Allow me to introduce myself . . . I'm a man of wealth and taste.' Sympathy? Not for me. No mercy for a criminal freak in Las Vegas. This place is like the Army: the shark ethic prevails — eat the wounded" (72). But of course, Duke's and Gonzo's car is the "Great Red Shark." The shame is of his own complicity in the commercial army of postmodern American culture, where "Sympathy for the Devil" has no subversive edge.

The chapter ends with Duke reading the Las Vegas paper, ostensibly to "stay calm" (72). The paper, not surprisingly, provides a synopsis of the horrors of late-sixties and post-sixties America: a young woman's fatal overdose of heroin, "GI DRUG DEATHS CLAIMED" (73), news of an anti-war protest at Selective Service Headquarters in Washington juxtaposed with "TORTURE TALES TOLD IN WAR HEARINGS" (73) concerning the notorious helicopter drops of Vietnamese prisoners, people shot in New York by a rooftop sniper with no apparent motivation, a Las Vegas pharmacist arrested in "a shortage of over 100,000 pills considered dangerous drugs" (74). Duke first claims this reassures him, since "against that heinous background my crimes were pale and meaningless" (74). But this ostensible complacency is undermined when he turns to the sports page and sees an item about Muhammad Ali, "sentenced to five years in prison for *refusing* to kill 'slopes'" (74), as they had been called by an army intelligence specialist in the report on torture in Vietnam. In Nixon's diabolical America, there is no sympathy for the sixties radical countercultural devil. Thompson uses Duke's alienation from Las Vegas to express his own horror at the emerging post-sixties configuration. However, again, it is precisely in Las Vegas that this post-sixties beast can be himself.

As Duke is on his way out of the Mint Hotel, making his escape from the hopeless bill he and Gonzo have amassed and the hopeless disaster they have made of their room, he receives a telegram from Gonzo in LA saying that he, Duke, has received a new assignment, from *Rolling Stone*, to cover the National Conference of District Attorneys' four-day seminar in Las Vegas on narcotics and dangerous drugs. The irony of this assignment powers the rest of the book. Duke initially repudiates the assignment — "I was in no mood or condition to spend another week in Las Vegas" (78) — but when his escape is ultimately thwarted by a highway patrolman, who declines to arrest him for any of the blatant offenses he has committed and instead, literally a figure of fate, blocks his escape route to LA, he accepts the inevitability of his return to Vegas: "I had no choice" (96). He will not only cover the District Attorneys' Las Vegas seminar on dangerous drugs, he will, of course, fit right in.

The conceit of Duke's total alienation from his environment is maintained throughout part 2, but the environment from which he is ostensibly alienated shifts, for most of the rest of the book, from Las Vegas in general to the District Attorneys' Convention in particular. He makes a distinction between covering the Mint 400 race and his new assignment:

> It was going to be quite a different thing from the Mint 400. That had been an *observer* gig, but this one would need *participation* — and a very special stance: At the Mint 400 we were dealing with an essentially simpatico crowd, and if our behavior was gross and outrageous . . . well, it was only a matter of degree.
>
> But this time our very *presence* would be an outrage. We would be attending the conference under false pretenses and dealing, from the start, with a crowd that was convened for the stated purpose of putting people like us in jail. We *were* the Menace — not in disguise, but stone obvious drug abusers, with a flagrantly cranked-up act that we intended to push all the way to the limit . . . [. . .] If the Pigs were gathering in Vegas for a top-level Drug Conference, we felt the drug culture should be represented.
>
> Beyond that, I'd been out of my head for so long now, that a gig like this seemed perfectly logical. Considering the circumstances, I felt totally meshed with my karma. (109–10)

He is meshed with his karma not just because he is on a mission to represent the drug culture right in the lair of its enemy, but also because he has moved fully from journalistic observation (he has conveniently forgotten that he made a stab at participating in the Mint 400) to new journalistic participation, and he has also become fully at home in Las Vegas. In a key sequence, Duke feels a kinship with the desk clerk at the Flamingo, who gives him, with his Vegas-friendly credit card, priority for a room over a cop who has already paid: "I had *been there* with these fuzzy little shitheads — and so, I sensed, had the desk clerk. He had the air of a man who'd been fucked around, in his time, by a fairly good cross-section of mean-tempered rule-crazy cops" (107). Las Vegas, postmodern market inheritor of Duke's sixties libertarianism, is on the side of commodity capitalism's anything-goes (as long as it makes a profit) and against "rule-crazy" law-and-order morality. Rules in Vegas, and their highly effective enforcement, have nothing to do with state-sanctioned morality or the rule of law. They are only there to protect the "Power," the controllers of this remarkable "gold mine": "security in a place like Caesar's Palace is super tense and strict. . . . The 'high side' of Vegas is probably the most closed society west of Sicily . . . A gold mine like Vegas breeds its own army, like any other gold mine. Hired muscle tends to accumulate in fast layers around money/power poles . . . and big money, in Vegas, is synonymous with the Power to protect it" (155–56). Wolfe, who acknowledges the ruling presence of the Mob in Vegas and the ultimate violent force of its rule, is never this explicit; for Venturi et al., the Mob has vanished into the postmodern commercial vernacular sublime.

This passage reminds Thompson of his horror of Vegas, his fear and loathing, which recurs even in the midst of Duke's appalled recognition, in part 2, of his belonging in this place, where he meshes with his karma, and where he finds the post-sixties incarnation of the American Dream. There is a sense in which Duke's identification with Las Vegas, rather than his fear and loathing, is the book's postmodern conceit, while Thompson's underlying horror at the place is the book's deep modernist truth. To the extent that *Fear and Loathing* still inhabits the sixties, it is truly a book of fear and loathing, not of the post-sixties self as most at home in and ultimately identified with Las Vegas, but simply of Las Vegas itself: "The Fillmore style never quite caught on here. People like Sinatra and Dean Martin are still considered 'far out' in Vegas. . . . A week in Vegas is like stumbling into a Time Warp, a regression to the late fifties" (156). To the sixties person, the late fifties (minus the Beats and Civil Rights) is the ultimate cultural anathema. There is no sense here of the postmodern irony of Debbie Reynolds singing the Beatles in a silver Afro wig.

The District Attorneys' Conference on Narcotics and Dangerous Drugs is anticlimactic, uneventful. Duke and Gonzo eventually just walk out in boredom, with contempt for the low-tech ignorance and cluelessness of the group. The major events of part 2 involve Duke's self-loathing complicity in the collapse of the sixties, the complicity that makes this conference so harmless for him. Several episodes revolve around contempt for and violence against subordinate women (a runaway teenager Gonzo picks up at the airport; a hotel cleaning person; a waitress), where Thompson presents Duke's and Gonzo's feelings and behavior in a more negative light than he has so far, narrating these sequences with a more heavy, ominous, though still comic tone than that of the lighter, more cartoonish outrageousness of part 1.[6] Duke himself, while acting on his violent contempt, fear, and loathing of women, also seems appalled by his own and Gonzo's behavior. This loathsome fear and loathing of women (in which Thompson, like Burroughs, one of his major influences, clearly participates at the same time that he distances himself from it) is part of the violent, crazed, self-destructive end of the sixties, the journey to the defunct, violated American Dream in the Great White Whale (the rented white Cadillac in which the heroes arrive at the end of the sixties line).

Duke and Gonzo do, actually and in fact, find the American Dream in Las Vegas. As advertised in its subtitle, this book is "A Savage Journey to the Heart of the American Dream." For this sequence, Thompson abandons Duke's first-person narration and switches instead to the device of the intervening "editor," who begins chapter 9 of part 2 by announcing, in an "Editor's Note," in italics, that

> *At this point in the chronology, Dr. Duke appears to have broken down completely; the original manuscript is so splintered that we were forced to seek out the original tape recording and transcribe it verbatim. . . . In the interests of journalistic purity, we are publishing the following section just as it came off the tape. . . . The rationale for the following transaction appears to be based on a feeling — shared by both Duke and his attorney — that the American Dream would have to be sought out somewhere far beyond the confines of the District Attorneys' Conference on Narcotics and Dangerous Drugs.* (161)

This device of course is intended to make the reader feel that s/he has reached the heart of the book's narrative authenticity, its "journalistic purity"; no longer a memoir-style, "subjective" reconstruction of events but a direct recording of dialogue that actually took place. The ensuing dialogue does indeed sound like real conversation, with repetition, interruption, and incoherent remarks left intact. The conceit of "journalistic purity" is yet another layer of Thompson's irony. The "tape-recorded" dialogue appears here because of its wonderful ludicrousness and absurdity, not because "Dr. Duke" has "broken down completely." Authenticity is precisely what cannot be found in Las Vegas: it has been banished in post-sixties postmodernity, as the heroes' arrival at the American Dream / heart of darkness makes clear.

The heaviness of the irony of this episode is signaled by the repetition of its location, alternately "Paradise Boulevard" and "Paradise Road," in the chapter title ("Breakdown on Paradise Blvd."), and the scene-setting by the "editor," whose prose style is suspiciously identical to Thompson's: *"The transcription begins somewhere on the Northeast outskirts of Las Vegas — zooming along Paradise Road in the White Whale"* (161). The Northeast outskirts of Vegas, or North Vegas, has already been established in the book as the down-and-out end of town, home of hookers over forty, drug dealers, and cheating gamblers banned from casinos at the center of town. Duke and Gonzo, hungry, go to Terry's Taco Stand, USA, which advertises five tacos for a buck. A long absurd interchange with the waitress ensues about whether the tacos are Mexican or "just regular," what a "taco burger" is, and whether or not to get a chiliburger: "as your attorney I advise you to get the chiliburger" (163), Gonzo says to Duke. Toward the end of this long comic-absurd interchange, which is precisely about Las Vegas as harbinger of postmodern American inauthenticity, Gonzo says:

> Let me explain it to you, let me run it down just briefly if I can. We're looking for the American Dream, and we were told it was somewhere in this area. . . . Well, we're here looking for it, 'cause they sent us out here all the way from San Francisco to look for it. That's why they gave us this white Cadillac, they figure that we could catch up with it in that . . .
> *Waitress:* Hey Lou, you know where the American Dream is?
> *Att'y* (to Duke): She's asking the cook if he knows where the American Dream is. (164)

Another absurd conversation follows, in which the waitress and Lou decide that the American Dream is a sort of discotheque on Paradise that used to be called the Psychiatrist's Club and is now "a mental joint, where all the dopers hang out . . . off Paradise around the Flamingo" (166; the Flamingo is where Duke and Gonzo are now staying). Gonzo summarizes Lou's and the waitress's information: "OK. Big black building [like the Fillmore], right on Paradise: twenty-four-hour-a-day violence, drugs" (167). The arrival at the American Dream is not included in the "tape-recorded" dialogue but is rather narrated by the "editor," in a statement, without further narration, that ends this chapter; the narration spirals into terminal absurdity after this chapter, as Duke and Gonzo, having virtually destroyed the White Whale, are on their inevitable way out:

> *Tape cassettes for the next sequence were impossible to transcribe due to some viscous liquid encrusted behind the heads. There is a certain consistency in the garbled sounds however, indicating that almost two hours later Dr. Duke and his attorney finally located what was left of the "Old Psychiatrist's Club"—a huge slab of cracked, scorched concrete in a vacant lot full of tall weeds. The owner of a gas station across the road said the place had "burned down about three years ago." (168)*

The irony here, and the representation of the book's theme, are as blatant as they can be. Like Nick Carraway at Gatsby's funeral, Duke and Gonzo bear solitary witness to the ignominious death of a corrupted American Dream. But unlike that of *The Great Gatsby, Fear and Loathing*'s irony is not so much tormented modernist ambivalence as self-mocking, absurd postmodern pastiche, with modernist torment at the betrayal of the Dream still simultaneously present in the text as a dominant but almost-residual formation. Out of the self-immolation of the sixties, culminating embodiment of the utopian American Dream, in drugged, violent insanity (the "Psychiatrist's Club"), the postmodern emerges. One of the primary ways in which *Fear and Loathing* is a characteristic sixties text is its horror, coexisting with hilarity, at this self-immolation; its deep regret for the loss of that utopian moment.

"Vegas is so full of natural freaks—people who are genuinely twisted— that drugs aren't really a problem. . . . Psychedelics are almost irrelevant in a town where you can wander into a casino any time of the day or night and witness the crucifixion of a gorilla—on a flaming neon cross that suddenly turns into a pinwheel, spinning the beast around in wild circles above the crowded gambling action" (190, a reference to an act at the Circus-Circus). On the next page, Duke talks to Bruce in the Circus-

Circus, from whom he is trying to buy this gorilla, his final failed act before departing Vegas:

> He seemed surprised. "You *found* the American Dream?" he said. In *this* town?"
>
> I nodded. "We're sitting on the main nerve right now," I said. "You remember that story the manager told us about the owner of this place? How he always wanted to run away and join the circus when he was a kid?"
>
> Bruce ordered two more beers. He looked over the casino for a moment, then shrugged. "Yeah, I see what you mean," he said. "Now the bastard has his *own* circus, and a license to steal, too." He nodded. "You're right — he's the model."
>
> "Absolutely," I said. "It's pure Horatio Alger, all the way down to his attitude." (191)

The American Dream Duke has found is now no longer the burned out, self-destroyed sixties on the down-market outskirts of Las Vegas, it is rather the Circus-Circus, the "main nerve" of Vegas, the ultimate simulacrum, marker of ironic postmodern commercial culture (Thompson endorses the notion that the Circus-Circus embodies the American Dream in his letter of May 9, 1971, to Jim Silberman, his editor at Random House; *Fear and Loathing in America*, 381–82). Duke ends by wanting to buy the gorilla: to become a full participant in the culture of the commercial simulacrum, the utopian jouissance bound and contained in the postmodern commodity. He fails. The ludicrous, tragic beast he wants to own, possess, buy with money — the man-ape whirling above the gambling tables of Vegas crucified on a neon cross — is Thompson himself.

LEARNING

Learning from Las Vegas is a postmodern manifesto.[7] Its title encapsulates the mission of the project of Robert Venturi, Denise Scott Brown, and Steven Izenour (Venturi et al.). Rather than judging Las Vegas, however ambivalently and with however much complexity, as both Wolfe and Thompson did, Venturi et al., just a year after Thompson and six years after Wolfe, want to suspend judgment (though in fact their relation to Las Vegas is fairly celebratory) and to position themselves as acolytes, or at least as interested students. "Las Vegas's values are not questioned here"

(6), they say, and, as they say in the second part of the book, on the "ugly and ordinary," "whether society was right or wrong was not for us at that moment to argue" (128). The fact of the Mob's origination and continuing control of Vegas is irrelevant, uninteresting, as I have mentioned. Las Vegas becomes instead a prime instance of postmodern valorization of popular desire, its embrace of commercial consumer culture and its vernacular styles, and of what Venturi et al. call the "ugly and ordinary" over against elitist modernist architecture's top-down aesthetic totalizations. *Learning from Las Vegas* has been a central text of postmodern ideology and advocacy.

The book began, as Venturi et al. explain in the preface, as a Yale architecture seminar (think of Wolfe!) with the sober, formalist title "Learning from Las Vegas, or Form Analysis as Design Research." Toward the end of the semester, as the spirit of Las Vegas got to them, the students changed the second name to "The Great Proletarian Cultural Locomotive" (xi). Sixties identification with proletarian politics and culture here comes to fruition as postmodern egalitarian populism, focused around manifestations not of working-class politics but of popular culture. Similarly, Venturi et al. open the book by claiming that "learning from the existing landscape is a way of being revolutionary for an architect" (3), again claiming and refunctioning for postmodernism a sixties keyword. They will be revolutionary "not in the obvious way, which is to tear down Paris and begin again, as Le Corbusier suggested in the 1920s, but another, more tolerant way" (3). Le Corbusier's suggestion appears here, of course, as monstrously arrogant and destructive, also fascistic. Venturi et al. distance themselves from modernist architecture throughout, which is consistently categorized as deludedly elitist and totalizing; "utopian and puristic" (3).[8] Modernism, as in many postmodern polemics, is the failed, destructive precursor from which postmodernism will save culture; against which it will champion the people and their "ugly, ordinary," commercial, consumer culture against the overweening, manipulative delusions of the cultural elite: "analysis of existing American urbanism is a socially desirable activity to the extent that it teaches us architects to be more understanding and less authoritarian [i.e., less modernist] in the plans we make for both inner-city renewal and new development. In addition, there is no reason why the methods of commercial persuasion and the skyline of signs analyzed here should not serve the purpose of civic and cultural enhancement" (6). In order to use Las Vegas as exemplum of "methods of commercial persuasion" and "skyline of signs," it is necessary for Venturi et al. to shift their attention from the economics of Mob control and enormous Mob profit and to focus it instead on popular desire: to substitute a postmodern model of multiple, fluid, multidirectional, indeterminate popular agency for a modern model of stark, binaristic domination and oppression.

Venturi et al. proceed by first identifying their project with that of pop art, a crucial sixties cultural pivot to postmodernism and postmodernity, in its at once ironic and celebratory relation to commercial consumer culture: "architects who can accept the lessons of primitive vernacular architecture . . . and of industrial, vernacular architecture . . . do not easily acknowledge the validity of the commercial vernacular. For the artist, creating the new may mean choosing the old or the existing. Pop artists have relearned this. Our acknowledgment of the existing, commercial architecture at the scale of the highway is within this tradition" (6).

For Venturi et al., the study of "commercial architecture at the scale of the highway" is a key to learning from Las Vegas, and the lesson is "anti-spatial," derived from an "architecture of communication over space; communication dominates space as an element in the architecture of the landscape" (8), a key postmodern trope (note the contradiction with Jameson's view of postmodernism as the replacement of modern temporality by postmodern spatiality; yet, both would agree on the primacy of communication). "If you take the signs away, there is no place" (18): we live in a postmodern hyperspace of communications and information (Jameson also defines "postmodern hyperspace").[9] Postmodern Las Vegas also teaches an architecture of commercial "persuasion" by means of this communication, particularly the giant billboards and casino signs that dominate and organize the visual experience of the Strip—communication and persuasion that dominate or supplant traditional, mappable (in Jameson's term) space.

In analyzing the gambling casinos, Venturi et al. come close to the question of immense profit and the Power (as Thompson would call it) that controls that profit as motive forces behind the phenomena of Las Vegas, including architectural phenomena. While the arrangement of signs that is the exterior architecture of Vegas is a characteristic postmodern manifestation of communication supplanting space, the design of the casinos seems to be, as they depict it, a manifestation of the top-down control they associate with modernist architecture: "the circulation of the whole [space of the casino] focuses on the gambling rooms. In a Las Vegas hotel the registration desk is invariably behind you when you enter the lobby; before you are the gambling tables and machines. The lobby is the gambling room. . . . The combination of darkness and enclosure of the gambling room and its subspaces makes for privacy, protection, concentration, and control" (49). This element of control, obviously in the interest of the massive gambling profits around which Vegas is constructed, is not the important architectural fact about the casinos to Venturi et al., however. Rather, it is the "monumentality" of these spaces, which Venturi et al. link to the monumentality of communal architectural spaces throughout human history, spaces that express and embody the "cohesion of the community" (50). There is no point, according to Venturi et al., in failing to acknowledge the true nature of contemporary communal spaces: "perhaps we should admit that our cathedrals are the chapels without the nave and that, apart from theaters and ball parks, the occasional communal space that is big is a space for crowds of anonymous individuals without explicit connection with each other. The big, low mazes of the dark restaurant with alcoves combine being together and yet separate as does the Las Vegas casino" (50). One would certainly now add the suburban mall to this list. (In fact, large sections of contemporary hotel-casinos on the strip contain what amount to high-end malls.) It is the casino's function as the architecture of postmodern popular, anonymous, fragmented, destabilized, multivalent, fluid, dynamic, shifting, commercially based community that most interests Venturi et al., not the profit-oriented control that dictates the construction of the Vegas spaces. Venturi et al. end the section on Las Vegas with an encomium to the postmodern:

> . . . the vitality that may be achieved by an architecture of inclusion or, by contrast, the deadness that results from too great a preoccupation [like modernism's] with tastefulness and total design. The Strip shows the value of symbolism and allusion in an architecture of vast space and speed and proves that people, even architects, have fun with architecture that reminds them of something else [the dehistoricized pastiche of architectural styles that has been the hallmark of postmodern architecture]. Allusion and comment, on the past or present or on our great commonplaces or old clichés, and inclusion of the everyday in the environment, sacred and profane—these are what are lacking in present-day Modern architecture. We can learn about them from Las Vegas. (53)

The everyday, the cliché, pastiche, fun, allusion, inclusion, and the lighthearted but biting irony of this powerful book are all watchwords and keywords of the postmodern. Venturi et al. open the world of Las Vegas to "ordinary" people, who are excluded from Wolfe's and Thompson's modernist Vegas rogues' galleries and freak shows of grotesques. The tastes of these ordinary, everyday people may be "ugly" by the lights of modernist aesthetics and of professional architecture, but these tastes — witty, complex, functional, and beautiful in their own ways — are in tune with the postmodern cultural dominant. This egalitarian opening out of meaningful subjectivity and agency to everyday, ordinary people is at the heart of postmodernity's populism.[10]

CHAPTER FIVE

Endnotes I: Sixties, Avant-Garde, Popular Culture

Marcuse, Adorno, and Barthes see the avant-garde as the primary cultural site of radical possibility — a potential alternative to the bankrupt, oppressive dominant culture, even if always implicated in and constructed by that culture.[1] Huyssen and others see the sixties avant-gardes as postmodern, emerging from a cultural history separate from, and opposed to, the history of modernism.[2] In the latter analysis, the twentieth-century avant-gardes, in their repudiation of art's separation from everyday life, oppose the modernist "great divide" between "high" and "low" culture; the sixties avant-gardes, therefore, directly ushered in postmodern popular culture. While I demur from Huyssen's somewhat monolithic categorization of modernism as elitist, and from his designation of those avant-gardes as fully postmodern, I agree with his assessment of the role of the sixties avant-gardes in the emergence of the postmodern.[3] The avant-garde renaissance of the sixties was a profoundly important cultural phenomenon, encompassing a wide range of movements in the visual arts, film, video, animation, theater, music, dance, performance, as well as all genres of writing. Pop art, for example, in its ironic populism, as Venturi et al. make clear, was one of the few most important sixties pivots from the avant-garde to the postmodern. It is not my purpose here to survey, account for, or evaluate these myriad vital movements. Rather, I want to focus, in highly abbreviated form, on a few manifestations of the nonliterary sixties avant-gardes that are most germane to my argument about the emergence of the postmodern. This brief discussion is included to make clear the pervasiveness throughout sixties cultural production, particularly in the avant-gardes, of the simultaneity of the dominant modern and the emergent postmodern. I will point out, briefly, a few key elements of this simultaneity.

Jean-Luc Godard is as good an iconic figure for this phenomenon as any. He was, of course, a key sixties avant-garde figure, one of the central luminaries of the French *nouvelle vague* in film. The *nouvelle vague*, like the sixties avant-garde movements in general, was an endpoint modernist movement, as well as incipiently postmodern. It was heroic, male-dominated; it operated in search of truth, depth, transcendence, unity in fragmentation; it was formalist, self-reflexive, mostly elitist in its appeal though not in its radical political ideologies, especially those of Godard, who was deeply involved in the French Maoist New Left. At the same time, however, Godard, the most experimental, formalist, and self-reflexive of the *nouvelle vague auteurs*, as well as the most political, was also the most involved in popular, consumer, commodity culture, and in fan and star culture. His movies repeatedly investigate and ironize not just their own status as film, as narrative, as aesthetic construction, but also as vehicles for "movie stars" (see particularly Godard's treatment of Anna Karina in *Pierrot le fou*).

Godard was also very interested in the kind of violence that has come to dominate popular film in postmodernity. His films were often quite violent and treated violence ambiguously: both comically and cartoonishly, with ludicrous gangsters and bungled crime or suicide, and also seriously, investigating the complex status of violence in both consumer capitalism and also in radical political movements, as well as in manipulations of the image. Godard's 1970 film *Weekend*, one of the latest of his more popular sixties movies, before he turned at once profoundly inward and also away from film and toward video, is filled with varieties of random, casual, as well as purposive violence. (Everyone leaves Paris for a summer weekend in the country; the road cannot handle the traffic and a massive traffic jam, in which violent, lethal collisions occur without much affect, ensues;

movement stops altogether so the protagonists leave their car and go off into the woods where they join a radical commune; the developments from this point are at once absurd, moving, comical, and violent.) Godard's treatment of this violence in *Weekend* is at once detached, amused, and horrified. Unlike violence in most popular postmodern movies, it is meant primarily to disturb, rather than to entertain, the audience: to insist on a profound critique of our culture and politics rather than to thrill us viscerally and momentarily, allowing us at once to experience and to displace violence with varyingly minimal critical or intellectual repercussions. Nonetheless, partly because Godard was interested in the meaninglessness, randomness, pervasiveness, and gratuitousness of contemporary violence, and partly because Godard understood that in order to disturb the audience the film must also appeal to the audience's attraction to violence that is itself disturbing, *Weekend* also has the effect of uncritical, visceral, entertaining thrill, in a way that is recognizable as a precursor of the pervasive violence, often accompanied by various modes of self-conscious ambivalence, of popular movies in postmodernity. Godard represents, in this analysis, the way in which the sixties avant-gardes at once continued the oppositional aesthetic tradition of the modernist avant-gardes and also ushered in the more affirmative, complicitously critical works of postmodernity.

No cultural phenomenon is more characteristic of the sixties than rock music; in no sixties cultural phenomenon is the simultaneity of the dominant modern and the emergent postmodern, and the emergence of the postmodern as the new cultural dominant, more clear.[4] I will discuss the Beatles as prime instance of this phenomenon in greater detail, by way of Richard Poirier's "Learning from the Beatles," in chapter 10. The most important characteristic of sixties rock in relation to my argument here, as my discussion of the Poirier essay will make clear, is its simultaneous status as popular culture and avant-garde. The popularity of this music, and its central role in the emergence of popular culture as dominant culture, is evident; its status as avant-garde culture is perhaps a bit less so. However, it is a truism that the lyrics of many sixties rock songs, particularly those by such great writers as Bob Dylan, Carole King, John Lennon, Joni Mitchell, Jim Morrison, and Neil Young, are of a piece with sixties avant-garde poetry (as I will argue in chapter 10, acknowledging the fact that these lyrics are frequently taught in high school and sometimes college English classes as poetry is different from arguing that they were part of a historically specific sixties literary avant-garde). Dylan and Lennon both wrote comic-fantastic books which are, literally, indistinguishable from other sixties avant-garde writing, and, like many of their song lyrics, derive from earlier twentieth-century and late-nineteenth-century symbolist, avant-garde, and experimental writing. In this writing, the determinate, sense-making function of communicative language is disrupted, replaced by open-ended, polysemous, suggestive linguistic juxtapositions, which are subversively, and utopically, liberatory: 'Oh, the ragman draws circles / Up and down the block, / I'd ask him what the matter was / But I know that he don't talk. / And the ladies treat me kindly / And furnish me with tape, But deep inside my heart / I know I can't escape."[5] These famous lines are highly suggestive — of self-mocking but ardent desire, of futility, also potential transcendent unity ("draws circles"); of imprisonment — the central theme of the song ("Stuck"; "I know I can't escape"); of frustrated sexuality; of recorded rather than live music, bondage, binding together, silencing ("tape"). The meanings, like the music, are multiple and indeterminate, lyrical and suggestive, ironic and passionate.

While Huyssen makes important points, particularly about the role of gender, in his analysis of the avant-garde subversion of the high-low divide, I do not agree with him (and the many other theorists and critics who either agree with him or develop their own versions of a similar thesis), ultimately, that the avant-gardes derive from a history markedly separate from that of modernism. Like Marcuse, I see modernism and the avant-gardes as ends of an oppositional continuum in the early twentieth century; by midcentury, both modernist and avant-garde aesthetic practice had come to be generally considered part of "high culture." These rock lyrics owe at least as much to French Symbolism, Eliot, and Stein as to Tzara.

Issues of race and gender are crucial to rock's central position in the emergence of postmodernity. The key role of African American music, particularly blues, in the emergence of rock, in Britain as well as the United States, is a commonplace. In general, rock is a form of popular culture just as much because of its emergence from African American and white folk roots as because of its mass appeal. Further, of course, British rock, in particular, emerges from the working class of the industrial north of England.

In the more agonistic narrative of sixties rock, white musicians, from Elvis to the Stones to Cream and Led Zeppelin, appropriated black music and displaced black performers. The virtually all-male "British invasion" of the mid-sixties ended the dominance in American popular music culture of Motown's black performers, many of whom were the women of the "girl groups." Sixties rock was indeed, like almost all other sixties cultural phenomena, dominated by white men. However, the "crossover" popularization of black music in the sixties was the pivot to the much more diverse, variegated racial scenes of postmodern popular music.

Although sixties rock was dominated by men, there were some highly visible, extremely successful women: first the Motown female artists and girl groups, and at the same time the great women's voices of the early-sixties folk revival, also a key precursor of sixties rock, such as Joan Baez and Mary Travers. Sixties rock divas such as Grace Slick and Janis Joplin were icons of female power and autonomy crucial in the emergence of second-wave feminism, itself, as we will see, a key pivot to postmodernity. Singer-songwriters such as Judy Collins, Carole King, and Joni Mitchell were also important presences in the rock scene, keeping open a space of and for the female voice.

Though there was a great deal of macho posturing in sixties rock — Jimi Hendrix and Mick Jagger come most immediately to mind — this masculinity, as was the case throughout the sixties countercultures, was complex. Hendrix and Jagger in particular, like many other male rock stars, also represented ambiguous sexuality. "Androgyny" was an ideal of sixties sexuality, at the same time that the culture was heavily misogynist and male-dominated. Sixties styles of masculinity, particularly visible in rock culture, were highly feminized, even at their most misogynist.[6] Some of the most frequently encountered clichés and epithets used by mainstream detractors of the counterculture had to do with this feminization. Ideal masculine affective and body styles and clothes were feminized. Sensitivity, intuitiveness, soulfulness, receptivity, and free expression of strong emotion were valorized as the hippie masculine ideal, in combination with long hair, willowy thinness, bodily grace rather than overmastering strength, deemphasizing muscularity. Men wore the same ("unisex") hiphugger bellbottoms and loose shirts that women wore. This conjuncture of hypersexism, androgyny, and masculine feminization in sixties rock is characteristic of sixties cultural formations as endpoint of modernity and incipience of postmodernity: at once modern utopian ideal of transcending gender difference and also postmodern gender-bending, multiplicity, diversity, and performativity of roles and sexualities; at once the traditional male dominance of the long durée of modernity and also the new hypermasculinity of the postmodern.[7]

The character or quality of voice in sixties rock was also a fascinating site of cultural change. Many of the great folk and rock voices of the sixties — those of Joan Baez, Bob Dylan, Rick Danko, Jerry Garcia, Janis Joplin, Paul McCartney, Robbie Robertson, Brian Wilson, Neil Young, for example, or the harmonies of Crosby, Stills, Nash (and Young) — were characterized by a deep, passionate, visionary sincerity; a clarity or purity; a directness of emotion. These qualities connected, again, to the utopian impulse of sixties rock: this was a music of liberation and transcendence, of untrammeled authenticity, of passion, truth, and love, even when it was either apocalyptically sardonic, as so often with Dylan's music, or mockingly ironic, a characteristic Beatles mode. The scathing bitterness and the sarcastic irony were in the service of a critique linked to Marcuse's Great Refusal. The possibility of a utopian alternative — "The Gates of Eden," "I Shall Be Released" — was always the implied alternative to the grotesqueries of "Maggie's Farm" or "Desolation Row," or being "Stuck Inside of Mobile with the Memphis Blues Again"; "Woodstock" the alternative to, coexisting with, "Tin Soldiers"; "A Box of Rain" to the persecutions of "Truckin'"; or, most evidently with the Beatles, "All You Need Is Love," "Lucy in the Sky with Diamonds," "Hey Jude," to "Paperback Writer," "A Day in the Life," or "When I'm Sixty-Four." "A Day in the Life," like many Dylan songs, contains its own transformative transcendence, in both music and lyrics, of the demoralized, bankrupt quotidian world it depicts. But beyond the lyrics and the music, again, the quality of voice in this sixties rock music was the key promise of modernity's utopian transcendence — of a world of pure truth, passion, freedom, justice, love.

At the same time, because this music was popular, both in origins and in reception, and because it was at the heart of the emergence of postmodern popular culture, these qualities of voice became trademark styles. Rock stars, as they quickly became and always already were, even or particularly when they continually changed their styles, as Dylan and the Beatles, Neil Young, the Stones, and the Beach Boys, most notably did, were recognized by a repertoire of unique, individual characteristics, of which quality of voice was a crucial component. It is interesting that unique quality of voice or style is also a key component of modernist artistic genius: the inimitable, auratic recognizability of Joyce, Eliot, or Woolf; of Debussy, Ravel, or Stravinsky; of Cézanne, Picasso, or Matisse. In postmodern popular culture, this uniqueness becomes, again, a trademark style, that can be marketed, often for enormous amounts of money, as in the case, particularly, of the Beatles; classic sixties rock appears so often now in television commercials that this phenomenon, at first shocking, is now completely unremarkable. The unique, trademark voice can also be appropriated, in the manner of postmodern pastiche, as has been the case throughout post-sixties rock, where vocal styles become stylings, and the unique, auratic, transcendent voice becomes available to imitation, transformation, institutionalization, fragmentation, (literal) commercialization, and the echt-pastiche of sampling: all forms of postmodern appropriation. In William Burroughs's formulation, as we will see in chapter 8, the unique, transcendent, utopian sixties rock voice becomes available to anyone who wants to (or can afford to) play the game: at once commodified and democratized, the key features of the undecidability of the postmodern.

I would like to address a final comment to a crucial issue: that of gender and popular culture. A great deal of feminist postmodernist work has been done on the gendering of popular culture, particularly consumer culture, as feminine, and the coincidence of the rise of popular culture in postmodernity with the rise of second-wave feminism. Key artists who developed this connection and made it visible are Cindy Sherman, Jenny Holzer, and Barbara Kruger; key theorists, critics, and historians of this phenomenon are Rachel Bowlby, Cora Kaplan, E. Ann Kaplan, Andreas Huyssen, Tania Modleski, Craig Owens, Kathy Peiss, Janice Radway, Lynne Segal, Brenda Silver, Jennifer Wicke, and many others. I do not wish to recapitulate this work here, or to add to it, but rather to point to the phenomena it so crucially explicates as a key factor in the emergence of the postmodern in the sixties. The importance of the emergence of women in the late sixties and early seventies out of the otherness of modernity's self-other hierarchical dualisms cannot be overestimated in the emergence of postmodernity (see chapter 14). Postmodern popular culture and consumer culture have been prime locations, in many ways, of women's moves into modes of agency in postmodernity — in cultural as well as economic and political terms. These forms of agency are, of course, like all features of postmodernity, complex — always complicitous in their modes of critique. Nonetheless, without the convergence of feminism and postmodern popular, consumer culture, second-wave feminism would not have become the pervasive cultural and political force that it did become in postmodernity.

PART THREE

Participatory Democracy to Postmodern Populism

CHAPTER SIX

Participatory Democracy in Port Huron

Participatory democracy is the primary informing concept of the profoundly influential 1962 document *The Port Huron Statement* (PHS), written by Students for a Democratic Society (SDS).[1] *PHS*, particularly in the sections that develop ideas relevant to notions of participatory democracy, became a crucial theoretical, ideological rallying point, self-explanation, and organizing tool for SDS.[2] As Arthur Marwick says, "The 'Port Huron Statement', with but one qualification [Vietnam], rehearsed all the major issues which were to form the essence of the New Left and the Movement throughout the High Sixties."[3] As James Miller explains, Tom Hayden, the primary author of *PHS*, learned about participatory democracy from his political theory teacher at Michigan, Arnold Kaufman, who coined the term in the 1960 essay "Human Nature and Participatory Democracy." *PHS* enacts the sixties pivot from modern democracy to postmodern populism, linked to a shift of the idea of the political toward constructions of subjectivity.[4]

The emphasis in participatory democracy, as developed in *PHS*, is on individual action, authenticity, and meaningfulness. As a mode of democratic politics, it was initially conceived as an adjunct to representative democracy—a means for individuals to become more directly involved than voting allows in making decisions that materially affect their lives, and in creating a vibrant public sphere. But as the New Left became increasingly radical in the course of the decade, participatory democracy more and more came to be seen as an alternative to representative democracy.[5] The latter was seen as inherently alienating, fostering passivity and noninvolvement, and also as susceptible to corruption and cooptation by big business—the military-industrial complex—whose interests were at odds with those of "the people."

The initial model for participatory democracy came from the Civil Rights movement. As Paul Booth, one of the authors of *PHS*, said in an interview with James Miller, " 'If everything could be restructured starting from the SNCC project in McComb, Mississippi, then we would have participatory democracy' " (Miller 144). The Civil Rights movement in the South was grassroots, activist, completely involving, meaningful, and authentic for its participants, and it demanded a significant degree of commitment, daring, exposure to physical danger—putting one's "body on the line." For Tom Hayden, participatory democracy "meant 'number one, *action*; we believed in action. We had behind us the so-called decade of apathy; we were emerging from apathy. What's the opposite of apathy? Active participation. Citizenship. Making history. Secondly, we were very directly influenced by the civil rights movement in its student phase, which believed that by personally committing yourself and taking risks, you could enter history and try to change it after a hundred years of segregation. And so it was this element of participation in democracy that was important. Voting was not enough' " (Miller 144). The emphasis for Booth and, most influentially, for Hayden, is clearly on the self—on changing history through personal, risk-taking involvement and direct action, rather than on communally instituting new social and political structures that would create a more democratic society. The personal meaningfulness derived from political activism seems at least as important to Hayden as the social and political change that are activism's goals. The communalist significances of participatory democracy that were also crucial in the New Left—the substitution of consensual group decision-making for the "alienated," distanced governmental structures of representative democracy—are not of first importance to Hayden.

The views of Sharon Jeffrey, another *PHS* author, epitomize the sense of participatory democracy as pertaining primarily to a politics of the self—of a modern, utopian ideal of a unified subject, a subject divided against itself by a corrupt society made whole in a utopia of participatory democracy:

> "On the one hand, it was a source of inspiration and vision and meaning: it was an idea that I could commit myself to from the depths of my soul. 'Participatory' meant 'involved in decisions.' And I definitely wanted to be involved in decisions that were going to affect *me*! How could I let anyone make a decision about me that I wasn't involved in? The other sentence [from *PHS*] that is essential to me is 'The goal of man in society should be human independence, finding a meaning of life that is authentic.' I think authenticity is something that we were deeply committed to discovering within ourselves. I had a very personalized sense of participatory democracy—but I could also connect it to black students, I could connect it to students in universities, I could connect it to the Third World." (Miller 144)

For Jeffrey, even more clearly than for Hayden, participatory democracy was primarily a politics of the self, only secondarily about what we conventionally think of as New Left and other sixties politics (the Civil Rights movement, the antiwar movement, free-speech and other university reform movements, third world liberation struggles).

Two other *PHS* authors Miller interviews have entirely different, more conventionally "political" views of participatory democracy. For Bob Ross, participatory democracy meant "socialism in an American accent," building on the indigenous "Jacobin tradition that had within it socialism—Tom Paine is not a bad example." Interestingly, Ross says he "thought it was what my colleagues meant by participatory democracy" (144), as if he has subsequently had to revise that notion. Richard Flacks also thought participatory democracy was about socialism—"Not just that it was another code word for socialism, it meant redefining the socialist tradition in terms of the democratic content of it . . . extending principles of democracy from the political sphere into other institutions, like industry, like the university" (145).

Miller uses these diverging explanations of participatory democracy to argue that it was a loose, flexible, shifting, capacious term that could encompass, in productive, useful ways, multiple, sometimes contradictory meanings. I agree with Miller, but would also argue that these meanings fall into two fairly clear clusters—what I am calling the politics of the self, represented by Hayden and most clearly by Jeffrey, as opposed, in Ross's and Flacks' views, not just to politics in some more traditional sense, though it is that, but in particular to the tradition of Enlightenment socialist utopianism. In *PHS* as a characteristic sixties text, these two meanings coexist as if they were the same thing, as they seemed to some extent to do in the minds of the *PHS* authors. But in postmodernity, the latter, socialist meaning recedes — defeated, discredited, disavowed. Note Bob Ross's tone of puzzled but defiant disillusionment in his mid-eighties interview with Miller: "To this day I know that this is what I meant ["socialism in an American accent"] and I thought it was what my colleagues meant by participatory democracy" (144).

PHS is at once a text in the tradition of utopian socialist modernity and also a text moving away from this Enlightenment metanarrative toward a politics of the local and particular, as well as a politics of the self that prepared the ground for, and was the immediate precursor of, postmodern politics of the subject (what I call, in part 4, "subject politics"). As a text of modernity, it uses the universal male pronoun and was written almost exclusively by white men (Miller's inclusion of Sharon Jeffrey as one of the key figures at Port Huron and in SDS is more a function of the intervention of feminism between the sixties and the eighties, when Miller was writing, than it is reflective of the prominence of women in SDS, until the emergence of feminism at the end of the decade). As a text of postmodernity, it finds its most powerful affective horizon continually drawn in toward the self in its particular place and time.

PHS opens with a proviso concerning its communal, processual authorship, and its provisionality. Its brief "Introductory Note" announces first that "this document represents the results of several months of writing and discussion among the membership, a draft paper, and revision by the Students for a Democratic Society national convention meeting in Port Huron, Michigan, June 11–15, 1962" (6). Like Julian Beck and Judith Malina in *Paradise Now*, as we will see in chapter 7, the authors of *PHS* emphasize both the collaborative, communal authorship of the "document" — calling it a "document" rather than a manifesto or a declaration downplays its authoritative status — and its evolution over time. The writing of the document is itself an instance of participatory democracy, with "the membership" as a whole participating communally in its development, drafting, and revision. Giving the precise location and dates of the SDS national convention that produced the current version of the document insists on its local particularity — its disavowal of the universal or timeless.

The second and third sentences of the three-sentence introductory note further insist on the provisionality of the document, its disavowal of the universal: "It is presented as a document with which s Ds officially identifies, but also as a living document open to change with our times and experiences. It is a beginning: in our own debate and education, in our dialogue with society" (6). These sentences speak at once with modern and postmodern voices. In "a document with which s Ds officially identifies," we hear the organizational voice, the gesture toward traditional socialist politics of the "official" position, even the "correct line." But the affective weight of these sentences falls heavily on the words "living," "open," "our," and "our own." The authors situate the document here within the politics of the self, and within the notion of time, human life, and authentic meaning as shifting, in flux, rather than fixed, "official."

The first section of *PHS*, "Introduction: Agenda for a Generation," contains some of its most important and influential writing. The phrase "agenda for a generation" is in itself very revealing. In its internal rhyme — "*agen*da for a *gen*eration" — it points toward characteristic Beat literary styles, bespeaking the link of New Left radical politics with the Beat-inspired counterculture. Its meanings are also characteristic of sixties texts. "Agenda" and "*a* generation," in the singular, indicate a unified, inclusive totality of both program and constituency. *PHS* claims to represent the coherent aspirations of a single, internally undifferentiated generation. This locates *PHS* within the totalizing universality of modernity. However, "agenda," rather than declaration, program, or even manifesto, points strongly toward action of a pragmatic sort. In its orientation toward "direct" action, born of and influenced in the first instance by the Civil Rights movement, and in general by immediate, particular, local political situations, the New Left moved away from the utopian politics of modernity premised on transcendent, totalizing theoretical master narratives. Further, in "agenda for a *generation*," *PHS* specifically rejects the universalist claims of modernity's utopian politics to be an agenda (or a worldview) for all humanity — for "Man" — and attaches its agenda, with the local-particular focus of postmodernity, specifically to the historical situation and geographical location of university students in the United States in the early sixties.

The opening sentence of "Agenda for a Generation" resonates at once with Allen Ginsberg's *Howl*, the Declaration of Independence, and the Constitution of the United States: "We are people of this generation, bred in at least modest comfort, housed now in universities, looking uncomfortably to the world we inherit" (7). In the famous opening line of *Howl*, Ginsberg also invokes his generation: "I saw the best minds of my generation destroyed by madness, starving hysterical naked." "Uncomfortably," as well as a contrast to "modest comfort," is a carefully moderated, restrained, toned-down gesture toward Ginsberg's "destroyed by madness, starving hysterical naked": a statement of what was often in the sixties called alienation.

"We are people of this generation" at once points clearly toward "We the People of the United States, in Order to form a more perfect Union," and also points powerfully away from the universalism of the Constitution: "We are people" instead of "We the People" specifies particular people, as does "of this generation," substituting limited particularity for the Constitution's generalizing, universalizing claims for "a more perfect Union." There is also a distant echo of the Declaration of Independence — "We hold these truths to be self-evident, that all men are created equal . . . Life, Liberty and the pursuit of Happiness" — and a stronger echo of the Gettysburg Address, in the second paragraph of "Agenda": "Freedom and equality for each individual, government of, by, and for the people — these American values we found good, principles by which we could live as men." PHS deliberately locates itself as inheritor of the greatest tradition of written American political self-fashioning.

This universalizing sentence, however, is preceded by a particularizing location of the experience of this generation: "When we were kids the United States was the wealthiest and strongest country in the world; the only one with the atom bomb, the least scarred by modern war, an initiator of the United Nations that we thought would distribute Western influence throughout the world" (7). Not just the historicizing references to postwar American dominance, the bomb, and the UN, but also the word "kids" pushes this document away from the great American precursors it at the same time invokes. That deliberate colloquialism gestures toward removing this document from the official pantheon of Great American Political Statements, not just by disqualifying it on the basis of inappropriate diction, but also in a positive way, by affirming the informal, the provisional, the unofficial: all positions at first occupied by the New Left as a powerful protest of and alternative to dominant culture, and subsequently forged by the New Left and the counterculture into new dominant (postmodern) cultural styles.

The references to U.S. postwar dominance, the atomic bomb, and the United Nations make a move opposite to that of the Declaration of Independence, where particular instances of British tyranny are catalogued but all as violations of universal, "unalienable Rights." PHS, by contrast, locate those rights — "freedom and equality for each individual, government of, by, and for the people" — in relation to a particular postwar U.S. history. It was because this generation grew up in that particular time and place, according to PHS, that they believed in the inevitable universal propagation of these rights, not because these rights are transparently "unalienable." The second paragraph concludes, "Many of us began maturing in complacency" (7).

As "Agenda for a Generation" proceeds, gathering force and eloquence as it delineates the ills of the present moment and the increasing motivation of "people of this generation" to take action to eradicate these ills, a subtle shift occurs. The document replaces the opening sense of "this generation" as inclusive of all those who grew up in the postwar period — what we now call the baby boomers — with a definition of "this generation" as those who are increasingly dissatisfied with American complacency and hypocrisy and are motivated to take concerted action to change them. In fact, the document had made several radically exclusionary moves in its opening sentence: "We are people of this generation, bred in at least modest comfort, housed now in universities, looking uncomfortably to the world we inherit." As the eloquent passages of PHS addressing racism and poverty make clear, far from all of the "people of this generation" were "bred in at least modest comfort" or are "housed now in universities," or, in fact, are destined under current political conditions to inherit the world at all, unless, as the biblical echo implies, it is precisely these disenfranchised, less and less "meek" population who *will* "inherit the world" (earth), if the "agenda for a generation" succeeds.

"Agenda for a Generation" proceeds chronologically with its saga: "As we grew, however [this immediately follows the sentence about maturing in complacency], our comfort was penetrated by events too troubling to dismiss" (7). The two most important of these "events," which are "too immediate and crushing in their impact, too challenging in the demand that we as individuals take the responsibility for encounter and resolution" (7–8), are the Civil Rights movement and the devastating nuclear politics of the cold war. The Civil Rights movement is referred to as the "Southern struggle against racial bigotry," which brought home to "us" the "permeating and victimizing fact of human degradation" and "compelled most of us from silence to activism" (7). Again and again, in discourses on the political and cultural impact of the sixties, the Civil Rights movement is cited as the catalyst both of the New Left and of all the postmodern "new social movements": feminism, gay rights, ethnic politics, politics based on age and disability discrimination, and to some extent the third world nationalist postcolonial movements with which the inheritor of Civil Rights, the nationalist Black Power movement, affiliated itself ideologically. Note here, as well, the consistent emphasis on the response of the individual, the call to personal commitment: "we as individuals" must "take the responsibility for encounter and resolution." The communal "we" of the New Left and the counterculture was always an aggregate of consenting, actively participating individuals. Only in the Marxist-Leninist or Maoist groups such as Progressive Labor, and in the communal religious cults, was this individualism suppressed or dissolved in a group identity, either a rigid "correct line" or a total submission to the will and teachings of a charismatic guru.

The second of these two crucial radicalizing factors is "the enclosing fact of the Cold War, symbolized by the presence of the Bomb," which "brought awareness that we ourselves, and our friends, and millions of absstract 'others' . . . might die at any time" (7). The viscerally palpable threat of total annihilation — as I remember it, not just instant death for all, which, though nearly unimaginable in its horror, does not include suffering, but massive instant death accompanied by the equally massive excruciating torture of radiation sickness leading inevitably anyway to death — truly did unite "people of this generation" with everyone else in the world, particularly in the first and second worlds. But the first "event," the Civil Rights movement, again, defines "people of this generation" as those who respond with committed personal activism to "the permeating and victimizing fact of human degradation." "People of this generation" do not include, therefore, those who are victimized by the "human degradation" of racism. This is a characteristic modernist universalizing gesture. The hegemonic white, bourgeois, male self identifies its particularity with a universal subjectivity, albeit in this instance a historically specified and localized subjectivity of "this generation" of American students. This is precisely the universal white, male, bourgeois European subject of modernity called into question and repudiated by postmodern/postcolonial epistemologies of situatedness and politics of subjectivity and particularity. Here, PHS, as a characteristic sixties text, at once particularizes and also universalizes its subjectivity and location.

The rest of "Agenda for a Generation" eloquently develops the sense on the one hand of frustration with the helpless apathy of "the vast majority of our people" (note the empowered possessive), and on the other the urgency "people of this generation" feel to bring about democratic change: "a yearning to believe there *is* an alternative to the present, that something *can* be done to change circumstances in the schools, the workplaces, the bureaucracies, the government" (9). These passages are most eloquent when describing and dissecting the apathy of postwar American complacency: "feeling the press of complexity upon the emptiness of life, people are fearful of the thought that at any moment things might be thrust out of control. . . . The dominant institutions are complex enough to blunt the minds of their potential critics, and entrenched enough to swiftly dissipate or entirely repel the energies of protest and reform. . . . Some would have us believe that Americans feel contentment amidst prosperity — but might it not better be called a glaze above deeply felt anxieties about their role in the new world?" (9). "The press of complexity upon the emptiness of life" and the "glaze above deeply felt anxieties" are brilliantly evocative phrases, informed by existentialist versions of alienation and by key social-political-psychic thinkers such as Herbert Marcuse (see chapter 1), C. Wright Mills, Erich Fromm, Wilhelm Reich, Norman O. Brown, R. D. Laing, Erik Erikson, and others, connecting that alienation specifically to the systemic human disenfranchisement wrought by bureaucratic, rationalized society, to be remedied by individual authenticity and liberation in participatory democracy.

These phrases invoke not just the radical separation of subject from society diagnosed by the New Left, but also a pandemic social neurosis in which a felt "emptiness of life" masks and defends against unacknowledged but "deeply felt anxieties," and in which the surface or conscious "glaze" of apathy and contentment fends off and defends against the unbearable "press of complexity" of alienated social, political, and economic institutions. It is the mission of the New Left to undo these defenses and to release the positive energy they hold in check, altering its affective valence from threat ("For most Americans, all crusades are suspect, threatening") to liberation. In this mission, the New Left allies itself with all the liberatory utopian agendas of modernity. Utopia is directly invoked in this passage, as American apathy and helplessness are linked to the despairing repudiation of utopian visions: "beneath the stagnation of those who have closed their minds to the future, is the pervading feeling that there simply are no alternatives, that our times have witnessed the exhaustion not only of Utopias, but of any new departures as well" (9).

"Agenda for a Generation" ends, not surprisingly, with gestures simultaneously toward the universal agendas of modernity and the local-particular agendas of postmodernity. The document is described as representing "an effort in understanding and changing the conditions of humanity in the late twentieth century" — a historically situated and contained (though vast) agenda ("in the late twentieth century" differs from the classical utopian vision of bringing about the just society for all time) — but at the same time "an effort rooted in the ancient, still unfulfilled conception of man attaining determining influence over his circumstances of life" (9): an agenda evoking Marx, and tellingly employing the universal male signifier, as PHS does throughout, at the largest possible level of human generality.

The second section of PHS, "Values," was most important in developing and promulgating notions of participatory democracy. (These sections are very brief, compressed, pungent — "Agenda for a Generation" is two pages, "Values" is a bit under five; this carefully crafted brevity helped PHS to achieve the wide distribution and influence it enjoyed.) The opening paragraphs of "Values" expand the earlier discussion in "Agenda for a Generation" of the apathy and alienation of postwar Americans, specifically in relation to the discrediting of the very notion of values, and urge an alternative vision of realizable utopia: "the decline of utopia and hope is in fact one of the defining features of social life today. . . . To be idealistic is to be considered apocalyptic, deluded. To have no serious aspirations, on the contrary, is to be 'tough-minded'" (10–11).

Into and against this alienated, antiutopian situation, PHS injects its utopian ethics and politics of authenticity and commitment. Unlike those party-line sloganeers their "liberal and socialist predecessors," SDS, "perhaps matured by the past," has "no sure formulas, no closed theories" (11). The values formulated in PHS are the fluid, unpredictable outcomes of continuing discussion and have achieved the status only of "tentative determination" (11). Nonetheless, these values are expressed with great urgency and conviction. Key sentences from this section again have the ringing eloquence, as well as explicit echoes, of the Declaration of Independence: "We regard *men* as infinitely precious and possessed of unfulfilled capacities for reason, freedom, and love [We hold these truths to be self-evident . . .]." "Men have unrealized potential for self-cultivation, self-direction, self-understanding, and creativity. It is this potential that we regard as crucial and to which we appeal, not to the human potentiality for violence, unreason, and submission to authority" (11).[6]

As these ringing statements make clear, the central impulse of the SDS articulation of participatory democracy is, again, directed not primarily toward the reconstitution of society, though that is in some sense the ultimate goal, but rather toward the reconstitution of the self. This articulation is divided into two sections, the first of which concerns not the ideologies or "values" informing political structures premised on participatory democracy, but rather "*Human relationships*," which "should involve fraternity and honesty." The "loneliness, estrangement, isolation" that characterize postwar human relationships would be supplanted, in participatory democracy, by "a love of man" overcoming "the idolatrous worship of things by man" (12). These formulations are clear evocations of the Romantic utopian humanistic and democratic traditions, particularly in the word "fraternity." But "fraternity" has moved up from third position, after "liberty" and "equality," into first place here. "Honesty" places personal authenticity and rejection of bland social hypocrisy — the "glaze" covering over the essential "emptiness of life" — on a par with the greatest values of the democratic tradition.

The second section, "*social system*," focuses almost as intently on the politics of the self as does the section on "human relationships." The central aims of "a democracy of individual participation," where "power rooted in possession, privilege, or circumstance" would be replaced by "power and uniqueness rooted in love, reflectiveness, reason, and creativity" — all attributes of individuals rather than of social systems — are "that the individual share in those social decisions determining the quality and direction of his life; that society be organized to encourage independence in men and provide the media for their common participation" (12–13). Again, the focus here is on the free self-determination and authenticity of the individual ("man"), participating democratically, rather than on the nature of the social structures participatory democracy entails. Even when social structure is addressed more directly, the emphasis in most of the particular formulations tends to shift back toward the impact on and role of the individual subject: "politics has the function of bringing people out of isolation and into community, thus being a necessary, though not sufficient, means of finding meaning in personal life; . . . the political order should . . . provide outlets for the expression of personal grievance and aspiration . . . channels should be commonly available to relate men to knowledge and to power so that private problems — from bad recreation facilities to personal alienation — are formulated as general issues" (13).

Economic as well as political principles of participatory democracy also revolve around the politics of the self: "work should involve incentives worthier than money or survival. It should be educative, not stultifying; creative, not mechanical; self-directed, not manipulated, encouraging independence, a respect for others, a sense of dignity, and a willingness to accept social responsibility, since it is this experience that has crucial influences on habits, perceptions, and individual ethics; . . . the economic experience is so personally decisive that the individual must share in its full determination" (13). Even "a willingness to accept social responsibility" has as its primary goal not creating a more just society but having a positive influence on the habits, perceptions, and ethics of the individual. Ultimately, the "economic experience" is of primary personal, rather than social, significance. Similarly, "like the political and economic ones, major social institutions — cultural, educational, rehabilitative, and others — should be generally organized with the well-being and dignity of man as the essential measure of success" (13). In developing its emancipatory, humanistic, utopian, socialist- and democratic-inspired politics, SDS paved the way for the postmodern subsumption of the politics of the social by the politics of the self.

"Agenda for a Generation" and "Values," constituting the introductory framework of *PHS*, are followed by "The Students" and "The Society Beyond": the mapping of the world implied here not only places "the students" at the center of a surrounding "society" but also assumes a separation of students from that society. Implicit throughout sixties ideologies is the utopian Enlightenment assumption of the capability of an avant-garde (by the end of the decade, a revolutionary avant-garde) to locate itself sufficiently outside of — at a critical distance from — society to see its ills clearly and to imagine alternatives that will cure them all.

These two sections, particularly "The Students," illuminate the scope and nature of social and cultural change wrought both by and against the sixties. "The Students" asserts again that it is students who have responded to the critical pressure of postwar contradictions, who "at least have felt the urgency of the times." Students have "moved actively and directly against racial injustices, the threat of war, violations of individual rights of conscience, and less frequently, against economic manipulation" (14). Students have brought some meaningful political discussion back to campuses frozen by McCarthyism, and have also made inroads against racism. But these gains are not the point, not what matters in *PHS*. On the contrary, and not surprisingly, "the significance is in the fact that students are breaking the crust of apathy and overcoming the inner alienation that remain the defining characteristics of American college life" (14).

Those students who have managed to break the crust of apathy, however, are decidedly in the minority, according to PHS; this in fact remained the case even at the height of campus political and countercultural radicalism in the late sixties. PHS goes on to condemn campus life in terms that make remarkably clear what was at stake in the emergence of postmodernity in the sixties: "the real campus, the familiar campus, is a place of private people. . . . It is a place of commitment to business-as-usual, getting ahead, playing it cool. It is a place of mass affirmation of the Twist, but mass reluctance toward the controversial public stance. Rules are accepted as 'inevitable,' bureaucracy as 'just circumstances,' irrelevance as 'scholarship,' selflessness as 'martyrdom,' politics as 'just another way to make people, and an unprofitable one, too'" (14). These sentences warrant close attention. In some ways, the campus of the sixties as described here is much the same as the campus of the present moment, which is also certainly a place of "private people," of "commitment to business-as-usual, getting ahead, playing it cool," of "mass affirmation" devoted primarily to modes of popular culture, of general student indifference to, and sense of inevitability about, university rules and bureaucracies, of little interest in "selflessness" or in the efficacy or meaningfulness of political involvement. However, the structures of feeling within which these comparable features of campus life reside, and which define their social and affective meanings, are radically different.

The tone of this passage—the righteous, almost bitter denunciation of student apathy and complacency—is a primary indicator of this reconfiguration of structure of feeling. Being primarily "private" and rejecting selflessness, as opposed to making profound, altruistic social commitments, is no longer necessarily associated with apathy, cynicism, amoral self-interest, with social resignation or indifference, or with a sense of the "press of complexity on the emptiness of life," or a contentment that is really a "glaze above deeply felt anxieties." Students now combine an unabashed commitment to self-advancement, careerism, the absolute priority of the "private" self, a "commitment to business-as-usual, getting ahead, playing it cool," and an indifference to both campus and local or national politics, with various modes of energized enthusiasm as a personal style, and with widespread social involvement in the form of community service, charity work, and grassroots, local, single-issue or

identity-based activism. In fact, community service is a graduation re-
quirement in many high schools, and has become a precondition for acceptance into the most competitive and prestigious colleges and universities. Stories of personal change and "growth" resulting from modes of
community service are a staple of the college admission "personal essay."
The genuine — *not* affectively alienated — personal meaningfulness the authors of PHS believed could only come from political engagement at the
largest level, from realizing fully the utopian potential of democracy, now
comes from modes of charitable social involvement or local, focused activism that were defined as coopted and "reformist" in the sixties — modes
that were seen as helping to maintain the unequal capitalist status quo by
alleviating the plight of some of its direct casualties. A sense of meaningfulness also comes now from full-throttle engagement with precisely
the late-capitalist consumer culture that in the sixties was perceived as the
enemy of progressive social change and of any possible personal meaningfulness. In postmodernity, particularly in the realm of minority popular
subcultures, and popular culture designated scornfully here by "mass affirmation of the Twist," popular culture is a site for what de Certeau calls
"tactics": the creative refunctioning of hegemonic formations, or, in other
terms of postmodern advocacy, "complicitous critique" and "resistance
from within." But even when there is no critique or resistance, fulfilling
personal meaningfulness is widely derived from success entirely within the
terms and parameters defined by hegemonic social and cultural structures,
as Marcuse predicts.

One particularly telling moment in the above passage is the invocation
of "irrelevance as 'scholarship.' " Among the most visible changes brought
about by the sixties are the change in the nature of university rules for
undergraduates and also the change in the nature of academic discourse.
The *"in loco parentis"* rules, attacked directly in PHS, against which
campus protest movements were waged, are for the most part gone. Here
the movement was almost completely successful. Rules are now "accepted
as inevitable" in part because they inhibit so little of students' behavior.

The rise of socially, politically "relevant" scholarship is a visible, palpable legacy of the sixties. It is conducted by former sixties radicals and
counterculturalists and those influenced by sixties movements, who became academics as an alternative to more alienated forms of labor and
also because the academy had become the haven of free speech and
thought the sixties movements wanted it to be. However, this scholarship
has not had, and does not have, the sort of transformative, revolutionary

impact it was thought in the sixties (and feared by right wing cultural warriors) would be its inevitable consequence. There is considerable debate concerning the actual social-political-cultural impact of scholarship derived from sixties ideologies and commitments.[7] However, even if one wants to argue that there is some meaningful impact, one cannot argue that this impact is revolutionary or even visibly transformative in any immediately perceptible way. The fact that the culture wars constituted by socially, politically committed scholarship along with the backlash against it have been waged so prominently in mainstream cultural and political venues does speak to the wide dissemination of sixties ideologies. But it also speaks very clearly to their failure to bring about the revolutionary change envisioned at the time by sixties radicals. Scholarship has become commonly, widely "socially relevant." Yet the revolutionary changes to campus and society that sixties radicals assumed would accompany this scholarly relevance not only failed to materialize, they became utterly dislodged from their connection to scholarly social-political relevance, so that the latter can exist by itself, in isolation from the universal Enlightenment revolutionary metanarrative of utopian social, cultural, political, human change of which it was, in the sixties, seen as only a single facet.

The campus is seen by *PHS* as a "place of mass affirmation of the Twist, but mass reluctance toward the controversial public stance." Two elements of this statement are of signal importance to my argument here. First, as is clear in its grammatical structure, this statement assumes that "the Twist" and "the controversial public stance" belong to opposed, or at least wholly divergent, universes. Second, it implies that there is a connection between "affirmation of the Twist," and "reluctance toward the controversial public stance." But in many post-sixties versions of the cultural and political changes that occurred in the sixties, the rise of mass teenage popular culture, much of it based on African American folk and popular culture, signaled here by "the Twist," is seen as part of the same general phenomenon as free speech, or the taking of a "controversial public stance." Both are subsumed under a general notion of cultural, social, political, sexual liberation. Distinctions that were of the first importance in the sixties have lost their urgency in this generalizing view of across-the-board liberation. While many or most sixties political radicals participated in popular youth culture and also in the counterculture, this was generally seen as an epiphenomenon of being "people of this generation." It would not have occurred to sixties radicals or counterculturalists to think that the Twist was of comparable significance to the Civil Rights movement or to SDS itself—it was in the category of fun, recreation, teenage "social life": of considerable affective importance but compartmentalized away from what was considered of "real" importance or meaningfulness. The privileging of "the controversial public stance"—of politics per se, in its traditional form—over either popular culture or the counterculture was taken for granted in radical ideologies. Politics as a mode of discourse had not yet become merged, as it is in postmodernity—in what is in fact a prime marker of postmodernity—with cultural politics. Further, many counterculturalists explicitly repudiated the mass popular culture signaled by "the Twist," seeing Top 40 pop music as empty, superficial, vapid, fully affirmative, in Adorno's terms; representing the soulless commercialism of contemporary capitalist consumer culture; controlled by, and a prime feature of, the culture industry—not yet the popular culture we now valorize and make a primary object of study. In the early sixties, the folk music revival, defining itself as an alternative to and repudiation of commercial pop culture, was a powerful manifestation of this countercultural formation.

All these meanings are at work in PHS's contempt for mass affirmation of the Twist. The authors of PHS could not have imagined the collapsing of these distinctions in the current sense of all sixties youth culture as subversive, in which the Twist itself is reconceived as a controversial, subversive public stance, nor could they have imagined that in postmodernity, popular culture would come to be seen as a, if not the, primary location of progressive political subversion or resistance (not, of course, of revolution).

Like academic "relevance," "the controversial public stance," as a result of the sixties, has become a common feature of discourse both in the academy and in the culture at large. Like socially-politically engaged scholarship, the controversial public stance no longer has the sort of transformative capability imagined in the sixties. In the immediate wake of McCarthyism, and in the midst of cold-war paranoia, the act of speaking or organizing against "the system"—free speech—was a radical political gesture. But in contemporary society, though there are controversies surrounding certain forms of "free speech" such as pornography and racial-ethnic-religious-sexual-gender-based hate messages (the fact that this is where "free speech" controversies currently reside is telling), a wide range of speakers regularly take public stances, without negative consequences or even public controversy, that are at extreme variance with mainstream or hegemonic views. As with socially-politically engaged scholarship in the current conjuncture, it is not so much that there is no social impact but that the sort of universally transformative, revolutionary impact imagined in the sixties is not expected to come about. The freedom to take the controversial public stance fought for in the sixties was won, and remains a crucial element of the diverse, resistant postmodern political scene, but the consequences of that freedom are not revolutionary, as they were imagined to be.

Jamesonian postmodernism would see in this phenomenon the flattening and death of meaning and of politics itself in postmodernity. Harawayan, Hutcheonian postmodernism would see the rise and emergence into audibility of minority voices and subversive points of view, heretofore inaudible and unheard, critiquing complicitously and resisting from within. Both, as I see it, are correct. In the proliferation of contestatory public voices speaking from myriad points of view, the transformative efficacy of a united oppositionality is diminished, and the impact of public speech itself is diluted. But this proliferation also makes of culture and politics a fluid, shifting scene of innumerable points of immediate, local complicitous critique and subversion from within. Social-political-cultural change is no longer measurable in leaps of revolutionary transformation, but rather in shifts that are difficult to quantify; that lose, regain, and shift the ground they win; that alter the tenor of life in subtle, complex ways.

In *PHS*, we can see, as the pivot on which this massive shift in structure of feeling turned, the primacy of individual meaningfulness—the politics of the self—over the utopian social-political transformation that had, throughout modernity, been the primary goal of radical democratic politics: "the significance of these scattered movements [for social change] lies not in their success or failure in gaining objectives. . . . the significance is in the fact that students are breaking the crust of apathy and overcoming the inner alienation that remain the defining characteristics of American college life" (14). "The Society Beyond," the brief, two-page section following "The Students," reiterates this message: "the apathy here is, first, *subjective*—the felt powerlessness of ordinary people, the resignation before the enormity of events" (18). Though this section, because it is about "The Society Beyond," continues by shifting the emphasis to the social—"But the subjective apathy is encouraged by the *objective* American situation"—this objective American situation is marked primarily by "the actual structural separation of people from power, from relevant knowledge, from pinnacles of decision-making" (18). The emphasis falls again on empowering the individual rather than on changing oppressive social structures. In the counterculture, and among sixties radicals who also participated in the counterculture, it was similarly assumed that any meaningful change in society would have to be at least accompanied, if not preceded, by a change in the nature and structure of subjectivity—a change in "consciousness."

The long central section of PHS does address "the society beyond" directly, with detailed, fact-based analyses and critiques. The first target is the economy, with subsections on "The Remote Control Economy," "The Military-Industrial Complex," "Military-Industrial Politics," "Automation, Abundance, and Challenge," "The Stance of Labor," and "The Horizon," in which the condemnation of the postwar U.S. economy is pungently summarized: "a more reformed, more human capitalism, functioning at three-fourths capacity while one-third of America and two-thirds of the world goes needy, domination of politics and the economy by fantastically rich elites, accommodation and limited effectiveness by the labor movement, hard-core poverty and unemployment, automation confirming the dark ascension of machine over man instead of shared abundance, technological change being introduced into the economy by the criteria of profitability—this has been our inheritance" (30). Again, as in the description of the campus, one is struck here by the extent to which this description applies to the economic situation of the current moment. The sea change in structure of feeling—the vast network of assumptions underlying the tone of this passage, making it perfectly characteristic of the sixties and highly unlikely in a document written now—is powerfully evident in the righteous outrage in PHS: its underlying sense that these facts are profoundly evil, are just the opposite of what the situation should be, and also are susceptible to total change by a mobilized population instituting participatory democracy.

The final sections of PHS, following inclusive, worldwide programs for political, economic, and social reform, return to the U.S. political scene where SDS intends primarily to operate. In "Towards American Democracy," PHS calls for abolition of the "political party stalemate," abolition of "institutions and practices which stifle dissent," making corporations "publicly responsible," the "allocation of resources" based on "social needs," and concentration on "genuine social priorities: abolish squalor, terminate neglect, and establish an environment for people to live in with dignity and creativeness" (57–66) through a nine-point program addressing poverty, civil rights, economic development, urban problems, mental health, prison reform, public education, agricultural policy, and progressive uses of science.

The second item in this section's numbered list of priorities, after "America must abolish its political party stalemate" (57) — an attack on conservative Dixiecrats — addresses the issue of participatory democracy directly: "Mechanisms of voluntary association must be created through which political information can be imparted and political participation encouraged" (58). PHS recommends that these participatory democratic "institutions," that will "engage people with issues and express political preference," should be "organized around single issues (medical care, transportation system reform, etc.), concrete interest (labor and minority group organizations), multiple issues, or general issues" (58–59). We see here an unusually clear instance of the simultaneity of modern and postmodern paradigms in sixties texts — a moment of inadvertence when ideology is most clearly revealed. Organization around single issues and "concrete interest" is seen as one of several possible strategies that can work in tandem with organization around multiple and general issues. No conflict or contradiction, or even difference of any important kind, is imagined between single-issue and universal political mobilization. Throughout the sixties, it was argued that any one liberation struggle — whether organized around race, gender, class, or nation — would inevitably lead to universal liberation and revolution. That causal link is not posited directly here (though it is implied elsewhere, in the penultimate, hopeful section of PHS on existing social movements, where the peace, civil rights, civil liberties, and labor movements are seen as having universal peace, freedom, and justice in common as an ultimate goal), but it is one possible understanding of the absence of conflict envisioned between single-issue and universal organizing. In fact, in postmodernity, single-issue politics has come to be seen as inimical to universalist politics, and vice versa. If they join together, it is through a conscious, temporary affiliation based on limited overlapping needs. In this moment of PHS, we can see both that single-issue and universal politics are still imagined not just as mutually enhancing but also as part of the same overall transformative project, and also, at the same time, that single-issue politics has been separated out from universal or "general issue" politics. The divergence that would structure and mark postmodern politics is clearly visible here, though not yet postmodern in affect or meanings.

PHS ends by returning to "this generation," in the universities, as the most promising starting point for social change. Student activism represents the best opportunity to "give form to the feelings of helplessness and indifference," and to transform "modern complexity" into "issues that can be understood and felt close up by every human being" (76): again, the politics of the self. In their particular, often single-issue struggles with university bureaucracies, students are seen here as providing the brightest, hottest spark to ignite universal social-political-cultural-psychic transformation. The statement, and the *Statement*, ends with a passionate utopian pledge: "as students for a democratic society, we are committed to stimulating this kind of [totally transformative, across-the-board] social movement, this kind of vision and program in campus and community across the country. If we appear to seek the unattainable, as it has been said, let it be known that we do so to avoid the unimaginable" (77). The pair "unattainable/unimaginable" echoes the initial pairing of "comfort" and "uncomfortably" ("We are people of this generation, bred in at least modest comfort, housed now in universities, looking uncomfortably to the world we inherit"), but PHS has traveled a long distance, from the tentative initial expression of dissatisfaction to the totalizing modern discourses of utopia and total annihilation. In the emphasis of the closing section on the local-particular issues of the student movement, juxtaposed with this ringing utopian totalization, we see how short a distance, how small a space, in the sixties separated the two radically disjunct paradigms of the modern and the postmodern.

CHAPTER SEVEN

Paradise Then

The experimental theater renaissance of the sixties was a quintessential form and embodiment of participatory democracy, and, partly for that reason, was one of the most characteristic cultural formations of the sixties avant-gardes. The convenient, largely consensual designation "experimental" includes guerrilla theater, street theater, and happenings as well as various modes of avant-garde directing, playwriting, and performance. Disparate as these theatrical modes were, they were united by their rejection of traditional, realist bourgeois theatrical forms and conventions, and by their embrace of various avant-garde, popular, and non-Western traditions and practices. They drew inspiration from a wide range of forebears, from Stanislavski, Artaud, Brecht, Meyerhold, Piscator, and Craig to Noh, Kabuki, Balinese puppet theater, commedia dell'arte, and mime. At the heart of this general phenomenon were the many communal theater groups that sprang up across the United States and in Europe, of which The Living Theatre, founded and codirected by Julian Beck and Judith Malina, was among the most influential, successful, and well known.[1]

The Living Theatre's *Paradise Now* was performed in numerous venues in Europe and the United States from 1968 through 1970.[2] *Paradise Now* is a remarkably pure distillation and inclusive compilation of central sixties ideologies and motifs, and of the sixties as dominantly modern/ emergently postmodern. Its mode of creation is characteristic and paradigmatic. In the 1971 Vintage paperback edition, *Paradise Now* is described as the "Collective Creation of The Living Theatre." The copyright page includes the following statement: "The play 'Paradise Now' is not private property: there are no performance royalties to pay: it is free: for any community that wants to play it." The members of The Living Theatre — the organic entity that developed and performed this collective creation — are listed in alphabetical order, with Julian Beck and Judith Malina given no extra recognition, though they are named on the cover and title page: "*Paradise Now*, Collective Creation of the Living Theatre, written down by Judith Malina and Julian Beck." "Written down by" strictly limits Malina's and Beck's role to that of scribes, merely recording the work of the theater commune, rather than authoring an original script. The egalitarian, participatory, improvisational, communal provenance of this production marks crucial sixties values and ideologies, as we saw in *The Port Huron Statement*. The term "collective creation" is carefully chosen, at least as revealing in what it repudiates as in what it affirms. It repudiates all traditional theatrical structures that establish hierarchies of separated functions and entities: play, playwright, producer, director, actors, crew, performance. It affirms both the communal nature and structure of this theater event and the Romantic ideology of sacred, authentic, unalienated creativity so central to the sixties counterculture.

After the alphabetical list of thirty-six names comes the following statement: "Writing down 'Paradise Now' did not begin until six months after the premiere. This means that it was not read by the actors until more than a year later, when the writing was completed, more than fifty performances after the premiere." Announcing this chronology in such a prominent location gives it the flavor of disavowal: of denying or undercutting the authority of this text. This gesture marks and circumscribes the act of publication as only one version of the "collective creation," one that omits the cumulative power and truth of "more than fifty performances." Unlike the traditional script, it has no privileged or authoritative status, any more than do the names "Judith Malina" and "Julian Beck." Quite the contrary: this text is marked as a partial, limited document, bound by its moment and circumstances of production. This statement, which, one suspects, was "written down" by Beck and Malina, gives priority, again, to the actors who developed those performances entirely without benefit of "writing down," and to the communal, improvisational practices that dictated the structures within which the performances evolved. It also emphasizes the processual nature of this "collective creation." The "writing down" is seen as freezing particular moments in time and therefore distorting the constantly shifting, fluid nature of the production, which varies according to specificities of location of performance, audience, and actors' changing states of being, and which also grows and changes organically over time.

Dominant modern and emergent postmodern paradigms are interlocked in this opening gambit of *Paradise Now* in characteristic sixties fashion. The utopian communal structure of The Living Theatre, emulated by all the other major sixties experimental theater groups, and at the heart of all their work, reflected here in "*Collective* Creation" and in the list of actors' names, as well as in the disclaimer about the "writing down" of the text, is characteristically modern. The valorization of sacred, agential creativity, lodged in and expressed by the authentic self of the actor, and foundational to the genesis of the piece, is also quintessentially modern, as is the improvisational basis of this "Collective Creation," deriving from that creative authenticity of the individual actor. In "more than fifty performances," we see an assumption of incremental growth, development, and strengthening through time—a version of modernity's paradigm of progress.

If the largest, most definitive structures of *Paradise Now* are modern, emergent postmodern paradigms are also clear. The elimination of the author, and the authorial function, in the development of the production and in the carefully produced account of the "writing down" of this text is characteristically postmodern, as is the crucial deauthorization of the text itself, and concomitant shift of valorization to performance. The emphasis on the specificity and local, locational particularity of each performance of the piece—the text includes a "Chronology of Performances" at the end—is also characteristically postmodern. As we will see, variation according to the particular location of the performance and the nature of audience response is built into the production.

Certain elements of the opening of the text reveal the ways in which postmodernity is an extension of as well as a break with modernity. The abolition of hierarchy within the company, and the elimination of separate functions and entities, and of the stratified relations among them, are at once modern and yet also incipiently postmodern, in ways that are crucial to the central arguments of *Utopia Limited*. This egalitarianism is a key premise of democratic modernity, though defined in contradiction to the hierarchies of class, race, gender, nation, empire which are also constitutive of modernity. In postmodernity, egalitarianism is extended, through expanded democratization, to the subaltern others of modernity's dominations. The way in which The Living Theatre pushes egalitarianism to its furthest reach is at once an expression of modernist egalitarian utopianism and of the populist democratization that is its postmodern inheritor. Similarly, the elimination of separate, distinct functions and entities expresses at once the potential interchangeability of roles implied by modernity's dislodging of inherited class-caste status, and also postmodernity's rejection of self-present authenticity and valorization of shifting subjective multiplicity: its indifferentiation, deauthorization, and fluidity of roles — its "performativity."

The processual model of continually shifting performance is also at once modern and incipiently postmodern. Enlightenment modernity is premised on diachronic chronological linearity. But modernism challenged that cause-and-effect structure of neatly separated past, present, and future. For modernism, time became what Gertrude Stein called a "continuous present" of steadily shifting present moments. This Bergsonian model is also reflected in various versions of stream of consciousness. In postmodernity, this breakdown of chronological linearity goes further: instead of a continuous present, which still implies a notion of the steady shift, and potentially the progress, of time, we live in an ahistorical simultaneity, an indifferentiated, rhizomatic timelessness, where there is nothing but process: the chronological (discredited as teleological) sequentiality of time has ceased to be a problematic. Any structuration of time is reasonable or valid, from the continual shifts of a present moment to the provisional linearity of chronological sequence and cause-and-effect historical narrative. Past, present, and future can be either distinct or indistinguishable because they exist simultaneously, in the present (see Jameson's *Postmodernism*).

Paradise Now is a total plan for utopian revolution. In contrast to its open, fluid, constantly changing, improvisational performance structure, it is premised on a putatively all-encompassing, remarkably rigid spiritual, political, psychic, physiological, and cultural program, based on a schematic, eccentric (and superficial) amalgam of disparate spiritual traditions. The traditions deployed here are Hasidism and Kabbalah (oddly separated into two distinct traditions), yogic Hinduism and the chakras, and the I Ching. The performance is modeled on a journey or "voyage" and is divided into eight "rungs," based on vertical, ascending steps derived from these spiritual traditions. On facing pages following the title page, we are given a handwritten, hand-drawn master chart of the eight rungs, each of them divided into various vertical and horizontal subsections including colors and body parts as well as spiritual and political abstractions. Some of these are marked on two full-frontal-nude male figures, one each from the Hebrew and Hindu traditions (see figure).

These premises are summarized in a brief preface called "Preparation": "The voyage is a vertical ascent toward Permanent Revolution. . . . The voyage is charted. The Chart is a map. The Chart depicts a ladder of eight Rungs. Each rung consists of a Rite, a Vision, and an Action which lead to the fulfillment of an aspect of The Revolution" (5). Again, in contrast to the open fluidity of the "collective creation," the content and underlying structure of the performance are fixed, totalized, and schematic. This contradiction, exceptionally stark in this instance, is characteristic of many sixties cultural formations. The ultimate totalizing move of revolutionary utopianism, convinced of revolution's immediate inevitability ("paradise *now*"), produces or is linked to all-inclusive, highly but simply structured intellectual schemes — the ultimate in modern "master narratives" — from various versions of Marxism, nationalism, and anarchism to appropriations and amalgamations of culturally-historically as well as ideologically distinct, complex Asian and Jewish spiritual traditions. This postmodern destructuration and flux dominated by the most extreme versions of modernist teleological totalization is characteristic, again, of sixties cultural productions.

The "Preparation" outlines the schema of the eight rungs; this schema takes the place of conventional division into acts and scenes. "Preparation" also outlines the way in which *Paradise Now* not only represents but also enacts and furthers the revolution: "The purpose of the play is to lead to a state of being in which non-violent revolutionary action is possible" (6). The Living Theatre's particular brand of New Left revolutionary politics was nonviolent anarchism. While the New Left was predominantly Marxist or democratic-socialist rather than anarchist, and was increasingly sympathetic to revolutionary violence, pacifist anarchism was in some ways a quintessential sixties ideology. Anarchism, which eschews all modes of political representation and centralization, projecting a system organized around small, autonomous, fully self-governing units, embodies the ultimate form of the participatory democracy at the heart of

אין סוף

כתר

חכמה

בינה

MODESTY		
PUSHING UPWARDS		
ABUNDANCE FULLNESS		VIII
CONFLICT		
DECREASE		VII
STANDSTILL STAGNATION		
PEACE		
BEFORE COMPLETION		VI
THE CAULDRON		
REVOLUTION		
FOLLOWING		V
DELIVERANCE		
OPPOSITION		
OBSTRUCTION		IV
CONTEMPLATION. VIEW		
RETURN THE TURNING POINT		
PEACE		III
ENTHUSIASM		
THE CREATIVE		
BREAKTHRU RESOLUTION		II
DEVELOPEMENT GRADUAL PROGRESS		
THE MARRYING MAIDEN		
INNER TRUTH		I
PROGRESS		

תפארת

יסוד

חסד   גבורה

נצח   הוד

מלכות

THIS CHART IS THE MAP

"This Chart Is the Map," frontispiece from Judith Malina and Julian Beck, *Paradise Now* (New York: Vintage Books, 1971).

New Left politics. Further, unlike the various versions of militant Marxism with their varying commitments to violent, armed struggle, nonviolent anarchism fused countercultural values (peace, love, joy, communalism, higher consciousness, total freedom and authenticity for the individual, living in the moment) with revolutionary politics. Marxism-Leninism, with its emphasis on ideological and political discipline, its embrace of an often macho working-class culture, and its scorn for the

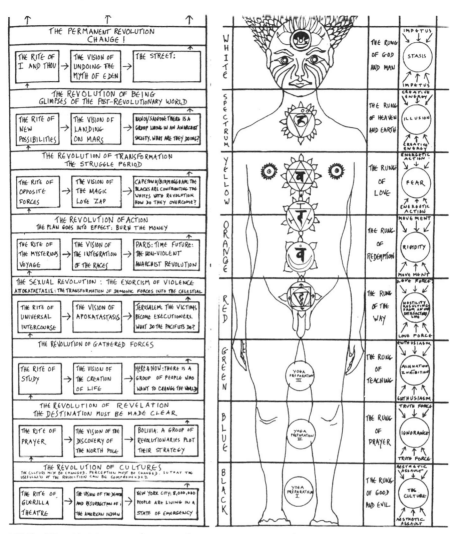

THE ESSENTIAL TRIP IS THE VOYAGE FROM THE MANY TO THE ONE   THE PLOT IS THE REVOLUTION

"carnival atmosphere" of public countercultural events, repudiated any such fusion.

Each of the eight rungs is divided into a rite, a vision, and an action; each has a "physical focus," three I Ching oracles (one each for the rite, the vision, and the action), a color, a yoga preparation, a "confrontation," and a "Kabbalistic Sefirah" (emanation or "attribute of the holy one"). For example, for Rung I, "The Rung of Good and Evil," the rite is "The

Rite of Guerilla [*sic*] Theatre," the vision is "The Vision of the Death and Resurrection of the American Indian," the physical focus is the feet, the color is black. This schematic structure bespeaks a modernist impulse toward totalization reminiscent of Joyce's correspondences in *Ulysses*, and also resonates with many parallel structures in the piece overall (fixed and clearly numbered time limits, for example, placed on putatively open-ended moments of actors' improvisation or audience participation). However, this fixed structure is at odds with what I would call the experience or feel of the production, which is unstructured, confusing, fragmented and fragmentary, seemingly aleatory and chaotic. Biner says, in his *The Living Theatre*, that the chart I have described, reprinted on facing pages following the title page, was handed to each spectator entering the performance, but I have no recollection of receiving or even seeing this chart (I saw a performance in Cambridge, Massachusetts, in 1968). Perhaps I did receive it, or at least I saw it at some point during the performance, but my experience of the performance was nonetheless of a confusing, chaotic, multidirectional, at times ludicrous, at times moving and exciting assault. The chart would have had little meaning to me — it would have had insufficient relation to my experience of the performance.

In its unmitigated, unqualified, universal utopian aspirations and assumptions, and in its schematic, teleological, spiritual-political progress narrative, again, *Paradise Now* is modern. In its locational particularities, its combination of psychic fluidity with identitarian concerns, its participatory, "interactive" structural emphasis, it is incipiently postmodern. These modern and postmodern formations coexist in the performance text as if there were no disjunction whatsoever between them — again, sixties cultural productions are characterized by precisely this seamless simultaneity of dominant modern and emergent postmodern paradigms, coexisting as if they were harmonious parts of one self-consistent whole, which in effect they were.

At times, this simultaneity resides in a single element of the performance. For example, what Malina and Beck call the "flashout" is used throughout *Paradise Now*, as a way of moving the performance forward: moving on from an otherwise potentially limitlessly open-ended moment to the next moment of the production. Flashout is used in lieu of conventional stage directions such as blackout (which it resembles verbally) or, ultimately, exit (since the actors never exit). In a note on page 16, flashout is defined as follows: "Whenever this [flashout] happens in the play, the actor by the force of his art approaches a transcendent moment in which he is released from all the hangups of the present situation." The first flashout in the play occurs at the end of Phrase 1 of Rung 1 (note again the consistent substitution of alternative structuring terminology that nonetheless reproduces, even more hierarchically, the conventional structure of acts and scenes). The opening "rite" of Rung I, The Rite of Guerilla [*sic*] Theatre, is structured around repeated phrases: "I am not allowed to travel without a passport," "I don't know how to stop the wars," "You can't live if you don't have money," "I'm not allowed to smoke marijuana," "I'm not allowed to take my clothes off." Actors roam around the performance space, where "stage" is undifferentiated from "audience," repeating these phrases and interacting with the audience in relation to the phrases. (These phrases provide a wonderful amalgamation of the libertarian, anarchistic, countercultural, pacifist sixties ideologies of The Living Theatre.) Preceding the first flashout is the following sequence: "by the end of two minutes [of repeating these phrases to the audience], all of the actors have reached a point close to hysteria. They are shouting the words with anguish and frustration. They are flipping out. . . . At the end of two minutes the actors go beyond words into a collective scream. This scream is the pre-revolutionary outcry. (Flashout.)" (16). This flashout, releasing the actor "from all the hangups of the present situation," seems of a piece with the modernist ideologies of transcendence that inform the notion of "paradise now." The space "beyond words" is a standard modernist formulation of transcendence. The collective scream is a characteristic vehicle of primal catharsis in this period. (One of the sixties psychic self-help therapy movements was called "primal scream"; people simply sat in a room together and screamed as loudly as they could, hoping thereby to release all their inhibitions and transcend their culturally induced "hangups.")

"By the force of his art" the actor reaches this transcendent moment of flashout: here we see clearly the modern reverence for the mysteries and agential powers of individual creativity; we see in fact its supreme valorization. The flashout is, however, at the same time incipiently postmodern, in its understanding of how change occurs, how time moves. After the first flashout, Beck and Malina write the following: "at this point the actors return to the artist's quiet center. They stand still and breathe. Pause and begin again" (16). After this, each flashout is followed by — or, actually, includes — "Pause and begin again." "Quiet center" and "breathe" mark The Living Theatre's extensive incorporation of yoga techniques and beliefs. But something else is going on here as well. In contradiction to the strictly linear, teleological progress of the eight rungs, the flashout instantiates a circular motion, moving almost randomly from one thing to the next with no apparent logic, certainly no apparent teleology or even forward progress. Again, that was certainly the feel of the production for me; I remember the abrupt cessation of the opening statements — "I am not allowed to travel without a passport," etc., addressed to the audience with mounting hysteria — as inexplicable and arbitrary. The repetitive, circular structure of the flashout — reach a point of crisis or climax which is indifferentiable from all other such points or moments in the production, then pause and begin again — also enacts this postmodern indifferentiation of time, of past-present-future — not as a modernist continuous present, or widening circular motion that increasingly covers and reveals more and more ground, but as a postmodern rejection of the meaningfulness of temporal progression and sequential change, of chronology itself.

The actors' mounting hysteria is written into the text. No matter how the audience responds, the actor is directed not to reply but to use this audience response to augment his outrage (the actor is designated throughout by the universal male pronoun): "he goes from spectator to spectator and repeats this phrase [the actors are instructed to do this with each phrase in turn]. With each repetition, his voice and body express greater urgency and frustration. He speaks only this phrase. If the spectator addresses him, he listens to the spectator but repeats only this phrase. The spectator may mock him, encourage him, question him. The spectator may be passive, sympathetic, superficial, witty, profound, cynical, hostile. The actor uses this response to increase his expression of the frustration at the taboos and inhibitions imposed on him by the structure of the world around him. . . . the Gates of Paradise are closed to him" (15). This unchanging fixity — an invariable response to the audience no matter what its input is — structuring an ostensibly open, fluid, participatory performance, is characteristic of *Paradise Now*. The actor's relation to audience response is entirely one-sided: no matter what the audience does, the actor will use the audience to produce a predetermined emotion. This one-sided relationship reflects the ultimate incompatibility of *Paradise Now*'s totalizing, comprehensively structuring impulses and its moves against predetermined, fixed structuration.

It could be argued that the frustrating lack of direct response by actors to audience *enacts* the unfreedom and disconnection that is the thematic content of this phase of the play. With the Gates of Paradise closed, "he [the actor] is separated from his fellow man" (15); "we may not act naturally toward one another" (17). However, this uniform, unchanging response to audience participation recurs throughout the play. Slightly later in Rung I, for example, at the end of Action I, Malina and Beck give the following explanation of the purpose of the text (the words the actors speak in each performance, comparable to the text of a conventional play) in the production: "the Action and its Text: the Text describes the basic condition. Its purpose is stimulus, suggestion, challenge, encouragement, to enable to the public to enact the revolutionary situation of each rung. The Text is a call to action" (22). Enacting the revolutionary situation inherent in each moment of the production seems quite different from being made to experience directly the frustration of the closure of the Gates of Paradise. It implies an interaction between the actors providing this "stimulus, suggestion, challenge, encouragement" and the audience so stimulated and encouraged. Further, within the text itself, the audience is instructed that "the theatre is yours. Act. Speak. Do whatever you want. / Free theatre. Feel free. You, the public, can choose your role and act it out" (23). However, at the end of Action I, the actors, "lying prone . . . wait one minute for the public to do anything it wishes to do. The public reacts. Anytime after one minute that there is a lull in the sound and activities of the public, the actors begin to beat a rhythm with their knees on the stage floor" (26). Again, the production must move forward, oblivious to the nature of audience response. Later in the performance, near the end, the audience is much more actively and directly included, but by that time they have become honorary or temporary members of The Living Theatre and are expected to do more or less what the rest of the actors are doing. They are included only insofar as they have achieved the prescribed state of consciousness.

That there is a fully formulated agenda for the audience, belying the ostensible freedom and openness of audience participation, is made clear in the explanation of the "Revolution of Cultures" at the end of Rung I. I will quote it in its entirety because it is such a forceful statement of the underlying ideological and political teleology of the production — the plan for controlling and directing audience response:

> In order to effect a social change, the old values must be replaced or destroyed and either new values set up or an open space of no values created for the wind to blow through. This destruction of old values is The Revolution of Cultures. This is the work of the revolutionary at this point in the struggle. It is represented here by the Indians as the

Natural Man who serve as examples of tribal and communitarian alternatives, bringing with them the gift of beads and the peace-pipe.

The actors have urged the spectators to discard the prohibitions, and to begin to undo the structures which make these prohibitions. Certain clues have been given that will be clear to the revolutionary and useful even to those who have not yet taken revolutionary action. These clues related to such subjects as the setting up of parallel cultures with hints from tribal cultures, the confrontation of the social structure with your naked body, the transformation of media, such as the theatre itself, from arenas of imitative action into areas [sic] of real action.

The public must now take the first step. (27–28)

In no uncertain terms we are told here that there is only one correct agenda for the audience, one endpoint of their enlightenment by this performance, and that they have been given "clues" to this endpoint in Rung I. No audience response is satisfactory other than the correct response of revolutionary action as defined by The Living Theatre.

The ideologies espoused directly throughout Rung I are mainstays of radical-anarchist/countercultural belief, thoroughly imbued with Romantic modern utopianism. The actors are instructed to remove "as much of their clothing as the law allows" (17) — much of the controversy surrounding this production had to do with nudity and sexual explicitness, in ways that seem quaint now. Nudity represented a breakthrough out of repressive, prudish antilife restriction, into liberation.

Vision I, "The Vision of the Death and Resurrection of the American Indian," mentioned above, enacts a classic noble-savage appropriative romanticization, with the Indian standing in for the free, unfettered, natural man, in holistic, fruitful relation to nature, which has been laid waste by the massed forces of capitalist oppression and destruction, and "resurrected" by the radical counterculture. In Vision I, the actors sit "cross-legged, silent, in a ceremonial circle. . . . They smoke the pipe of peace until they become Indians" (19–20). Here a scene strongly evocative of hippie marijuana ritual is used to connect the counterculture with those the counterculture saw as the true inheritors and redeemers of the earth, and also to suggest that by "smoking the pipe of peace" — by giving themselves over to the heightened consciousness induced by marijuana — a group of hippies can almost instantaneously *become* Indians. This implication is made explicit later in the Action: "it is the hippies who have risen up from the pavement, reincarnations of the American Indian, aspiring to be the Natural Man as represented by the great Indian culture, the great suppressed cultures. The culture is assaulted from below. It is the first step in revolutionary action to change the culture" (27). This was just the sort of easy, appropriative identification with subaltern cultures characteristic of the sixties counterculture, an opressive appropriation that has been powerfully debunked and resisted by the particularist politics of postmodernism.

Further, "the Natural Man knows he can travel without a passport, that he can smoke marijuana, that he can find ways to live without money, that he can take off his clothes. He knows how to stop the wars" (27). This sentence of course refers directly to the statements made by the actors at the beginning of the play — "I am not allowed to travel without a passport," etc. By the end of what is only the first of eight rungs, or acts, of this production, the blocked, thwarted actor of the opening rite, or scene, has been transformed, by becoming the American Indian, therefore the Natural Man, into the revolutionary man — he has opened the Gates of Paradise. It was really considered to be that easy, not just by The Living Theatre but by the radical counterculture in general. The rest of *Paradise Now* will move us through those gates.

Rung II, the "Rung of Prayer," opens with "The Rite of Prayer," in which the actors move among the spectators, speaking "two words of sanctification" to each individual they address, praising random body parts and objects as "holy": "Holy hand. Holy shirt. Holy smile. Holy teeth. Holy hair. Holy asshole. Holy chair. Holy feet. It is a prayer of praise. A prayer of the sacredness of all things. It rises gently toward a very quiet ecstasy, ending when the feeling of the prayer, the feeling of universal identification or oneness, has filled each of us. When the holy relationship has been established. (Flashout.)" (36). The audience is expected at once to participate fully in this "Rite" (which borrows freely from Allen Ginsberg's "Footnote to HOWL"),[3] to respond openly to the actors touching and speaking to them, but yet to feel exactly what the actors feel, and what the production expects everyone present to feel. Again we see the contradictory simultaneity of openness and fixed, predetermined structure that permeates the production. Moreover, the audience is expected not simply to feel a readily available, basic emotion, such as anger, or fear, or delight, but to achieve rapidly a state that is the mainstay of the spiritual practice of the counterculture but which is nonetheless supposed to be the result of arduous, or at least informed and dedicated, spiritual practice: "the feeling of universal identification, or oneness." From the distance of the beginning of the twenty-first century, it is mind-boggling to remember how simple, "natural" it seemed to bring together not just a roomful of fellow hippies but an auditorium full of hundreds of diverse strangers and expect them to achieve almost instantaneous simultaneous spiritual transcendence. This phenomenon could be said to have its parallel traditionally and presently in revival meetings, other evangelical gatherings, and modes of ecstatic or meditative worship prevalent throughout the world's religions. But these manifestations occur among groups of people already united in belief, gathered precisely for the purpose of achieving a heightened common spiritual state, and generally practiced in doing so. Members of audiences for *Paradise Now*, even those fairly advanced in the modes of countercultural spiritual belief and practice employed by The Living Theatre, had come to see a dramatic performance.

Later in Rung II, the actors are directed to "wait at least sixty seconds for the public to initiate the action" (45). If this action accords with the "revolutionary theme" or the "plateau to which we have been brought by the Rite and the Vision," the actors "join with the spectators in giving support to the scene that the spectators are playing." But if the spectators' action "digresses" from this predetermined revolutionary content, the actors are instructed to "guide the scene back to the meaning of the Rung. If the public is extremely passive and unresponsive, the actors will initiate spontaneous/improvised action" (45). Again, seemingly completely open-ended audience participation is in fact confined, within fixed ideological limits, to a predetermined agenda.

Further, one of the central events of this rung is the disrobing of the actors. Again, nudity was a major controversy in this production and in experimental sixties theater in general. It represented freedom and liberation from repressive inhibitions to the counterculture, while it represented indecency and the defiance of public order to the establishment. The fact that nudity has become relatively unremarkable—though still policed, it has none of the attendant frisson of radical disruption and violation it had then—in the wake of the sixties is generally taken as a measure of the success of sixties liberationism, for better or worse. I would argue that it is rather a measure of the breakdown in postmodernity of the affect attached to dualistic distinctions; in this case, naked/clothed.

The audience of *Paradise Now* is expected to see the light about nudity as it should do in every other phase of making the revolution:

> As the actors work with the public in the Actions, one of the motivating factors of the actor/public relationship is the actors' semi-nudity in

confrontation with the spectators' attire. And all its psychological amplifications. As the play progresses, and the involvement and communication between actors and spectators deepen, the psychological balance
should reverse. At first the appearance of the actor's body seems strange
and the spectator's attire proper. At the end of this contestation it is the
spectators' clothing which seems embarrassing and alienating. The su-
perobjective of the scene is to plan The Non-Violent Anarchist Revolution and to make the meaning and aims of The Revolution clear. . . . the
actor's aim is always to take the scene into the paradisial and hopeful
situation. (45–46)

The seemingly free, fully participatory function of the audience in this
production is in fact a ruse — almost a lure to make the audience feel free
in "choosing" revolution. This relation to the audience is diametrically
opposite to the Brechtian liberation of the audience from identification
through the alienation effect, intended to produce an audience of emo-
tionally detached spectators rather than vicarious participants, freely ex-
ercising their critical intellectual faculties in relation to the production. In
Paradise Now, we have more than a return to the emotional identification
of traditional theater. We have in fact a move toward a literal identification, through actual incorporation, of the audience into the production,
similar to the agenda for the audience in fascist spectacle. But this invitation is not made openly. It is made in the guise of an invitation to free self-
expression on the part of the audience.

I devote so much attention to this issue because it seems to me characteristic of the inherent authoritarianism of many ostensibly free, egalitarian, open sixties countercultural practices and formations; authoritarianism that revealed itself most fully, perhaps, in the many communal
cults, with both political and spiritual emphases, built around charismatic
authoritarian male leaders. Following these leaders was always presented
of course as a free choice on the part of the followers, but in fact enormous
psychological and sometimes physical pressure and coercion were applied
to ensure obedience, submission, conformity. The enactment of the egalitarian communal ideal of modernity in the sixties contained the seeds of
one of the most characteristic formations of postmodernity: the rise of
mass-movement authoritarian fundamentalisms. In *Paradise Now*, we see
precisely this coercive structure, where there is only one possible truth
(anarchist revolution) and everyone must be made to see, adhere to, and
enact this truth.

Much of *Paradise Now* is a meditation on, as well as an enactment of, the content and nature of this revolution. The spoken text of the play frequently addresses this question directly: "after the Revolution there will be no useless work. . . . After the Revolution there will be no money. . . . The Revolution does not want power but meaning" (39). "What is the Revolution?/ Free theatre. . . . Because in the society we envisage, everyone is free" (45; this sequence is set among a group of Che Guevara's revolutionaries in a jungle of Bolivia). Just before forming the word ANARCHISM and then the word PARADISE with their bodies, the actors severally speak the following lines, in response to the question "WHAT DO YOU WANT?":

> To make the world glow with creation. / To make life irresistible. / To feed all the people. / To change the demonic forces into the celestial. / To remove the causes of violence. / To do useful work. / To work for the love of it and not the money. / To live without the police. / To change myself. / To get rid of the class system. / To re-invent love. / To make each moment creative. / To be free of the force of the State. / To be free to create. / To get rid of a life of material greed. / To free all the energy wasted in financial transaction. / To cut all the bureaucratic wasted time out of life. / To free men from armies. / To stop distorting the mind of the people. / To stop crippling the human body with frustration. / To learn how to breathe. / To live longer than we do. / To be free of the system. / To get rid of central control. / To supply what we need. / To seek what we desire. / To stop wasting the planet. / To stop dying of competition. / To break down the walls that alienate. / To get to know God and His madness. / To make the destination clear. (40–41)

This random amalgamation of vaguely, loosely formulated tenets of a variety of radical, anarchist, and countercultural systems is characteristic not just of this production but of sixties ideologies in general. Revolution was imagined as occurring simultaneously on all fronts—political, economic, spiritual, physical. The "withering away of the state" that Marx imagined as the endpoint of proletarian revolution is here imagined as occurring instantaneously. Ecology, ecstatic spirituality, Reichian libidinal libertarianism, Romantic creativity, anarchist refusal of all forms of centralized power, Marxist repudiation of the class system, pacifism, and what might be called the American Dream—limitless self-improvement, material well-being, increasing longevity, the satisfaction of all desires—are fused in a casual revolutionary potpourri that is quintessentially modern and utopian. However, at the same time, in choosing opportunistically among so many diverse radical, spiritual, and utopian traditions, reducing complex, difficult bodies of thought and practice to easy, simple notions and throwing them together so casually and randomly, erasing worlds of difference among them (a criticism regularly leveled at the New Left and the counterculture at the time), this characteristic sixties text produces the culture of surface and pastiche of postmodernity at the same time that — in fact, by the way that — it distills central traditions of modernity.

The formation of the words ANARCHISM and PARADISE using the bodies of the actors — the latter memorably recorded in a photograph included in the text — is one of the most remarkable features of this production. It is a literalization of the creation of "paradise now" from, on, and with the bodies of the members of The Living Theatre. The actor's body, and — to the extent that the audience members are all potential Living Theatre actors, at least for that performance — the body of each audience member as well, is literally at the center of this play's move into paradise. In Rung III, "The Rung of Teaching," which employs yoga practices, Malina and Beck write "every motion must find its source in the center of the actor's body" (56). Here again, it is within a prime representation and enactment of this play's utopian modernity that it moves toward postmodernity. Embodiment becomes a key focus and problematic in postmodernity, where the body is seen, especially in Foucauldian, queer, and feminist analyses, as the prime site of both the inscription of hegemonic power and also of potentialities of resistance. The "marked" body is also a location of particularity, the specificity of subjectivity embedded in particular histories of race, gender, class, nation, over against the abstract, universal, but always implicitly white-male-bourgeois-European, transparent subject of modernity. In literally making P-A-R-A-D-I-S-E out of particular bodies, so that the shape of each letter, and therefore of the word overall, depends on the shape and size of the bodies comprising it, *Paradise Now* announces this postmodern regime of the particularity of the marked body.

Throughout *Paradise Now*, opportunities are written into the text for variation according to the political specificities of the particular performance venue. Action III of Rung III, "The Rung of Teaching," is described as follows: "the Text for this scene varies with the location. Information is researched ahead of time on the actual social and political situation in that locality and the Text altered in accordance with what seems appropriate" (62). The text for the first performance of the play in Avignon in July 1968 includes both general and specific language: "Avignon. / How The Rite of Study and The Vision of the Creation of Life lead to The Revolution of Gathered Forces. / How can the City of Avignon be transformed? / Free theatre. Theatre of freedom, of spontaneous joy and action. / Avignon. Free theatre. Imagination takes power. / What actions are the Communists planning? / What tactics are the Anarchists planning? / What are the Gaullists doing? / Be the people in jail in Avignon. / Be the people in the Monoprix. / Be the police in the street. / Be the Pieds Noirs. / Be the Algerians. / The hand can gather. / The hand can write. / The hand can reach" (62–63). While significant details of this text pertain directly to the concrete situation of Avignon in 1968, the structure of the text overall does not depend on these particularities. Details from other locations could easily be substituted without altering the sequence, rhythm, basic content, or political thrust of the speeches. This section is designed to produce immediate revolutionary action relevant to the location of the performance: "discussions are begun on the formation of cells. Radical Action Cells to continue work during and/or after the performance are formed" (64). While this model of political action is premised on the anarcho-syndicalist view of a fully participatory, local, grassroots foundation for action as the only viable and legitimate road to revolution ("A basic cell, says Bakunin, should have five members" [63]), the interchangeability of these specific locations in the structure of the text points to the totalized, utopian nature of the sixties revolutionary vision so characteristically represented here. The specificity of location in this text, again a pivot of modern to postmodern, points at once, in the interchangeability of locations, to modernist utopian totality, and also, in the careful emphasis on the particularity of the local, toward postmodern refusal of generalizing, totalizing metanarrative. *Paradise Now* is one of the clearest instances I have found of the defining simultaneity within characteristic sixties radical and countercultural texts of the dominant modern and emergent postmodern.

CHAPTER EIGHT

William Burroughs: Any Number Can Play

We generally think of characteristic sixties cultural products as looking more or less like *Paradise Now*: characterized by formal avant-gardeism, radical or revolutionary political ideologies, alternative cultural and spiritual orientations. If one were to construct a composite sixties cultural artifact, one would want it to include characteristics from most of the following: the radical formal innovation — developed within the twentieth-century traditions of modernism and the avant-garde — of North American antirealism, Latin American magic realism, the French *nouveau roman* and *nouvelle vague*; the cultures of authenticity and immediacy of Beat and confessional poetry; the comic, apocalyptic, anarchistic musical styles of sixties rock, most notably those of Dylan and Lennon; the communal, improvisational modes of happenings and the experimental and guerrilla theater movements; the Asian- and Native American–inspired spirituality of the counterculture and its texts, from the Bhagavad Gita and Tibetan Book of the Dead to Watt and Castañeda; the biting, satirical left politics of the underground press, popularized in Mailer's *Armies of the Night* or *Miami and the Siege of Chicago*; the ironic, self-mocking edge of pop art and the austerity of minimalism and conceptual art; the left liberationist political, spiritual, and psychoanalytic theories of Marcuse, Reich, N. O. Brown, Fromm, Laing; the revolutionary politics of the international left, from Marx and Lenin to Mao, Che, and Fanon; the revisionary, subjectivity-oriented texts of the "new social movements," especially Civil Rights, Black Power and the Black Arts movement, second-wave feminism, gay liberation, and postcolonial movements. In short, this artifact would be comprised of all the central sixties cultural and political formations *Utopia Limited* encompasses.

As the impossible diversity of this composite artifact suggests, the cultural products of the sixties are characterized by a wide, heterogeneous array of aesthetic practices and historical provenances, in which formal, political, cultural, theoretical, and spiritual ideologies intermingle and varyingly predominate. No genre, set of formal practices, group of authors or cultural practitioners, or system of beliefs or ideas, no matter how loosely defined, can stand as representative of the multifariousness of "the sixties": there can in fact be no composite sixties artifact. William Burroughs's work of the sixties, however, comes as close as any single author's work can to representative status (Burroughs was central to my own experience of the sixties).[1] Burroughs develops a number of avant-garde formal techniques, and works within the legacy of high modernism as well. He was particularly influenced by Eliot and the Symbolists — he lists "The Waste Land," Tzara, and the "Camera Eye" sequences in Dos Passos's *U.S.A.* as his crucial formal antecedents.[2] He writes from within both gay and drug subcultures. He advocates extreme anarchistic-liberationist ideologies popular among both certain strains of New Left politics and hippie countercultural ideologies. He does so by constructing an excessive, outrageous verbal-imaginary universe that marks an extreme point in the project of exploding and offending the bourgeois status quo, unleashing the comic-grotesque nightmare barely covered over by the ersatz (one of Burroughs's favorite words), "white-bread" fifties American dream. He is strongly influenced by Wilhelm Reich, one of the gurus of the counterculture. Though he did not consider himself a Beat writer, he is generally included in the sixties-precursor Beat pantheon; he had close, long-standing friendships with Kerouac, Ginsberg, Corso, and others at the center of the Beat movement. His disjunctive tone, alternating between voices of a sort of cosmic carny hucksterism and high-serious poetic apocalypse, is characteristic of many kinds of sixties subjective self-positioning in language. His verbal juxtapositions, evident in the titles of his major sixties tetralogy

(*Naked Lunch*, *The Soft Machine*, *The Ticket That Exploded*, *Nova Express*), hark back to Gertrude Stein, one of his primary influences, and also both characterize and influence a dominant sixties style of word association, most visible perhaps in the names of rock groups and their album titles (Led Zeppelin, for example, or Jefferson Airplane's *Surrealistic Pillow*).[3] Further, Burroughs's work and thought are characterized by the sort of extreme separatist gender ideology that also characterizes the work of certain radical feminists influential in early second-wave feminism, such as Valerie Solanas and Shulamith Firestone (see chapter 14).

In Burroughs's work, the characteristic sixties textual pivots from dominant modern to emergent postmodern modes, the textual traces of shift in structure of feeling that are my primary concern in this book, are strongly apparent. As in the other sixties texts I discuss, this dominant modern/ emergent postmodern simultaneity centrally concerns the shift from a utopian, revolutionary, totalizing, humanist, Eurocentric, high-cultural, dialectical modernity to a post-utopian, complicitous, local, partial, subcultural-minoritarian, hybrid, popular, ordinary, cyborg, global, antinomous postmodernity. On the pivot of Burroughs's sixties democratizing egalitarianism, modernist utopian transformation—the revolution of the word—becomes postmodern empowerment of the "minoritarian and excentric" (Hutcheon) through literary practice.

William Burroughs's "novels" of the sixties are at once modernist/ avant-garde and also thoroughly implicated in such popular genres as science fiction, hard-boiled detective fiction, pornography, horror film, and superhero comics.[4] Unlike high modernist works, which draw on popular modes but absorb and transform them within a self-consciously unique or individual, innovative modernist style, Burroughs's incipiently postmodern works leave the popular genre material more or less intact, only exaggerating it through parody and skewing it toward his own obsessions. This opportunistic deployment of popular modes within the literary is characteristic of postmodern writing, as we have seen.

Burroughs's quasi-satirical, apocalyptic gay pornographic sequences, especially those involving hanging, for example "A.J.'s Annual Party" in *Naked Lunch*, are well known. (Burroughs has claimed that these sequences constitute an argument against capital punishment.) The tetralogy is full of science fiction/horror film figures, from junkies who morph into bloblike protoplasm to absorb heroin, to "Uranian Willy," "The Heavy Metal Kid" (possible source of the rock designation heavy metal), the evil "Divisionists," "Liquefactionists," and the criminal "Nova Mob" itself. Many of his characters are satiric versions of superheroes of the comics, especially Inspector J. Lee of the Nova Police, Burroughs's primary narrative persona. Burroughs's tone often simultaneously reproduces and mocks that of the hard-boiled narrator, as is evident in the opening of *Naked Lunch*: "I can feel the heat closing in, feel them out there making their moves, setting up their devil doll stool pigeons, crooning over my spoon and dropper I throw away at Washington Square Station, vault a turnstile and two flights down the iron stairs, catch an uptown A train. . . . And right on time this narcotics dick in a white trench coat . . . hit the platform."[5]

At the same time, Burroughs's work in many ways looks stylistically no different from a high modernist/avant-garde text, making allowances for the content marked by its origins in sci fi, hard-boiled detective fiction, porn, and comics. In a television news obituary for Burroughs on the occasion of his death, in the summer of 1997, *Naked Lunch* was described as a "stream-of-consciousness novel," thereby marking it with a prime code or metonym for experimentalist high modernism. Here is a sequence from *Nova Express* that is characteristically avant-garde/experimental: "could give no other information than wind walking in a rubbish heap to the sky — Solid shadow turned off the white film of noon heat — Exploded deep in the alley tortured metal Oz — Look anywhere, Dead hand — phosphorescent bones — Cold Spring afterbirth of that hospital — Twinges of amputation — Bread knife in the heart paid taxi boys — If I knew I'd be glad to look anyplace — No good myself — C'lom Fliday — Diseased wind identity fading out — Smoke is all — We intersect in the dark mutinous door — Hairless skull — Flesh smeared — Five times of dust we made it all — consumed by slow metal fires."[6] Burroughs's obsessions are evident here, particularly in the pervasive presence of certain forms of gay sex ("paid taxi boys" and "five times of dust we made it all," which is a transformation of "made it five times," a recurring description of a sexual encounter), sci fi-tinged apocalypse, and idiosyncratic lore of the drug subculture ("C'lom Fliday," a recurrent motif throughout the tetralogy, refers to a sequence in *Naked Lunch* where the narrator explains that "in 1920s a lot of Chinese pushers around found The West so unreliable, dishonest and wrong, they all packed in, so when an Occidental junky came to score, they say: 'No glot. . . . C'lom Fliday.' " [144] — the racist orthography is characteristic of Burroughs's satire, which is broad, utterly uninhibited, and no respecter of any kind of persons, particularly himself).

Despite the presence of this subcultural material, more characteristic of the postmodern than the modern, this passage, in its formal structure, is representative of Burroughs's positioning within the modernist/avant-garde/experimentalist tradition. It is constructed of loosely, associatively linked fragments comprised of poetically suggestive verbal juxtapositions, in the characteristic modernist experimental manner. These links and juxtapositions are constructed by means of a technique Burroughs calls "cut-up and fold-in," which in itself stands as a marker of the simultaneity of the modern and the postmodern in transitional sixties texts such as Burroughs's. Fold-in harks back to Steinian experimental writing and the modernist cult of what Barthes calls "the writerly": a transformation of literature from the passive consumption of commodified mass culture to the active participation of the enlightened reader of open-ended, "difficult" modernist/avant-garde texts. At the same time, cut-up/fold-in looks forward to the democratizing, deauthorizing imperatives of postmodernity.

Cut-up/fold-in aims for a modernist authenticity that Burroughs unashamedly calls the "Truth": "No one can conceal what is saying cut-up . . . You can cut the Truth out of any written or spoken words//" (*The Third Mind* 73). Yet at the same time, the cut-up/fold-in method works through postmodern pastiche, based on the deauthorization of the author, the vitiation of the uniqueness of the authorial literary voice, and therefore of the authenticity on which modernism depends.

In Steinian experimental writing, as in Burroughs's cut-up and fold-in method, conventional word associations, syntactical patterns, and literary sequences are broken apart to make room for new modes of thought. These literary methodologies aspire to change the world by opening out new possibilities of thought-in-language, on the assumption, common in sixties countercultural ideologies, that revolution must come not through politics alone but through an accompanying, or even preceding, changed consciousness as well (as we have seen, most significantly, in Marcuse). This experimentalism was characteristic of a good deal of sixties culture, notably the mystic-apocalyptic-sardonic lyrics and prophetic, cosmically sincere musical styles of Bob Dylan, John Lennon, Jerry Garcia, Neil Young, and others. This was a new language for the new world, the utopia in the making, to be made flesh by the arts and lives of the counterculture. This is also the essence of the modernist/avant-garde revolution of the word; the logical endpoint of what Virginia Woolf calls, in *A Room of One's Own*, "breaking the sentence" and "breaking the sequence," phases that have become clichés of modernist (especially feminist modernist) experimentalism. Art is transformative, potentially redemptive, in this ideology, in its unique ability to reinvent the world through reinventing thought-in-language.

As Burroughs develops its ideology, however, the cut-up and fold-in method is more actively democratic, egalitarian, and participatory than modernist/avant-garde experimentalism. While modernist aesthetics, as we have seen, wanted to transform consciousness in order to rescue it from the degradations of the mass, "one-dimensional" "culture industry," depending on the power and unique genius of the imaginative artist who can effect this transformation, cut-up/fold-in can be used immediately by anyone, working on any sort of cultural material, to liberate the self from the stranglehold of authoritarian "control," as Burroughs calls it. Cut-up/fold-in works through pastiche and universal accessibility to deauthorize the artist-genius and to undercut uniqueness and authenticity. Burroughs invites "all peoples of the world" to "cut the enemy beam off your line" (*Nova Express* 14). The open, universally accessible, participatory nature of Burroughs's method marks it as characteristic of the prime sixties political ideology of participatory democracy, and as the site of emergent postmodern ideologies of the popular.

In *The Job*, a series of interviews conducted by Daniel Odier in the late sixties, supplemented by Burroughs with excerpts from a range of his other publications, Burroughs elaborates at some length his cut-up/fold-in technique, and its cultural-political-ideological implications. In these discussions, Burroughs moves back and forth between characteristically modern and characteristically postmodern paradigms. In the section titled "Journey through time-space," the opening section of the original version of *The Job*, Burroughs gives the fullest account of cut-up/fold-in available in his works. This account is prefaced with a question and answer that vividly demonstrate the simultaneity of the dominant modern and the emergent postmodern in Burroughs's work (the following sequence opens this section of the book):

QUESTION: *Your books, since* The Ticket that Exploded *especially, are no longer "novels"; a breaking up of novelistic form is noticeable in* Naked Lunch. *Toward what end or goal is this break-up heading?*
ANSWER: That's very difficult to say. I think that the novelistic form is probably outmoded and that we may look forward perhaps to a future in which people do not read at all or read only illustrated books and magazines or some abbreviated form of reading matter. To compete with television and photo magazines writers will have to develop more

precise techniques producing the same effect on the reader as a lurid action photo.[7]

Odier's question about the breaking up of novelistic form draws on the assumptions, characteristic of high modernism and avant-garde experimentalism, that traditional genres must be dismantled and redefined.[8] Odier is locating Burroughs within this tradition, expecting from him, presumably, a reply about the inadequacy of traditional genres to represent modernity.

Burroughs, however, gives a very different sort of reply. He doesn't invoke the Woolfian distinction, in "Modern Fiction," between realism's "series of gig lamps symmetrically arranged" and the "luminous halo or envelope" of modernist fiction. He does not sound any modernist or avant-garde call to a realer realism of the twentieth century, true to its fragmentation, mechanization, alienation, reification, commodification, self-consciousness, or depth psychologies. While he agrees that "the novelistic form is probably outmoded," he does not think it needs to be replaced by a truer, realer prose fiction that at once represents and transforms the twentieth century (the modernist credo). Instead, it needs to be replaced by "more precise techniques producing the same effect on the reader as a lurid action photo." The reflex effect on the reader of a lurid action photo, invoking passive, prepackaged, visceral responses rather than consciousness-altering engagement in the invention of new meanings, is precisely what the modernist/avant-garde ideology of the writerly intends to blast apart. Burroughs looks directly here, along with McLuhan though with far less utopian optimism, at the end of the Gutenberg Galaxy: the advent of postmodern postliteracy.[9] Burroughs's tone is neutral — he neither welcomes nor abhors this paradigm shift. Rather, he hopes to use it to the advantage of his liberatory aesthetics.

Odier moves quickly to a set-up question, designed to allow Burroughs to explain his alternative to the outmoded novel form: "*What separates* Naked Lunch *from* Nova Express? *What is the most important evolution between these two books?*" (27). This question initiates Burroughs's discussion of cut-up/fold-in, which, of course, is what separates *Naked Lunch* from *Nova Express* — he evolved the technique in the post-*Naked Lunch* books of the tetralogy. As Burroughs explains, "the simplest way [to do a cut-up/fold-in] is to take a page, cut it down the middle and across the middle, and then rearrange the four sections" (*Job* 29). His deployment of the technique became much more elaborate than that, involving piecing together fragments of a range of literary and nonliterary texts, as well as of tape recordings made at different times and places, along with similarly cut-up and rearranged fragments of his own writing.

Burroughs immediately swerves away from this postmodern post-literacy, locating his literary practice firmly within modernist/avant-garde aesthetics. He adverts to the Steinian sentiment (see, for example, *Lectures in America*), derived for Burroughs most immediately from the artist Brion Gysin, his collaborator, that " 'writing is fifty years behind painting.' Why this gap? Because the painter can touch and handle his medium and the writer cannot. The writer does not yet know what words are. He deals only with abstractions from the source point of words. The painter's ability to touch and handle his medium led to montage techniques sixty years ago. It is to be hoped that the extension of cut-up techniques will lead to more precise verbal experiments closing this gap and giving a whole new dimension to writing. These techniques can show the writer what words are and put him in tactile communication with his medium" (27–28). Burroughs invokes here the long tradition of modernist/avant-garde self-referentiality — the focus on the medium itself, on the plasticity of language; the need to make language as directly, concretely, immediately expressive as daubs of paint or notes of music. This focus is a primary impetus of experimental writing.

Burroughs follows Stein again in insisting on the conscious artistry of the cut-up/fold-in process (Stein explained, in a 1946 interview conducted just before her death, that her seemingly random or arbitrary experimental word juxtapositions were in fact carefully chosen). Odier asks him *"When you have arrived at a mix or montage, do you follow the channels opened by the text or do you adapt what you want to say to the mix?"* Burroughs's reply becomes a classic defense of the experimental method from within a traditional definition of artistic practice: "I would say I follow the channels opened by the rearrangement of the text. . . . It's not unconscious at all, it's a very definite operation. . . . It's quite conscious, there's nothing of automatic writing or unconscious procedure involved here" (29). Stein repudiated in very similar terms the notion that her writing was in any way automatic or unconscious.[10] Discussing cut-up/fold-in of tape recordings, Burroughs says, "you get very interesting juxtapositions. Some of them are useful from a literary point of view and some are not" (28). Again: "As to the sequences and rhythms organizing themselves, well, they don't. The cut-ups will give you new material but they won't tell you what to do with it" (32). Note the emphasis on "sequences

WILLIAM BURROUGHS **169**

and rhythms" here, core concerns of the "literary point of view." Burroughs finds "texts which try to describe the visions offered by drugs . . . for the most part dull. The writer has forgotten that he is a writer" (160).[11] Burroughs praises Conrad and Ford; "Beckett and Genet I admire without reservation" (55).[12]

In an answer to a question about his desire for clarity, Burroughs locates himself firmly within the representational ideology of the modernist/ avant-garde tradition:

> When people speak of clarity in writing they generally mean plot, continuity, beginning middle and end, adherence to a "logical" sequence. But things don't happen in logical sequence and people don't think in logical sequence. [Remember Woolf's "luminous halo or envelope" replacing the falsifying "series of gig lamps symmetrically arranged."] Any writer who hopes to approximate what actually occurs in the mind and body of his characters cannot confine himself to such an arbitrary structure as "logical" sequence. Joyce was accused of being unintelligible and he was presenting only one level of cerebral events: conscious sub-vocal speech. I think it is possible to create multilevel events and characters that a reader could comprehend with his entire organic being. (35)

We are in a different universe, here, from the postliterary anti-aesthetics of the lurid action photo.

However, in "Prisoners of the earth come out," in response to Odier's provocative question "*How do you feel about human beings?*," Burroughs switches readily to that postmodern, postliterary orientation: "nothing basically wrong with the human beings themselves, but they certainly will have to take a very basic forward step in evolution. . . . I think the next step will have to be beyond the word. The word is now an outmoded artifact. Any life form that gets stuck with an outmoded built-in artifact is doomed to destruction. The dinosaurs survived because they were large and then they got larger and larger and this ultimately of course led to their extinction. The present form of human being quite possibly results from words, and unless they get rid of this outmoded artifact, it will lead to their extinction" (98).

This simultaneity of irreconcilable modern and postmodern modes of self-positioning is vividly apparent in Burroughs's theorizations of language itself. On one hand, he believes that the word is not only an "outmoded artifact" but also the primary vehicle of what he calls "control," the seamless domination of the world by various linked, interchangeable repressive forces, which encompass the standard sixties villains — capitalism, imperialism, the military, the police, organized religion, sexual repression, the family, the nation, the law; "power in all its forms," as Daniel Odier says. Burroughs says, "you must leave the old verbal garbage behind: God talk, country talk, mother talk, love talk, party talk. You must learn to exist with no religion no country no allies" (*Job* 21).

> Q: *What is the importance of power, in all its forms, in the machinery of destruction?*
> A: The exercise of power for power's sake is precisely the machine of destruction. This would seem to be something we have had throughout history. . . . [but] to confuse this old-style power with the manifestation of control madness we see now on this planet is to confuse a disappearing wart with an exploding cancer.
> Q: *And what of money, ownership, property?*
> A: Vested interest of power and/or money is perhaps the most potent factor standing in the way of freedom for the individual. (*Job* 59–60)

Even in theorizing the end of "the word," then — the postmodern end of the Gutenberg Galaxy — Burroughs constructs a revolutionary/redemptive scenario derived from central paradigms of modernity. In this paranoid ideology, characteristically modern in its binaristic totalization of domination and resistance, "the word" or "word-and-image" stand as the vehicle of domination, and "silence," beyond the word, is the utopian mode of resistance: "You must learn to live alone in silence" (*Job* 21). Yet at the same time, as we will see, Burroughs believes contradictorily that, through cut-up and fold-in's liberation of the word or word-and-image from its conventional "association tracks," language itself can effect its own rehabilitation, if not redemption. Further, the "message of resistance," as he calls it, involving destruction of all conventional language, is, at times in Burroughs's work, only a partial, compromised message. When asked directly, he says he does not believe in the possibility of pure or total resistance, and this statement accords with many of his fictional representations of compromised modes of resistance. As he says in the introduction to *Nova Express*, "to speak is to lie, to live is to collaborate" (14). This is a quintessential postmodern position, rejecting the utopian hope of modernity for total liberation, a position outside or beyond the history of social-political determinations. This position is linked to postmodern complicitous critique and resistance from within. These contradictory modern and postmodern relations to liberatory possibility coexist seamlessly, undifferentiated, within Burroughs's work.

Burroughs rails regularly against the forces of control, of which the most important and pervasive is language: "The word of course is one of the most powerful instruments of control as exercised by the newspaper and images as well. . . . Now if you start cutting these up and rearranging them you are breaking down the control system" (*Job* 33). (Other vehicles, embodiments, or metaphors for control are heroin ["junk"], virus, Mayan thought control, the Nova Mob; word-and-image, junk, virus become interchangeable, metonymic for one another and for control itself.) Again, this is a classic modernist/avant-garde position, in which conventional language is seen as the tool of the bankrupt, oppressive status quo, the mass-culture industry. Experimental writing is its antidote, bringing the possibility of freedom, authenticity, truth. Burroughs differs from these avant-garde, experimentalist language theories (of which language poetry is the most recent incarnation) only through the extreme literalness of his view of linguistic mechanisms of control, in which certain word-and-image combinations exert the same sort of direct biological power as addictive drugs, holding the word junkie (all of us) in the same sort of absolute vise/vice.

As tool of the world enforcers of power, the language of control — as in some "jewels gathered from one of the periodicals admittedly subsidized by the CIA" — is "blind prose. It sees nothing and neither does the reader. Not an image in a cement mixer of this word paste" (*Job* 104). Cut-up/ fold-in can both expose the deadness and manipulativeness of this prose and substitute a mode of language capable of releasing us from it, connecting us with the true, authentic expression of the free human imagination:

As a literary exercise I pick up the Penguin translation of Rimbaud and select images to place in congruent juxtapositions with this colorless vampire prose which having no color of its own must steal color from the readers such contractually accessible linguistically structuralized preparations on blue evenings I shall go down the path in a dream feeling the coolness on my feet starved of direction or vector by derivationally confluent exasperations five in the evening at the Green Inn huge beer mug froth turned into gold by a ray of late sunshine perspective of illiterate human beings would traduce or transfigure fecundate with orifices potential the Watchman rows through the luminous heavens and from his flaming dragnet lets fall shooting stars and precisely reciprocal latent consensus. (*Job* 104–5)

Burroughs regularly exhorts his readers to resist these forces of control through an apocalyptic refusal or negation, which he generally calls "silence," or "the message of resistance": "Q: *Is the introduction of what you call "the message of resistance" the most important thing in the montage? Why?* A: Well, yes, I would say it's a very important factor in the montage because it does tend to break down the principal instruments of control which are word and image and to some extent to nullify them" (*Job* 34–35). This modest, tentative, qualified reply belies the apocalyptic tone of Burroughs's call to his readers in his fiction:

> What scared you all into time? Into body? Into shit? I will tell you: "*the word.*" Alien Word "*the.*" "*The*" word of Alien Enemy imprisons "*thee*" in Time. In Body. In Shit. Prisoner, come out. The great skies are open. I Hassan i Sabbah *rub out the word forever.* . . . [Hassan i Sabbah is one of Burroughs's many narrative aliases—others are Inspector J. Lee of the Nova Police, and Uranian Willy or Willy the Rat.] And what does my program of total austerity and total resistance offer *you?* I offer you nothing. I am not a politician. These are conditions of total emergency. . . . cut the enemy beam off your line. Apomorphine and silence. I order total resistance directed against this conspiracy to pay off peoples of the earth in ersatz bullshit. (*Nova Express* 13–14; apomorphine is a chemical derivative of morphine that successfully ended fifteen years of heroin addiction for Burroughs—again, Burroughs conflates drug addiction with language as control)

Note the modernist ideology of transcendence here—we are exhorted to leave the body behind, through total austerity and total resistance. We are offered nothing in return but freedom, purity, liberation from the ersatz universe of capitalist commodity culture. Burroughs advocates the totalized, apocalyptic revolutionary scenario of modern/sixties redemptive ideologies, in which the realization of utopia must be preceded by wiping the contaminated slate clean: "Q: *Does total destruction seem to you a desirable outcome?* A: I would say total destruction of existing institutions, and very rapidly, may be the only alternative to a nuclear war which would be very much more destructive. . . . I certainly prefer the total destruction of the present system of society to a nuclear war, which is the inevitable result of its remaining in operation" (*Job* 108).

Burroughs says that in *Naked Lunch*, "the title means exactly what the words say: NAKED lunch — a frozen moment when everyone sees what is on the end of every fork" (*NL* xxxvii). He wants us to "see what is on the end of that long newspaper spoon" (*NL* xliv). A recurring motif for Burroughs is the notion, linked to the "message of resistance" — the breakup of conventional word-and-image enacted by experimental writing — that there is some unmediated truth accessible to the person liberated from the enforced "association tracks" of control. There is a utopian location outside social construction, in which this truth resides and is available to the initiated, those who have cut the enemy beam off the line: "Q: *Is the ability 'to see what is in front of us' a way of escaping from the image-prison which surrounds us?* A: Very definitely, yes. But this is an ability which very few people have. . . . For one thing, because of the absolute barrage of images to which we are subjected so that we become blunted . . . and this makes a permanent haze in front of your eyes, you can't see anything. Q: *When you say that when you're in a world of simple images you see them more clearly what do you mean by clearly?* A: There's nothing between them and the image. A farmer really sees his cows, he really sees what's in front of him quite clearly, it isn't a question of familiarity, it's a question of something being between you and the image, so that you can't see it" (*Job* 34). "Nothing between them and the image": the unmediated vision of the "innocent eye" viewing the unsituated, in some sense absolute truth. This is a notion located in modernity, unavailable to postmodernity. The back-to-the-land communal movement of the sixties counterculture believed similarly that it could establish a pure, unmediated relation to nature, wholly unimplicated in and uncontaminated by the dominant technological-commodity culture it repudiated.

In *Naked Lunch*, Burroughs indicates that mediated vision is peculiarly American — indigenous to our thoroughly mediated, commodified, consumer-capitalist culture:

> Into the Interior: a vast subdivision, antennae of television to the meaningless sky. In lifeproof houses they hover over the young, sop up a little of what they shut out. Only the young bring anything in, and they are not young very long. . . . there is no drag like U.S. drag. You can't see it, you don't know where it comes from. Take one of those cocktail lounges at the end of a subdivision street — every block of houses has its own bar and drugstore and market and liquorstore. You walk in and it hits you. But where does it come from?

Not the bartender, not the customers, nor the cream-colored plastic rounding the bar stools, nor the dim neon. Not even the TV. . . . Motels with beaverboard walls, gas heater, thin pink blankets. (*NL* 12–13)

The "subdivision" is a prime sixties symbol of American conformity and the empty, sanitized, "meaningless," "lifeproof" routine of postwar bourgeois culture: "they're all made out of ticky tacky and they all look just the same." Burroughs focuses on the addiction to modes of escape from what he would consider unmediated truth and reality necessitated by subdivision life — the bar, drugstore, liquor store. He claims that the "U.S. drag" does not come from the bartender, customers, cream-colored plastic, dim neon, beaverboard, thin pink blankets, or "even the TV," but this contemptuous, depressed instantiation of what he calls elsewhere "ersatz bullshit" indicates at least a strong connection.

The ersatz bullshit of the U.S. drag has a political dimension as well, as it does in general in the sixties: "Back through Lake Charles and the dead slot-machine country, south end of Texas, nigger-killing sheriffs look us over and check the car papers. Something falls off you when you cross the border into Mexico, and suddenly the landscape hits you straight with nothing between you and it, desert and mountains and vultures; little wheeling specks and others so close you can hear wings cut the air . . . that shattering bloody blue sky of Mexico . . . barking dogs and the sound of running water" (*NL* 14). From television, bars, drugstores and liquor stores, plastic, beaverboard, and thin pink blankets — habitat of "nigger-killing sheriffs" — we go straight to a direct sensory apprehension of nature: desert, mountains and vultures, shattering bloody blue sky, barking dogs, running water. The "something" of the falsifications of control "falls off you" when you leave the United States, and you are face to unmediated face with a utopian naturalized nature outside culture, like the farmer with his cows.

"Vested interest of power and/or money is perhaps the most potent factor standing in the way of freedom for the individual" (*Job* 60). Burroughs believes in that quintessential tenet of liberal modernity: individual freedom — the absolute right to self-determination of the unique individual. He also believes in the liberated imagination, liberation in general, and the dream: "Q: *You have described America as a nightmare. Would you enlarge on this point?* A: America is not so much a nightmare as a *non-dream*. The American non-dream is precisely a move to wipe the dream out of existence. The dream is a spontaneous happening and therefore dangerous to a control system set up by the non dreamers" (*Job* 102). The evil characters in Burroughs's fiction are often described as having "dead, undreaming eyes." At the end of *The Job*, Burroughs indicts contemporary academia because "research that could be used to free the human spirit is being monopolized by paltry intellects in the name of 'national security'" (224). Freeing the human spirit is the Romantic-humanist agenda par excellence, and it is also the legacy of modernity most strongly endorsed by sixties countercultural ideologies.

While the dominant paradigms of modernity discussed above are most evident in Burroughs's work, emergent postmodern paradigms are also pervasive.[13] Cut-up/fold-in may liberate us from the obsessional association tracks of control, but it also introduces postmodern pastiche, de-authorizing and deconstructing the unique individual free human spirit of the literary author: "a writing machine that shifts one half one text and half the other through a page frame on conveyor belts . . . Shakespeare, Rimbaud, etc. permutating through page frames in constantly changing juxtaposition the machine spits out books and plays and poems — The spectators are invited to feed into the machine any pages of their own text in fifty-fifty juxtaposition with any author of their choice any pages of their choice and provided with the result in a few minutes."[14] The result evidently is quintessential postmodern pastiche. Further, "the spectators are invited": anyone can participate in this process; anyone can use the cut-up/fold-in method. The priestlike power of the modernist artist, the transcendent greatness of imagination and highly evolved artistry, are rejected here. Literature becomes a site of sixties participatory democracy that opens directly onto postmodern egalitarian ideologies of the popular.

In postmodernity, anyone can be a writer; no one can be totally free. In direct contradiction to Burroughs's central advocacy of modernity's utopian, unmediated, universal, psychic-artistic-individualistic liberation, he also writes from within a postmodern practice and ideology — multiple, cyborg, hybrid, immersed in popular culture, particularist, subcultural, minoritarian, global, limited, partial, ordinary, complicit, collaborationist. (We have already seen the pervasiveness of genre and subcultural material in his work: sci fi, gay porn, hard-boiled detective fiction, horror film, comics.)

In direct contradistinction to the modernist artist-as-priest, Burroughs considers himself a "recording instrument. . . . I do not presume to impose 'story' 'plot' 'continuity'" (*NL* 221).

Q: *Your characters are engulfed in a whirlwind of infernal happenings. They are bogged in the substance of the book. Is there a possible way to salvation for them?*

A: I object to the word salvation as having a messianic Christian connotation, of final resolution.

Q: *Do free men exist in your books?*

A: Free men don't exist in anyone's books, because they are the author's creations. I would say that free men don't exist on this planet at this time, because they don't exist in human bodies, by the mere fact of being in a human body you're controlled by all sorts of biologic and environmental necessities. (*Job* 37)

There are no free men or women in Burroughs's fiction — all his positive characters are implicated in the forces of control. Even Uranian Willy of the Nova Police, or Willy the Factualist (factualists can see unmediated reality and are the primary enemies of the forces of control, the latter represented in the fiction by Doc Benway, Mr. Bradly-Mr. Martin, Mayan Thought Control, virus, junk, the Nova Mob, the Interzone Parties of the Senders, Divisionists and Liquefactionists), is also Willy the Rat, a former member of the Nova Mob whose full defection is somewhat in doubt. The fact that the "good guys" are Nova Police, given Burroughs's extreme version of standard sixties feelings about the law in general and police in particular, indicates the intermittently compromised status of all forces of resistance in his fictional universe: "Q: *Do Good and Evil really exist?* A: Not in the absolute sense. Something is good or evil according to your needs and the nature of your organism. . . . I think it's naive to predicate any absolutes there; it only has reference to the conditions of life of a given organism or species or society" (*Job* 75).

There can in fact be no free men or women in Burroughs's fiction because there are no coherent characters: there are no men or women. Personae, voices, with many, overlapping, sometimes interchangeable names, gender identities, sexualities, races and ethnicities, and general biological status, slide in and out of the montage. These "characters" are not only of shifting, indeterminate gender-race-ethnicity-nation, they are just as often part animal, part monster, part chemical or other inanimate object as they are recognizably human: they are quintessentially postmodern, boundary-crossing, Harawayan cyborgs (intermeshings of human and machine or human and animal). The integrity of the free human being Burroughs advocates from the foot planted in modernity is countermanded by what he writes standing on the foot planted in postmodernity, from which he can see only a kaleidoscopic view of morphing, multivalent, dedefined subjectivities. These cyborg subjectivities are constituted emphatically by an indeterminate, shifting, quintessentially performative "transitional" sexuality ("positively no Transitionals in either direction will be allowed in this decent hall" [NL, 85]), and a postmodern global racial hybridity that sees white supremacy as a primary world-historical force of control (at one point Burroughs says "this leads us to the supposition that the word virus assumed a specially malignant and lethal form in the white race" [*Job* 13]): "the room seems to shake and vibrate with motion. The blood and substances of many races, negro, Polynesian, Mountain Mongol, Desert Nomad, Polyglot Near East, Indian — races as yet unconceived and unborn, combinations not yet realized pass through your body. Migrations, incredible journeys through deserts and jungles and mountains. . . . The Composite City where all human potentials are spread out in a vast silent market" (NL 106). This nomad, hybrid, market-contained subjectivity is quintessentially postmodern. In the *Paris Review* interview that opens *The Third Mind*, Burroughs speaks solidly and prophetically from within postmodern refunctioned consumerism: "I see no reasons why the artistic world can't absolutely merge with Madison Avenue. Pop art is a move in that direction. Why can't we have advertisements with beautiful words and beautiful images?" (7).

Burroughs's fiction itself partakes formally of the same kaleidoscopic shape-shifting, in the realm of the ordinary, the apocalyptic, the illicit, and the popular: "this book spill [*sic*] off the page in all directions, kaleidoscope of vistas, medley of tunes and street noises, farts and riot yipes and the slamming steel shutters of commerce, screams of pain and pathos and screams plain pathic, copulating cats and outraged squawk of the displaced bull head, prophetic mutterings of brujo in nutmeg trances, snapping necks and screaming mandrakes, sigh of orgasm, heroin silent as dawn in the thirsty cells" (NL, 229).

The binaristic systems of modernity Burroughs disrupts here, rejected by postmodern theory, are not only inadequate but linked to the dynamics of control. Burroughs considers

> classical philosophical thought . . . completely outmoded, as Korzybski, the man who developed general semantics, has pointed out, the Aristotelian "either-or" — something is either this or that — is one of the great errors of Western thinking, because it's no longer true at all. That

sort of thinking does not even correspond to what we now know about the physical universe.

Q: *Why has it been accepted for so long?*

A: There are certain formulas, word-locks, which will lock up a whole civilization for a thousand years. Now another thing is Aristotle's *is* of identity: this *is* a chair. Now, whatever it may be, it's not a chair. . . . Yes, I would agree emphatically that Aristotle, Descartes, and all that way of thinking is extremely stultifying . . . and particularly disastrous in that it still guides the whole academic world. (*Job* 48–49)

Burroughs is on the cusp here of the advent of structuralist and poststructuralist thought.

Even as Burroughs advocates the modernist-utopian "message of resistance" and "silence" through cut-up/fold-in, he also sees that this avantgarde method can use language to save it from itself, participating in a form of postmodern complicitous critique and resistance from within. In *Naked Lunch*, one of his distanced, self-mocking but partly sincere narrative voices says, " 'So I got an exclusive why don't I make with the live word? The word cannot be expressed direct. . . . It can perhaps be indicated by mosaic of juxtaposition like articles abandoned in a hotel drawer, defined by negatives and absence' " (NL 117). The "live word" is different from silence. It points toward a complicit, compromised language ("to speak is to lie, to live is to collaborate") which nonetheless resists the dead, deadly, "blind prose" of control.

In the wake of the progressively extreme experimentalism of the sixties tetralogy, Burroughs's fiction, like postmodern fiction in general, retrieved and redeployed opportunistically many aspects of conventional narrative: resistance from within. Burroughs discusses this new direction in *The Job*, which, again, was written in the late sixties:

Q: Finnegans Wake *is generally regarded as a magnificent literary dead end. What is your opinion?*

A: I think *Finnegans Wake* rather represents a trap into which experimental writing can fall when it becomes purely experimental. I would go so far with any given experiment and then come back; that is, I am coming back now to write purely conventional straightforward narrative. But applying what I have learned from the cut-up and the other techniques to the problem of conventional writing. It's simply if you go too far in one direction, you can never get back, and you're out there in complete isolation, like this anthropologist who spent the last 20 years of his life on the sweet-potato controversy. (*Job* 55)

As emerging postmodernist, Burroughs has no desire to be stranded in the vanishing avant-garde of the failed revolution of the word.

Writing for Burroughs was an act of self-reconstruction that he wanted to share with the world. Concerted writing and emerging from heroin addiction were concomitant for him, and he saw them as linked manifestations of one process. Since "junk *is* image" (*Nova Express* 15), liberating himself from the control of heroin was equivalent to liberating language (word-and-image) from the control of its oppressive conventional structures of association and meaning. He says in the introduction to *Naked Lunch* that "I awoke from The Sickness at the age of forty-five, calm and sane, and in reasonably good health except for a weakened liver and the look of borrowed flesh common to all who survive The Sickness. . . . Most survivors do not remember the delirium in detail. I apparently took detailed notes on sickness and delirium. I have no precise memory of writing the notes which have now been published under the title *Naked Lunch*" (xxxvii). Yet in *The Job*, in answer to the question "What does the discovery of apomorphine represent in your life," he says, "The turning point between life and death. I would never have been cured without it. *Naked Lunch* would never have been written" (145). He distinguishes between notes taken in the "delirium" of heroin addiction, an apparently nonvolitional activity, and the active, volitional "writing" of *Naked Lunch*. Notes were taken during his heroin addiction, of which he has no precise memory. Though these notes somehow became *Naked Lunch* (with extensive help from Allen Ginsberg), they do not inhabit the same universe as the *writing* of *Naked Lunch*. Writing as an activity represents to him the sign, manifestation, embodiment of agency — the opposite of addiction, which is a state of utter passivity, in the grip of junk's control.

Further, this act of self-construction in the act of writing, in the literary as practice, is not limited to the artist, to one who has been set apart and elevated as a practitioner of a demanding, difficult, redemptive calling, as in the modernist ideology of the artist as cultural savior. It is potentially available to everyone, as we have seen. Burroughs repeatedly calls on his reader to try cut-up and fold-in, to try splicing together tapes of ordinary life to produce new meaning. He repeatedly, in fact, gives fairly detailed instructions for how to do it, developed within elaborate comic scenarios of saturnalia invading humdrum office or suburban life:

record your boss and co-workers analyze their associational patterns learn to imitate their voices oh you'll be a popular man around the office but not easy to compete with the usual procedure record their body sounds from concealed mikes the rhythm of breathing the movements of after-lunch intestines the beating of hearts now impose your own body sounds and become the breathing word and the beating heart of that organization become that organization . . . why not give tape recorder parties every guest arrives with his recorder and tapes of what he intends to say at the party recording what other recorders say to him it is the height of rudeness not to record when addressed directly by another tape recorder (*Job* 163)

Satire aside, Burroughs sees the egalitarian diffusion of the power of word-and-image, the appropriation of cut-up/fold-in to tape splicing by "millions of people," as a powerful subversive force. In "Playback from Eden to Watergate," a 1973 piece that prefaces the revised edition of *The Job*, Burroughs fantasizes the disruption of the political forces of control epitomized by the Nixon presidency ("tape recorder three," which plays back spliced-together pieces recorded separately on tape recorders one and two, is the crucial factor both in control and in Burroughs's plan for subverting it): "the basic operation of recording, pictures, more pictures, and playback can be carried out by anyone with a recorder and a camera. Any number can play. Millions of people carrying out this basic operation could nullify the control system which those who are behind Watergate and Nixon are attempting to impose. Like all control systems, it depends on maintaining a monopoly position. If anybody can be tape recorder three, then tape recorder three loses power. God must be *the* God" (*Job* 20).

A multitude of gods (critiquing logocentrism); critiquing binary thought: Burroughs's links to poststructuralism here are clear. Burroughs can even sound like an underground comic version of Derrida (representative sixties sensibility that he is, Burroughs believes that the underground press in general "serves as the only effective counter to a growing power and more sophisticated techniques used by establishment mass media to falsify, misrepresent, misquote . . . I suggest that the underground press could perform this function much more effectively by the use of cut/ups" [*Job* 177]): "it is generally assumed that the spoken word came before the written word. I suggest that the spoken word as we know it came after the written word. In the beginning was the Word, and the Word was God —

and the word was flesh . . . human flesh . . . in the beginning of *writing*,
Animals talk. They don't write. Now, a wise old rat may know a lot about
traps and poison but he cannot write "Death Traps in Your Warehouse"
for the *Reader's Digest*. . . . My basic theory is that the written word was
actually a virus that made the spoken word possible" (*Job* 11–12).

Like Derrida, Burroughs attacks the either-or of classical philosophy
not only as outmoded but as the structure of thought expressing, linked
to, necessitated by, and adequate to all binaristic forms of hierarchical domination. This is the central Derridean insight so crucial to anti-
phallogocentric feminist theory, which sees the binary as the necessary
intellectual form of gender inequality and domination. Yet the link to
feminist theory must be made carefully. Burroughs was, at least until
certain careful retractions late in his career, a committed misogynist, who
argues in one interview for the elimination of women altogether.[15] Given
the advances of reproductive technologies, Burroughs hopes women will
become unnecessary: "in the words of one of a great misogynist's plain Mr
Jones, in Conrad's *Victory*: 'Women are a perfect curse.' I think they were
a basic mistake, and the whole dualistic universe evolved from this error.
Women are no longer essential to reproduction as this article indicates:
OXFORD SCIENTISTS REPRODUCE FROGS FROM SINGLE CELLS by
Walter Sullivan" (*Job* 116). Interestingly, in fact, Burroughs is very close
here, both in sentiment and in tone, to the thought of early second-wave
radical feminists such as Valerie Solanas and Shulamith Firestone, and
also to the antibinaristic theories of Luce Irigaray and Hélène Cixous.
They agree that the "whole dualistic universe" was produced by the initiation of the hierarchized gender binary, and that the elimination of this
hierarchy is the precondition for universal liberation. Solanas feels exactly
about men the way Burroughs does about women — their positions neatly
mirror one another (Solanas's *The SCUM Manifesto* argues for the elimination of the male gender). Firestone, in *The Dialectic of Sex*, argues as
well that the elimination of sexual reproduction is the basis of universal
liberation, and that the advent of reproductive technologies is a harbinger
of this liberation (see chapter 14).[16]

Generally, in moving away from a dualistic, dialectical universe and
toward an indifferentiated or antinomous universe (see Jameson, *The
Seeds of Time*) Burroughs, while remaining primarily within the modernist dominant, enacts a crucial element of the shift from modern to postmodern. In this shift, the antithetical/dialectical either-or of modernity,

whether in resolved or unresolved dialectic, is replaced by unlimited ands, consisting of elements incommensurable with one another, and in a state of limited, partial overlap/dehiscence. All subjectivities come to morph about performatively, like the human/animal/vegetable/mineral blobs that ooze freely through Burroughs's sixties works.

CHAPTER NINE

Endnotes II: Sixties, Avant-Garde, Popular Culture

William Burroughs was one of the sixties avant-garde writers who moved, through the relevant elements of his own work, into postmodernism. In the novels succeeding his sixties tetralogy, including *The Wild Boys*, *Cities of the Red Night*, and *The Place of Dead Roads*, he returned to refunctioned modes of conventional narrative, just as he said he would in *The Job*. There were a number of writers who did the same: Susan Sontag, for example, a key figure of the intellectual avant-garde of the sixties, wrote two highly experimental, recherché novels in the sixties — *The Benefactor* and *Death Kit* — that were restricted in readership to an avant-garde intellectual elite. Like Burroughs, she has moved on since the sixties to write popular, successful postmodern novels deploying refunctioned conventional and subgeneric modes, most notably the romance plot: *The Volcano Lover*, and the National Book Award winner, *In America*. Thomas Pynchon, whose *V.*, *The Crying of Lot 49*, and *Gravity's Rainbow* were among the most important novels of the sixties avant-garde renaissance in fiction, is of course one of the two or three most important postmodern novelists in the United States, with *Vineland* and *Mason & Dixon* not only quintessentially postmodernist in their eclectic, wide-ranging deployment of an enormous variety of formal strategies and blending of disparate high-literary, popular, and subgeneric modes, but also profound works on precisely the issues involved in the shift to postmodernity: the political and ethical betrayals that destroyed the sixties (*Vineland*) and the depredations of the *longue durée* of the Enlightenment (*Mason & Dixon*). Don DeLillo, less well known in the sixties, has also become a key figure of postmodern fiction, with *White Noise* a top candidate for quintessential postmodern novel. E. L. Doctorow and Kurt Vonnegut, whose work was always more accessible, popular, and situated within refunctioned modes of conventional narrative than that of the fully experimental, formalist sixties avant-garde fiction writers, have also survived the end of the sixties and moved into postmodern prominence.

Many of the fiction writers associated with the American sixties avant-garde, who were used by groundbreaking, highly influential critics — premier among them Ihab Hassan — to define postmodernism in the seventies and eighties, and whose work is still read, studied, taught, and written about by many academic and public intellectual critics of postmodern fiction, did not shift in the same way that Burroughs, DeLillo, Doctorow, Pynchon, Sontag, or Vonnegut did into the version of postmodernism/postmodernity I have developed here. Their fiction is much less widely read than that of the above writers, except among critics and readers committed to this version of postmodernism. For a representative (though not of course inclusive or exhaustive) list of these writers, I draw on Brian McHale's highly influential 1987 book *Postmodernist Fiction*. The American writers he discusses (he also discusses a number of British and European writers), in addition to Burroughs, DeLillo, Doctorow, Pynchon, and Vonnegut (not Sontag), include John Barth, Donald Barthelme, Richard Brautigan, Leonard Cohen, Robert Coover, Stanley Elkin, Raymond Federman, William Gass, John Hawkes, Russell Hoban, Steve Katz, Thomas McGuane, Clarence Major, Leonard Michaels, Ishmael Reed, Gilbert Sorrentino, Ronald Sukenick.[1] These writers have remained committed to the experimentalism of sixties avant-garde fiction, derived from the great fiction of modernism and the earlier twentieth-century and mid-century avant-gardes, epitomized in the works of Beckett, Nabokov, Borges, Robbe-Grillet (McHale discusses these late-modernist European writers at some length). The European avant-gardes, represented in fiction by writers such as Walter Abish, Italo Calvino, Umberto Eco, Günter Grass, and Peter Handke, and of course the great global magic realists, most notably García Márquez and Rushdie (all of whom McHale also discusses, though he does not discuss Isabel Allende or other women global magic realists) have, unlike the Americans McHale discusses, crossed over into the popular postmodern. Those Americans did not shift toward refunctioned convention, subgeneric modes, and forms of the popular, as did Burroughs, De-Lillo, Doctorow, Pynchon, Sontag, Vonnegut.

I hope it is evident that, with the exception of Susan Sontag, all the writers I have listed here are male. (McHale also includes the British women Christine Brooke-Rose and Angela Carter and the French Monique Wittig, but not the Americans Kathy Acker, Grace Paley, or Sontag.)[2] Further, all but Ishmael Reed are white. Sixties avant-garde fiction was almost entirely dominated in America by heterosexual white men. The high-literary, writerly experimentalism of this fiction, despite its interest in and intermittent sympathy for various modes of popular culture, was, as I see it, an endpoint of modernism. It assimilated popular culture to the oppositional codes of the avant-garde, rather than entering into its force field complicitly, as postmodern writing does. The white male domination of this fiction, often accompanied by sexism and misogyny, accords with its stance as arbiter of the popular, and artistic transmuter of the popular into oppositional high art. It was with the emergence of postmodernity that women writers, of a broad range of racial, ethnic, and geographical locations and diverse sexualities, adapting some methods of the sixties avant-gardes to the forms of postmodernism, emerged into prominence, as I will discuss in chapter 14. One of the most striking features of McHale's list of American writers, a list that includes several fairly obscure writers, is the absence from it, even in 1987, of Toni Morrison, and of all of the other great African American women writers, and other women writers of color, of postmodernity. The white male sixties experimentalists who did persist into postmodernity not only shifted into refunctioned conventional, popular, and subgeneric modes, they also took seriously and engaged directly the questions of otherness the sixties raised revolving around issues of gender, race, ethnicity, sexuality, and location, issues that have become central in postmodernity. The emergence of postcolonial, transnational, global fiction in this period, by men as well as by women of a broad, diverse spectrum of racial, ethnic, and geographical backgrounds and sexual orientations, is also, evidently, characteristically postmodern. This fiction reinvents and forges new possibilities of a vastly multiple and diverse global/local popular and literary imaginary, immersed in hybridity, boundary-crossing, and modes of dislocation. It is, I would argue, the most important, vibrant development in contemporary fiction.

PART FOUR

Subject Politics

CHAPTER TEN

Politics of the Self

In the preface to his 1971 collection *The Performing Self*, Richard Poirier begins by discussing the unfinished Michelangelo sculpture reproduced on the front cover of the book. The sculpture, "one of the four 'Captives' displayed at the Accademia in Florence," depicts a male body that is "emerging from stone, the right leg, thick and powerful, is straining up as from the elements that imprison it; the left arm is raised, the elbow forward, and the hand and forearm push at what would be the back of the head. Except there is no head. Where it would be is instead a heavy block of stone." Poirier describes the "communicated effect" of this sculpture as an "elemental will toward the attainment of human shape and human recognition," with "the imagined head . . . as part of the material that will not willingly yield itself to the head's existence."[1]

While these "possible impressions . . . are not . . . available for easy translation into politics of any fashionable kind, they do, at least for me, allow a political response. . . . that any effort to find accommodation for human shapes or sounds is an act that partakes of political meaning" (viii). This political meaning emerges from the effort, represented by the statue, to achieve a self. The statue "involves negotiation, struggle, and compromise with the stubborn material of existence, be it language or stone. The fact that the statue was left in its unfinished state provides a surpassingly eloquent image of the strenuousness, even, sometimes, the violence, required by this effort" (viii). Poirier goes on to make explicit the parallel between Michelangelo's activity as a sculptor and the subject Michelangelo depicts: "the workings of Michelangelo with the stone are thus of a piece, quite literally so, with the seeming exertions of the captive within it: both of them would summon the power required for the composing of a self otherwise lost to the material from which it might be formed. This book is in part based on the conviction that this activity, when it is found in writing, offers a traceable exemplification of possible political and social activities" (viii).

Poirier expresses here, with an eloquence and precision that make his work part of what he describes, a version of the modernist view of the artist as hero, struggling, against the massive resistance of the literary as well as the social-political medium, in Joyce's words in *A Portrait of the Artist as a Young Man*, to "forge the uncreated conscience of [his] race," where that uncreated conscience is seen as human subjectivity itself, epitomized as well as produced by the exemplary artist. What inflects this analysis toward the sixties, and the postmodern, is its emphasis on the political content of subjectivity, and its focus on politics anchored in questions of subjectivity rather than in what was traditionally viewed as the social. Interesting and important politics, in this view, concern subjectivity, unlike "what is usually considered political, especially by most Americans": politics "of any fashionable kind," into which "translation" of aesthetic works is "easy." Throughout sixties political expression, as we saw so clearly in *The Port Huron Statement*, the meaningfulness and authenticity of the subject's relation to self and world is primary. This sixties politics of the self is rooted, as we see here, in a modernist view of the heroic struggle for selfhood of the exemplary subject against a resistant, hostile world. During the course of the sixties, this modernist politics of the self, that radiates out from the exemplary subject to a potentially transformed society and culture, shifts into a postmodern politics that coincides with and is contained by formations of subjectivity. "The personal is political," the great New Left–derived slogan of second-wave feminism, was originally meant to break down the artificial separation of the political and social from the intimate and subjective, a separation that relegated the lives of women to a sphere of "nature" and its inevitabilities, outside the potentially transformative struggles of politics. It was intended to link subjectivity to the political, thereby transforming both, not to define the political as or through subjectivity. In the sixties shift to postmodernity, "the personal is political," which annexes subjectivity to the social, becomes reconfigured as what might be dubbed "the political is personal," where political struggles are defined by, and located most meaningfully within, the realm of subjectivity, that includes or projects local, particular political allegiances and goals. Political ambitions for a totalizing, universal, transformative social change come to seem at best distant, "utopian" in the negative sense of illusory; at worst, repressive.[2]

The title essay of Poirier's volume develops the notion of the politics of the struggle for subjectivity as what we now call a politics of performance, or performativity.[3] Poirier argues that writers such as Robert Frost, Norman Mailer, and Henry James (but he could "almost as profitably consider the self as performance in Byron, in Yeats, or in Lawrence . . . Andrew Marvell as well as Thoreau") "treat any occasion as a 'scene' or a stage for dramatizing the self as a performer" (86); "what excites [each writer] most in a work is finally himself as a performer" (87). It is telling that Poirier's three writers include two modernists and one contemporary whose sixties work, particularly *The Armies of the Night*, which Poirier discusses here, is crucial to the sixties phenomena I discuss in this book (Yeats and Lawrence are of course also modernists; Byron, Marvell, and Thoreau were all important to the sixties sensibility — Byron in his flamboyant, defiantly unconventional subjectivity, Thoreau in his views of the correct human relation to nature and of democracy, and Marvell, less popularly, in his complex poetry of humans inextricably interlinked with nature). Performance involves "the act of doing" rather than its end product: "the gap between the completed work, which is supposed to constitute the writer's vision, and the multiple acts of performance that went into it is an image of the gap between the artist's self as he discovered it in performance [which is what interests Poirier and his three writers] and the self, altogether less grimy, discovered afterward in the final shape and the world's reception of it" (88). Poirier emphasizes here not only performance, which, again, comes to be a crucial trope in postmodernity, but also "process" — the act of doing rather than its end product. This valorization of process is characteristic of various modes of sixties aesthetic practice (see chapter 7), particularly experimental theater, the happening, guerrilla theater and street theater, experimental writing and music (think of John Cage), and a range of styles in film and the visual arts. Rooted in the modernist/avant-garde notion of authenticity, fidelity to the medium, and living in/expressing the present moment, epitomized perhaps by Gertrude Stein's notion of the "continuous present" and by Ginsberg's Beat aesthetic, this aesthetic of process, wryly taken for granted, made smooth, largely relieved of its "griminess"—its history of revolutionary breakthrough in struggle against aesthetic linearity and the valorization of the end product—becomes a key tenet of postmodern theory (especially in work derived from Derridean deconstruction) as well as art forms. Sixties aesthetics were performative as well as processual, and so were sixties politics. The performative, improvisatory character of sixties public political events, memorialized by Mailer in *The Armies of the Night*, clearest perhaps in the performance politics/political performance of the Yippies, and culminating in May '68 in France, has become a truism. Street theater and guerrilla theater, quintessentially performative and open-ended, are characteristic sixties political/aesthetic forms.

All the writers he discusses, according to Poirier, "are preoccupied with the possible conjunctions of acts of poetic with acts of public, sometimes even political power" (93). For example, the punning practice of Thoreau and Marvell, inherited from Shakespeare and Donne and anticipating Joyce, "is a way of showing that the words by which the world carries on its sensible business are loaded with a radical content. It is within the subversive power of the poet to release that radical content" (95). But with Mailer, particularly in his account of the 1967 march on the Pentagon, *The Armies of the Night*, which is a mock-heroic performance of his own role in the march and the self he constructs for the purpose of writing about it, "we have the case of a writer who really believes that when he is 'working up the metaphor' he is involved in an act of historical as well as of self-transformation" (93). *The Armies of the Night* is in fact, again, a key, characteristic sixties text. It is structured by a dominant modern narrative of the sickness of American society and the need for massive social-political-psychic transformation, a narrative Mailer builds toward steadily and arrives at in full-blown form at the center of the text. This dominant modern narrative is juxtaposed with Mailer's postmodern self-conscious, ironic narrative gamesmanship (the book is divided into two sections: "History as a Novel" and "The Novel as History") which invokes central postmodern tropes, always ironic, of the narrativity of history and the historicity of narrative. Mailer's narrative voice is quintessentially performative, in Poirier's sense of being primarily interested in the improvisatory, heroic (even if mock-heroic) modernist act of forging an exemplary, anticonventional self rather than in whatever self is ultimately produced by this process. At the same time, this voice is performative in the postmodern sense of understanding all subjectivity as the result of a series of performances that produce the illusion of a coherent, predictable subject rather than expressing any underlying coherent essential self. In postmodern theory, such a thing does not exist: all subjects, in the predominant postmodern Lacanian view, are non-self-identical. The key shift from dominant modern to emergent postmodern connections of politics to subjectivity here turns on the pivot of this sixties notion of subjective political performance, or political performance of subjectivity. This pivot is based on the replacement of the exemplary, heroic, struggling, unique, modernist individual, defying convention in order to adumbrate a transformed culture and society, parallel to the revolutionary vanguard of sixties ideologies (still dominant in Mailer as in sixties texts in general), by a popular, egalitarian notion of all subjectivity. This egalitarian subjectivity is limitlessly differentiable both from others and from itself, constituting and constituted by the infinitely, continually shifting fields and flows of difference of postmodernity. At the same time, this modern-to-postmodern shift also encompasses the replacement of a vision of universal, utopian social-political transformation — led by this heroic individual or vanguard — by temporary affinity groupings constituted around local, particular, limited, clearly defined issues. In these temporary coalitions of affinity, certain interests, forming a small piece of these continually shifting, performatively produced, nonessential, non-self-identical subjectivities, can be seen temporarily to coincide.

"Learning from the Beatles," originally published in *Partisan Review* in 1967 and reprinted as the sixth essay in *The Performing Self*, is an instance (I think an exemplary one) of the postmodern genre, initiated in the sixties, of rock criticism as serious cultural criticism (one wonders whether Venturi et al.'s *Learning from Las Vegas* is indebted to Poirier's title; Venturi et al. cite Poirier's 1967 *New Republic* essay "T. S. Eliot and the Literature of Waste," also collected in *The Performing Self* as "The Literature of Waste: Eliot, Joyce, and Others," on the first page of the book).[4] Poirier connects his project in this essay to the sort of careful, detailed close reading he helped to develop in Harvard's renowned undergraduate course Humanities 6 — reading that gives the most alert, clear, sophisticated possible attention to the moment-by-moment experience of the work: "talking about the experience of any work of art is more difficult than talking about the theory of it, or the issues in it, or the history around it" (117). While the close reading practiced by Poirier and others in "Hum 6" could be used to read any literary text of a complexity and richness capable of rewarding such careful scrutiny, it was modernist writing that most concertedly, consciously devoted itself to, and defined itself by, the production of this complexity and richness. Hum 6, like the New Criticism with which it had much in common, was a historical outgrowth of the triumph of modernism in the midcentury academy (two of Poirier's other books are on Henry James and Robert Frost). Poirier refers to a wide variety of writers throughout these essays, ranging through the centuries from the Renaissance to the present, with no national or historical constraint on his sense of which writers are germane to his arguments. It is only the inventive, performative richness and complexity of the work that interests him, though he does open the essay by "proposing that a line of force in literature beginning with some American works of the last century and passing through Eliot and Joyce to the present has offered a radical challenge to customary ways of thinking about expression in or out of the arts" (112). However, it is the great modernists, particularly Eliot, whom he invokes most frequently; one could also argue that the "line of force" he proposes, in which Emerson is a crucial figure and Stein is of increasing importance in his later work, is essentially modernist. In "Learning from the Beatles," for example, he compares "A Day in the Life," the masterpiece of the 1967 album he focuses on in this essay, *Sgt. Pepper's Lonely Hearts Club Band*, to Eliot's *The Waste Land*: "it is, as I've suggested, a song of wasteland, and the concluding 'I'd love to turn you on' has as much propriety to the fragmented life that precedes it in the song and in the whole work as does the 'Shantih, Shantih, Shantih' to the fragments of Eliot's poem" (138). Poirier goes on to make a larger comparison of the Beatles to Eliot: "Eliot can be remembered here for still other reasons: not only because he pays conspicuous respect to the music hall but because his poems, like the Beatles' songs, work for a kaleidoscopic effect, for fragmented patterns of sound that can bring historic masses into juxtaposition only to let them be fractured by other emerging and equally evocative fragments" (138–39). Poirier here attributes a modernist/avant-garde aesthetic sensibility to the Beatles, and argues for a critical practice derived primarily from modernism in order to understand and write adequately about their music.

This argument may seem to be, but in fact is not, another version of the pervasive, standard practice, common in high school and some college English courses, of presenting rock lyrics, not just by sixties writers such

as Dylan and Lennon but also by contemporary lyricists, on poetry, on a
continuum with the complex poetry, much of which is modernist, students
must also try to read. This pedagogical practice is designed to make poetry
itself more accessible to teenagers who find poetry alien, by using material
(rock lyrics) they feel more comfortable with than they do with "Poetry,"
which has become embedded in fear and loathing in contemporary academic culture. (The public cultures of hip-hop, spoken-word poetry, and
the poetry slam are an entirely different, quintessentially postmodern populist phenomenon.) This pedagogical practice reveals rock lyrics as themselves poetry, thereby demystifying poetry. This practice has nothing to do
with the historical continuity of rock music with modernism and the
avant-gardes that I am discussing here.

Poirier's brilliant readings of the *Sgt. Pepper's* songs are the best argument for the critical practice he advocates. Instead of imposing monolithic, simplifying intellectual, critical, historical, social, or political inter-
pretive categories on the songs (which would be part of "the shelving
process," as he calls it), he responds to the moment-by-moment experience of listening to them, bringing to bear on his acute, precise responses a
wide range of knowledge in order to understand the meanings not just of
the lyrics, or of the music, but of the performance. The result, again — very
much a critical performance of "learning from the Beatles" — is one of the
few accounts of Beatles songs that does justice to the often contradictory,
incongruous complexity of their effects, fully justifying the comparison to
Eliot. Poirier's reading of "A Day in the Life," by general agreement the
greatest song on this album and one of the few greatest in all rock music, is
the high point of the essay in this regard. It is difficult to quote from this
reading without quoting at length, since its texture is as richly interwoven
with references, readings, and responses as the song itself is with multiple,
densely layered meanings:

> In "A Day in the Life," the last song and a work of great power and
> historical grasp, the hapless man whose role is sung by Lennon wants to
> "turn on" himself and his lover — maybe us too — as a relief from the
> multiple controls exerted over life and the imagination by various and
> competing media. He is further confounded by the fact that these con-
> trols often impose themselves under the guise of entertainment. "Oh
> boy" — that sad little interjection of enthusiasm comes from Lennon's
> sweet, vulnerable voice into orchestral movements of intimidating,
> sometimes portentous momentum [the first verse of the song is quoted

here]. . . . The news in the paper is "rather sad" — as is the pun on "making the grade," a reference both to a man's success and to a car's movement up the road to what will be a crash — but the photograph is funny, so how does one respond to the suicide; suicide is a violent repudiation of the self but it mightn't have happened if the man had followed the orders of the traffic lights; . . . Lennon and McCartney in their songs seem as vulnerable as the man in "A Day in the Life" to the sights and sounds by which different media shape and then reshape reality. But their response isn't in any way as intimidated, and "turning on" isn't their only recourse. They can also tune in, literally to show how one shaped view of reality can be mocked out of existence by crossing it with another. (133–36)

At the same time, however, Poirier does not at all want to assimilate the Beatles, anachronistically, to high modernism. Quite the contrary — he discusses them (and frequently mentions Bob Dylan, also briefly The Who, as their peers) as part of contemporary youth culture and popular culture. He connects his project in this essay to the emerging field of cultural studies as "has been proposed for some years by Richard Hoggart and his colleagues at the Centre for Contemporary Cultural Studies at Birmingham University" (114–15), the founders of the field. The study of popular culture, which Poirier advocates here in addition to arguing for the great cultural significance and high aesthetic quality of the Beatles, has, as we know, become equated with cultural studies and with postmodern academic study in the humanities in general. In its democratization of all culture, which both contributes to and is produced by the undoing of the high-low divide of modernity, in which popular culture can, as Poirier demonstrates here, fully reward the sort of close critical scrutiny previously reserved for high-cultural productions, cultural studies links, as we saw with Barthes's *Mythologies*, the critical methods derived from modernism and the avant-gardes with the production and the study of popular culture. In "Learning from the Beatles," which immediately follows the title essay in *The Performing Self*, Poirier makes the further link, crucial to the emergence of postmodernity in the sixties, and to my argument here, of the subjective aesthetics of performance with the study and practice of popular culture. Poirier analyzes *Sgt. Pepper's* as a performance, not just in the obvious sense (the songs are performed by the Beatles) but in the senses he develops in "The Performing Self." In this analysis, the Beatles' performative constructions of subjectivity can be seen as a locus of political meanings. "Learning from the Beatles," therefore, enacts the sixties shift from modern heroic, transformative subjectivity, still clearly dominant in Poirier's work, to postmodern subject politics, through the democratizing vehicles of performative subjectivity and popular culture.

Poirier shows that the Beatles, as we have seen in his reading of "A Day in the Life," comment on the sort of media control of consciousness that Adorno, Horkheimer, and Marcuse attack in their modernist analyses, at the same time that they (the Beatles), as postmodern performers, preeminently use and extend the power of popular media. He shows us a range of postmodern aesthetic practices in the Beatles' work: the pervasive use of pastiche of clichéd popular musical styles throughout the album; repeated "mixing of styles and tones" (120); the pathos, vulnerability, and isolation of the subject position established in several of the songs, particularly, again, "A Day in the Life"; the continually redefined, reinvented subject positions from which the Beatles sing, within each song and across the album: "any self is invented as soon as any purpose is conceived" (122). Here is a characteristic moment of Poirier's analysis: "especially in the later songs, one of the interwoven strands is likely to be an echo of some familiar, probably clichéd musical, verbal, or dramatic formula. These echoes, like the soap-opera background music of 'She's Leaving Home' or the jaunty music-hall tones of 'When I'm Sixty-four,' have the enriching effect that allusiveness can bring to poetry: of expanding a situation toward the simultaneous condition of pathos, because the situation is seen as recurrent and therefore possibly insoluble, and comic, because the recurrence has finally passed into cliché" (120). No distinction is made here among what now appear incompatible modern and postmodern intellectual paradigms, social-political-cultural meanings, and aesthetic practices (the "enriching effect that allusiveness can bring to poetry" of modernism; the postmodernism of ironically displaced use of cliché).

This simultaneity of modern and postmodern modes is clearest in Poirier's introduction to these readings:

> In proposing that a developed appreciation of the popular arts can redirect and enhance an appreciation of all the arts, I am not suggesting that the only way lies in some unhistorical and unlearned close attentiveness to aspects of performance. An artist performs with the materials at hand, and these include whatever accents, phrases, images have gotten into one's head or voice, ears, or eyes. This poses, as we've seen,

a problem of *self*-expression and "sincerity." It also offers an enormous opportunity to certain artists who feel challenged by it. Such artists tend, as in the examples of Joyce, Eliot, and others discussed in earlier chapters, to be unusually allusive both in their direct references and in their styles. They aren't sure — and in this they are classical and Johnsonian in tendency — that anything in their modes of expression really belongs to them. The *Sgt. Pepper* album is an example of how these same tendencies are at work in areas of the popular arts and are perhaps indigenous to the best art of any kind now being performed. (119)

We see here immediately the seamless intermeshing of Poirier's postmodern advocacy of the study of popular culture and "the popular arts," his understanding of what is most important about the aesthetic practices of the popular arts of the sixties, and his study of high modernist writers. He points particularly to a key postmodern aesthetic of unoriginality — both the questioning of the possibility of originality ("an artist performs with the materials at hand . . . [these artists] aren't sure . . . that anything in their modes of expression really belongs to them"), and also the deliberate abrogation of the modernist drive toward and valorization of originality and heroic individualism: the pastiche of styles, historical periods, and subjectivities that, perhaps more than any other aesthetic practice, characterizes postmodern cultural production. But rather than using the notion of what we now call pastiche to distinguish contemporary (sixties) from modernist aesthetic practice, he links these sixties aesthetic practices, within the dominant modernity of the moment — again, as if they were part of a single, self-consistent formation — to the allusiveness of Joyce and Eliot (and to canonical literary history in general through "classical and Johnsonian"). At this historical moment in the sixties, the dominant modern and the emergent postmodern were in fact indistinguishably intermeshed, intertwined. The allusiveness of modernism and the pastiche of postmodernism, which now seem clearly distinct from and even opposite to one another (particularly to Jameson), not only appear to be, but they *are*, indistinguishable in the sixties; not just for Poirier, but in the general sense of continuity with the liberatory, oppositional aesthetic and political projects of modernity experienced by participants in the sixties movements practicing modes of pastiche. And at this utopian historical moment in the sixties, modernism is not yet seen as the elitist, hegemonic high culture that becomes the obverse of democratic, oppositional popular culture in postmodernity. Poirier can imagine that "a developed appreciation of the popular arts can redirect and enhance an appreciation of all the arts." The "best art of any kind" is the proper object of attention, and we can understand it better by "learning from the Beatles." Popular culture and high culture are one. The contrast between Poirier's position here and Venturi et al.'s contemporaneous, polemically pro-postmodern, antimodernist position in *Learning from Las Vegas* could not be more stark, and yet their projects, of "learning from" popular culture while situating it powerfully in relation to the history of what we now consider high culture, overlap to a very great extent. The difference is precisely the difference the sixties made, in the evolution of its democratizing, egalitarian, populist projects, between the modern and the postmodern.

CHAPTER ELEVEN

Laing's Politics of the Self

R. D. Laing's highly influential 1967 book *The Politics of Experience* (PE) is characteristic of a crucial sixties genre, which includes works, mostly philosophical but also psychoanalytic and/or largely unclassifiable, by writers such as Norman O. Brown (whose 1959 *Life Against Death* and 1966 *Love's Body* were on a par with PE in iconic importance and influence, and also in subsequent oblivion), Carlos Castañeda (whose work became a New Age cottage industry), Erich Fromm, Paul Goodman (whose 1960 *Growing Up Absurd* was an initiatory text of the sixties), A. S. Neill (*Summerhill*, 1960) and other gurus of the progressive education movement, Wilhelm Reich of orgone fame (an earlier avatar, for Marcuse as well), and Alan Watt, who popularized Buddhism for the American sixties. These writers and their works, represented here by PE, inhabit and expound a characteristic sixties lifeworld of manifest alienation and thwarted, stifled authenticity. Their message is a call to a spiritual, psychic, Marcusean Great Refusal. Like Marcuse, Laing locates hope for change — which must be revolutionary change to count at all — in individual consciousness: "this book begins and ends with the person."[1] Unlike

Marcuse, and like the other writers he represents here, Laing, a psychoanalyst, does not attach the potentiality for revolutionary change to material social conditions. Rather, change for Laing can come only as a result of a collective set of acts of willed individual self-liberation. This view, in effect redefining politics as a question of subjectivity (consciousness) rather than structural social change, made Laing profoundly influential for the counterculture, and for those in the New Left who believed that revolutionary social change must be preceded, or at least accompanied, by a change in consciousness, as Marcuse himself argued. For Marcuse, only a liberated consciousness could act to realize the liberatory potentiality inherent in advanced technology. For Laing, the liberation of authentic consciousness from the constraints of alienation is itself sufficient to bring about revolutionary social change. Laing's emphasis on what I am calling here "the politics of the self," or "subject politics," resonated throughout sixties ideologies, not just countercultural but also political, as we saw in *The Port Huron Statement*. Again, this "subject politics" is at once an endpoint of the modern and an inception of the postmodern.

The Politics of Experience now seems at once quaint in its rage, disgust, and radical fervor, and also, with a slight realignment of tone, much like the innumerable New Age and popular psychological self-help books of postmodernity. When it appeared, PE seemed, at least to me and the people I knew in the university New Left and counterculture, to be one of the few most important and powerful statements yet to appear, not so much of what we already knew or believed, or what would be easy to embrace, but rather of what we must, with enormous difficulty and painful self-reconstitution, come to understand and use to reshape our lives and world. For me, in any case, Laing, more than anyone else I had read, spoke through his passionate, poetic intellectual writing to my sense of what was most deeply wrong with the world and what must be done to right it. News of this book spread rapidly among my peers; most people I knew read it. Laing seemed to me a more passionate, literary Marcuse, saying roughly the same things but in a more moving and compelling way.

The paucity in Laing's writing of Marxist or other explicitly political language and thought did not at the time separate his work from Marcuse's or any of the other political or sociological writing that influenced the New Left — it did not place his work in a distinct "psychoanalytic" or "spiritual" category over against a "political" category. Laing cites not just Marcuse and Fanon, who also deploy psychoanalytic ideas in their political analyses, but also Baran and Sweezy's *Monopoly Capital*, for example (another bible for sixties radicals), the violent ravages of North American and European colonialism, the war in Vietnam, as well as (like Marcuse) Romantic, modernist, and avant-garde poets and novelists. He was part of a continuum of radical thought and writing influential in the sixties, with Carlos Castañeda or Alan Watt at one end and Mao or Marx and Engels at the other.[2] Like Marcuse, Laing was part of the ongoing modern, particularly twentieth-century, synthetic project, generally rejected by postmodernity, of conjoining not just Marx and Freud — politics and psychoanalysis — but also philosophy, aesthetics, ethics, cultural history, in a unified, integrated theory and critique of all human culture and society, culminating in a totalized, utopian plan for revolutionary change: the ultimate "master narrative."[3] Laing describes his project as a response to the "need for a strong, firm primary theory that can draw each practice and theory into relation to the central concerns of all forms of psychotherapy. . . . Most fundamentally, a critical theory must be able to place all theories and practices within the scope of a total vision of the ontological structure of being human" (48).

The central message of PE, which resonates clearly with that of *One-Dimensional Man*, can be summed up in a sentence from Laing's introduction (ODM is in fact cited in the introduction): "humanity is estranged from its authentic possibilities" (second page of unpaginated three-page "Introduction"). This estrangement, as the word "authentic" signals, is primarily a Sartrean existential alienation (Sartre was a major influence for Laing), at once psychic, political, social, spiritual, and phenomenological. For Laing, as for Sartre and Marcuse, human beings in alienated society introject their reified lifeworld, substituting it for the authenticity from which they have been utterly, but possibly not irrevocably, divorced. Laing attacks "the disarray of personal worlds of experience whose repression, denial, splitting, introjection, projection, etc. — whose general desecration and profanation — our civilization is based upon. When our personal worlds are rediscovered and allowed to reconstitute themselves, we first discover a shambles. Bodies half-dead; genitals dissociated from heart; heart severed from head; head dissociated from genitals. Without inner unity . . . Man cut off from his own mind, cut off equally from his own body — a half-crazed creature in a mad world" (55). Most of PE consists of jeremiads such as this against the condition of estrangement from authenticity — "this book attempts to document some forms of our contemporary violation of ourselves" (unpaginated third page of "Introduction"); most of this jeremiad is located within modernity's utopian project.

The opening language of the introduction, particularly, reflects the pervasive sense among sixties radicals and counterculturalists that existing conditions were utterly intolerable and must be changed totally in order not just for life to improve, or for humanity to realize its authentic or liberated potential, but for life to continue at all in any meaningful way. This apocalyptic sense of imminent upheaval, either annihilating or redemptive, is one of the least currently accessible aspects of the sixties structure of feeling, but one of the most decisive.[4] Laing's opening language is also characteristic of the dramatic intensity of his tone and address to the reader, an intensity that now, in postmodernity's cool, ironic affective landscape, rings melodramatic, exaggerated, overly earnest and impassioned, but is characteristic of much sixties writing: "few books today, are forgivable. Black on the canvas, silence on the screen, an empty white sheet of paper, are perhaps feasible. There is little conjunction of truth and social 'reality.' Around us are pseudo-events, to which we adjust with a false consciousness adapted to see these events as true and real, and even as beautiful. In the society of men the truth resides now less in what things are than in what they are not. Our social realities are so ugly if seen in the light of exiled truth, and beauty is almost no longer possible if it is not a lie" (unpaginated first page of "Introduction").[5] (The closing sentence of the book, culminating a visionary "trip" that acts as a coda for the text, narrating Laing's own quest for truth and authenticity, which, Joyce-like, he glimpses in the figure of the "Bird of Paradise," the title of this section, is equally characteristic: "If I could turn you on, if I could drive you out of your wretched mind, if I could tell you I would let you know" [190; also 185–86]). Laing here speaks Marcuse's Great Refusal. He speaks it in part in the language of the avant-garde: the black canvas, the silent screen, the empty white sheet of paper are familiar avant-garde tropes signifying a transcendent silence or emptiness that is the only authentic aesthetic response to an utterly bankrupt social order. This avant-garde aesthetic is not postmodern — it is informed by modernity's belief in a real, unitary, transcendent "truth" that is "exiled" by alienated society, and a similarly knowable, potentially consensual "beauty" that is "almost no longer possible" because it is so utterly divorced from that "truth."

The introduction is characteristic of the text. Most of *PE* is located clearly in the modern: "our task is both to experience and to conceive the concrete, that is to say, reality in its fullness and wholeness. But this is quite impossible, immediately. Experientially and conceptually, we have fragments" (22). This formulation evokes the works of literary high modernism, where "fullness" and "wholeness" are the elusive, yearned-for ultimate goals of complex texts that map, in form and content, the bleak modern terrain of fragmentation. The revolutionary Freud who underwrites this apocalyptic ideology would be unrecognizable to a postmodern, Lacanian Freud: "the relevance of Freud to our time is largely his insight and, to a very considerable extent, his *demonstration* that the *ordinary* person is a shriveled, desiccated fragment of what a person can be" (25–26).

Laing's first chapter, "Persons and Experience," establishes the parameters of the book's central arguments. Laing poses the question, "can human beings be persons today? Can a man be his actual self with another man or woman? . . . *are persons possible* in our present situation? . . . Is love possible? Is freedom possible?" (23). (Note, crucially, the characteristic prefeminist assumption that "person" or "human being" equals "man"; Laing wants to know whether a "man" can "be his actual self with . . . a woman," but not whether the reciprocal might be possible — the woman is still fully other here.) This language is, again, characteristic of the sixties in its passionate tone and unapologetically high level of generality.

The authentic self is associated for Laing with the innocent child, as it is in much Romantic sixties ideology (Blake was a crucial figure in the sixties) — particularly that of the progressive education movement, with Neill's *Summerhill* among the most visible and popular of its texts. This idealized child figure, unwarped by alienation, is associated with derepressed bodily desire (Marcuse's Reichian eros), and with the liberated unconscious, as we have seen in Burroughs, of fantasy and dream: "as adults, we have forgotten most of our childhood, not only its contents but its flavor; as men of the world, we hardly know of the existence of the inner world: we barely remember our dreams, and make little sense of them when we do; as for our bodies, we retain just sufficient proprioceptive sensations to coordinate our movements and to ensure the minimal requiements for biosocial survival . . . an intensive discipline of unlearning is necessary for *anyone* before one can begin to experience the world afresh, with innocence, truth and love" (26).

Laing proposes the realm of fantasy, in which alienated humans can gain access to their childhood, their dreams, and their bodies, as a potential antidote to this "almost unbelievable devastation of our experience" (27). He then links fantasy to poetry, or the literary, which "enabl[es] being to emerge from nonbeing," and "can be the occasion of that great liberation when one makes the transition from being afraid of nothing [the dissociated condition of alienation in which fear is repressed] to the realization that there is nothing to fear [the liberated condition in which disabling fear is transcended]" (42). These positions, though framed very differently by Laing, in much more mystical terms, are familiar from Marcuse, for whom the "aesthetic dimension" is the most accessible currently available location of an incipient revolutionary consciousness.

The above cursory summary is not intended to do justice to Laing's work, which has far more intellectual gravitas than I have so far indicated.[6] He draws not just on a deep knowledge of Sartrean existentialism, which also assumes a knowledge of the Marxist intellectual tradition, but also on an eclectic array of psychoanalytic thought, including Winnicott's object relations theory, and on Husserlian phenomenology, as well as on his own earlier, pioneering work on the dynamics of schizophrenia (particularly in *The Divided Self*, 1965, another key sixties text). My purpose in the above summary is not so much to elucidate Laing's thought, whose precise contours, merits, and/or deficiencies are not germane to my argument, but rather, in addition to understanding this book as a marker of the politicization of subjectivity, and subjectification of politics, in the sixties and in postmodernity, to demonstrate the forceful, dominant presence in it of modernity's metanarratives.

Even in the first chapter, however, dominated as it is by characteristic ideologies of sixties modernity, Laing stakes out postmodern positions. In his object relations–informed, incipiently postmodern analysis of what would now be called intersubjectivity, which Laing calls "interexperience," he attacks, as did Marcuse, the Cartesian dualism on which much modern thought is premised. While Marcuse found in Cartesian dualism a rationalistic corruption of the thesis/antithesis binary informing the dialectic, a corruption that enabled the development of scientific rationality as domination, Laing, in utter contradiction of his own Manichean view of alienation squelching authenticity, seems, in one phase of his argument, to want to dispense with dualism altogether. The attack on dualism, on the binary, is pervasive in postmodern thought. In discussing what he means by his key term "experience," Laing refuses the Cartesian dualism of "inner" and "outer":

Experience is invisible to the other. But experience is not "subjective" rather than "objective," not "inner" rather than "outer." . . . This distinction between outer and inner usually refers to the distinction between behavior and experience; but sometimes it refers to some experiences that are supposed to be "inner" in contrast to others that are "outer." More accurately this is a distinction between different modalities of experience, namely, perception (as outer) in contrast to imagination, etc. (as inner). But perception, imagination, fantasy, reverie, dreams, memory, are simply different *modalities of experience*, none more "inner" or "outer" than any other. (20)

Laing goes on to discuss the way in which the reification of "inner" and "outer" "does reflect a split in our experience. We seem to live in two worlds, and many people are aware only of the 'outer' rump" (21). The false inner-outer dualism thus becomes reintegrated into, or reabsorbed by, a modern paradigm, as a measure of the alienation Laing attacks in this book, just as Cartesian dualism is a location of the domination Marcuse attacks in ODM. Laing actually cites Marcuse here: "it is not enough to destroy one's own and other people's experience. One must overlay this devastation by a false consciousness inured, as Marcuse puts it, to its own falsity" (57). In a characteristically impassioned, eloquent, visionary personal statement, Laing makes clear his Manichean vision of an ultimate truth and good that is "desecrated" and "profaned" by this false consciousness: "I am a specialist, God help me, in events in inner space and time, in experiences called thoughts, images, reveries, dreams, visions, hallucinations, dreams of memories, memories of dreams, memories of visions, dreams of hallucinations, refractions of refractions of refractions of that original Alpha and Omega of experience and reality, that Reality on whose repression, denial, splitting, projection, falsification, and general desecration and profanation our civilization as much as on anything is based. We live equally out of our bodies and out of our minds" (58–59). Underlying the repudiation of the Cartesian dualism is the bedrock sixties dualism of alienation and authenticity. The incantatory, repetitive language, and the tone of prophetic outrage, just as much as the totalized, apocalyptic vision, are characteristic of sixties writing as final flowering and endpoint of modernism/modernity.

Similar dualisms underlie Laing's vision: "love and violence, properly speaking, are polar opposites. Love lets the other be, but with affection and concern. Violence attempts to constrain the other's freedom, to force him to act in the way we desire, but with ultimate lack of concern, with indifference to the other's own existence or destiny. We are effectively destroying ourselves by violence masquerading as love" (58). Throughout *PE*, Laing denounces this split between authentic and alienated worlds, as we have seen, as the central deformation of human life, assuming that the inner/outer split is real rather than apparent. In referring to his earlier book *The Divided Self*, for example, he says, "I devoted a book, *The Divided Self*, to describing some versions of the split between experience and behavior. . . . The therapists, too, are in a world in which the inner is already split from the outer . . . we are a generation of men so estranged from the inner world that many are arguing that it does not exist" (54). But with "*seem* to live in two worlds" (emphasis added), Laing, again, undermines, or shifts toward the postmodern, his own analysis of the radical split between an alienated actuality and an authentic potentiality, realized in fantasy, dreams, and the aesthetic. Though the split is unnecessary, according to Laing — it represents the violation of the deeper truth of the unity of inner and outer — it also marks the necessity of the Marcusean Great Refusal: if "inner" and "outer" constitute a false dualism, deformed and ideal reality do not. Yet the commitment to the indifferentiability of inner and outer underlying Laing's vision is different in its implications from his fully modern notion of an authentic inner world of fantasy, the dream, the child, and eros, corrupted by an alienated, violent, exploitative external social order. This indifferentiability of inner and outer undoes the revolutionary dialectical structure of opposition, resistance, refusal — Marcuse's terms. For both Laing and Marcuse, the attack on dualism, born of and articulated in the service of a utopian modern agenda, is a pivot to the postmodern transformation of dualism into a limitless field of difference, or indifference, and of the ideological repudiation of all dualism as the defining structure marking and produced by the oppressive self-other binary.

At the beginning of the chapter titled "Us and Them" — an attack on precisely the self-other binary, particularly in the form of the fearful, defensive demonization of the other that culminates in the cold war — Laing articulates explicitly a position that will become the postmodern repudiation of all master narratives. He attacks the conformism that had become a familiar object of contempt in the wake of the fifties, as we saw in *The Port Huron Statement*: "the history of heresies of all kinds testifies to more than the tendency to break off communication (excommunication) with those who hold different dogmas or opinions; it bears witness to our intolerance of different *fundamental structures of experience*. We seem to need to share a communal meaning to human existence, to give with others a common sense to the world, to maintain a *consensus*" (77). Beyond the alienated blandness and passivity of conformism as it was denounced in PHS, we have here a nearly demonic Sartrean mode of alienation, in which "reified projections of our own freedom are then introjected"; "these projected-introjected reifications . . . tak[e] on the appearance of things. They are not things ontologically. But they are pseudo-things" (77). Although Laing is working from a profoundly modern, Marxist-existentialist view of aliena-tion, his attack on this "pseudo-thing" of "projected-introjected" con-sensus expands to include all versions of "communal meaning to human existence." For Laing, the existence of consensus, or communal meaning, is a sign of alienation, which assumes the Marcusean domination of power elites over relatively or varyingly disenfranchised people. Laing refers reg-ularly, throughout the book, to the Vietnam War and third world libera-tion struggles as well as to the alienation from potential authenticity of white, Western "man." It is a short step from that position to the postmod-ern view of consensus as oppressive master narrative, always working in the service of precisely the hegemony attacked and deconstructed by the postmodern post-'s.

One key master narrative both undermined by postmodernity and re-pudiated by much postmodern ideology is the natural or organic biolog-ical nuclear family (second-wave feminism and gay liberation are also crucial here, as we will see in chapter 14). Later in this chapter, Laing's analysis of group identity as "mirage," with the family as key instance and prime villain, also comes very close not only to postmodern attacks on the family but also to more general postmodern, particularly queer, critiques of the phantasmatic nature of the processes of identification that produce group identity, or formations of a "we." For Laing, all such group identi-ties are versions of the alienated, defensive, projected-introjected "us" that exists on the basis of demonizing an othered "them." Laing argues that any group in which all members experience the group as a "we" "is not a social object out there in space. It is the quite extraordinary being formed by each person's synthesis of the same multiplicity [of identifications] into "We," and each person's synthesis of the multiplicity of syntheses. Looked at from the outside, the group comes into view as a social object, lending, by its appearance . . . credence to the organismic illusion. This is a mirage; as one approaches closer there is no organism anywhere" (86). The mirage "we" par excellence for Laing is the conventional nuclear family, in which "each person may . . . act on the other person to coerce him (by sympathy, blackmail, indebtedness, guilt, gratitude or naked violence) into maintaining his interiorization of the group unchanged" (87). Laing repeatedly writes of the family as the primary vehicle and location of the general violence done to human beings. But all groups that exist by means of a consensual "we," from nations to political parties to utopian communes and radical political movements — "we the people" — come under the purview of this attack. Again, though Laing is ultimately writing in defense of a deeply modern view of potential authenticity and wholeness — "We and They must be transcended in the totality of the human race" (98) — his critique of the oppressive "we," with that modern underpinning, crucial for him and for the sixties, simply fallen away, becomes a central tenet of postmodern thought. It is a powerful presence in the postmodern structure of feeling, where all articulations of "we" are either oppressive if accorded a false essentiality, or self-consciously partial and performative in their constructedness.

Much more could be said about this book, again, from the points of view of a variety of intellectual preoccupations. But for my concerns in this argument about *PE* as one of the few most important and vanished sixties radical-countercultural texts, the significant issue is that its overall intellectual structure depends on the undifferentiated contiguity and seamless intermeshing of dominant modern and emergent postmodern paradigms, which have subsequently sundered into clearly differentiable, in fact often antithetical, paradigms, in the postmodern dominant.

CHAPTER TWELVE

Tell Me Lies about Vietnam

It was the war in Vietnam, and the experience of protesting against it, that "radicalized" most of the students who joined the New Left in the sixties ("radicalized" was the term used to describe the process of opting for a Marcusean Great Refusal, as opposed "working within the system," as many "liberal" antiwar organizations continued to do). I do not think (and this is essentially by now a truism) that the New Left agendas for universal social and economic equality and justice, personal meaningfulness, and participatory democracy embodied in *The Port Huron Statement* would have taken hold as they did without the urgency of the war, particularly the urgency of the war drafting, wounding, and killing college students. Everyone in this cohort knew someone who was killed or wounded in Vietnam; most male students were in danger of being drafted.

It had been possible to support the Civil Rights movement ardently and avoid radicalization. Civil Rights was an optimistic movement, based on faith in the potential fairness of the U.S. democratic system, and on an underlying belief that sufficient moral pressure would push the nation toward realizing its inherent, true, as yet unrealized democratic destiny.

Kennedy and Johnson seemed to be sympathetic to the movement's ultimate goals, if not to its tactics. It appeared to be just a question of overcoming local, (what then seemed) residual, antiquated racism — manifesting
itself as segregation and remediable by integration — with determination at
the national level. The late-sixties shift from Civil Rights to Black Power
divided liberals from radicals among both blacks and whites, but liberals of
any race, class, region, or ethnicity could support Civil Rights unambivalently while at the same time supporting Kennedy and Johnson with
equal confidence.

The Vietnam War was an entirely different story. It was waged by the
authors of the New Frontier and the Great Society. My friends and I
worked for Young Citizens for Johnson in the 1964 election — we were
saving the world from the terrifying Barry Goldwater, making it safe for
racial equality and the end of poverty, first in the United States and then, in
our poignantly ignorant optimism, everywhere. Like most of the rest of
the population, I did not actively oppose the war — I suffered it in a detached, passive way — until the nature of the war changed, and the "body
counts" began piling up, in late 1965 and early 1966. I did not like the idea
of the war, but I told myself that those great wise men, who were going to
end racism and poverty, must know what they were doing — they must
know things I, like any ordinary citizen, could not possibly know; things
that made fighting this war, which seemed so pointless and needlessly
destructive, a necessary thing to do. It was precisely this sort of passive
deference to (white, male, middle-aged) authority, and sense of separation
from and inadequacy to decision-making, that the sixties radicalism of
participatory democracy and empowerment of minorities and women
challenged. One of the primary inspirations for that challenge was the
increasingly apparent horror of the Vietnam War. The fact that it was the
orchestrators of the Great Society, not Barry Goldwater and his ilk, who
were waging this war, and continually, repeatedly telling unconscionable
and egregious lies about it, created the powerful conviction of the deeply
untrustworthy hypocrisy of all vested authority, of anyone in any way
associated with "the establishment," whatever his (no women yet) ostensible claims to enlightened liberalism, that characterized sixties radicalism.

I joined SDS in 1967, relatively late. Though much about its vociferous,
defiant stance and lawbreaking tactics frightened me and put me off, it had
far and away the strongest commitment of any group I saw on campus to
ending the war, and by then it appeared to me that ending the war must be
the highest priority of anyone with a conscience. It would be difficult to

overestimate the horror of the Vietnam War as a daily fact of U.S. life, especially campus life, in the late sixties. The vividness of the death, maiming, burning, terror, and unthinkable destruction of a small country on the evening news, coupled with the immediacy of the draft, made it feel as if nothing else, nothing good in life, could have any meaning or reality while this savagery continued.

Hundreds of important books, stories, and essays, from a number of points of view and in a number of genres and styles, were written, and continue to be written, about this war; many important films were and will be made and works of art produced.[1] As with texts emerging from or connecting to the other defining historical events I discuss in this book, I do not survey or account for the range of these works.[2] Instead, I will discuss Frances FitzGerald's 1972 *Fire in the Lake* (FL), certainly one of the few best Vietnam War books, as a text whose treatment of the war is particularly relevant to my concerns here.[3]

FL is as scathing, definitive an attack on the war in all its aspects and manifestations as any that was produced. FitzGerald's magnificent writing was then, and still remains to me, one of the most eloquent and moving denunciations of the war I have seen, most powerful in the almost cool, understated but burning lucidity of its passion. The following passage from FL also makes clear the emotional investments of the sixties antiwar movement in the Vietnamese people and against the U.S. government, investments that seem scandalous in the current ultrapatriotic moment, in which the victims of the Vietnam War are seen in the United States as primarily, almost exclusively, the American soldiers who fought in it. For the antiwar movement, however, the Vietnamese people were the heroes, and the U.S. government was the colonialist aggressor:

> American officials, who have witnessed only the division and paralysis their presence has created among their own "allies," tend to underestimate the capacities of the Vietnamese. The American war has created a social and economic chaos, but it has not stripped the Vietnamese of their vitality and powers of resistance. The Vietnamese survived the invasions of the Mongol hordes, and they may similarly survive the American war.
>
> The first source of strength in the south is the National Liberation Front. With North Vietnamese help the NLF has fought the United States for over a decade and remained undefeated. Standing in the place of all Vietnamese, it has carried on the tradition of Le Loi and those

other Vietnamese heroes who waged the millennium long struggle against foreign domination. . . . Their victory would not be the victory of one foreign power over another but the victory of the Vietnamese people — northerners and southerners alike. Far from being a civil war, the struggle of the NLF was an assertion of the principle of national unity that the Saigon government has endorsed and betrayed. With the North Vietnamese the Front leaders faced up to the threats, the promises, and finally the overwhelming military power of the United States. They held out against a country that could never be defeated by force of arms, and they provided an example of courage and endurance that measures with any in modern history. (583–84)

FitzGerald delineates in scrupulous detail the history not just of the American war but of the continuous, thirty-year French-American colonial war in Vietnam, supplying names, dates, numbers, and facts in great and devastating abundance. But what makes this book so remarkable is not so much the wealth of detail but the fact that it narrates the history of the war just as much from the Vietnamese as from the American point of view. When we in the United States think now of the Vietnam War, we think primarily of what it did to American society, and to Americans, particularly the soldiers who fought there.[4] Most American books and films about the war focus on the American experience of it, however opposed to the war they are or sympathetic they are to the Vietnamese. But the protests against the war in the sixties focused primarily not on damage to Americans but on the unspeakable damage inflicted by the United States on the Vietnamese. FitzGerald weaves together both kinds of damage.

FitzGerald focuses primarily not on the Vietnam War within U.S. history but on the position of this war within the centuries-long cultural and political history of Vietnam, and on the Americans' cataclysmic ignorance and lack of interest in this history ("an extreme removal from reality" [485]) — a lack of interest in who the Vietnamese actually are and what war the Vietnamese were actually fighting: "an American reporter, experienced in Vietnam, once said to me, 'I finally realized we'd never win this war when I noticed that all of the streets in Saigon were named after Vietnamese heroes who fought against foreign invaders.' The street names were in a sense the perfect metaphor for the resistance of Saigon. Though written in Roman letters and used every day by Americans, they were perfectly incomprehensible to those who did not know a great deal about

Vietnamese history. The xenophobia of Saigon was hidden in plain sight"
(512).

This lack of interest in Vietnamese history, as FitzGerald makes clear —
this is one of her central themes — is not a result merely of perverse ignorance, criminal indifference, willful self-deception, or arrogant ethnocen-
trism, though all of those play a significant role at various junctures and in
the decisions of various major figures. Rather it is produced by a worldview so at odds with the realities of the Vietnamese worldview that the
latter becomes literally invisible to Americans. The essential invisibility of
Vietnam as it sees itself to Americans pursuing the war is in large part a
result of the fact that the United States was continuing the French colonial
war, and adopting with it the essential assumptions and relations of colonialism. The Vietnamese were never seen as having an ancient, rich, complex, particular social, political, economic, spiritual, and cultural way of
life entirely separate and different from that of the West and legitimate in
its own terms. They were rather the "gooks," orientalized, barely human,
inferior in every way; lazy, stupid, shiftless, slow, devious, dishonest, unreliable, backward, corrupt: "American officers liked to call the area ouside
GVN control 'Indian country' . . . the Americans were once again em-
barked upon a heroic and (for themselves) painless conquest of an inferior
race" (491–92). My Lai was "not exceptional to the American war"
(494), because (quoting an American soldier) "when you shot someone
you didn't think you were shooting a human" (496).[5] There could be no
question that the "mission" of the Americans, like that of their European
colonial predecessors, was to crush these backward upstart barbarians,
then civilize them and haul them into modernity. FitzGerald calls the
American war against the Vietnamese "a policy of genocide" that "no one
in the American government consciously planned" (502) — it was rather
the logical result of the view of the Vietnamese as "gooks," in which
arbitrary "beating and crude torture" of "Viet Cong suspects" was routine, and "many soldiers used to carry around in their wallets pictures they
had taken of Vietnamese men and women in obscene positions, obscenely
wounded" (496; Herr and others confirm this fact).

FitzGerald uses, in a way that is now familiar in postcolonial studies,
the narrative of *The Tempest* to dramatize and make clear this colonial
paradigm. Prospero is the colonialist, first French, then American, who
invades and takes over the land; Caliban is the Vietnamese whom Prospero degrades and enslaves, but who is ambivalent toward Prospero because of the great power and the riches of wealth and knowledge Prospero

might one day share with Caliban. Ariel is the puppet South Vietnamese power elite, utterly dependent on and in thrall to Prospero, his tool and confidante, who, like Caliban, is deeply resentful of Prospero and wants freedom from him, but, unlike Caliban, cannot afford to express his rage and resistance directly, so must resort to passive resistance and concealed subversion.

Even this "civilizing" colonial mission, however, to whatever extent Americans actually believed in it, was a cover or rationalization for the underlying cold war mission, which was to "fight Communism." Vietnam was a domino that must not fall, a pawn that must not be taken by the wrong player, in that East-West game of world-historically high stakes. (Finally, even "fighting Communism" became a cover for not losing a war.) The notion that America was intervening to support a "freely elected democratic government" in South Vietnam in a "civil war" resulting from an "invasion" by the "Communist" north of the "democratic" south was always a fiction the Americans waging the war consciously and cynically used to cover their actual cold war agenda (even the communism of the North Vietnamese and NLF was a very particular, Vietnamese version of communism, just as traditionalist and nationalist as communist). In fact, as FitzGerald demonstrates at great length and with great particularity and precision, there was no real political entity "South Vietnam," nor was there ever a real government of that entity that had any shred of legitimacy. The governments of South Vietnam during the American war were entirely puppets of the Americans: "created, financed, and defended by Americans, the Saigon regime was less a government than an act of the American will — an artificial military bureaucracy that since the beginning of the Diem regime had governed no one and represented no one except upon occasion the northern Catholics. The U.S. attempt to polarize the Vietnamese between communists and noncommunists made as much sense as an attempt to polarize the American people between Southerners and Catholics: the two groups were not in any way equivalent. Indeed, there were not two sides at all" (422–23). The Vietnam War was a war of the West — the French and then the Americans — against the only legitimate indigenous political entity in Vietnam that had any degree of widespread support among the Vietnamese people, which was the government of North Vietnam and, in the south, the NLF.

What makes *FL* so important to my concerns in this book is not just the power with which FitzGerald narrates, demonstrates, and documents these conclusions (this is a brilliantly written book), and not just the great extent to which she narrates the war from the point of view of the Vietnamese. It is the particular way in which her underlying assumptions, the premises on which her view of Vietnam, and her approach to writing about it, are based, are at once dominantly modern and emergently postmodern. In the clash she constructs of a vast, stark, dualistic, abstract universe of the United States and a local, particular, personalized, embodied universe of Vietnam, FitzGerald makes a postmodern case for the catastrophic limitations and destructiveness of Western modernity. For example:

> Over the years of war American officials spoke of the NLF as if it were an illustration of some larger principle, some larger menace to the security of the United states. To Walt Rostow the National Liberation Front was but one instance of the "disease of Communism." . . . To Robert McNamara it was a test case for the "new" Communist strategy of promoting "wars of national liberation" around the world. To many American military men it was but an example of the threat that guerrillas in general provided to the established governments of the earth. By this attempt at generalization . . . the officials reduced the NLF to the status of a symbol and, again, obscured its achievement. For the Vietnamese revolution in the south was in many ways unique. If it belonged to a category, then that category was extremely small. (187)

At the same time, as this passage also implies, FitzGerald's treatment of the U.S. conduct of the war is premised on the quintessential modern paradigm, at the center of her book, of the big lie (the Big Lie): repeatedly, what U.S. military and government officials say for propaganda purposes, in order to continue pursuing the war, is a deliberately manufactured lie, a wilful reversal of the underlying truth: "in 1966 Senator George Aiken of Vermont suggested that the United States government simply announce that it had won the war and then withdraw its troops from Vietnam. In refusing to take this plausible alternative of ignoring reality altogether, Johnson condemned his officials who worked on Vietnam to the excruciating mental task of holding reality and the official version of reality together as they moved farther and farther apart" (488). Like Marcuse, FitzGerald wants her readers to see through and refuse this lie: to enact the Great Refusal. On one side there is the lie of wealthy, all-powerful authority; on the other, the truth of the poor, beleaguered, horribly oppressed people. This is a quintessential sixties paradigm. It is also a quintessential paradigm of modernity, where truth and lies are as separate and totally opposed to one another as socialism and capitalism, good and evil, revolution and repression, resistance and domination, utopia and one-dimensional society. In postmodernity, these dualisms are complicated, internally differentiated, interwoven, and relativized, in the Foucauldian field of multiple power flows and the Deleuze-Guattarian universe of nonhierarchically branching rhizomes. Knowledge in postmodernity is no longer governed by neatly, diametrically opposed "truths" or "lies"; there are situated knowledges, complex, overlapping, intersectional affinities and differences, mutually constitutive or opposed particularities, varyingly incommensurable points of view. FitzGerald also, in her treatment of the particularity of Vietnamese history and culture, invokes these postmodern paradigms of specificity and difference; in her predominantly nonjudgmental tone, and her careful precision concerning particular people's motivations and material circumstances at particular historical moments — people from among every major American and Vietnamese set of actors involved in the war — she also juxtaposes the emergent postmodern universe of complex, intersecting relationality with the dominant modern universe of the Big Lie.

The lies of Vietnam produced and culminated in the lies of Watergate. The drama of uncovering and punishing the Watergate lies is a good candidate for marker not just of the end of the long "decade" of the sixties but also of modernity itself. After Watergate, in postmodernity, we expect and take for granted not the Big Lie, or any massive, totalized hidden truth it covers, but rather ambiguous evasions, partial truths, inevitable "spin" and selective manipulation of fact; multiple, conflicting, variously interested, situated, and relative versions of reality, all part of the language games of politics. When there is no longer any unitary, transparent truth, there can be no Big Lie.[6]

The title of FitzGerald's book, as she explains in her opening "Note on the Title," is taken from the I Ching, the Chinese "Book of Changes." "Fire in the Lake" is "the image of revolution," as FitzGerald states in her first sentence. The book does not address directly the question of revolution as it was discussed and understood among sixties radicals (total, utopian transformation of all political, social, and cultural structures), nor is the word "revolution" used in the book to describe the war as fought by North Vietnam and the NLF. Nonetheless, using the I Ching hexagram for revolution as the title of the book, taken from the title of the closing chapter, in which FitzGerald's damnation of the war is closest to the surface of the writing, is a signal gesture toward locating the book within the discourse of sixties radicalism, the primary goal and slogan of which was to "make the revolution." But it also, especially in its use of the I Ching, locates the book within the particular, historically specific meaning of "revolution" for the Vietnamese, for whom "it forms the mental picture of change within the society" (vii) — a meaning quite different from the meanings of revolution in the Western, Marxist, or participatory-democratic contexts. And at the same time, in this complex layering of reference and context, the use of the I Ching connects the book to the counterculture as well as to radicalism and to the history of Vietnamese culture — the I Ching was central to the sixties countercultural appropriation of modes of Asian spirituality.

Most of the brief (slightly over a page) "Note on the Title" is a quotation from Richard Wilhelm's introduction to his 1967 edition of the I Ching, explaining the origins and development of its sixty-four hexagrams. The I Ching began centuries ago, Wilhelm explains, as "a collection of linear signs to be used as oracles," with single lines indicating "yes" — an unbroken line — and "no" — a broken line. But this dualistic system became inadequate, "at an early date," to express the complexities of the answers necessary to the questions posed to the book. The

> single lines were combined in pairs. To each of these combinations a third line was then added. In this way the eight trigrams came into being. These eight trigrams were conceived as images of all that happens in heaven and on earth. At the same time, they were held to be in a state of continual transition, one changing into another, just as transition from one phenomenon to another is continually taking place in the physical world. . . . Attention centers not on things in their state of being — as is chiefly the case in the Occident — but upon their movements in change. The eight trigrams therefore are not representations of things as such but their tendencies in movement. (Wilhelm, xlix–li, qtd. in FitzGerald, vii–viii; the eight trigrams were later combined into sixty-four hexagrams, each of which expresses a state of transition)

Wilhelm's explanation is profoundly important to FitzGerald's book, and to the dominant modern/emergent postmodern pivot of the sixties. His conceptualization is based on a massive dualism of "Occident" and "Orient" — a dualism, as we know from the pathbreaking work of Edward Said and from so much ensuing work in postcolonial studies, crucial to the thought of Western modernity. Like so many in the sixties, Wilhelm seems to valorize the "Oriental" over the "Occidental" worldview, in a way that has come to seem a patronizing, usurping appropriation — an extension rather than a repudiation of an imperialist Western hegemony.

At the same time, Wilhelm, seemingly unaware that his own work is based on this massive founding modern dualism, repudiates dualism (or valorizes the I Ching's move beyond dualism) because dualism is far too simple a model of the complexity of the universe. At the heart of this Chinese representational system's adequacy to the complexity of the universe is its privileging of transition, fluidity, change ("The Book of Changes") — "movements in change," "tendencies in movement" — over the "Occidental" privileging of "things in their state of being," "things as such" (one of the most frequently used countercultural slang phrases in the sixties was "going through changes," to indicate a fruitful, convention-renouncing turbulence in one's life). This view of a universe of fluidity and continual change rather than static states of being has become a central, defining concept of postmodernity. This concept has made impossible the notions of "Occident" and "Orient" — two massively static states of being and things as such — that underlies Wilhelm's conceptualization, characteristic of the sixties, of the significance of the I Ching. The unconscious, seamless, contradictory simultaneity of dominant modern and emergent postmodern paradigms in sixties consciousness here could not be more clear.

FitzGerald's use of Wilhelm's introduction, and of the figure "Fire in the Lake," frames her discussion of the role in Vietnamese history of the notion of continual change. Throughout the centuries-long history of Vietnam, no government, however long-lived, has been considered permanent; rather, empires wax and wane, and are understood as always waxing and waning. At the conclusion of their waning a cataclysmic change brings in a new government. For the Vietnamese, then, the thirty-year war against the French and Americans is an unusually protracted and violent episode in a permanently recurring cycle. The "Fire in the Lake" will bring on a new era for Vietnam. Only the North Vietnamese and the NLF were in a position to take Vietnam into this new era — only they inserted themselves into the position of the new empire in the "hearts and minds" of the Vietnamese. The utter failure of the United States to understand this system of meaning is one of FitzGerald's central objects of critique. She uses the local, particular, embodied history of Vietnamese culture, of the sort practiced by current, postmodern history, in which the war has an entirely different significance from the Americans' "fight against Communism" and "support of a democratically elected government in South Vietnam in its civil war against the invading North," in order to undercut these cold war dualisms. These dualisms are also, in their stark good/bad, self/other structure, (terminal) instances of the massive dualisms of modernity. The paradigms of fluidity and change, and of local-particular, historically embodied specificity, so central to postmodernity, are at the heart of FitzGerald's representation of Vietnamese culture. Yet at the same time, the terms she uses, particularly "revolution," have another significance: they garner a great deal of meaning and emotional force from their position not in the Vietnamese worldview, but in the modern, Western, Marxist, and democratic political traditions within which sixties radicalism was situated. Similarly, the valorization of the I Ching aligns FitzGerald with those who think they can repudiate hegemonic Western culture altogether and establish a utopian counterculture uncontaminated by it, and in total resistance and opposition to it. As the book gathers devastating force through its nearly 600 pages, the "Fire in the Lake" becomes, retroactively, an image of the modernist utopian revolution that, in the dominant modern utopianism of the sixties radical view, may be the only hope for saving the world from the Americans and the Americans from their government.

FitzGerald's opening chapter, "States of Mind," establishes some central assumptions of the Vietnamese worldview that underlie the differences between American and Vietnamese universes of assumption and structures of feeling ("two different dimensions," as FitzGerald says [4]), differences that are crucial in producing the cataclysmic history of the war. The delineation of these differences depends on a construct of the divergence between a regime of the local, rigidly hierarchical, cyclical tradition (Vietnam) and a regime, tragically destructive and irrelevant outside the West, of vast, starkly dualistic "states of being" (the United States). The particularity of Vietnamese culture, history, and general lifeworld is established by FitzGerald as profoundly different from those of the West in almost every key dimension: "In their sense of time and space, the Vietnamese and the Americans stand in the relationship of a reversed mirror image, for the very notion of competition, invention, and change is an extremely new one for most Vietnamese" (10).

Note here that, even in establishing the incommensurability of Vietnamese and American lifeworlds, FitzGerald deploys a dominantly modern dualistic figure of the "reversed mirror image." In every particularity of the Vietnamese lifeworld FitzGerald emphasizes, we see a negation or reversal of Eurocentric American assumptions:

The Vietnamese pride themselves less on their conquests than on their ability to resist and to survive. . . . For traditional Vietnamese the sense of limitation and enclosure was as much a part of individual life as of the life of the nation. . . . The population of the village [the essential unit of Vietnamese society and culture] remained stable, and so to accumulate wealth meant to deprive the rest of the community of land, to fatten while one's neighbor starved. . . . In this continuum of the family [in the Vietnamese religio-socio-cultural system of Confucianism linked to ancestor worship] "private property" did not really exist. . . . To the Vietnamese the land itself was the sacred, constant element: the people flowed over the land like water, maintaining and fructifying it for the generations to come. (10–11)

Traditional Vietnamese law rested not upon the notion of individual rights, but the notion of duties — the duty of the sovereign to his people, the father to his son, and vice versa. Similarly, the Confucian texts defined no general principles but the proper relationship of man to man. Equal justice was secondary to social harmony. This particular form of social contract gave the individual a very different sense of himself, of his own personality. In the Vietnamese language there is no word that exactly corresponds to the Western personal pronoun I, *je*, *ich*. When a man speaks of himself, he calls himself "your brother," "your nephew," "your teacher," depending upon his relationship to the person he addresses. (30)

FitzGerald summarizes: "Americans live in a society of replaceable parts — in theory anyone can become President or sanitary inspector — but the Vietnamese lived in a society of particular people, all of whom knew each other by their place in the landscape" (13). This opposition of the "replaceable," interchangeable parts of modernity's abstraction with the embodied specificity of "particular people" with a "place in the landscape" is part of FitzGerald's general "mirror image" duality of modern American and traditional Vietnamese culture, but in her treatment of it here, it becomes inflected toward a modern/postmodern differentiation (a differentiation that is clearly FitzGerald's construction). FitzGerald is not literally or directly constructing Vietnamese culture as postmodern, nor am I in any simplistic way arguing here that Vietnam is postmodern while the United States is modern. But FitzGerald repeatedly emphasizes the elements of Vietnamese cultural difference that bear on the shift from dominant modern abstraction and generality to emergent postmodern local particularity: "In going to Vietnam the United States was entering a country where the victory of one of the great world ideologies occasionally depended on the price of tea in a certain village or the outcome of a football game" (5–6). Or, "the Chinese system of orthography, used by the Vietnamese until the mid-nineteenth century, was not, like the Roman alphabet, composed of regular, repeatable symbols. It was built of particulars. The ideograms for such abstract notions as 'fear' or 'pleasure' were composed of pictures of concrete events" (24). In characterizing the traditional, hierarchical, fixed Confucian structure of Vietnamese culture, so at odds with American Western modernity, FitzGerald is, again, drawn toward emphasizing those elements of Vietnamese culture that resonate with the emergent postmodern.

One of the most important incommensurabilities of Eurocentric and Vietnamese worldviews, for FitzGerald, is their divergent understanding of "revolution": "revolution for Westerners is an abrupt reversal in the order of society, a violent break in history. But the Vietnamese traditionally did not see it that way at all. For them revolution was a natural and necessary event within the historical cycle; the problem of revolution was merely one of timing and appropriateness. . . . To him [the Vietnamese villager] revolution meant no alarming break from the past, but simply a renewal. The Chinese character for revolution meant in its original sense an animal's pelt, which is changed in the course of a year by molting" (41–42). Again, only the North Vietnamese and the NLF were legitimate agents of this renewal. To the extent that she premises her account of the war on the particularity of the Vietnamese worldview, and its difference from that of the Americans, and in her sympathy for the Vietnamese universe as one of specificity and flux, as opposed to her disdain for the tragically irrelevant American universe of static, warring vast abstractions, FitzGerald locates herself within postmodernity's emergent values. However, as we will see, a great deal of the book is preoccupied with establishing the American war as an instance not so much of the assumptions of modernity coming a cropper of those of a traditionalist culture inflected toward or emphasizing its postmodern aspects (while downplaying its hierarchical traditionalism), but of the Big Lie, where reality is the opposite of official accounts of it, which are fabricated with varying degrees of cynical self-consciousness. To the extent that the book's purpose is to expose and denounce the Big Lie, it is located within dominant modernity.

Most of the book is devoted to exposing the Big Lie. In lengthy, detailed chapters on the French colonial war, the Diem regime and its fall, the

Buddhist resistance, the rise of Ky and Thieu, Ho Chi Minh, North Vietnam and the NLF, and the ongoing tragedy of American errors that constituted the history of the U.S. war in Vietnam, through the Eisenhower, Kennedy, Johnson, and Nixon administrations, FitzGerald again and again contrasts Vietnamese reality with American lies (or, at best, willfully self-deluded misconceptions) about it. The war as waged by Nixon and Kissinger becomes the ultimate enactment of the Big Lie, because Nixon and Kissinger, unambivalent about the destruction they perpetrate, unhampered by the limits Johnson had placed on what he was willing to do (bombing and invading Cambodia and Laos, mining the harbors of Hanoi and Haiphong, inflicting death and destruction on Southeast Asia on a far greater scale than Johnson was willing to undertake), are the least deluded about the nature of what they are doing, and therefore are the clearest about the contradiction between the truth of the war and the lies they tell the American people. Johnson appears in FitzGerald's account as deeply ambivalent (by now the standard view of Johnson), knowing the truth, lying deliberately, motivated primarily by a macho refusal to lose a war, but halfheartedly resisting military pressure to go much further, and allowing himself to be shielded by intermittent, ineffective denial. Johnson emerges as a lesser villain than Nixon: Johnson, whose murderous pursuit of the war dominates this 1972 book, is almost a tragic figure in comparison to Nixon; Johnson is a Macbeth (as he is in Barbara Garson's great sixties political farce *MacBird*) to Nixon's Iago.

The lies the American government told its people (and that countless more or less honorable self-deluded "experts" told themselves) were not even self-consistent. FitzGerald points this out with characteristically careful understatement of tone, making clear the "inconsistencies" in American propaganda's misrepresentations of Vietnamese reality rather than using the word "lies":

> It was one of the inconsistencies of American public relations that while the American officials painted over these acute national differences [among Southeast Asian countries] with the rubric of "Asian dominoes" or "Free World Allies," they simultaneously brought into sharp relief the differences between northern and southern Vietnamese. The American public thus had the impression that while all Southeast Asians were alike — that nationality stood for little among them — the South Vietnamese were a nation distinct from the northerners [this of course was never the case]. Certainly there were differences between

the two groups of Vietnamese, but these were small by comparison with the separate culture and the thousand years of history that distinguished the Vietnamese from the Thais and the Cambodians. (55–56)

The American ability to intervene in the affairs of South Vietnam was not, then, at all in question: the southern politicians were ready to accept any foreign power that would feed and protect them. It was the hope of building "a strong free nation" that was absurd. How should the south build a strong anti-Communist government when most southerners continued to obey the old authorities of the family, the village, and the sect? Communist, anti-Communist, the next war would begin in a language that few of them understood. (95)

American lies about Vietnam invoke abstract, universalizing cold war dualisms; Vietnamese reality, in FitzGerald's incipiently postmodern version of it, emphasizes local, specific histories of multiple difference and embodied human particularity:

in passing over the drama of the Ngo family [in dealing with the fall of Diem] the [American] officials overlooked something essential to the outcome of the entire American effort in Vietnam. Ngo Dinh Diem was only one man; the private psychological drama of Diem and his family was as nothing beside the grand strategies and global concerns of the United States in Vietnam. But, as the French historian, Philippe Devillers, once wrote, "In our age of mass society, where all history seems to be determined by forces so powerful as to negate the individual, the Vietnamese problem has the originality to remain dominated by questions of individuals. Indeed, the problem becomes almost incomprehensible if one transforms men into abstractions." (100–101)

Remaining "dominated by questions of individuals," Vietnamese politics constitutes, as FitzGerald presents it, a version of the subject politics of the postmodern. At the same time, however, this postmodern reality is, for FitzGerald, the "truth" side of a massive modern "truth" / "lies" dualism. The deceptions and self-deceptions of vested American authority are "absurd": a crucial sixties modern paradigm, inherited from existentialism and embodied in the "theater of the absurd," of the hopeless incommensurability of underlying truth and official lies. Knowing that the NLF would win any truly democratic election in South Vietnam, for example, the Americans insist on the empty ritual of a democratic constitution and popular elections while countenancing and encouraging Diem's violation of all tenets of democratic rule and his blatant theft of the election. In this section of her narrative, FitzGerald adopts the bleakly ironic tone of the literature of the absurd (she alludes, for instance, to Sartre's *No Exit* in the following: "the dialogue of Saigon turned around on its own axis, giving no exit into reality" [456]): "Dr. Fishel presumably felt that the fact that Diem had so generously adopted a constitution excused him from all obligation to abide by it. . . . In fact, of course, American officials in Saigon were not at all anxious to see Diem adopt an electoral democracy. Their attitude sprang less from a principle than from a prediction. According to all intelligence estimates, the Communists would win more than a majority of the votes in a free election" (119, 121). Better-intentioned (one cannot quite say well-intentioned) American officials "would go so far as to suppress their awareness of the Diemist repressions, while others would rationalize them on the grounds that such measures were necessary in this moment of crisis. . . . The Diem regime would, in other words, become a fiction to them, an autonomous creation of the mind" (122–23; note the echo of *Macbeth*). This is the lesser lie of willful self-deception, which alternates in FitzGerald's account with the deliberate, conscious lie required by the American war: "but the American aid to the Saigon government was not merely useless. In the days of the Diem regime the desire for profit persuaded at least some of the officials to try to keep the peasants alive, productive, and moderately discontented, but now they could forget the peasants entirely and concentrate on filling out forms" (464). The nature of the lie is less important than its end result, which is always absurd, as in that quintessential sixties text *Catch 22*: "while in Malaya the British had fortified Malay villages against Chinese insurgents, in Vietnam [in the disastrous "Strategic Hamlet" program] the Vietnamese would have to fortify Vietnamese hamlets against other Vietnamese who had grown up in those hamlets" (165); "in [this] hamlet as in so many others, the circle of artillery and barbed wire enclosed a political void that waited for the NLF" (168). Or, "while the Ngo brothers were essentially pathetic figures, their regime was an indissoluble mixture of nightmare and farce" (135), a "mixture" that underlies the sixties absurd. And the absurd becomes monstrous when the difference between farce, which "lay generally in the cities," and nightmare, which "lay generally in the countryside, among the rice farmers further impoverished by the American importation of food . . . and where no laws held," is "invisible to most Americans" (135).

This invisibility, again, is not so much understandable and remediable ignorance as it is a willed commitment to the Big Lie: "even as late as 1968 many American liberals, including many of the journalists in Saigon, believed the official claims that the United States was at least making an effort to develop South Vietnam and to improve the welfare of the South Vietnamese people [one of the central propaganda rationalizations of the war]. But as a look at the aid budget would show, the claims were, and always had been, false" (161). It was the transparency of the Big Lie that sixties radicals seized upon: anyone who wanted to could see that "throughout the Diem era the United States spent approximately 90 percent of its aid on the creation of an army and a military bureaucracy" (162).

In the war of "Occident" against "Orient," in Wilhelm's terms, it would be easy to mystify the North Vietnamese and the NLF as representing a superior, ancient, timeless, unchanging, traditionalist culture and society, unseating upstart "helpless giant" modernity, the way the counterculture mystified and simplistically appropriated traditional modes of spirituality and ways of life. But FitzGerald does not do this. In her valorization of and emphasis on the historical specificity, particularity, fluidity, and embodied difference of the North Vietnamese and NLF, their incorporation, refunctioning, and resignification of modern technology into local, particular cultural practices, at the expense of the hierarchical, traditionalist features of Vietnamese culture and society, she in fact constructs them as postmodern (I would emphasize here that this is her construction), with, as postmodernity has, the mark of modernity on their culture. Again, I am not arguing that, in some anachronistic, ahistorical way, Vietnamese culture "is" postmodern. Rather, I am arguing that FitzGerald, in line with the dominant modernity/emergent postmodernity of this sixties text, focuses on what she construes or represents as postmodern elements of Vietnamese culture, postmodern only in her mode of describing and understanding them. In doing this, she constructs Vietnamese culture as a postmodern alternative to a failed Western colonialist modernity:

> Brown as the earth itself, the cache [part of the NLF's alternative underground world of tunnels and caches] would look as much like a part of the earth as if it had originated there — the bulbous root of which the palm-leaf huts of the village were the external stem and foliage. And yet, once they were unwrapped, named, and counted, the stores would turn out to be surprisingly sophisticated, including, perhaps, a land mine made with high explosives, a small printing press with leaflets and

textbook materials, surgical instruments, Chinese herbal medicines, and the latest antibiotics from Saigon. The industry clearly came from a civilization far more technically advanced than that which had made the external world of thatched huts, straw mats, and wooden plows. And yet there was an intimate relation between the two, for the anonymous artisans of the storerooms had used the materials of the village not only as camouflage but as an integral part of their technology. (191–92)

The Diem regime had shown a few of them a way out of the village. The NLF had shown all of them a way back in, to remake the village with the techniques of the outside world. (194)

The elements of Vietnamese culture and practice FitzGerald focuses on here — the integral relationship between the ancient village and technological modernity; the hybridity, fluidity, malleability of Eastern and Western, reinvented and intermingled traditional and modern cultural materials, ideologies, and practice — are characteristic of global, postcolonial postmodernity. By finding in Vietnamese culture what she delineates and valorizes as a "postmodern condition" with such lucidity, power, and persuasiveness, FitzGerald positions it to break free, in the postmodernity so soon to follow, from the modern paradigm of Truth and Lie that dominates her analysis, and within which this delineation and valorization of the postmodern is situated.

CHAPTER THIRTEEN

Fire Next Time or Rainbow Sign

If one had to choose (and many before me have done so) the most important force underlying the political and cultural phenomena of the sixties in
the United States, the Civil Rights movement, and its inheritor, sibling,
and (to some extent) rival, the Black Power movement, would be that
force. Without Civil Rights and Black Power, as many analysts and historians of the sixties have argued, sds in particular, the New Left in general,
second-wave feminism, gay liberation, and the other new social movements would not have had either the grounding in concrete activism and
organizing or the emotional and intellectual frames of reference that enabled the development of political radicalism in the sixties. (The Vietnam
War, again, was responsible for widening the radical movement well beyond the dimensions it would have achieved otherwise, but Civil Rights
was the sine qua non of that movement.) Without Civil Rights, African
American musical and cultural traditions, so crucial to the founding and
evolution of rock, and of the sixties counterculture in general, may well
not have "crossed over" to mainstream white youth culture. For the purposes of my argument here, perhaps the most important fact about Civil

Rights and Black Power is their development of an "identity politics" based on race, and the simultaneous location of that development in the liberatory humanist universalism of modernity and the local, particularist subject politics of postmodernity.

The gulf, as it appeared then to both blacks and whites, between Civil Rights and Black Power now appears as a continuum — two facets, in some ways obviously opposed, but also at once simultaneous and historically sequential, of the same movement, the same phenomenon. As Malcolm X said, in his *Autobiography*:

> Sometimes, I have dared to dream to myself that one day, history may even say that my voice — which disturbed the white man's smugness, and his arrogance, and his complacency — that my voice helped to save America from a grave, possibly even a fatal catastrophe.
>
> The goal has always been the same, with the approaches to it as different as mine and Dr. Martin Luther King's non-violent marching, that dramatizes the brutality and the evil of the white man against defenseless blacks. And in the racial climate of this country today, it is anybody's guess which of the "extremes" in approach to the black man's problems might *personally* meet a fatal catastrophe first — "non-violent" Dr. King, or so-called "violent" me.[1]

In this remarkably prophetic statement — the "non-violent" King did survive the "violent" Malcolm, but not by much — Malcolm makes clear the close link between Civil Rights and (what became) Black Power: the proximity and shared goals of the two outweigh the differences so palpable and important to most blacks and whites at the time.[2]

Civil Rights and Black Power initiated and defined postmodern identity-based movements. Feminism, gay-lesbian-queer rights and power, Latino/a and other racial, ethnic rights and power movements, movements based on age or disability, are all offspring of Civil Rights and Black Power. In its inception, the broad African American rights and power movement, including Civil Rights and Black Power, combined, without recognizing a distinction between them, what we now think of as postmodern identity politics — characterized by limited agendas and goals, particular and exclusive to its own identity category — with the universalist, liberatory goals of modernity. Both King and Malcolm X, and also all the other great African American leaders and writers of the sixties, thought the black movement could "save America from a grave, even fatal catastrophe." Civil Rights and Black Power were seen as revealing the national soul — the national

disease, rottenness, corruption — and pointing the way toward full realization of American democratic potential.

It is generally known and not surprising that King had these goals. One
of his most famous and oft-quoted statements, from the "Letter from
Birmingham Jail," espouses this position: "injustice anywhere is a threat
to justice everywhere. We are caught in an inescapable network of mutuality, tied in a single garment of destiny."[3] He argues that the "disinherited
children" who "sat down at lunch counters" in the South "were in reality
standing up for the best in the American dream and the most sacred values
in our Judeo-Christian heritage, and thusly, carrying our whole nation
back to those great wells of democracy which were dug deep by the
Founding Fathers in the formulation of the Constitution and the Declaration of Independence" (100).

Even more radical writers, however, associated with black separatist
repudiation of white culture and politics — writers openly opposed to and
scornful of the integrationist agenda of Civil Rights, and in their turn
repudiated by the Civil Rights ideology of nonviolence — saw Black Power
as offering not just an end to black oppression but a cure to the diseased
and distorted American psyche and polity as a whole. On the same page of
the *Autobiography* on which Malcolm says he has "dared to dream . . .
that my voice . . . helped to save America from a grave, possibly even a
fatal catastrophe," voicing the view of the black liberation struggle as
agent of revolutionary American transformation, he also discusses the
role of whites in the movement as entirely separate: "let sincere white
individuals . . . form their own all-white groups" and "go and teach nonviolence to white people!" (377).

In *Soul on Ice*, Eldridge Cleaver, one of Malcolm's most influential
disciples, a key exponent of Black Power, Minister of Information of the
Black Panther Party, and eloquent articulator of black rage, refers to "the
central event of our era" as "the national liberation movements abroad and
the Negro revolution at home."[4] The foundations of authority have been
blasted to bits in America because the whole society has been indicted,
tried, and convicted of injustice" (74). Generally, Cleaver mingles particularist African American politics with general apocalyptic-utopian world-
revolutionary politics, as if they were indistinguishable from one another
and seamlessly, invisibly interlinked, in a way that was characteristic of
sixties radicalism but would not be possible now. Typically for the sixties as
modern/postmodern pivot, he sees all these political movements as interwoven, mutually dependent, inseparable, at the same time that he sees

them as separate; he does not seem to be aware of a contradiction. For example, unlike Malcolm, he welcomes the presence of whites in Civil Rights demonstrations because "the presence of whites among the demonstrators emboldened the Negro leaders and allowed them to use tactics they never would have been able to employ with all-black troops. The racist conscience of America is such that murder does not register as murder, really, unless the victim is white" (75). But this statement, in which the role of whites in the movement is to serve and hasten the black cause, comes within a section on the "rebellion of white youth" which "has gone through four broadly discernable stages" (74; participation in Civil Rights demonstrations is the third stage). Cleaver is discussing "the rebellion of white youth" because "it is among the white youth of the world that the greatest change is taking place" (72), a change that has "transform[ed]" the "Negro revolution . . . into something broader, with the potential of encompassing the whole of America in a radical reordering of society" (76–77). Again, Cleaver perceives no contradiction between his particularist African American and his universalist revolutionary goals.

Angela Davis's 1971 essay "Reflections on the Black Woman's Role in the Community of Slaves" is a powerful analysis of American slavery's complex, particular historical circumstances, focused exclusively on the experience of African and African American women: "this was one of the supreme ironies of slavery: in order to approach its strategic goal — to extract the greatest possible surplus from the labor of the slaves — the black woman had to be released from the chains of the myth of femininity."[5] This insight has become a central tenet of postmodern African American feminism, or womanism, in Alice Walker's coinage, where the histories and conditions of black and white women in this country are viewed as profoundly divergent, in particular ways that make white feminism's emphasis on repudiating the traditional constraints of femininity irrelevant to black women. However, Davis ends her essay on modernity's universalizing revolutionary note, a note that would not now be struck by a writer making the case Davis makes about black women's "release from the chains of femininity":

> black women have made significant contributions to struggles against the racism and the dehumanizing exploitation of a wrongly organized society. In fact, it would appear that the intense levels of resistance historically maintained by black people and thus the historical functions of the black liberation struggle as harbinger of change throughout the society are due in part to the greater *objective* equality between the

black man and the black woman. Du Bois put it this way: "In the great rank and file of our five million women, we have the up-working of new revolutionary ideals, which must in time have vast influence on the thought and action of this land." (126)

Davis's language seems almost to take for granted the idea that the "historical function" of the "black liberation struggle" is to serve as "harbinger of change throughout the society." This position, where there is no contradiction between a black liberation struggle that is a struggle at once for black liberation and for universal utopian social change, is characteristic of a wide array of African American thought and writing in the sixties.

Frantz Fanon — whose 1961 *The Wretched of the Earth*, translated into English in 1963, was enormously influential in the New Left and, along with his *Black Skin, White Masks*, written in 1952 but not translated into English until 1967, has been crucial to the third world liberation and postcolonial movements — saw the colonizer/colonized relationship as organizing all human society in a universal, totalizing system that he describes in both books as "Manichean."[6] He argues that his analysis of this massive global dualism would require that "everything up to and including the very nature of precapitalist society, so well explained by Marx, must here be thought out again" (*Wretched* 40). He also says, matter-of-factly, that "decolonization . . . sets out to change the order of the world" (*Wretched*, 36). For Fanon, as for the theorists of Civil Rights and Black Power in the U.S. context, the revolutionary decolonization movements of third world liberation would at once aim toward particular goals of the group for whom, by whom, and in whose name the liberation struggle is being waged, and also, at the same time, serve as harbinger or advance guard or agent of a universal, revolutionary, utopian transformation of all society worldwide. In the postmodern aftermath of these movements, the universal revolutionary agenda, taken for granted by everyone politically active in the sixties, either fell away or was repudiated as antithetical to each movement's particularist goals, defined by what has become identity politics, in which the metanarratives of universalism are revealed as inherently exclusionary, hierarchical, and founded on the interests of the white European male, and therefore hostile to the local, specific agendas of separate, distinct nonhegemonic groups.[7]

James Baldwin is in some ways an atypical luminary of the Civil Rights and Black Power movements. His name may not come to mind first when one is thinking of leaders of the African American struggles of the sixties. Unlike Malcolm, King, Cleaver, Davis, and others who wrote influentially as well as serving as political leaders, Baldwin is thought of, and thought of himself, primarily as a writer. For him, the essay, even when it has clear and ascendant political agendas, is a literary genre. He wrote powerfully and influentially in many other genres as well and is, of course, as eminent a novelist and playwright as he is an essayist (he also wrote poetry). Nonetheless, I would argue that his books of essays, particularly the early books, *Notes of a Native Son* (1955), *Nobody Knows My Name* (1961), and *The Fire Next Time* (1963), were as important and influential in forging and representing the sensibility, the structure of feeling, of the African American movements, and of radical sixties movements in general, as anything written in the period.[8] They are also, in many ways, particularly in the richness and complexity of their treatment of the politics of subjectivity, ideal for discussing the role of Civil Rights and Black Power in the emergence of postmodern from modern identity politics in the sixties.

Baldwin has the advantage of being a great writer. His work is a masterful, eloquent, varied, powerful literary treatment of some of the most profound cultural, political, psychic, and aesthetic materials of his time. He was working within the traditions of Euro-American twentieth-century literary modernity — early-century modernism and midcentury existentialism — as well as within the African American traditions of the slave narrative, the blues, jazz, gospel, preaching, call-and-response, and other oral folk traditions. The informing presence of these African American literary and cultural traditions in his work is well known. His self-location within modernist and existentialist traditions is apparent throughout his work in his masterful development of the artist or writer as isolated loner struggling against an uncomprehending, hostile social order, against authority both familial and social; striving to construct an authentic, liberating, fully expressive voice and subjectivity.

Baldwin's discussion in the essay "Princes and Powers," in *Nobody Knows My Name*, of the contrast of African and Western aesthetic practices reveals clearly his self-location within Euro-American modernism, and his understanding of Western culture as dominated by that tradition:

> The distortions used by African artists to create a work of art are not at all the same distortions which have become one of the principal aims of almost every artist in the West today. (They are not the same distortions

even when they have been copied from Africa.) And this was due entirely to the different situations in which each had his being. Poems and stories, in the only situation I know anything about, were never told, except, rarely, to children, and, at the risk of mayhem, in bars. They were written to be read, alone, and by a handful of people at that — there was really beginning to be something suspect in being read by more than a handful. (150)

Baldwin goes on to say that only in jazz does Western art approximate African communal aesthetic production as described by Leopold Senghor. However, "the ghastly isolation of the jazz musician, the neurotic intensity of his listeners, was proof enough that what Senghor meant when he spoke of social art had no reality whatever in Western life" (151). Even the communal readings of the Beats, let alone the jazz jam sessions he describes, seem unreal in their claim to communality to Baldwin. He is entirely within the modernist and existentialist paradigm of heroic, tormented individualism. At the same time, however, he can speak of the communal art Senghor describes as "a way of life which I could only very dimly and perhaps somewhat wistfully imagine" (150). He can imagine the anti-individualist valorization of group creative practice of African aesthetics that, in a very different mode, has become a staple of postmodern sensibility, but as a modernist he cannot imagine its realization in the cultural scenes he knows and inhabits. Like other sixties writers, Baldwin used literary writing as a high-stakes existential arena for constructing and performing complex, shifting, dynamic versions of his own heroic subjectivity as at once representative and unique, yet also self-consciously performative — a characteristic sixties political "performing self."

The essay "In Search of a Majority," in *Nobody Knows My Name*, originally delivered as a lecture at Kalamazoo College, is remarkable for the multiple, contradictory fluidity of the subject positions Baldwin uses it to construct. This fluidity is noteworthy not only because it predicts the self-conscious performative malleability of postmodern subjectivity, but also because the contradictory positionalities in question are themselves crucial to the formation of identity politics in the sixties, and therefore to the emergence of postmodernity. Baldwin uses the first-person plural pronoun throughout the essay, but the reference of this pronoun slips and shifts between a particular African American "we" and a general, inclusive American "we."

The essay is specifically concerned, as the title indicates, with the question of "minority" and "majority" in American society. Baldwin refuses to assume that the meaning of either of those racially coded terms is self-evident. As he announces in his opening statement, "I am supposed to speak this evening on the goals of American society as they involve minority rights," but "before we can begin to speak of minority rights in this country, we've got to make some attempt to isolate or to define the majority" (215) — in effect, as the terms "isolate" and "define" imply, to contain and assert power over this "majority." The "I" of the opening sentence becomes a "we" who must try to "isolate or to define the majority." This initial "I" who has been invited to speak on minority rights is instead going to "invite you to join me in a series of speculations. Some of them are dangerous, some of them painful, all of them are reckless" (215). This dangerous, painful, reckless joint endeavor then is understood, by Baldwin and, by extension, his audience and the reader, as generating the daring "we" who will try to "isolate or to define the majority."

Baldwin has performed a complex series of moves in this opening sequence. He first defines himself as an innovative resister of conventional expectation. He rejects the topic he is "supposed to speak" on — "the goals of American society as they involve minority rights": a bland, relatively safe topic on which uncontroversial sentiments might easily be expressed. Instead, he first breaks down the separation of speaker and audience/reader implied by "I am supposed to speak" in order to propose a common or mutual "we," which will undertake a dangerous, painful, reckless speculative journey: exciting and important rather than bland and predictable. This "we," constructed around Baldwin's experimental ("speculative") enunciative or literary subjectivity, becomes a characteristic sixties vanguard, valorizing moral bravery, honesty, and authenticity, defining itself in opposition to the safe and conventional. This biracial or multiracial vanguard, precisely the vanguard to which he will appeal in *The Fire Next Time*, itself undercuts the static structure of "minority" and "majority" that Baldwin is "supposed" to address.

With his audience/reader now joined with him in a common project, occupying, at least for the moment, a common subject position, Baldwin defamiliarizes the conventional American meaning of the term "majority," which equates numerical majority in the population with racial whiteness. He says first that "majority is not an expression of numbers . . . you may far outnumber your opposition and not be able to impose your will on them or even to modify the rigor with which they impose their will on you"; he gives as examples "Negroes in South Africa or in some countries, some sections, of the American South" (215). Further, majority is not, as this may imply, simply a question of power: "you may have beneath your hand all the apparatus of power, political, military, state, and still be unable to use these things to achieve your ends" (215; a prophetic remark in light of the Vietnam War). He gives here another two examples, again one from the postcolonial and one from the African American struggle — de Gaulle in Algeria, and Eisenhower "forced to send paratroopers into Little Rock" (215). He concludes that the "only useful definition of the word 'majority' does not refer to numbers, and it does not refer to power. It refers to influence" (216). With this definition of "majority," Baldwin frees himself to insert the daring, vanguard "we" he constructed at the beginning of the speech/essay into the position of putative "majority" of national moral influence, filling the vacuum left by the displaced, vanished New England aristocracy. He makes this substitution clear in his assessment of the enormous task facing this "we": "Someone said, and said it very accurately, that what is honored in a country is cultivated there. If we apply this touchstone to American life we can scarcely fail to arrive at a very grim view of it. But I think we have to look grim facts in the face because if we don't, we can never hope to change them" (216).

Baldwin goes on to discuss the "national self-image" from a characteristic sixties position. The "national self-image" is one which "suggests hard work and good clean fun and chastity and piety and success," thereby "leav[ing] out of account, of course, most of the people in the country, and most of the facts of life," and "has almost nothing to do with what or who an American really is. Beneath this bland, this conqueror-image, a great many unadmitted despairs and confusions, and anguish and unadmitted crimes and failures hide" (218). Baldwin then makes a crucial shift from the general "national self-image" and what it hides to himself, in order to root a different sense of the national American identity — a different "we," corresponding to the "we" he premised at the beginning of the speech/essay — in the subjectivity he represents himself as embodying:

> To speak in my own person, as a member of the nation's most oppressed minority, the oldest oppressed minority, I want to suggest most seriously that before we can do very much in the way of clear thinking or clear doing as relates to the minorities in this country, we must first crack the American image and find out and deal with what it hides. We

cannot discuss the state of our minorities until we first have some sense of what we are, who we are, what our goals are, and what we take life to be. The question is not what we can do now for the hypothetical Mexican, the hypothetical Negro. The question is what we really want out of life, for ourselves, what we think is real. (218)

Baldwin speaks "in his own person" as a member of "the nation's most oppressed minority, the oldest oppressed minority." This is the characteristic self-positioning of identity politics, where personal identity, invoking an embodied subject, is equated with and defined by membership in a particular, historically oppressed, disempowered, nonhegemonic, here racially marked group. But Baldwin also speaks, simultaneously, with no sense of self-contradiction, and in the same sentence, as part of a "we" that is at once the vanguard of right-minded, antiracist Americans he invoked at the opening of the essay/address, and also in some sense the general, putatively dominant, influential, "majority" American conscience itself. He contrasts the abstract markers of identity politics — "the hypothetical Mexican, the hypothetical Negro" — with the "we," a word repeated, along with "our" and "ourselves," eleven times in these sentences, who possess, include, and are responsible for "our minorities"; who must define and take responsibility for a group identity, set of values, sense of reality, and national-cultural agenda.

This slippage in subjectivity is of course in part a powerful rhetorical strategy of Baldwin's to annex his audience and persuade it to embrace his point of view. But it is a strategy made possible by its sixties historical moment, when identity politics were at once the vanguard of modern, universal utopian revolutionary change and also the emergent locus of postmodern, anti-universal particularity. His purpose is both to undercut the notion of a hegemonic "majority," a postmodern agenda, and also to replace oppressive hegemonic politics and ideologies with his own progressive, egalitarian, antiracist politics and ideologies, a key agenda of modernity. A significant part of Baldwin's power comes from the way he forges a literary space at the intersection of these sensibilities, these modes of subjectivity, these structures of feeling. My experience of reading Baldwin as a young white teenager was precisely at once of being included with and by him in a moral-political-intellectual-literary vanguard that might change the world, and also of being deeply challenged by the difficult particular truths he revealed about African American life.[9]

Toward the end of "In Search of a Majority," Baldwin seems to catch himself in this contradiction, brought up short by his own shifting pronouns:

> No one in the world—in the entire world—knows more—knows Americans better or, odd as this may sound, loves them more than the American Negro. This is because he has had to watch you, outwit you, deal with you, and bear you, and sometimes even bleed and die with you, ever since we got here, that is, since both of us, black and white, got here—and this is a wedding. Whether I like it or not, or whether you like it or not, we are bound together forever. We are part of each other. What is happening to every Negro in the country at any time is also happening to you. . . . I think that what we really have to do is to create a country in which there are no minorities—for the first time in the history of the world. (221)

From the position of the "we" Baldwin has forged with his audience, "the American Negro" is "he." But in the rising emotion of "watch you, outwit you, deal with you, and bear you, and sometimes even bleed and die with you," the "he" of "the America Negro," female ("bear you") as well as male, becomes Baldwin's particular African American "we" of "ever since we got here," recalling the slave trade. He then catches himself, corrects himself, in "that is, since both of us, black and white, got here," and moves on from there to reconstruct the (polymorphously gendered and sexualized) "wedding" of black and white that produces the righteous, revolutionary vanguard.

Baldwin's peroration makes explicit his construction of the audience/reader as this transformative "majority" of progressive influence; the "we" he had so carefully produced becomes a "you" of the college students, the potential radical sixties youth movement he addresses and to which he proposes to pass on the high revolutionary task of modernity: "the majority for which everyone is seeking which must reassess and release us from our past and deal with the present and create standards worthy of what a man may be—this majority is you. No one else can do it. The world is before you and you need not take it or leave it as it was when you came in" (221; "a man" is again modernity's universalizing metonym for human). What had been a high-wire act of fluid, experimental, performative subjectivity comes to ground at last on what now sounds like a commencement-speech platitude. However, it was not a commencement-speech platitude at the time. It was a disarmingly simple, modest, direct statement of what was in fact a revolutionary agenda. In the process of arriving at this end point, Baldwin opened out a version of identity politics at once universal and particular, thereby helping to shift the American structure of feeling toward an identity politics in which the universal, especially in its utopian goal of social transformation, is at once discredited and also recontained as the particular.

This simultaneity of dominant universalist and emergent particularist identity politics recurs throughout Baldwin's three great, definitive volumes of essays so influential in the sixties — *Notes of a Native Son*, *Nobody Knows My Name*, *The Fire Next Time* — with the particularist themes of the Black Power movement emerging more forcefully in the last volume, but with the universalist theme of the African American movement as transformative national and international vanguard also dominant in all three volumes. The general American "we" appears throughout, though with greater frequency in the two earlier volumes; in *The Fire Next Time*, "we" is more likely to signify a universal humanity.

"Many Thousands Gone," in *Notes*, a scathing discussion of Richard Wright's *Native Son*, seems to anchor its subjectivity entirely within a general, white-dominated American "we." In the beginning of the essay, Baldwin establishes his subject position very clearly as generally American, with "the Negro" identified as an (again universally male) other, "him": "the ways in which the Negro has affected the American psychology are betrayed in our popular culture and in our morality; in our estrangement from him is the depth of our estrangement from ourselves. . . . What we really feel about him is involved with all that we feel about everything, about every one, about ourselves. The story of the Negro in America is the story of America — or, more precisely, it is the story of Americans" (19). Even here, however, the gulf between the American "we" and the "Negro" "him" is established only to be discredited: the history of subjectivity of "the Negro" constitutes the deepest, truest story of American subjectivity. Later in the essay, following his discussion of the novel, Baldwin moves close to a particular, embodied, masculine African American subject position: "It is this image [of African Americans as "hewers of wood and drawers of water," out of which "our image of Bigger was created"], living yet, which we perpetually seek to evade with good works; and this image which makes of all our good works an intolerable mockery. The 'nigger,' black, benighted, brutal, consumed with hatred as we are consumed with guilt, cannot be thus blotted out" (28). The "we," clearly African American in the above sentence, becomes more clearly white, however, and the black woman joins the black man in the othered third-person position, as the passage progresses—"he stands at our shoulders when we give our maid her wages, it is his hand which we fear we are taking when struggling to communicate with the current 'intelligent' Negro" (28)—but in the sentence beginning "it is this image, living yet, which we perpetually seek to evade with good works," the "we" shifts close, I would argue, to Baldwin's own subject position as an African American man.

In the extremely powerful autobiographical title essay of this volume, "Notes of a Native Son," Baldwin writes from an explicitly African American subject position. However, the essay moves toward a sense of the indissoluble mutual imbrication of black and white American subjectivities: "the Negro's real relation to the white American. This relation prohibits, simply, anything as uncomplicated and satisfactory as pure hatred. In order really to hate white people, one has to blot so much out of the mind—and the heart—that this hatred itself becomes an exhausting and self-destructive pose. . . . One is always in the position of having to decide between amputation and gangrene" (82–83).[10]

In "Encounter on the Seine" and "Equal in Paris," Baldwin explicitly writes from an African *American* subject position, arguing that African Americans in Europe discover their ineluctable Americanness, their difference not just from white Europeans but also from black Africans in Europe. It is explicitly in constructing a black identity ("the battle for his own identity" [88]), in fact, that the African American (man, assumed) discovers his American identity: "in this need to establish himself in relation to his past he is most American . . . this depthless alienation from oneself and one's people [the alienation from Africa Baldwin feels] is, in sum, the American experience" (89). Further, in a glimpse forward to postmodernity, Baldwin claims in this essay that African American identity is ineluctably hybrid: "they face each other, the Negro and the African, over a gulf of three hundred years—an alienation too vast to be conquered in an evening's good-will . . . this alienation causes the Negro to recognize that he is a hybrid" (89). This hybridity, however, is not so much of Africa and America, but, in an explicitly erotic register, of black male African American and white male European American: "in white Americans he finds reflected—repeated, as it were, in a higher key—his tensions, his terrors, his tenderness. . . . he is bone of their bone, flesh of their flesh; . . . therefore he cannot deny them, nor can they ever be divorced" (89). Baldwin looks at Africa in order to see American racial hybridity. This recognition of American hybridity, a recognition that we are all "on a dangerous voyage

and in the same boat," "will bring Americans . . . at last their own identity," and will allow "the American Negro" to "make peace with himself
and with the voiceless many thousands gone before him" (90). As Baldwin
repeatedly says, this has nothing to do with blacks being "accepted" by
whites. It has to do with a recognition of racial hybridity and mutual
subjective imbrication that is postmodern, at the same time that it denies
the version of postmodern identity politics of the local and particular that
is based on histories of racial "origins."

In "Stranger in the Village," the great essay that concludes *Notes*, Baldwin's peroration shifts seamlessly in point of view between an African
American identity that envisions a gulf between blacks and whites, in
which American identity is white, and a general black/white American
identity in which this visible gulf is recognized as catastrophic, and in
which it must be overcome: "Americans are as unlike any other white
people in the world as it is possible to be. I do not think, for example, that
it is too much to suggest that the American vision of the world—which
allows so little reality, generally speaking, for any of the darker forces in
human life, which tends until today to paint moral issues in glaring black
and white—owes a great deal to the battle waged by Americans to maintain between themselves and black men a human separation which could
not be bridged" (128). Here, "Americans" are exclusively white; "black
men" (again, the universal male) are the stark other of this pathologically
white America. But immediately following this sentence, without a paragraph break or transition of any kind, Baldwin continues: "it is only now
beginning to be borne in on us—very faintly, it must be admitted, very
slowly, and very much against our will—that this vision of the world is
dangerously inaccurate, and perfectly useless. For it protects our moral
high-mindedness at the terrible expense of weakening our grasp of reality"
(128–29). Suddenly, Baldwin produces an interracial or biracial American
"us" that bears the burden of insight into the impossible racial dynamic of
American identity, and the burden of overcoming and reversing it. This
American subjectivity is, again, the transformative moral-political vanguard of the sixties.

Baldwin ends the essay with a statement of another of his key recurring
themes, which is also a key recurring theme, as we have seen, of many
other major African American writers of the period—that the African
American political movements constitute the catalyst for universal social
change: "the history of the American Negro problem is not merely shameful, it is also something of an achievement. For even when the worst has

been said, it must also be added that the perpetual challenge posed by this problem was always, somehow, perpetually met. It is precisely this black-white experience which may prove of indispensable value to us in the world we face today. This world is white no longer, and it will never be white again" (129). Baldwin says here that the African American movements, a catalyst for universal social change — a key idea of modernity — produce not a universal brotherhood of supraracial egalitarianism, modernity's goal, but rather a postmodern world which supersedes the racial dualisms of modernity, not by erasing or transcending race but by eliminating the hegemonic construction of whiteness.

In *Nobody Knows My Name*, the theme of the human universality of African American subjectivity predominates. Repeatedly in this volume, Baldwin sees the project necessary for the salvation of American society and psyche as the recognition of African American humanity. This theme is clearly located within the ideologies of modernity. In "Fifth Avenue, Uptown: A Letter from Harlem," this theme is connected to the notion of the African American movements as universal revolutionary vanguard, which also recurs throughout this volume:

> The white policeman standing on a Harlem street corner finds himself at the very center of the revolution now occurring in the world. . . . One day, to everyone's astonishment, someone drops a match in the powder keg and everything blows up. Before the dust has settled or the blood congealed, [everyone wants] to know what happened. What happened is that Negroes want to be treated like men. *Negroes want to be treated like men*: a perfectly straightforward statement, containing only seven words. People who have mastered Kant, Hegel, Shakespeare, Marx, Freud and the Bible find this statement utterly impenetrable. (177)[11]

The American and world revolutions led by African and African American liberation movements will bear apocalyptic, potentially redemptive fruit because "Negroes want to be treated like men": blacks claim a subject position of universal humanity, so clearly indicated in the universal use of "men" to indicate humanity. In "A Fly in the Buttermilk," Baldwin says, of a white high school principal, "he impressed me as being a very gentle and honorable man. But I could not avoid wondering if he had ever really *looked* at a Negro and wondered about the life, the aspirations, the universal humanity hidden behind the dark skin" (194). In "Nobody Knows My Name," again making the connection between the revolution led by the African American movements and the necessity to recognize the

universal humanity of black people, Baldwin says, of the coming upheaval: "the trouble will spread to every metropolitan center in the nation
which has a significant Negro population. . . . because the nation, the
entire nation, has spent a hundred years avoiding the question of the place
of the black man in it. . . . what this evasion of the Negro's humanity has
done to the nation is not so well known" (207–08).

"East River, Downtown: Postscript to a Letter from Harlem" develops
the theme of the African American movements as an American revolutionary vanguard: "the Negro student movement . . . I believe, will prove to be
the very last attempt made by American Negroes to achieve acceptance in
the republic, to force the country to honor its own ideals. . . . The goal of
the student movement is nothing less than the liberation of the entire
country from its most crippling attitudes and habits" (181–82). At the
same time, "East River, Downtown" also looks forward to postmodern
racial subjectivity in the identity politics of black pride and black cultural
nationalism. Baldwin says of black youth: "the power of the white world
to control their identities was crumbling as they were born; and by the
time they were able to react to the world, Africa was on the stage of
history. This could not but have an extraordinary effect on their own
morale, for it meant that they were not merely the descendants of slaves in
a white, Protestant, and puritan country; they were also related to kings
and princes in an ancestral homeland, far away. And this has proved to be
a great antidote to the poison of self-hatred" (185).

At the end of "Alas, Poor Richard," his fiercely ambivalent three-part
meditation on the career of Richard Wright, the penultimate essay of
Nobody (the final essay is Baldwin's more indulgently ambivalent meditation on Norman Mailer, "The Black Boy Looks at the White Boy"), Baldwin interweaves these central themes in a way that makes very clear his
location between dominant modern and emergent postmodern identity
politics. In his final paragraph, Baldwin begins by invoking the unique
position of the African American, with one face turned toward black
Africa and the other toward white America, struggling to forge an identity
in the space between: "Time brought Richard, as it has brought the American Negro, to an extraordinarily baffling and dangerous place. An American Negro, however deep his sympathies, or however bright his rage,
ceases to be simply a black man when he faces a black man from Africa"
(267). As we have seen, this is a recurring motif for Baldwin: the African
American discovers her/his (again, named by the universal male) Americanness in the difference s/he feels from the African. The implication

here is that "black" in itself is not a sufficient source of identity or self-definition — an adequate locus of subjectivity — for the African American. This position reflects primarily the race-transcending universalism of modernity but also the complex postmodern subject politics of historical and locational specificity, where race is too ahistorical, uninflected, reductive, and socially constructed a category to be capable of full alignment with actually existing, multiple, hybrid, non-self-identical subjectivities.

Baldwin's closing paragraph continues to move through his central preoccupations, brilliantly using each statement to propel his writing to the next idea: "when I say simply a black man, I do not mean that being a black man is simple, anywhere. But I am suggesting that one of the prices an American Negro pays — or can pay — for what is called his 'acceptance' is a profound, almost ineradicable self-hatred. This corrupts every aspect of his living, he is never at peace again, he is out of touch with himself forever" (267; is this "black man" modernity's universal figure that includes black women, as we have seen elsewhere in Baldwin's work, or is the experience of black women different and omitted here?). This theme is the primary subject of the volume's title essay, "Nobody Knows My Name," which elaborates on this self-hatred, arguing that it is just as much the core of northern as well as of southern black experience in America; arguing that there is far less difference between racism in the two regions than northern whites would like to think.[12] It also invokes Du Bois's crucial formulation of African American double consciousness, in which the black subject is "out of touch with himself forever." Note also that "American Negro" is postulated here as a particular, unique identity category, defined in its differentiation at once from black African and from white American.

Baldwin then moves, after his statement of ineluctable (under the regime of racism) African American self-alienation, toward an imbrication of these two other, definingly differentiated racial-national categories: "and, when he faces an African, he [the white American male] is facing the unspeakably dark, guilty, erotic past which the Protestant fathers made him bury — for their peace of mind, and for their power — but which lives in his personality and haunts the universe yet" (267–68). Baldwin refers here to a central idea not only in his work but also in the work of many other African American writers of the period, notably Eldridge Cleaver and also Malcolm X: the notion of the black man as fantasy surrogate and scapegoat for puritanically repressed white male sexuality (the figure of the lynched and castrated black man, a national fantasy all too frequently acted out, is the terrorist and monitory realization of this racial-sexual pathology), with the black woman serving then as actual as well as fantasy object and embodiment of this violent illicit sexuality, and the white woman as idealized marker, repository, possession, and reward of this also violent white male sexual repression. Here Baldwin locates the burden of this buried sexuality within the African American man himself, clearly now particularly male rather than universally black: again, in "fac[ing] an African, he is facing the unspeakably dark, guilty, erotic past which the Protestant fathers made him bury — for their peace of mind, and for their power — but which lives in his personality and haunts the universe yet." This sentence bridges the embodied blackness of the African with the violent, guilty sexual repression accorded to the black man by dominant white American men, across the riven body of the African American man. This positioning of African American men is postmodern in its multiplicity, complexity, local-particular historicization, self-differentiation, emphasis on (queer) sexuality and embodiedness.

At the same time, however, this "unspeakably dark, guilty, erotic past . . . haunts the universe": the situation of the African American man, again, as we have seen over and over in these essays, has universal transformative implications. Indeed, Baldwin moves from here immediately into a universal register: "the war in the breast between blackness and whiteness, which caused Richard such pain, need not be a war. It is a war which just as it denies both the heights and the depths of our natures, takes, and has taken, visibly and invisibly, as many white lives as black ones. And, as I see it, Richard was among the most illustrious victims of this war. This is why, it seems to me, he eventually found himself wandering in a no-man's land between the black world and the white" (268). The "no-man's land between the black world and the white" in which Baldwin says Wright was tragically and unnecessarily condemned to wander, constructed here as a self-inflicted, transcendable doom, had just a few sentences back been constructed as the inevitable location of the African American man, defined in the space of sexual abjection between black African and white American masculinities. However, from the perspective of Baldwin's utopian modernity, as we have seen, this space is transcendable by the conscious few, the revolutionary vanguard, white as well as black, building on the groundwork laid by African American history and subjectivity, and the African American political movements: "it is no longer important to be white — thank heaven — the white face is no longer invested with the power of this world; and it is devoutly to be hoped that it will soon no longer be important to be black. The experience of the American Negro, if it is ever faced and assessed, makes it possible to hope for such a reconciliation. The hope and the effect of this fusion in the breast of the American Negro is one of the few hopes we have of surviving the wilderness which lies before us now" (268).

In *The Fire Next Time*, perhaps his most influential, greatest, and certainly his most enduring book of nonfiction prose, Baldwin moves, along with history, much closer to the ideas and emotions of the Black Power movement than he had in the two previous volumes.[13] He does not, however, relinquish his utopian belief in the universal, transformative potentiality of vanguard radicalism: "for this is your home, my friend [he addresses his nephew James, in the brief opening section 'My Dungeon Shook,' a letter on the occasion of the hundredth anniversary of Emancipation], do not be driven from it; great men have done great things here, and will again, and we can make America what America must become" (294).

In the autobiographical essay "Down at the Cross: Letter from a Region in My Mind," which occupies most of *The Fire Next Time*, and which recapitulates the material on which Baldwin's great first novel, *Go Tell It on the Mountain* (1952) was based, Baldwin's tone overall is significantly angrier and more apocalyptic than it was in the earlier essays, as the title, and the epigraph, and the closing lines of the book, taken from one of the spirituals, from which it is derived, would predict: "God gave Noah the rainbow sign, / No more water, the fire next time!" The essay also recounts in detail a visit Baldwin made to Elijah Muhammad. In a characteristically thoughtful and complex narration of this visit, Baldwin makes powerfully vivid the appeal of the Nation of Islam's message, and of Elijah Muhammad himself, as a charismatic leader. This narration makes equally clear Baldwin's ultimate refusal of this leader and his message: his refusal, one that Malcolm X himself had arrived at just before he was assassinated, to endorse or embrace the Nation's stark Manichean racial dualism, despite his admiration of the compelling dignity and power the Nation accorded African Americans, his sympathy for the Nation's analysis of the continuing global history of monstrous white crime against black people, and for its analysis of the strength and greatness of black people.

Baldwin's expression of rage in this essay, particularly as he remembers his Harlem childhood and youth, is frequently clear, direct, unmodulated, and unmuted: "neither civilized reason nor Christian love would cause any of those [white] people to treat you as they presumably wanted to be treated; only the fear of your power to retaliate would cause them to do that, or to seem to do it, which was (and is) good enough. There appears to be a vast amount of confusion on this point, but I do not know many Negroes who are eager to be 'accepted' by white people, still less to be loved by them; they, the blacks, simply don't wish to be beaten over the head by the whites every instant of our brief passage on this planet" (299). His expressions of love for and pride in black people and African American culture, and concomitant contempt for white American culture, are also direct, clear, and passionate:

> We had the liquor, the chicken, the music, and each other, and had no need to pretend to be what we were not. This is the freedom that one hears in some gospel songs, for example, and in jazz. In all jazz, and especially in the blues, there is something tart and ironic, authoritative and double-edged. White Americans seem to feel that happy songs are *happy* and sad songs are *sad*, and that, God help us, is exactly the way most white Americans sing them—sounding, in both cases, so help-lessly, defenselessly fatuous that one dare not speculate on the tempera-ture of the deep freeze from which issue their brave and sexless little voices. (311)

> When I was very young, and was dealing with my buddies in those wine- and urine-stained hallways, something in me wondered, *What will happen to all that beauty*? For black people, though I am aware that some of us, black and white, do not know it yet, are very beautiful. (346)

Nonetheless, Baldwin cannot join the Nation of Islam, or embrace its repudiation of all whites, because "I had many white friends. I would have no choice, if it came to it, but to perish with them, for (I said to myself, but not to Elijah), 'I love a few people and they love me and some of them are white, and isn't love more important than color?' " (327). Baldwin's move closer to Black Power does not obviate his belief in the revolutionary role of the enlightened vanguard, beyond race. In fact, this move only makes clearer to him the pressing necessity of universal transformation beyond the massively destructive political divisions of race ("Color is not a human or a personal reality; it is a political reality" [345–46]):

> For the sake of one's children, in order to minimize the bill that *they* must pay, one must be careful not to take refuge in any delusion—and

the value placed on the color of the skin is always and everywhere and forever a delusion. . . . If we — and now I mean the relatively conscious whites and the relatively conscious blacks, who must, like lovers, insist on, or create the consciousness of the others — do not falter in our duty now, we may be able, handful that we are, to end the racial nightmare, and achieve our country, and change the history of the world. If we do not now dare everything, the fulfillment of that prophecy, re-created from the Bible in song by a slave, is upon us: *God gave Noah the rainbow sign, No more water, the fire next time!* (346–47; emphasis in original)

The Fire Next Time, like the earlier essays but more vividly and starkly, primarily endorses a utopian/apocalyptic, universalist narrative of progressive blacks and like-minded whites either at the vanguard of redemption or, failing in that endeavor, falling along with the unenlightened into damnation, while it also adumbrates a racially marked, identity-based postmodern subject politics.

In the wake of the urban fires of the mid- and late sixties, literal and figurative, which Baldwin here, in 1963, uncannily predicts; following on the assassinations of the two greatest leaders of the African American political movements, and of the white politician of national stature most closely allied with the black movements (Bobby Kennedy); and in the aftermath of the failure of all sixties political and cultural agendas arising from the revolutionary paradigms of modernity, at least in their totalized utopian form, Jesse Jackson's Rainbow Coalition, based on postmodern identity politics of difference and affiliation around local, particular, limited goals, entirely opposite to Baldwin's modern postracial revolutionary vanguard which was to bring about total, utopian transformation, unnaturally (counternaturally) reverses this sequence of rainbow and fire. Jackson's rainbow is produced in the aftermath of fire — it is explicitly not the sort of rainbow produced by the salvific aftermath of apocalyptic flood. It certainly is not premised on the end of racial difference — it is premised instead on racial difference itself, as well as on other identity-category differences such as gender, sexuality, ethnicity, ability, age, geographic location. It is a deliberately socially constructed rainbow, not in fact a rainbow at all — rather, a postmodern simulacrum, very consciously deploying the readily available, accessible, popular cultural symbolism of the rainbow, as advertising does, to achieve contained, specific, perhaps even realistically feasible political ends.

CHAPTER FOURTEEN

Personal and Political

This chapter discusses not just the pivotal status of key texts of second-wave feminism between the dominant modern and the emergent post-modern, but, more explicitly, the pivotal role of second-wave feminism in the emergence of postmodernity. I will not be making reference to the many important feminist analyses linking feminism with postmodernism, or to postmodern analyses of the puzzling failure of that linkage.[1] Nor will I invoke Andreas Huyssen's argument about mass culture as woman, modernism's other, or Craig Owens's argument about women's theories and practices of difference coinciding with postmodernism. I will discuss, rather, the structure and impact of second-wave feminist thought and writing itself. I will be building shamelessly and gratefully on preceding work, and in the interest of doing anything at all beyond making continual reference to great works of feminist theory, history, and criticism of the past thirty years, I will assume, with a few exceptions that are most directly germane to my discussion, that the work I am building on will be evident.[2]

Feminism was at the heart of the emergence of the postmodern from within the ultimate, culminating modernity of the sixties. This is partly because its analysis claimed a totalizing revolutionary content superseding that of any other analysis. The "dialectic of sex" — the dualistic sex/gender binary — is seen, especially in radical feminism, as the foundation of all other hierarchical binaristic oppressions: a characteristic formulation reads "male supremacy is the oldest, most basic form of domination."[3] At the same time that this analysis promised to eradicate all modes of domination and bring about utopia, it focused on an identity-defined group of people — "women" — who were not the vanguard party of this revolution just because of their structural location within an oppressive system, like the working class in the Marxist analysis of capitalism, but who were oppressed because of what was seen as their nature, either inherent or constructed, and must rally together around an affirmation of this nature, even as they worked to eradicate the gender categorizations that constructed it. Universal, transformative revolution at the most profound structural level, then, came to be lodged in and equated with a particular identity category. As the 1977 "Combahee River Collective Statement" says, "we realize that the only people who care enough about us to work consistently for our liberation are us. . . . This focusing upon our own oppression is embodied in the concept of identity politics. We believe that the most profound and potentially most radical politics come directly out of our own identity, as opposed to working to end somebody else's oppression. In the case of Black women this is a particularly repugnant, dangerous, threatening, and therefore revolutionary concept because it is obvious from looking at all the political movements that have preceded us that anyone is more worthy of liberation than ourselves" (Schneir, *Feminism in Our Time* 179–80). The revolutionary concept of "identity politics," steeped though it still was in dominant universalist revolutionary goals (Combahee also says, "We might use our position at the bottom, however, to make a clear leap into revolutionary action. If Black women were free, it would mean that everyone else would have to be free, since our freedom would necessitate the destruction of all systems of oppression" [Schneir 183]), was a crucial pivot to the postmodern repudiation of these universalist emancipatory goals of modernity. While Civil Rights and Black Power operated on the same pivot from modern universal liberation to postmodern "subject politics," as we saw in chapter 13, it is in second-wave feminism that this shift is most clearly embedded and formulated in theoretical self-articulations and also enacted in the history and impact of feminism as a social-cultural-political movement.

Like poststructuralism, second-wave feminism attacked the binary itself—all dualisms structured by a dominant self-term and a subordinated other-term (self-other dualisms)—as inherently hierarchical and oppressive. Mammalian reproductive biology could no longer be either the material basis or the ideological metaphor governing the socialization of gender, and with the repudiation of this foundational reproductive dualism all dualism must and would be repudiated. Feminism would rid the world of gender itself, bringing about an egalitarian utopia where all domination, based on the original domination of man over woman, would be eliminated, and we would all be simply human, with the commonality of humanity emphasized over its diversity. We see clearly here the seamless simultaneity, with the difference between them invisible, of dominant modern and emergent postmodern paradigms in second-wave feminism: its postmodern attack on the binary coincides with its modern humanist universalism.

Postmodernity did undo or reconfigure the binary, with feminism at the vanguard of the binary's dismantling, but the result is not a utopia of the human, but rather a field—sometimes battlefield—of the play of relational differences, alongside, and in disjunction or antinomy with, an extreme form of capitalist economic and cultural globalism. Human commonality as utopian ideal, as we have seen, has been repudiated by postmodernism as an enforced uniformity, the exemplary oppressive Enlightenment master narrative. This Enlightenment universal guarantees the normativity of the hegemonic, founded on the denial of full subjectivity to subaltern others. In postmodernity, again, differentiation becomes the locus of oppositional politics. The radical feminist attack on the binary hoped to produce a utopia of equals premised on the elimination of politically meaningful differentiations of subjective positioning, believing those differentiations to be the basis of all oppression. What the critique of the binary actually produced was the emphasis on those differentiations, not just as primary structure but also as locus of progressive political possibility. In this postmodern subject politics, "identity" is no longer in any way essential or self-present. It is characterized by the play of shifting, malleable, constructed differences, with race, ethnicity, location, gender, and sexuality predominant, but no one axis of difference inherently more important than others. Juxtaposed with globalism, this field of difference characterizes postmodernity.

The "difference" advocated by the greatest of the endpoint modern feminist theorists, the poststructuralist-Lacanian "French feminists," because it valorizes fragmentation, has sometimes been collapsed with this relational field of subjective differentiations. French feminist difference, however, is ultimately a very different thing. It is a universal, totalizing, transformative utopia, in the tradition of modernity, like poststructuralism itself, rather than of postmodern politics of differential subjectivity (again, I would argue that this differential subjectivity does not necessarily imply or claim a self-present, coherent stability). French feminist difference implies a world in which any identity categorizations have lost their meaning, based as they are seen to be on the subjectivity produced by the masculine, patriarchal psychic politics of the self-same: the self-identical, self-present white male European subject. French feminist difference repudiates all self-other dualisms and is marked by its open play of difference, its polysemous, semiotic indeterminacy and fragmentation, its subversion of the repressions of masculine reason and the symbolic cultural order of the Father.

As is clear, or at least implicit, in this account, contained within this modern, universalist, utopian analysis is the embryo of the postmodern: the valorization of difference, of limitless, multidirectional flow, of the local-particular, of fragmentation, and of fluid, non-self-present but historically marked and embodied subjectivities themselves, rather than the coherence of master narratives. Further, the patriarchal formation attacked by French feminism is specifically Western, white, and bourgeois; the others of patriarchy to be liberated in the French feminist vision are not just feminine but are also the subaltern others of race, class, sexuality, and location. In positing the elimination of these hierarchical differentiations, French feminism inevitably names and brings into focus as agents and beneficiaries of utopian transformation precisely the othered, "minoritarian" identity categories the affirmation of which, in postmodernity, becomes a political end in itself.

At the same time, in positing "the feminine" as the utopian alternative to patriarchical domination, French feminism implicitly argues that the achievement of a feminine subjectivity and/or cultural-political-psychic practice is, itself, the revolution. The goal of utopian transformation, lodged in modernity, thereby comes to be identified with the achievement of a certain kind of subjectivity. This subjectivity is not just a precursor or prerequisite of revolutionary transformation, as it is, for example, for Marcuse. It is, itself, that transformation.

This notion of the feminine as difference is highly indebted to the poststructuralist and Lacanian paradigms in which the French feminist theo-

rists were immersed. Like Derridean poststructuralism and Lacanian psychoanalysis, French feminism is at once quintessentially modernist in the
totalizing reach of its theorizations — all Western culture, in the case of
poststructuralism, and all cultural, psychic, subjective phenomena, in the
case of Lacan — and at the same time postmodern in its emphasis on the
play of difference, the critique of dualism, and the notion of subjectivity as
split, multiple, non-self-identical. This embrace of the feminine as fragmentation, jouissance, and difference contains a contradiction that is a
major factor in the current postmodern feminist repudiation of French
feminism: this fragmentation is at odds with the universalism of the key
French feminist notion of "the feminine," even though that notion is seen
in the major works of Cixous, Irigaray, and Kristeva as a cultural position
rather than as embodied in actual women. It is this universalism, and the
collapse or merging of "the feminine" as Western historical cultural position with the notion of "woman" as an oppressively disembodied abstraction, obliterating the historical specificity of actual, embodied women in
all their difference, that led to the repudiation of French feminism as
essentialist. "Woman," or even "women," which originated in second-
wave feminism both as an identity category and also as a place-marker for
the agency and content of revolutionary transformation, became, in postmodernity, itself an oppressive universal. In key works of early second-
wave American radical feminism, we see many of the same pivotal, dominant modern/emergent postmodern structures that characterize French
feminism.

Robin Morgan's introduction to her influential radical feminist anthology of 1970, *Sisterhood Is Powerful*, is a representative text of what was
then called the women's liberation movement.[4] Not only does it encapsulate most of the central arguments, emotions, postures, attitudes, and
vocabularies of radical feminism, mostly derived from those of the New
Left, it also enacts the ways in which radical feminism, like French feminism but more explicitly socially-politically, marked at once the culmination of modernity and the inception of postmodernity, and was instrumental in that shift.

Morgan titles her introduction "The Women's Revolution." This formulation is subtly but tellingly different from either "Women's Liberation," the most common name for the movement in the late sixties and
early seventies, or "Feminist Revolution," as in Redstockings' *Feminist
Revolution* or Shulamith Firestone's *The Dialectic of Sex: The Case for
Feminist Revolution*.[5] "Women's Liberation" names an explicitly political

movement, invoking the Romantic tradition of the left, and deliberately linking feminism to the third world liberation movements (in fact directly imitating that formulation) that were such an integral part of the sixties radical conjuncture.[6] While these movements were organized by and focused on specific third world peoples, they were understood to be premised on a global revolutionary analysis that conceived third world liberation as part of the overthrow of the capitalist, racist foundations of imperialism, and the institution of some form of socialism in its place, beginning in the third world but ultimately, inevitably, in the first world as well. It was not merely a question of the banding together and rising up of oppressed peoples against their oppressors as an end in itself. This rising up was conceived teleologically, as a stage in the historical sequence of capitalism, imperialism, and world socialist revolution.

"Feminist Revolution," as opposed to "The Women's Revolution," similarly implies a teleology. Feminism names a set of political analyses and priorities — an alternative, gender-egalitarian system that would replace the systemic oppressions of patriarchy. Feminist revolution generally understood and subsumed socialist revolution and allied itself with black and third world liberation movements. It aimed at a totally egalitarian society, with no politically meaningful categorical differentiations.

"The Women's Revolution," however, is, or can be, an end in itself. It implies that the banding together and rising up of members of the category "women," independent of their political analysis or purposes, is in itself inherently revolutionary. It is in who and what "women" are, rather than in what they think or propose to do, that the revolutionary capacity resides. Sisterhood as well becomes an end in itself, producing its own subculture, rather than a means toward the end of transformative social-political-cultural change. Critiques of this version of feminism as ahistorical, hegemonic, and essentialist, from Alice Echols's analysis of what she calls "cultural feminism" to the wide and powerful range of works of feminist postcolonial, African American, ethnic, third world, postmodern, and queer theory, are crucial, and very well known.[7] The important observation for my purposes here is that Morgan's "women's revolution" encompasses not only this essentialist significance of the category "women" but also the feminist significance in which "women" names not an ahistorical essence but rather a necessary political category of analysis, with a wide range of historical variability and specificity.

The political meaningfulness that adheres to subjectivity in postmodernism adheres as well, of course, to more traditional or overtly political modes of activism. I am in no way suggesting that these modes are superseded in postmodernity. Quite the contrary. However, this political activism is often organized around particularist agendas and goals linked to modes of subjectivity and subjective location. Again, it is the focus on the politics of subjectivity, rather than either the mode of activism or the way in which subjectivity is understood, that is at issue. The postmodern battles over the politics of subjectivity ("identity politics") having to do with the question of essentialism as opposed to social constructionism (inherent and immutable, or malleable, shifting results of political, social, cultural structures), with whether subjectivities are stable or in flux, consistent or non-self-identical, are, again, not in question here. What is characteristic of postmodernity in fact is precisely the field in which the postmodernism of flux, performativity, shifting affiliation, relationality, and constructedness contests various modes of identitarian essentialism. Both sides of this debate are lodged within, and the debate itself defines or marks, the postmodern location of the political within questions of subjectivity (again, I am not addressing here the long, rich, important debates around these questions of "identity politics"). The point is that the focus of political contestation, of what is considered political, has shifted markedly to questions of identity and subjectivity, particularly in relation to cultural practice. Second-wave feminism's defining contribution to this shift was its core belief and organizing tool, embodied in and marked by the phrase "the personal is political."

"The personal is political" began in the Romantic tradition of adequation of transformed self with transformed world—recognizing the marks of general oppression in the specific facts of personal life, and remaking the world by remaking the self—but rapidly became instead a politics of living a feminist life without therefore necessarily transforming the system that produced the oppressed life. This is a familiar story, as Sara Evans's revolutionary "personal politics" become Alice Echols's apolitical, as she sees it, "cultural feminism." The additive accumulation of individual feminist lives became equated with political transformation. Analyses of patriarchal systems as premised throughout history on the subordination of women were superseded, as politics shifted to the realm of particular subversive or resistant or counterhegemonic identifications, modes of subjectivity, tactics of the everyday, and cultural or subcultural practices. The result is not, as it is often judgmentally labeled, the apolitical new age inward-turning self-cultivation so frequently seen as the fallen progeny of the sixties, but a non- or antisystemic politics in which personal transformation is equated with political transformation, and in which cultural and subcultural practices not necessarily overtly directed toward political change are often seen as the most interesting, dynamic locations of politically progressive resistance. A reconfigured postmodern understanding of what constitutes the political, primarily in the conception of power and resistance as shifting, multidirectional, local, partial, "capillary," "nomadic," "rhizomatic," dynamic flows rather than massive dualisms of domination and revolution, most closely associated with the theories of Foucault and of Deleuze and Guattari, accompanied this shift.[8]

In Robin Morgan's "Women's Revolution," I see the beginnings of this shift. "Women's Revolution" implies that the aims and ideologies of this revolution are less important than who is involved in it, whom it serves: "women." Accordingly, Morgan begins her introduction by stipulating the exclusive involvement of women in the project of the book: "It was conceived, written, edited, copy-edited, proofread, designed, and illustrated by women" (xiii). This statement is preceded, in Morgan's opening line, by an important political statement: "This book is an action." Along with the use of the keyword "revolution" in the introduction's title, this opening line carefully contextualizes women's liberation in general, and this anthology in particular, within the discourses of the New Left, which was committed to spontaneity, creativity, and diversity in its political expression. An "action" could range from the familiar modes of march, rally, sit-in, leafleting, petition, and protest, to various forms of street or guerrilla theater, to a bombing or a bank holdup, in the final violent years of the movement. The women's liberation movement, indebted to the New Left, deployed and in some ways extended this practice. It was particularly creative in its street and guerrilla theater actions, such as the "hexings" of the WITCH groups. The way the New Left extended the domain of the political, and women's liberation extended it further, so that "actions" could be almost anything and appear almost anywhere, was again a prelude to postmodernity, where resistance is as pervasive and diffuse as power itself, and, again, is seen to inhere in everyday cultural tactics, practices, and modes of performance not themselves necessarily overtly political.

Morgan considers *Sisterhood Is Powerful* an "action" specifically *because* "it was conceived, written, edited, copy-edited, proofread, designed, and illustrated by women." This opening provides a direct enactment of the anthology's title: by banding together as women, in sisterhood, placing commonality as women above any differentiations along other axes, women through sisterhood acquire power—the power to transform the world. Sisterhood must override all other forms of solidarity as well as all other forms of differentiation.

In the context of the male-dominated public sphere faced and resisted by early second-wave feminism, an exclusively woman-produced book can certainly be seen as a feminist action. Even in publishing, where women had gained entry in relatively lowly jobs in some numbers, positions of decision-making power and authority were still overwhelmingly held by men. In the case of *Sisterhood Is Powerful*, the women by whom the book was "conceived," etc. were acting as feminists. But implicit in Morgan's celebration of this all-female anthology is the assumption that the fact of the presence of women, the substitution of women for men, implies or produces a politics.

Herein lies the contradiction that resulted in the late-second-wave feminist split between what came to be thought of as difference feminism on one side, and both socialist or materialist feminism and liberal egalitarian or equality feminism on the other. I am not interested in rehearsing yet again what the substance of this split was or how it came about. For my purposes here, the crucial issue is the way in which contradictions within radical feminism prefigured, marked the shift to, and enabled or even produced postmodern configurations. On the one hand, radical feminism located the foundational oppression in the gender division itself and premised its political movement on eradicating gender difference. On the other hand, radical feminism argued that women as the oppressed group must band together as women, shunning men, the oppressor, because gender oppression as policed by the patriarchal family is founded on the primary attachment of individual women to individual men, and on a "divide and conquer" separation of women from one another by means of sexual rivalry between women over men. Difference feminism, especially the utopian theories of the French feminists, finessed this contradiction by viewing not women per se but "the feminine," a cultural force historically located in women but not inherent in women, and potentially available to all humans, as a revolutionary alternative to patriarchy. Equality or liberal feminism never set out to eliminate gender difference by revolutionary means but rather to minimize or even eliminate the unequal differential social impact of gender difference. Their goal was to give women equal access to public power, and to equalize the burden of housework and child rearing—to allow everyone regardless of gender to occupy the privileged position of man, and to bring about a sharing of the oppressed position of woman by men (or, in some versions, to revalorize "women's work," though that position is more commonly associated with cultural feminism).

I want to take a moment here to discuss the close presence in this argument of the work of Joan Scott and of Ann Snitow. In her 1996 book *Only Paradoxes to Offer: French Feminists and the Rights of Man,* Joan Scott argues that modern feminism is rooted in a foundational contradiction between women's political claims as women, a class wrongfully excluded from citizenship and full humanity, and women's political claims as humans, regardless of, and repudiating the meaningfulness of, gender difference.[9] In Scott's words, "in order to protest women's exclusion, they had to act on behalf of women and so invoked the very difference they sought to deny" (x). This contradiction remains inevitable in feminist thought and politics. Ann Snitow articulated a similar inevitable and foundational feminist contradiction, focusing on her own experience in the second wave, in her essay "A Gender Diary," in Marianne Hirsch and Evelyn Fox Keller's collection *Conflicts in Feminism,* published in 1990.[10] Snitow discusses the contradiction between the second-wave feminist desire to affirm the strengths of women and the simultaneous desire to eliminate gender difference, therefore to eliminate the category "women" altogether. Clearly, my work here is indebted to these arguments. But rather than emphasizing either the foundational status or the continuing simultaneity of these contradictory positions, I am arguing that in the early second wave, this simultaneity constructed the elimination of gender difference as the utopian goal of overcoming all dualistic hierarchical oppressions, founded on the primary gender oppression, as an agenda of modernity, while the particularist, subjectivist goal of affirming women as an identity category was constructed as an agenda of postmodernity.

The opposite argument could also be made: that the elimination of gender difference became the postmodern agenda of queer theory, while the affirmation of women as an identity category is modern in its universalist essentialism. I would argue, however, that the object of queer theory (whether or not it has a "proper object"; see Judith Butler's "Against Proper Objects") is not that of feminist modernity, to eliminate completely the binary gender differentiation of compulsory heterosexuality, but rather to derealize or deconstruct it by performances of queer subjectivities. Binary gender differentiation, in queer theory, will not disappear but rather will be constantly reinstituted and constantly deconstructed (Judith Butler is the preeminent theorist of the performativity of queer subjectivity). Moreover, cultural feminism, after its radical phase, which (though it continues in some essentialist versions of ecofeminism) culminated in Greenham Common and other women's peace movements of the eighties, despite its essentialism, is not universalist. It is marked as postmodern by its subjectivist particularism: its affirmation of women is generally an end in itself, and often a personalistic end for particular women, not a means to a larger end of general utopian transformation.

Morgan's introduction is characteristic of the radical feminist moment in which emergent subjectivist postmodern politics were in suspension with, and undifferentiated from, dominant modern utopian revolutionary politics. In line with the latter — with the concepts, rhetoric, and goals of universal revolution — Morgan considers the "non-hierarchical" women's movement "the first movement that has the potential of cutting across all class, race, age, economic, and geographical barriers — since women in every group must play essentially the same role, albeit with different sets and costumes: the multiple role of wife, mother, sexual object, baby-producer, 'supplementary-income statistic,' helpmate, nurturer, hostess, etc. To reflect this potential, contributors from those different groups speak in this book — and frequently disagree with each other" (xviii). Further, "the women's movement has set itself the task of analyzing divisions (race, class, age, hetero- and homosexuality) that keep us apart from each other, and is working very concretely to break down those divisions" (xxv). It is precisely this universalist sisterhood, this desire to "cut across all . . . barriers" and to "break down those divisions," that has been repudiated in postmodern feminism as constituted by an appropriative, oppressive, straight, white, middle-class hegemony. It is no longer a question in postmodernity of "disagreement" or "divisions," it is a question of the diversity and conflict of often incommensurable differences. Note also Morgan's formulation "the first movement": like the New Left, radical feminism saw itself as new in history, eclipsing and leaving in the dust the sad failures of all previous radical left and feminist movements.

Morgan sees the sexism engendered by patriarchy as "the primary oppression" (xxxv); she sees "a worldwide Women's Revolution as the only hope for life on the planet . . . the genuine radical movement" (xxxv). The "profoundly radical analysis beginning to emerge from revolutionary feminism" is "that capitalism, imperialism, and racism are *symptoms* of male supremacy — sexism" (xxxiv). The Women's Revolution is the same here as feminist revolution, and it will unify under the umbrella of its all-inclusive analysis all revolutionary movements of the oppressed; it will change, transform, save the world.

At the same time, literally — the same paragraph that begins with the statement that the "worldwide Women's Revolution" is "the only hope for life on the planet . . . the genuine radical movement" — Morgan continues: "I can no more countenance the co-optive lip-service of the male-dominated Left which still stinks of male supremacy than I can countenance the class bias and racism of that male 'Movement.' I haven't the faintest notion what possible revolutionary role white heterosexual men could fulfill, since they are the very embodiment of reactionary-vested-interest-power. But then, I have great difficulty examining what men in general could possibly do about all this. In addition to doing the shitwork that women have been doing for generations, possibly not exist? No, I really don't mean that. Yes, I really do. Never mind, that's another whole book" (xxxv). Morgan's enraged attack on men here speaks of much more than the general rage at male oppression and exploitation of women, and rage at one's own oppressive men in particular, that inevitably accompanied women's arrival at feminist consciousness and analysis. Beyond this feminist rage, Morgan's formulation speaks, again, of the substitution of identity categories for positioning in an unequal, oppressive political system. It is not systems of patriarchy or male dominance that Morgan identifies as the source of oppression here. But beyond that, it is also not even sexist behavior, or men with power in sexist institutions, that she wants to "not exist," rather it is men in general. Nor is it "men" as an abstract category, the necessary antithesis to "women" in the oppressive gender binary, and therefore gender difference itself, that Morgan wants to eliminate, any more than she wants to eliminate "women" — quite the contrary, she wants women to bond in revolutionary sisterhood. Again, this aim exists in contradiction and suspension with the desire Morgan expresses elsewhere to do away with the founding oppressive gender binary. It is men as individuals, as "embodied" male people, that she conflictedly, ambivalently, but passionately wants not to exist. She wants not just insight and change from men, she wants retribution, possibly to the extent of total annihilation. This position is elaborated much more fully and unambivalently by Valerie Solanas in the scum Manifesto, a work I think we read now as mainly funny, but that was read then by many with dead seriousness. This is very different from eliminating oppression, or even from anarchist acts of targeted assassination. The target here is an entire identity category rather than a position of power, or its symbolic representative, within an oppressive system.[11]

Slightly earlier in the introduction, Morgan herself seems almost conscious of the confusion generated by the seamless, invisible mix in women's liberation of modern with postmodern formations: "the only thing I know is that *this* time we women must seize control over our own lives and try, in the process, to salvage the planet from the ecological disaster and nuclear threat created by male-oriented power nations. It is not a small job, and it does seem as if women's work is never done" (xxxiv). *In the process* of "seiz[ing] control over our own lives": the connection between women seizing power over our own lives, for the first time since the early matriarchies, as radical feminism has it, and salvaging the planet from militaristic patriarchal capitalism is not clear to Morgan; she describes it not as an inevitable outcome of women ending patriarchy, but as something else women would have to do in addition to, though somehow as part of ("in the process of"), not ending patriarchy but seizing control over our own lives — doing, so ironically, "women's work." The idea of connection between women's revolution and general utopian transformation is still primary, but the elements are beginning both to disaggregate and to change in nature. Feminist revolution is becoming women's self-determination and autonomy; the general goal of egalitarian revolution is becoming a specifically ecological, antinuclear salvaging.

Morgan also pays a great deal of attention to personal experience: the politics of subjectivity that defined the New Left in general and the credo "the personal is political" that has defined second-wave feminism. Morgan describes her feminist radicalization: "speaking from my own experience, which is what we learn to be unashamed of doing in women's liberation, during the past year I twice survived the almost-dissolution of my marriage, was fired from my job (for trying to organize a union and for being in women's liberation), gave birth to a child, worked on a women's newspaper, marched and picketed, breast-fed the baby, was arrested on a militant women's liberation action, spent some time in jail, stopped wearing makeup and shaving my legs, started learning Karate, and changed my politics completely. That is, I became, somewhere along the way, a 'feminist' committed to a Women's Revolution" (xiv). This passage is remarkable for the deliberate leveling indifferentiation of Morgan's gendered experience. We see here so clearly how the category of "experience" is constructed: the more traditionally political activities of union organizing, marching and picketing, being arrested and spending some time in jail are interspersed with and undifferentiated from the near-dissolution of a marriage, the birth and breastfeeding of a baby, abandoning feminine rituals of makeup and leg-shaving, and learning karate. We learn that Morgan "changed [her] politics completely," but we do not hear how (in fact it is assumed we know this, but I would still argue that it is important that Morgan does not make reference to the content of these changed politics here), nor are we to assume that her changed politics are in a different category from ceasing to wear makeup or to shave her legs. Quite the contrary.

This passage is meant to exemplify what it means to say that "the personal is political." At the time, resisting what was seen as conventional, "oppressed" femininity was political. It was a rebellion against the markings of an oppressed gender identity that enforced the subordination of women. But what appears in this passage incipiently is the postmodern world in which "a woman's politics" are indistinguishable from decisions about makeup, body hair, childbearing and breastfeeding, saving or ending a marriage. This passage exemplifies dramatically just how the revolutionary modern "the personal is political" became the subversive postmodern "the political is personal." In this passage, the two are as yet indistinguishable. Shortly thereafter, they became profoundly sundered. The familiar narrative of a depoliticizing fall from radical to cultural feminism by means of substitution of the personal for the political does not allow us to understand this shift of the postmodern from emergent to dominant formation, nor does it allow us to understand the key role of second-wave feminism in this shift.[12]

Morgan also discusses her experience of consciousness-raising (c-r), the primary tool and political structure of the women's liberation movement, and home of "the personal is political." She credits c-r, along with working on this anthology, with the feminist transformation of her life and political ideas. C-r is another prime instance of how early second-wave feminism was on the cusp between dominant modernity and emergent postmodernity and was instrumental in the shift. Its goal was to radicalize women and bring about feminist revolution, but its methods emphasized what came to be considered individual "lifestyle choices." These questions of how one lives one's life were then questions of how individual women could transform their consciousnesses and thereby change the oppressed conditions not just of their own lives but ultimately of all women's lives. But the emphasis on changing one's own life clearly led to the postmodernity of the construction or performance of subjectivity as in itself inherently political. Again, this is not a process of depoliticization but a transformation of the meaning of the political. As far as the future of feminist theory and practice is concerned, understanding the nature of this transformation might help us to understand the various modes of intellectual impasse that currently receive so much attention and that have led many of us to turn our attention elsewhere. I agree with Barbara Johnson that impasse can be seen instead as an empowering ambivalence of "holding on to more than one story at a time," as she says in her introduction to *The Feminist Difference*, and I agree with bell hooks that, as she says in *Conflicts in Feminism*, "we have to be willing . . . to work with . . . contradictions and almost to celebrate their existence because they mean we are in a process of change and transformation."[13] This link of contradiction to change is intellectually proximate to the kind of transformation I am discussing here. If we can understand our impasses as historically dynamic rather than ideologically static, we might have a better chance of moving beyond them.

Shulamith Firestone's *The Dialectic of Sex: The Case for Feminist Revolution* of 1970 would appear to be located entirely within the Enlightenment/modern, utopian revolutionary moment of early second-wave feminism, untouched by the pervasive incipience of postmodernity we have seen in Robin Morgan's introduction to *Sisterhood Is Powerful*. Firestone's book indeed may be the most thorough, explicit, systematic, defining argument for utopian world-transforming feminist revolution produced by early radical feminism. Nonetheless, *The Dialectic of Sex*, just as much as the Morgan text, vividly reveals the inherence of postmodern configurations within the most fully, quintessentially modern-revolutionary ideas and programs of early second-wave feminism.

Dialectic is marked as Enlightenment/modern most obviously by its (ostensible) adherence to that quintessentially modern intellectual paradigm, the dialectic, and not only by its content overall but also by its form and structure. It purports to offer a total, systematic, systemic analysis of the "dialectic of sex" as "the missing link between Marx and Freud," as the Bantam edition back-cover blurb claims; an analysis that covers all relevant topics and issues, and covers them in a coherent, organized fashion. Firestone writes in a fairly traditional, formal, distanced, rationalistic, logical, orderly, cool style — a style that had already been rejected by a wide spectrum of sixties writers, and that came to be considered "male" or "patriarchal" in later phases of radical feminism. In this regard, Morgan's introduction moves much further toward that later stage of radical feminism, and toward styles popularized in the sixties that have become standard postmodern essayistic writing practices in general. These practices are characterized by informality, associative structure, first-person narration, personal tone and autobiographical reference, nonsuppression or noncensorship of controversial, "shocking," or generally taboo opinions and emotions ("letting it all hang out," in sixties terminology), as in her desire for men to "not exist," rejection of formal or rigorous logical argumentation, as what Morgan in fact calls a "linear, tight, dry, boring, male super-consistency." Morgan boasts of the "blessedly uneven quality noticeable in the book, which I, for one, delight in" (xvii), an unevenness that stands as a repudiation of that "linear, tight, dry, boring, male super-consistency." By Morgan's standards, Firestone's book largely conforms to that repudiated "male" style of thought and writing.

The fact that Firestone's book was a bestseller, a Bantam paperback with multiple printings, is indicative of its postmodern elements: despite the fact that its analysis of patriarchy and calls for total revolution, which occupy most of the book, would interest only a small minority of its readers, Firestone's ideas about the future of gender, sex, sexuality, the family, and, most important, the lifestyles indicated by these insights spoke to the shifts already under way in Western cultures/societies, shifts that produced and were produced by postmodernity. The fact that this book was until very recently out of print for many years indicates, I would argue, both the extent to which the radical utopian revolutionary moment it bespeaks and represents is superseded, and also the extent to which its postmodern programs have become commonplace.

Firestone gives full voice to the radical feminist analysis of sex-gender oppression as the ultimate and primary oppression from which all others derive, and also as the source of the hierarchical, binary, self-other structure of all oppression. She opens on a powerful, resonant note: "Sex class is so deep as to be invisible" (1). She expands this observation: "this is painful: No matter how many levels of consciousness one reaches, the problem always goes deeper. It is everywhere. The division yin and yang pervades all culture, history, economics, nature itself; modern Western versions of sex discrimination are only the most recent layer. To so heighten one's sensitivity to sexism presents problems far worse than the black militant's new awareness of racism [note the competitiveness with Black Power]: Feminists have to question, not just all of *Western* culture, but the organization of culture itself, and further, even the very organization of nature" (2). Before second-wave feminism emerged, gender differentiation in the midcentury West — what Firestone calls "sex class" — was at once a pervasive, constitutive social-cultural determinant, and also a nonissue, something too unimportant or irrelevant or trivial to mention, let alone to think about or take seriously. Firestone does not have far to go from that dynamic of pervasiveness and invisibility to an analysis of "sex class" as the ultimate source of all oppression.

A great deal of the book is devoted to recounting Marxist analysis, especially Engels's, of gender, to outlining what Firestone understands as Marxist dialectical materialism, and to reviewing Freudian analysis of the family. In her treatment of Marx and Engels, Firestone wants to embrace dialectical or historical materialism but take the analysis, as she sees it, one significant step deeper or further back, to (again) the ultimate oppression, biological sex differentiation, with its ensuing or concomitant unequal division of reproductive labor, inherently prejudicial to women. In her treatment of Freud, she wants to accept his analysis of the dynamic of the bourgeois patriarchal family, but she also wants to historicize that analysis as a brilliant profile of the dynamics of sex-gender oppression under patriarchy. A feminist extension of Marx-Engels, Firestone argues, gives us the ultimate material base of all oppression, superseding and providing the structural model and grounding for class and race oppression. A feminist contextualization of Freud gives us an analysis of the social and psychic mechanism that maintains and enforces the oppression of women in the patriarchal bourgeois family.

Firestone's version of Freud became one form of standard feminist ideology, and its details are far too familiar now to require rehearsal here, but her version of Marx-Engels was exceptional. It forms the basis of Firestone's emergent postmodernism. Most feminist adaptations of Engels's argument in his crucial text, *The Origins of the Family, Private Property and the State*, accepted his linkage of the development of private property with the initial oppression of women. Despite this linkage, Engels considers the oppression of women the foundational oppression, on which all subsequent oppressions were based. Only when men acquired private property and therefore a reason for guaranteeing inheritance did there come to be any material basis for social control of women's reproductive sexuality. This necessity produced the subordination of women to men within the family, and the denigration of women's labor, which had heretofore been equal to men's. Men rather than women first acquired private property because they happened to be responsible for herding within the gendered division of labor, and herds happened to be the first private property (this is by far the weakest element of Engels's argument).

Firestone does not accept Engels's linkage of the oppression of women with the development of private property. She claims, as we have seen, that the oppression of women is grounded in biology itself. She intends to learn from Marx and Engels their dialectical materialist method rather than their conclusions — "we are dealing with a larger problem [than class antagonism], with an oppression that goes back beyond recorded history to the animal kingdom itself" (2): "the immediate assumption of the layman that the unequal division of the sexes is 'natural' may be well-founded. We need not immediately look beyond this. Unlike economic class, sex class sprang directly from a biological reality: men and women were created different, and not equally privileged. Although, as De Beauvoir points out, this difference of itself did not necessitate the development of a class system — the domination of one group by another — the reproduction *functions* of these differences did" (8). Firestone's emphasis on Freud's analysis of the family derives from her belief that the "*biological family*—the basic reproductive unit of male/female/infant, in whatever form of social organization" (8) — is the construct that dictates the inevitable oppression of women, for four neatly ordered reasons. First, female biology, including "menstruation, menopause, and 'female ills,' constant painful childbirth, wetnursing and care of infants, all of which made them dependent on males . . . for physical survival" (8) controls women's lives, or at least it has done so "throughout history before the advent of birth control" (8). Second, human infants' long period of dependency oppresses women, their caretakers. Third, this oppressive dependency constructs women's psyches, presumably as also themselves dependent or cripplingly bonded with the dependent child. Fourth, "the natural reproductive difference between the sexes led directly to the first division of labor at the origins of class, as well as furnishing the paradigm of caste (discrimination based on biological characteristics)" (9).

The solution to the foundational inherent biological inequality of men and women based on differential reproductive function, for Firestone, lies in the full human triumph over nature, including the elimination of mammalian sexual reproduction from human life (or at least its drastic curtailment so that it is not the reproductive norm). In this belief, Firestone is at once quintessentially modern and incipiently postmodern. Her "biological essentialism" has come to be seen by postmodern feminism as the hallmark and primary pitfall of feminist modernity. The triumphant rationalism of every aspect of her thought and textual form finds its culmination in her utopian commitment, which she shared with Marcuse, to modern technology's progressive ability to "liberate" humankind from the constraints of this essential, but transcendable, nature Unlike Marcuse, or Horkheimer and Adorno, she does not take into account the devastating domination of nature by instrumental rationality that has been one of modernity's most dangerous legacies. At the same time, her commitment to eliminating the social significances of sexual difference, along with her belief in the potential of technology to liberate women from those significances, has deep resonance with a range of postmodern feminist thinking, from queer theory, with its denaturalization and disruption of male-female sex as well as gender dualisms, to Harawayan cyborgian socialism, with its vision of the ineluctable, and potentially liberatory, interpenetration of the human and the technological. Firestone not only uncannily inhabits and articulates the sixties moment of shift from modern to postmodern, but, in both the wide proliferation of her text and its subsequent near disappearance, she marks and enacts the crucial role of second-wave feminism in facilitating that shift.

Second-wave feminism exploded in the late sixties out of cumulative rage at the male supremacism of sixties radicalisms. No sixties movement has had a greater social, political, cultural impact than second-wave feminism, including its key impact on the shift from modern to postmodern. There is widespread debate concerning the nature and extent of the changes wrought by various modes of sixties political and cultural activism, but, despite the extensive effects of the backlash and the persistence of deeply resistant sex-gender inequities, few would dispute the contention that feminism has had an enormous impact. (Those on the right who deplore the effects of feminism perhaps would accord it a greater impact than would those disappointed feminists who view the revolution as having failed.) The general nature of this impact (again with the proviso that the backlash has been extremely effective in innumerable areas), involving women's massive entry into the workforce and seismic shifts in social, cultural, psychic expectations and practices concerning sex and gender, does not need to be recounted here. I want to focus instead on the seismic shift in literary production.

In line with the shift of sixties activism from the social-political to the cultural-intellectual arena, second-wave feminism has found an important home in the academy. My own career, like the careers of many other women academics over the past quarter century, has been enmeshed in, made possible, and constructed by the feminist transformation of the academy. Literary study has been powerfully affected by feminist theory and criticism. Just at the time, in the seventies, that feminist critics and theorists shifted our focus to questions of gender and sexuality, and to the study of women writers, literary production itself also underwent a massive shift. In the case of many important women writers, this shift was a direct result of involvement in the women's movement.[14] Poetry was an enormously important component of second-wave feminism; poems often served as the most powerful, rich, galvanizing movement statements. Poems are included, for example, in *Sisterhood Is Powerful* and in Miriam Schneir's *Feminism in our Time*; Florence Howe's *No More Masks!* was a crucial collection for second-wave feminism, particularly in literary academia.[15] Sylvia Plath, Anne Sexton — the great precursors/foremothers whose tragic ends prevented them from stepping into the promised land — Adrienne Rich, and Audre Lorde have iconic status in the movement. Many other poets were, and continue to be, vital to its evolution, its self-understanding and self-representations. Fiction was also crucial. Doris Lessing's Martha Quest novels, and, even more important, *The Golden Notebook*, were enormously influential, as were novels by a wide range of feminist writers. Further, second-wave feminism inspired, produced, influenced, and was influenced by a general renaissance in women's literary writing. My purpose here is not to revisit these gratifying, self-congratulatory truisms but rather to discuss literary production, by men as well as women, in relation to second-wave feminism as shift from modernity to postmodernity.

Many writers of the feminist renaissance are women of color; many writers, male and female, are from the third world; many are lesbian and gay; many write from within nonhegemonic, hybrid, border-crossing ethnic, racial, religious, and other positionalities. I mention this not merely as a celebratory observation but rather as an indicator of feminism's crucial position in the shift to postmodernity. Feminism's politics of subjectivity, again, simultaneously inhabited modernity and postmodernity, and operated as key pivot from the former to the latter. Sisterhood was intended to supersede differences among women, yet the powerful force of subject politics itself, articulated at once by feminism and by black, third world, and other racial and ethnic politics, opened the door for the empowerment and voicing of a broad array of nonhegemonic subjectivities. Because of the great impact of feminism in the cultural and intellectual arenas, this has been extremely important not just for writing by women but for the wide range of postmodern writing which is informed by feminism and the other new social movements (see chapter 9). I would like to argue here that the ways in which the literature of (representing, enabled by) second-wave feminism, while primarily deploying postmodern literary modes, is deeply informed and powered by second-wave feminism's modern/postmodern simultaneity. This simultaneity is evident not just in the broad proliferation and success of work by writers who occupy what Linda Hutcheon calls minoritarian and ex-centric positionalities (of race, class, sexuality, ethnicity, religion, location as well as gender), who move into audibility in the aftermath of postmodernity's decentering of modernity's hegemonies, but also in characteristic formal elements of postmodern literary writing in general.

Of these writers, Toni Morrison is for me exemplary, partly because I work primarily on fiction, partly because she is simply so great a writer, and partly because her postmodern work is so clearly informed by modernist literary traditions. There are many other writers whose work is similarly structured by and located within a postmodernism strongly marked by the modernist legacy — Morrison is exceptional only in the quality, power, influence, and popularity of her work.

Morrison is also crucial to me because of her post-utopian utopianism, or utopian post-utopianism. Along with a range of other postmodern fiction, Morrison's novels, as I will discuss in the final chapter, can be characterized precisely as mapping a domain of "utopia limited."[16]

CHAPTER FIFTEEN

Utopia Limited

Utopianism, like postmodernism, has been seen as a quintessentially or characteristically American phenomenon.[1] This chapter will analyze, in the realm of postmodern American fiction, which is a crucial inheritor of sixties cultural and political movements (see chapter 9), the interrelations among the sixties, postmodernism, and utopianism that I have been investigating throughout this book. I will begin (appropriately, I hope, for a chapter on "historiographic" fiction)[2] by sketching a brief history of American utopianism.

The real heyday of American utopianism was not in the sixties but rather in the nineteenth-century antebellum period, which saw the blossoming of hundreds of communities, the names of some of them at the heart of our cultural history (Brook Farm, the Shakers, the Icarians, Oneida, Amana, to mention a few of the best known). Socialist and, in the case of the Owenite communities, feminist egalitarianism were crucial to these utopian communities.[3] This historical utopian cornucopia also coincided, of course, with the heyday of slavery. The utopian movements overlapped with and sometimes embraced (fostered, were committed to) abolitionism, with

Brook Farm a prime instance. It is clear that nineteenth-century utopianism and abolitionism shared the universalist, Enlightenment ideals of human equality and freedom so central to the modernity that is so deeply
problematized in the sixties and in postmodernity. I would argue that
Radical Reconstruction, including most notably the Freedmen's Bureau
(1865–72), hoped and even attempted to realize the goals of utopianism
and abolition, and that the destruction of Reconstruction marked the
defeat, at least for that historical moment, of the social goals and visions of
both.[4] The period in the 1870s and 1880s following the dissolution of the
Freedmen's Bureau, and the ultimate defeat of Reconstruction, was a post-
utopian historical moment (utopianism of course reemerged throughout
the twentieth century, until its endpoint and transformation in the sixties).
These decades witnessed the breakup and disappearance of most of the
antebellum utopian communities, contemporaneous with the institution
of slavery by other means in the sharecropping Black Belt South, and of
systemic, often murderous racism throughout the country. At the same
time, this period encompassed the stunning growth of industrial capitalism
in the urban North, with its rampant social miseries as yet unchecked by
subsequent radical and reformist movements.

American utopianism's next major renaissance was, again, in the sixties, with hundreds of communities (none of them as famous or successful as their nineteenth-century predecessors) springing up all over the
country. Like their predecessors, these communities were committed to
egalitarianism and crucially linked to a resurgence of socialism, though
there were many differences: sixties utopias were generally marked by an
anarcho-syndicalist version of socialism, emphasizing personal, individual freedom, pleasure, and fulfillment at the expense of group unity or
coherence (see chapter 7 on The Living Theatre).[5] They were therefore
much more ephemeral and fragile than the generally more group-oriented,
and sometimes rigidly rule-governed, nineteenth-century communities.[6]
Despite this difference of emphasis, however, the sixties communes were
varyingly, loosely, but consistently committed to ideals of common owner-
ship, equitably shared labor, and an egalitarian power structure based
on the crucial ideal of participatory democracy (the hierarchical, guru-
governed religious communes were an exception).[7] As I have argued, the
antagonisms between the political New Left and the countercultural hippie utopian communes are well documented, but they should not obscure
the fact that the New Left and the counterculture were two facets of
a broad, general movement that had at its core a commitment to social-

ist egalitarianism — liberty, equality, community — including racial, class, and, sometimes, gender equality. These issues were highly complex and troubled: most hippies were white and came from middle-class backgrounds. Further, because both radicalism and the counterculture were exaggeratedly macho and male dominated until the emergence of second-wave feminism in the final phase of the sixties (see chapter 14), they usually reproduced dominant gender inequalities, often in exaggerated versions, despite their egalitarian ideologies.

Like the post-Reconstruction period, the post-sixties, postmodern present is also a post-utopian moment; unlike post-Reconstruction, the current postmodern, post-utopian moment seems definitive.[8] Many studies mark the decline or end of egalitarian, socialist-based or -inspired utopianism in postmodernism.[9] In this chapter, I will discuss the status of utopianism in two postmodernist works of fiction, both of them set in the post-utopian early 1870s. I have chosen these two seemingly unrelated novels because they are both set just at the moment of the demise of the Freedmen's Bureau, with, in both cases, that historical moment a simultaneous representation and displacement of the sixties, used at once to account for and also to parallel our current situation: Toni Morrison's *Beloved* and E. L. Doctorow's *The Waterworks*.[10] Both of these writers also have iconic status for me in relation to this study, since Morrison is (perhaps) the greatest "minoritarian" writer to emerge out of the upsurge of writing by women of color galvanized by second-wave feminism (as I have argued in chapter 14), and I consider Doctorow to be one of the most important white male "postmodernists" (as defined in the seventies, when "postmodernism" was seen as a formalist phenomenon inhabited almost exclusively by white males) to move his work, actively and constitutively, into the field mapped by the postmodern inheritance of sixties participatory democracy and subject politics (see chapter 9). I will discuss the connections between these novels' visions of utopianism, their post-sixties, postmodern politics, and their deployments of postmodernist narrative strategies. It may seem strange that I am writing about postmodern novels set in historically displaced versions of the post-utopian post-sixties, rather than novels written directly about the sixties and their aftermath, of which there are, of course, many. I do so because at this point in this study I want to engage the question of the utopian and the post-utopian in postmodernity directly. The historical displacement in these novels to the post-utopian situation of the 1870s, based on rather than representing directly the post-utopian 1970s, allows a clarity of focus on the question of postmodern post-utopian hope itself, rather than on the specificities of the 1960s.

Both *Beloved* and *The Waterworks* are engaged with utopian visions; in both, history destroys or distorts potential or attempted utopias. Both novels are thoroughly postmodernist in their narrative strategies, interweaving popular with high literary modes of fiction writing.[11] In both novels the failure or destruction of utopia is connected to slavery and its racist sequelae: the utopian possibilities of the late sixties — both 1860s and 1960s — are defeated by the intractability of slavery's legacy. For Doctorow, that defeat coincides with the deformations of urban industrial capitalism and its concomitant political corruption (capitalism appears in *Beloved* in the muted or displaced but crucial form of schoolteacher's brutal, dehumanizing, efficiency-oriented rationalism). At the same time, both novels express a postmodern skepticism about utopia as well as regret for its defeat.

Morrison and Doctorow both delineate in the post-utopian 1870s the present of post-sixties postmodernity. Doctorow saturates his 1870s New York with the crude inequality of vast, ill-gotten elite wealth in dialectic with mass poverty, squalor, and wretchedness. Both are linked to the thoroughgoing corruption and degradation of public politics, everywhere suggestive of what Fredric Jameson calls the global triumph of capitalism in its purest form. *Beloved*, though less explicitly than *The Waterworks*, evokes the aftermath of the sixties by using the end of the Freedmen's Bureau, signaling the nearing defeat of Reconstruction itself, to suggest the failed utopian goals of Civil Rights, Black Power, and early second-wave feminism.

A characteristic postmodernist narrative strategy works in both novels to handle the dilemma of at once representing a powerful utopian desire and representing a thoroughgoing skepticism, in the wake of both the defeat and the discrediting of the utopian in the sixties, concerning both the desirability and the possibility of its fulfillment. This strategy is the refunctioning of sentimental, sensationalist popular genres — melodrama/ghost story for Morrison,[12] detective fiction for Doctorow — along with the traditional heterosexual romance plot, both to resolve and also to refuse to resolve or absolve the loss and defeat, and at the same time to represent the postmodern skepticism at the center of each novel.[13] An excess of apocalyptic fictional material, which cannot be integrated into the resolutions conventional narrative forms enforce, pushes into the ending of each novel and also erupts through the prose surface of each throughout. This excess connects to the anticonventional writing in each novel, which I consider the persistence of utopianism as modernist form within the reconfigured formal conventionality of postmodernism.[14] What I am calling modernist writing is most evident in the ellipses Doctorow uses throughout the novel, and also in the explicitly visionary passages in his prose. Morrison's poetic prose in general pushes at the limits of conventional writing; in *Beloved*, the ultimate scene of putative but ultimately murderous utopian fulfillment is written in fully experimental prose. I consider this persistence of utopian desire in tension with post-utopian assumptions characteristic of the most important postmodern fiction.

"Sweet Home" is Morrison's ineluctably clear indictment of the possibility of utopia in a slave country.[15] The acerbic irony of that plantation's name exceeds its allusion to "Home Sweet Home," forcefully undercutting America's claim to Edenic status. As in Eden, the power of naming at Sweet Home belongs to the patriarch; in this case, in this country, he is the white patriarch. The power of naming, both oneself and one's children, is crucial to this novel. Sethe and her mother insist on their right to name their children; Baby Suggs and Stamp Paid insist on the right to name themselves. The fact that all but two of the Sweet Home men are named Paul both highlights the deindividuation of slaves and also provides yet another ironic reference to the master's Christian tradition. The tree planted on Sethe's back by schoolteacher's student's whip is the Edenic tree of knowledge with a vengeance. There is no possibility of antebellum utopia in *Beloved*, because, simply, of slavery.

The novel acknowledges the white utopian aspirations of the antebellum period, in Mr. and Mrs. Garner's enlightened relations to their slaves, in the name "Sweet Home," and in the almost livable life Sethe leads with Halle before the advent of schoolteacher. Utopia, however, is always already contaminated by slavery: even at their best, the slaves' lives are only almost livable, and nothing like autonomous or free. The unusual (for slavery) autonomy of the "Sweet Home men" proves empty when Mr. Garner dies and Mrs. Garner feels that "she needed her brother-in-law [schoolteacher] and two boys 'cause people said she shouldn't be alone out there with nothing but Negroes" (197). Because their "freedom" was created by Mr. Garner, it died with him.

Toward the end of the novel, Morrison comments, by means of Paul D, on the nonfulfillment of America's Edenic promise: "in five tries he had not had one permanent success. Every one of his escapes . . . had been frustrated. Alone, undisguised, with visible skin, memorable hair and no whiteman to protect him, he never stayed uncaught. . . . And in all those escapes he could not help being astonished by the beauty of this land that was not his. He hid in its breast, fingered its earth for food, clung to its banks to lap water and tried not to love it" (268). This passage evokes the beautiful (withheld rather than promised) land as the nurturant maternal body. The linkage of the utopian to the maternal, found frequently throughout Western figurations and analyses of utopia, is an important element of the fictional configurations I analyze here. The conscious deployment of this linkage is characteristic of the self-conscious engagement with gender politics of post-sixties postmodernist fiction, forged in the heat of second-wave feminism and the other sixties new social movements.

Abolition is similarly at once given its due and undercut by Morrison. The Bodwins—the abolitionists who enable Baby Suggs and her family to find shelter and employment—are clearly "good people." Bodwin remembers with nostalgia, as "heady days," the time "twenty years ago when the Society was at its height in opposing slavery," when " 'bleached nigger' is what his enemies called him, and . . . had caught him and shoe-blackened his face and hair" (260). For Bodwin, the heyday of abolition was indeed a utopian time, betrayed in the postwar period. His thoughts resemble those of some current veterans of the 1960s: "Those heady days were gone now; what remained was the sludge of ill will; dashed hopes and difficulties beyond repair. . . . Nothing since was as stimulating as the old days of letters, petitions, meetings, debates, recruitment, quarrels, rescue and downright sedition" (260).

The irony of Sethe seeing Bodwin as schoolteacher, when she attacks him with an ice pick at the end of the novel, is nonetheless sharply pointed. While the Bodwins expose themselves to considerable risk in the service of their abolitionist beliefs, and they manage Sethe's release from prison, they do not see or treat African Americans as equal to whites. Baby Suggs and later her granddaughter Denver both enter the Bodwin house through the back door. Denver, having obtained the "Service" (see below) employment in the Bodwin house that will allow her and Sethe to survive, affirms that the Bodwins are "good whitefolks." As she is about to leave through that back door, she sees, "sitting on a shelf . . . a blackboy's mouth full of money. His head was thrown back farther than a head could go, his hands were shoved in his pockets. Bulging like moons, two eyes were all the face he had above the gaping red mouth. His hair was a cluster of raised, widely spaced dots made of nail heads. And he was on his knees. His mouth, wide as a cup, held the coins needed to pay for a delivery or some other small service, but could just as well have held buttons, pins or crab-apple jelly. Painted across the pedestal he knelt on were the words 'At Yo Service'" (255). Beyond exploitation, dehumanization, degradation, reification, and theft of labor, this remarkable figure suggests the tortures both of slavery and of postwar violence against African Americans that are among Morrison's central concerns in this novel.[16] The "head thrown back farther than a head could go" and the "gaping red mouth . . . wide as a cup" suggest not only lynching (that suggestion reinforced by the bulging eyes) but also the humiliation and torment of the collar and bit suffered by Paul D.[17] The nails driven into the head suggest at once a generalized violence and also the most drastic sort of bodily imprisonment. "At Yo Service" and "on his knees" remind us of the view of African Americans held by (almost) all whites, even "good whitefolk" abolitionists like the Bodwins.[18]

Both the New World Eden and white abolitionism are vitiated by slavery and racism, but there exists in this novel a much more potent, promising, and therefore more tragically destroyed utopian possibility, opened up by sixties spiritual countercultures, African American politics, and second-wave feminism. We see it first in the preaching Baby Suggs, holy, does in the Clearing, during the period between Halle's purchase of her freedom and Sethe's arrival at 124 Bluestone Road with Denver in her arms and the tree of knowledge on her back. Baby Suggs had

> decided that, because slave life had "busted her legs, back, head, eyes, hands, kidneys, womb and tongue," she had nothing left to make a living with but her heart — which she put to work at once. Accepting no title of honor before her name, but allowing a small caress after it [holy], she became an unchurched preacher, one who visited pulpits and opened her great heart to those who could use it. . . . Uncalled, unrobed, unanointed, she let her great heart beat in their presence. When warm weather came, Baby Suggs, holy, followed by every black man, woman and child who could make it through, took her great heart to the Clearing — a wide-open place cut deep in the woods nobody knew for what at the end of a path known only to deer and whoever cleared the land in the first place. (87)

The Clearing has strong utopian resonance, with its anonymous provenance, its anti-instrumentality, its spaciousness, and its depth in the woods — the primeval nature of the American Eden. Baby Suggs, self-named, is literally free of tainted institutions, "unchurched." Her congregation is a spontaneous egalitarian bonding, in nature, of the oppressed, for the purpose of mutual salvation.

They achieve this salvation not through any acceptance of dogma or practice of ritual or belief in divine intercession. Morrison explicitly circumvents Christianity: "She did not tell them to clean up their lives or to go and sin no more. She did not tell them they were the blessed of the earth, its inheriting meek or its glorybound pure. She told them that the only grace they could have was the grace they could imagine" (89). They achieve salvation through the inspiration of Baby Suggs's great heart and her moving language, by means of ecstatic laughing, dancing, singing, sobbing. Morrison represents in the Clearing the release through the body into love of the black body despised by white America: " 'Here,' she said, 'in this here place, we flesh; flesh that weeps, laughs; flesh that dances on bare feet in grass. Love it. Love it hard. Yonder they do not love your flesh. They despise it. . . . *you* got to love it, *you!*' " (88).

We learn of Baby Suggs's ministry in the Clearing only after it is long since lost, as Sethe yearns for it in order to be able to bear the information Paul D has given her about Halle's end, information that has begun to catalyze her "rememory." Baby Suggs renounced her ministry in the wake of the unbearable events at the center of this novel, the "unspeakable unspoken" of slavery itself, whose objective correlative for Morrison is the necessity for a mother to murder her child in order to save her: "no notebook for my babies [to write down their 'animal characteristics'] and no measuring string neither" (198). Baby Suggs says " 'those white things have taken all I had or dreamed . . . and broke my heartstrings too. There is no bad luck in the world but whitefolks.' . . . Her faith, her love, her imagination and her great big old heart began to collapse twenty-eight days after her daughter-in-law arrived" (89).

The event that empties the Clearing and deprives Baby Suggs of faith, love, imagination, and her heart itself, the historical event around which Morrison constructed this novel, takes us back to the linkage, crucial to French feminism, of the utopian and the maternal (see chapter 14; see particularly Irigaray's *Speculum of the Other Woman*, Cixous's "The Newly Born Woman," and Kristeva's *Revolution in Poetic Language, About Chinese Women*, and "Stabat Mater"). Beloved is the child Sethe has been driven by the Fugitive Slave Act to kill in order to save her from slavery, the child she then named by paying by the letter with her body for a tombstone inscription. This child returns to claim her mother, into a space opened in Sethe for her by the reappearance of Paul D and the eruption of rememory into Sethe's life. The watery world of death from which Beloved returns is endowed by Morrison with deliberately multiple, ambiguous, undecidable suggestions at once of the womb, the underworld or afterlife, the specific circumstances of Beloved's death, and the general historical circumstances of the Middle Passage. This literally miraculous return restores mother and daughter to one another, and sister to sister (though that relation is largely nonreciprocal, with Denver desiring Beloved and Beloved desiring only Sethe).

Morrison constructs this space of maternal restoration and completion very explicitly as utopian. The three women form a closed whole of perfect mutual gratification. Paul D has decamped, leaving the three women alone at 124 Bluestone. First he had exorcised the ghost Beloved had become, enabling her return in bodily form. When that bodily presence becomes unbearable to him, he repudiates Sethe's action in murdering/saving Beloved by accusing Sethe of precisely the "animal characteristics" ("four feet," as he puts it) attributed to her by schoolteacher. The attribution of "animal characteristics" is what Sethe killed Beloved in order to save her from. In his bitterness at his recognition that Sethe's love for her children outstrips anything she might feel toward him, and in his fear at the danger of a black woman loving her own, therefore herself, with such an absolute claim, he has accused her of a love that is "too thick" (164).

Ultimately, Morrison endorses Paul D's view. At first, the self-contained, absolute, world-excluding mother-daughter bond Sethe forms with Beloved appears to be a redemption not only of the crime against both their lives forced on Sethe by the law of slavery, but also of the pre-Oedipal connection of the girl child to the mother's body advocated in much feminist theory as the ground for a revolutionary feminist praxis. This bond, however, proves to be monstrous and nearly itself murderous.[19] Beloved's absolute love for and dependence on Sethe gradually, steadily emerges as lethal to Sethe: Beloved is literally sucking away Sethe's life, growing fat on it as Sethe declines (Beloved looks pregnant as Sethe nears death). It is Denver, with her refusal of an absolute bond with Sethe, her link to her father (she looks like and yearns for Halle), her fear of her mother's "too-thick love," and her independence, who pushes outside this self-contained female utopia/dystopia, out into the community, and thereby saves herself and her mother.

Sethe's limitlessly abundant milk is a central figure in the novel of the utopian maternal, suggesting the revolutionary, sixties-inspired feminist utopianism of écriture féminine, specifically Hélène Cixous's call to women to write the female body in the "white ink" of mother's milk. In fact, the sequence culminating the bonding of the three women, a bonding so extreme that they become interchangeable with one another, is written in a version of écriture féminine, or experimental prose. It is filled with imagery of mother-daughter merging, and is reminiscent of Cixous's own writing:[20] "in the night I hear chewing and swallowing and laughter   it belongs to me   she is the laugh   I am the laugher   I see her face which is mine   . . .   her face comes through the water   a hot thing   . . .   my face is coming   I have to have it   I am looking for the join   I am loving my face so much   my dark face is close to me   I want to join   she chews and swallows me   I am gone   now I am her face   my own face has left me   I see me swim away   a hot thing   . . .   I want to be the two of us   . . .   she is my face smiling at me   doing it at last   a hot thing now we can join   a hot thing" (212–13). This writing is the embodiment, the literalization, of Sethe's "too-thick" maternal love, the "chewing and swallowing" of mutual engulfment. The theft of self perpetrated by slavery on Africans is represented by the violence of the theft of Sethe's milk — to Sethe this theft is even more intolerable than the brutal whipping that produces the "tree" on her back. Despite this theft, her milk is still miraculously ample and available for both daughters when Sethe arrives at the home of Baby Suggs, the matriarch of 124's maternal utopia. When Beloved returns, it appears as if the promise of Sethe's miraculous milk will be fulfilled in the face of, in defiance of, beyond and outside the history of slavery and the violent defeat of Radical Reconstruction. But a utopia that excludes Stamp Paid is a utopia that denies black solidarity, the only hope located within the limiting specificities of history rather than, as utopian constructions inevitably are, projecting beyond or outside it (I refer to the important scene where Stamp Paid, hearing the three merged voices within the house, feels he cannot enter, cannot even bring himself to knock on the door when in fact, given what he has done, he has the right to enter any African American house without knocking). Sethe's miraculous milk drains off into the succubus Beloved has become; its seemingly limitless flow is in fact limited by the extent of Sethe's own life.

The community of women, catalyzed by Denver, saves Sethe; Paul D returns to tell her that she, not her children, is her own "best thing" (273). The radical, absolute mother-daughter bond is broken, and lighter, thinner, reformist rather than revolutionary bonds take its place: individualist self-realization ("you your own best thing"), the romance plot (reconciliation with Paul D), and intermittently activated, saving but potentially rejecting community (the praying circle of women who had turned their backs on Sethe's "too-thick love"). Radical black feminist utopia turned deadly gives way to uneven, local, partial, particular, historically embedded resistance (black feminist rather than simply feminist because its maternality is a defiance of and alternative to the deformations of slavery).

Denver's successful move out into the world, her reintegration into the community, bringing Sethe with her, and the return of Paul D do not end the novel. The postmodern, post-utopian ending derived from the conventions of mainstream bourgeois fiction (just as the central narrative structures of the novel are dependent on the ghost story, and sentimental, sensationalist melodrama) is succeeded, and to some extent supervened, by the final, two-page section. Morrison gives the last word to the uncontainable, apocalyptic excess Beloved represents: "Disremembered and unaccounted for, she cannot be lost because no one is looking for her"; she "erupts into her separate parts"; "They forgot her like a bad dream. . . . Remembering seemed unwise" (274). But "down by the stream in back of 124 her footprints come and go, come and go" (275) and her name is the last word of the text.[21] The experimental prose cited above and, more pervasively, the dense, magnificent poetic writing Morrison uses throughout are the footprints of Beloved on the form of this novel. Further, the repeated refrain, "It was not a story to pass on," twice, then "This is not a story to pass on" (274–75), represents, in its contradictory double-entendre of "pass on" as transmit and "pass on" as walk away from, the persistence of utopian desire in a postmodern fiction that at once passes on it and passes it on.

While *Beloved*'s evocations of sixties utopianism, and post-sixties post-utopianism, are implicit, Doctorow's in *The Waterworks* are explicit, or as nearly so as they can be in a novel set in the 1870s.[22] Morrison deploys refunctioned narrative conventions of sensationalist sentimental melodrama; Doctorow deploys those of sensationalist detective melodrama. I have already alluded to the strong parallel *The Waterworks* establishes between the brutal urban capitalism of the late nineteenth and the late twentieth centuries. Augustus Pemberton, one of the novel's villains — the father of one of its heroes, Martin — made his fortune first from the illegal slave trade, and then from Civil War profiteering: selling lethally inferior goods to the Union Army. He has built for himself, as the robber barons in fact did, a massive estate on the Hudson, Doctorow's descriptions of which evoke the unnatural monstrosity of the houses on the shore of Fitzgerald's West Egg (*Gatsby* is a profound influence on this novel, as we will see). In his megalomania, his wholehearted belief in his own invulnerability, which corresponds to Boss Tweed's fatal hubris (the breakup of Tammany Hall is one of the novel's subplots), Augustus Pemberton fakes his death and turns all his money over to the amoral genius Dr. Sartorius, who promises him longevity of indefinite term. He thereby impoverishes his young second wife and child, sentimentalized paragons in this stark moral melodrama.

Dr. Sartorius is a figure of scientific/technological modernity, the Enlightenment progress concerning which Doctorow is deeply skeptical. Dr. Sartorius promises Pemberton a version of eternal, or at least indefinitely prolonged life, which he hopes to achieve through his medical "experiments." These fiendish experiments are based on vampirizing the vital essence of poor orphan children and transfusing it into rich old men. Martin begins to unravel the plot when he digs up his father's supposed grave and finds there instead an oddly withered child — "a very shrunken corpse . . . in odd clothing . . . with a tiny leathered face with its eyes closed and lips pursed" (107).[23] Like Pemberton, Sartorius had taken advantage of the Civil War to make his career. He had established his reputation as a brilliant army surgeon: "he had marched and ridden through the worst of our Civil War unscathed . . . either by its cannon and shot or by its issues. The seemingly endless carnage ended upon the table before him in his field surgery . . . as one continuously fascinating . . . wonderfully torn and broken and dying body . . . with endless things to be fixed" (213).

Sartorius's experiments are performed in a secret laboratory constructed within the "Waterworks" of the title, the upstate pumping station for New York City's water supply (the heart for its lifeblood). He establishes there what Martin explicitly calls an "obverse Eden" (188). Unlike Yeats's ambiguous utopia, Byzantium, it is a country exclusively for old men — old evil plutocrats who want to live forever by feeding off the lives of the impoverished young. Here is Martin's description of this perverse utopia:

> It was in the nature of an indoor park, with gravel paths and plantings and cast-iron benches. It was all set inside a vaulted roof of glass and steel which cast a greenish light over everything. The conservatory was laid out to effect a forbearing harmony and peacefulness. [. . .] Enormous clay urns sprouted profusions of fronds and leaves that I knew on

sight were not native. A kind of tepid steam or diffusion of watered air hissed out of ports or valves inset in the floor, so that the atmosphere was cloyingly humid. I could feel through the floor vibrations of the dynamo that was responsible. [. . .] It was as if I had stepped into another universe, a Creation, like . . . an obverse Eden. (187–88)

Late-nineteenth-century capitalism as unchecked greed and exploitation, in unholy alliance with modern science and technology as amoral instrumentalist megalomania, has converted the American Eden into its obverse, an anti-Eden, with the machine dynamo vibrating with a vengeance in the ersatz garden.

Doctorow's post-utopianism is even more explicit elsewhere in the novel. The harbinger of Sartorius's demonic obverse Eden at the Waterworks is his Home for Little Wanderers, the seemingly benign but in fact lethal orphanage where children are housed in order to die into the unnaturally prolonged lives of plutocrats. The narrator-hero, the journalist McIlvaine, accompanies the policeman-hero, Donne, on a stakeout of the orphanage, which is at 93rd Street and the East River. McIlvaine gives a long, loving description of the still-pastoral landscape in process of urbanization:

At this time, the city north of Seventy-second Street was no longer country, but not yet city either. The houses were few and far between. Whole blocks had been scraped clear and laid out with surveyor string, but nothing was on them. [. . .] Here was a street set with paving stones that stopped at the edge of a pasture, there was a scaffolded half-risen apartment house through whose unframed windows you saw the sky. [. . .] From Park Avenue and Ninety-third the unpaved road ran downhill in a gentle slope to the river. In the fields on either side pumpkins were scattered and trees were beginning to turn. The sounds of the city were distant, almost imperceptible. Donne and his men were encamped beneath a stand of yellowing weeping willow halfway between First and Second avenues. [. . .] Here and there in the field around us birds were scooting about in their dustbaths or hopping from brush to tree. High up over the river an undulant arrow of geese pointed south. (154–56)

Rearing up out of and violently negating this bucolic scene is the Home for Little Wanderers: "a Romanesque structure of red stone trimmed in granite and with the turrets and small windows of an armory. The bottom half was obscured by a brick wall. A cast-iron gate gave on to a courtyard. It

looked its part — a very substantial building, lending substance to those
who lived there. It was an outpost of our advancing civilization . . . like all
our other institutions out at the edges — poorhouses, asylums for fallen
women, homes for the deaf and dumb" (156). McIlvaine so detests this
manifestation of "our advancing civilization" that he is moved to the
following reflection: "I fervently wished there were no buildings of any
kind on this island. I envisioned the first Dutch sailors giving up on the
place as a mosquito-infested swamp, and returning in their longboats to
the ships" (156).

Doctorow is alluding explicitly here to the famous ending of *The Great
Gatsby*, where Nick imagines the Dutch sailors' vision of America, specifically New York, as the "fresh green breast of the new world . . . commensu-
rate to [man's] capacity for wonder." Unlike the modernist Fitzgerald, for
whose narrative vision the "inessential houses" of Long Island can "melt
away" so that he can see again the "fresh green breast of the new world"
that "flowered once for Dutch sailors' eyes," the postmodernist Doctorow
sees those Dutch sailors not as surrogate Adams, beholders of utopia, but
as emissaries of the "advancing civilization" that destroyed utopia. While
Fitzgerald can see utopia again through the Dutch sailors' imagined eyes,
Doctorow can only wish that those eyes had perceived not utopia but a
"mosquito-infested swamp." Utopia can be reimagined by Doctorow/
McIlvaine not through European eyes but only as the pre-Columbian home
of Native Americans, those "savage polytheists of [his] mind":

> Ever since this day [the day of the vision quoted above at the Home for
> Little Wanderers] I have dreamt sometimes . . . I, a street rat in my soul,
> dream even now . . . that if it were possible to lift this littered, paved
> Manhattan from the earth . . . and all its torn and dripping pipes and
> conduits and tunnels and tracks and cables — all of it, like a scab from
> new skin underneath — how seedlings would sprout, and freshets bub-
> ble up, and brush and grasses would grow over the rolling hills [. . .] A
> season or two of this and the mute, protesting culture buried for so
> many industrial years under the tenements and factories . . . would rise
> again . . . of the lean, religious Indians of the bounteous earth, who
> lived without money or lasting architecture, close to the ground [. . .]
> always praying in solemn thanksgiving for their clear and short life in
> this quiet universe. Such love I have for those savage polytheists of
> my mind . . . those friends of light and leaf . . . those free men and
> women . . . (163–64)

The remarkable image of industrial-capitalist Manhattan lifted like a scab to permit the regeneration of a pre-European New World Eden, peopled by what is self-consciously, admittedly a fantasy of prerationalist and therefore free "friends of light and leaf," marks Doctorow's post-utopian utopianism: utopia, as for Morrison, can only be imagined outside, and in explicit negation of, history.

As for Morrison, as well, utopian desire persists powerfully in this novel. Like those of *Beloved*, its narrative structures are mainly governed by the popular fictional conventions that make both novels bestsellers, capable of reaching a wide audience. Doctorow uses the conventions of the detective novel (unraveling the crime of the Waterworks, and bringing its perpetrators to justice, controls the plot: the novel's "hero" is a police detective, Donne) and of the closed or neatly resolved heterosexual romantic plot (in this novel's more-or-less happy ending, Donne marries Augustus Pemberton's young widow, and Martin finally marries his long-suffering childhood sweetheart). Also as in *Beloved*, however, the apocalyptic excess of the novel pushes against the closure installed by those conventions. At the most obvious level, McIlvaine himself (like Beloved) cannot be absorbed into the closing structure of heterosexual coupling. Similarly, McIlvaine's language, the prose of the novel itself, is broken throughout, as the lengthy citations here must have made clear, by erratic use of ellipsis. The ellipsis, like Faulkner's use of italics in *The Sound and the Fury*, is inconsistent — sometimes clearly motivated and sometimes not. It is a mark of what Morrison calls "the unspeakable" breaking into, disrupting, the smooth prose surface we would otherwise expect, marking the place of an absented, discredited, repudiated, historically defeated, but nonetheless persistent utopian desire. The unspeakable, like the Nietzschean abyss of the modernists, deforms and reforms narrative convention. It is precisely this undecidable aggregation of popular convention with anticonventional, modernist or experimental narrative elements that marks for me the domain of serious or ambitious postmodernist fiction.

In *The Waterworks*, as in *Beloved*, the novel's ending is reserved for such an eruption of fictional excess, in this instance in a passage of powerfully evocative poetic prose reminiscent of the great modernists and of Morrison:

> I remember how still the city was that afternoon as I walked uptown from the church. It was brilliantly sunny and terribly cold and the streets were empty. The footing was treacherous. Everything was thickly

glazed. . . . Horsecars were frozen to their rails, as were the locomotives
on their elevated railway of ice. . . . The masts and sheets of the ships in
the docks were ensheathed in ice. . . . Ice floes lay in the viscous river. . . .
The ironfronts of Broadway seemed in the sun to be burning in ice. . . .
The trees on the side streets were of crystal. [. . .] my illusion was that the
city had frozen in time. [. . .] all still, unmoving, stricken, as if the entire
city of New York would be forever encased and frozen, aglitter and
God-stunned. (252–53)

Like the riverside ground behind 124 carrying and erasing Beloved's
footprints, this frozen, God-stunned city is marked, by its prose as well as
by its figuration of apocalypse outside time and history, as the site of a
defeated, discredited, absented, inevitably recurring utopian desire.[24]

The maternal is the locus of defeated utopia for Morrison, and maternality itself becomes monstrous in its historical deformation. For Doctorow, it is the paternal that has become the site of the betrayal, defeat,
and discrediting of utopian possibility: *The Waterworks* is a father-quest,
not for an idealized dead father but for a despised, criminally alive father.
Beloved's utopian excess is lodged in the vanishing/returning footprints of
a water-lost daughter; *The Waterworks*' in the curse of frozen water inflicted by God the Father. But in the postmodern destabilization of the
characteristically modern Oedipal configuration and its attendant gender
dualism, enabled and constructed, again, by second-wave feminism, this
difference (the maternal orientation of one novel, the paternal orientation
of the other) loses defining significance. Morrison's maternal feminine
African American world, as victim of history, is no more capable of transcending history's depredations (surviving, defying, but not transcending)
than Doctorow's paternal masculine Euro-American world, agent of that
victimization, is capable of transcending itself (dissecting, repudiating,
but not transcending).

As postmodern narratives, in which oppositional modernist writing
cohabits with popular fictional convention, both novels choose and enact
a postmodern form of resistance-from-within. They leave behind the
modernist/avant-garde mode of wholesale opposition, in which the new
aesthetic stands as representation, harbinger, embodiment of a world
made new. As Marcuse—the greatest advocate of the modernist/avant-
garde, utopian model of totalized oppositionality, the most wholehearted
sixties believer in the liberatory, transformative power of antirealist aesthetics—said, the "new sensibility" is the de-repressed human conscious-

ness that would bring into being a "realm of freedom which is not that of the present . . . a liberation which must precede the construction of a free society, one which necessitates an historical break with the past and the present" (*Essay on Liberation*, viii).

In postmodernity, as I have argued throughout this book, we are beyond the moment of imagining that revolutionary political/aesthetic intentionality can produce such utter rupture with the past and the present. I also argue, nonetheless, that we live in the aftermath of a profound historical rupture — postmodernity itself — a rupture that did not break along the lines revolutionary (or any other) intentionality had in mind. Utopia in postmodernity is multiply defeated and discredited, yet it persists in the form not only of desire for the amelioration of suffering, inequality, and oppression but also of desire for the total elimination of those conditions: a condition of joy, justice, and freedom. Morrison and Doctorow, in a manner characteristic of the most important, interesting postmodern fiction, suffuse their post-utopian, genre-inflected bestsellers with high modernist affect and form. Similarly, the political imagination of postmodernity cannot encompass a universal utopia, but it can encompass building "piecemeal . . . a democratic society that will be as imperfect as the people who live in it": an imagination of struggle for local, partial, limited, shifting, diffuse, complicit versions of the freedom, justice and equality, and joy that mark the utopian project.

The words quoted above are from a letter by a victim of Soviet-style utopia, written in Prague two days before the invasion of 1968. He is disgusted by what he considers the romantic unreality of Western radical utopianism of the late sixties, particularly that of Marcuse:

> The men I met are all properly repelled by the realities of authoritarian rule, but they keep on preaching the same weary Utopian ideologies that can lead to nothing else. They live in a romantic dream-world in which their dear radical rhetoric is perfectly consistent with their apparently sincere faith in freedom and justice. But do they really think they could apply their radical Utopia in a real world and still respect their libertarian commitments? Do they really think their utopia could be benign if their revolutions were not comic-opera coups on indulgent campuses but real ventures in the exercise of power? . . . It was not until I started visiting the West that I began to understand that a Sartre or a Marcuse can simply afford a great deal of illusion. You all live in a different era — you still believe in Utopia. . . . We've had our fill of

Utopia. No more. Now we are building piecemeal, building a democratic society that will be as imperfect as the people who live in it. It will be socialist because it is an industrial and a democratic society — it just doesn't work the other way around. It won't be a Utopia, but it will be a human kind of society, fit for people to live in.[25]

As for Morrison and Doctorow, the utopian for this "friend from Prague" is not only unrealizable but also utterly discredited, discarded, "of a different era." He not only settles for, but actively prefers, the limited possible. Yet like them, he still powerfully desires the freedom and justice, the liberated, egalitarian socialist democracy, that have constituted the core vision of modernity's secular utopias. In "a human kind of society, fit for people to live in," the formulation conceived as definitive repudiation of and alternative to utopia, the emancipatory Enlightenment-humanist project echoes. The intensity of this utopian desire is clear throughout his prose as well, in the very bitterness of his tone, just as the intensity of Morrison's and Doctorow's utopian desire is palpable in the push of their literary writing past the defeat and repudiation of utopia. Postmodern, post-sixties utopia is limited, in all senses — local-particular, embodied, multiple, diffuse, provisional; contained, subdued, partial, and incorporated.[26] Nonetheless, its footprints come and go, come and go.[27]

CONCLUSION

Post-Utopian Promise

I began this book by saying that I have no interest in engaging the ongoing political and cultural battle over the legacies and meanings of the sixties. That was a necessary assertion to make at the outset, since most books on the sixties have been written, more or less polemically, precisely to engage those crucial questions, and this book definitely has a different agenda. However, the agenda this book does have — to understand the massive shift that occurred during and in the wake of the sixties — has, by definition, an inevitable connection to our contemporary relation to the sixties. In understanding the emergence of the postmodern in and through the sixties, I am charting in fact precisely the relation of the sixties to the present — a relation Fredric Jameson says we must always imagine in light of the utopian project (*Postmodernism* 159).

As I have said in many ways throughout this book, neither defeatism nor triumphalism in relation to the modern, to the sixties, or to the postmodern that emerged from the sixties is of interest or of use. The sixties conjuncture, as endpoint of modernity and modernism, for better and worse, is no longer available. The shifted ground we stand on offers many possibilities as well as difficulties for the egalitarian, popular, local, limited, marked, partial, affiliative, complicitous, embodied liberatory projects postmodernity affords. Informing, perhaps even underlying these postmodern possibilities and difficulties is a set of intellectual and affective relations to "the sixties" as assimilated into the contemporary cultural-political imaginary. The range of these relations is as wide and diverse as the range of political and cultural positionalities of the present moment. And though careful, thoughtful, responsible, penetrating, illuminating histories and analyses of the sixties are fortunately available (see bibliography, part II), simplistic mythologizing dominates popular views of this period. As Ellen Willis argues in her *New York Times* review of Robert Greenwald's *Steal This Movie*, his fictionalized film account of Abbie Hoffman's life, such mythologization is inevitable if only because the sixties radical countercultures, most notably Hoffman's and Jerry Rubin's Yippies, were so often already created as media self-constructions.[1] This media orientation is itself a central move of/in the sixties into postmodernity (see Todd Gitlin's crucial book, *The Whole World Is Watching*, which early on, and still most importantly, made this argument). Willis, a well-known journalist and veteran of sixties radicalism and one of the founders of second-wave feminism, devotes much of her review to a tough-minded critique of this nostalgic mythologizing of the sixties, a critique based on an analysis of the grandiose self-mythologization of so many sixties radicals. Willis ends her review, however, on a profoundly, movingly different note, in writing that deploys an emotive tone diametrically opposite to the cool, distanced, ironic, analytical tone of the rest of the review. In this closing section, Willis argues that what is missing from current debates about the sixties is its "emotional experience," which is a version of what I have been calling the structure of feeling of the sixties, totally recircuited, reconstructed, reconstituted by/in/through the emergence of the postmodern:

> Two kinds of voices dominate the present conversation about the
> 60's: those who condemn the utopianism of the time as a totalitarian
> delusion, and those who sentimentally endow it with a moral purity
> unknown to today's era of rampant materialism and cynicism about
> politics. What's missing from both accounts is the 60's as emotional
> experience: the desire to live intensely, the hope that people could have
> more than Freud's ordinary unhappiness. For my generation, the pur-
> suit of happiness was not a slogan; it turned our guts inside out and left

us with a bone-deep sense of loss. "Steal This Movie" makes a stab at expressing this dimension, but in the end it sentimentalizes. (19)

Despite the defeat ("bone-deep sense of loss") of that intensely utopian sixties structure of feeling, for which some of our generation were, or thought we were, willing to sacrifice everything ("turn our guts inside out"), Willis ends not with despair but rather with an assertion of the persistence of utopian hope and desire in post-utopian, postmodern culture: "to my mind, the movie that gets closest to the heart of the matter isn't about the 60's at all: it's 'Thelma and Louise.' Two female outlaws are transformed by unspeakable hopes for freedom, for a wholly different way of being. They can't go back no matter what. As they leap to their deaths, for one last defiant (and mythic) moment, they are complete. I imagine Abbie would have loved it" (19).

Despite the "bone-deep sense of loss," if we understand how our current postmodern conjuncture emerged from the utopian modernity of the sixties, and still, in very different forms, carries some of its promise,[2] we can recognize the popular, egalitarian, specific, muted, ironic, ambiguous, carefully pitched, disconnected, multiform, multigenre, cross-cut, sampled, electronic, hybrid, transnational, border-crossing, nomadic, multilingual, wavering or roaring voices, often misheard or misinterpreted, of that promise when they speak.

NOTES

Because so many critical and theoretical works have informed my understanding of post-modernity and postmodernism, I have listed them in an annotated critical bibliography (bibliography, part I) rather than citing them in notes that would threaten to become overwhelming in number and length. I have taken the same approach to general works on the sixties (bibliography, part II). Works in either part I or part II are cited parenthetically in the text by short title and page number. Likewise, when they are cited in the notes, I have omitted city, publisher, and date of publication.

Preface

1 New York: Atlantic Monthly Press, 1977.
2 I will explain my use of Raymond Williams's term "structure of feeling" in the introduction. "Lifeworld" is a word Herbert Marcuse uses.
3 Neil Young's song by this title can be used to express so many and varied sixties emotions and experiences.
4 Katha Pollitt makes this argument powerfully in her "Subject to Debate" column titled "War and Peace," in *The Nation*, November 5, 2001, 10. With the American war in Iraq, Vietnam reemerges frighteningly into view.
5 In a "News of the Week in Review" piece in the *New York Times* on November 11, 2001, 14, James Sterngold argues that, in the aftermath of September 11, there is little sympathy, not just in the general populace but specifically among former sixties radicals, for violent sixties activists such as Sara Jane Olson. He quotes Todd Gitlin, a former radical, now very much disenchanted, and one of the most

important historians of the sixties, as saying: "It's not that the country is more reactionary, but I think the prevalent feeling is impatience with the claims made back then that violence can contribute to the political good."

6   See for example books such as Dilip Parameshwar Gaonkar, ed., *Alternative Modernities* (Durham: Duke University Press, 2002).

7   See Fredric Jameson, *Postmodernism, or, The Cultural Logic of Late Capitalism* and *The Seeds of Time*. See also Benjamin R. Barber, *Jihad vs. McWorld* (New York: Ballantine, 1995), and Barber's post–September 11 development of his ideas in "Beyond Jihad vs. McWorld: On Terrorism and the New Democratic Realism," *The Nation*, January 21, 2002, 11–18, for pungent analyses of the contemporary simultaneity of consumer-capitalist globalism and fundamentalist local particularism.

Introduction

1   For example, in her wonderful, richly documented study of New York avant-gardes in the early sixties, *Greenwich Village 1963: Avant-Garde Performance and the Effervescent Body*, Sally Banes argues that the sixties renaissance of the avant-garde itself wholly constituted the beginning of postmodernism (not the emergence of postmodernism from dominantly modern formations, as I argue; evidently, Banes focuses exclusively on the postmodern elements of these movements).

2   David Harvey, *The Condition of Postmodernity*, 42.

3   Despite Jameson's generally critical tone in his accounts of postmodernism and postmodernity, he argues powerfully against any such judgmental stance, as both irrelevant and detrimental to a constructive engagement with the present: "if post-modernism is a historical phenomenon, then the attempt to conceptualize it in terms of moral or moralizing judgments must finally be identified as a category mistake. . . . [we are] now so deeply immersed in postmodernist space, so deeply suffused and infected by its new cultural categories, that the luxury of the old-fashioned ideological critique, the indignant moral denunciation of the other, becomes unavailable. . . . in a well-known passage [of the *Communist Manifesto*] Marx powerfully urges us to do the impossible, namely, to think this development [of capitalism] positively and negatively all at once; to achieve, in other words, a type of thinking that would be capable of grasping the demonstrably baleful features of capitalism along with its extraordinary and liberating dynamism simultaneously within a single thought, and without attenuating the force of either judgment" (*Postmodernism*, 46–47). Note the word "infected," which of course reflects Jameson's general tone in relation to the postmodern phenomena he describes; nonetheless, his efforts at grasping simultaneously its baleful and liberating aspects contribute significantly to the power and usefulness of his work.

4   There are numerous categorizations of the present moment in other terms, deliberately avoiding or moving beyond the seeming datedness or limitations of the term "postmodern": "the information age," various formulations, concerning computer technologies, using the prefix "cyber-" and/or having to do with the "information superhighway"; "globalism," "empire," "new world order," "cosmopoli-

tanism," variations on "postcolonialism" and "post nationalism," formulations using the word "modernity" or "modernities," such as Gaonkar's *Alternative Modernities* or Arjun Appadurai's *Modernity at Large: Cultural Dimensions of Globalization* (Minneapolis: University of Minnesota Press, 1996), "hybridity," "nomadism," Barber's *Jihad vs. McWorld,* "the new millennium," "the twenty-first century"; formulations of "neoliberalism," or based on versions of refunctioned concepts of democracy; formulations having to do with the power of new media, spectacle, simulacrum, popular culture, and the visual; formulations engaging paradigms of performativity and fluid, constructed, marked, ethnically, racially, geographically located and/or queer subjectivities; formulations based on conjunctions of ethics or affect with culture, psyche, and politics; formulations based on paradigms or theories of trauma, mourning, repression and recovery, and witness; formulations based on paradigms of the secular or postsecular. However, though each term maps a particular space of the current conjuncture, and emphasizes crucial aspects of it, and though some of these terms are at odds with one another and, particularly, postcolonialism is at odds with some versions of postmodernism, none of these terms names or describes phenomena substantially different from those included in the understanding of postmodernism/postmodernity I develop here.

5 As evidence of the pervasiveness and nearly consensual status of key elements of the view of the postmodern I am developing here, an article by Edward Rothstein in the "Arts and Ideas" section of the *New York Times,* March 2, 2002 (B9, 11), titled "Damning (Yet Desiring) Mickey and the Big Mac," featuring pictures of Britney Spears in Rio de Janeiro, an old woman in a babushka smilingly greeting Ronald McDonald in Kiev, and Mickey and Minnie Mouse at a Disney theme park in Tokyo, summarizes, in simplified, widely accessible, but nonetheless recognizable and substantive terms, the undecidably mixed view of postmodern (he does not use the term, but it is nonetheless what he is describing) American popular consumer culture as at once loathsome and irresistible globally, offering limitless gratifications, abundant objects (literally) of desire, dislocations, particular local resignifications, enraged culturally protective resistances, leveling of the high/mass cultural distinction associated with class stratification, and democratic, egalitarian possibility in general.

6 See Susan Buck-Morss, *Dreamworld and Catastrophe: The Passing of Mass Utopia in East and West* (Cambridge: MIT Press, 2000), for a brilliant analysis of the reciprocity and mutuality of capitalist and socialist utopianism as constitutive of modernity. For Buck-Morss, it is precisely the mass utopian vision based on technological progress that defines modernity for both capitalist and communist paradigms and states: "The construction of mass utopia was the dream of the twentieth century. It was the driving ideological force of industrial modernization in both its capitalist and socialist forms" (ix). This modernity ended, for Buck-Morss, in 1989, with the fall of the Soviet Union; I would argue that 1989 marks the final completion of the shift to postmodernity that began in the sixties.

7 Modernism of course was in no simplistic way "elitist," or scornful of popular culture. Many modernists were immersed in various modes of popular culture and

incorporated some of those modes into their work. Modernism was, however, constructed by its critical, autonomous self-positioning in opposition to a degraded, affirmative culture industry. The shift in the sixties from "culture industry" to "popular culture" is one of the central topics of this book.

8   "Jihad" and "crusade" — the stark, dualistic, totalizing worldviews of good and evil — subscribe, in a terrible, ironic twist, to the totalizing dualisms of modernity. Nonetheless, again, these are compensatory fantasies and mobilizing ideologies in a world that no longer supports such dualisms as functional political, cultural, or psychic realities. See Benjamin Barber's *Jihad vs. McWorld*, and, in a different register, Arjun Appadurai's *Modernity at Large*, for powerful analyses of the unsustainability and reactive ideological function of this dualism.

9   Again, many of these modes of theory are skeptical of certain white, Western, theory-oriented strains of postmodernism, but they exist within the large scope of postmodernity as I understand it here.

10 See Judith Butler, *The Psychic Life of Power* (Stanford: Stanford University Press, 1997), for a powerful and helpful theoretical discussion of the difference between the "individual" and the "subject." For my purposes here, the shift in connotations and political significances of these terms that occurred within the sixties shift to the postmodern is most germane. Subjectivity becomes a powerful theoretical tool and locus of political valence in postmodernity. While the "subject" is a locus of progressive political meaning in postmodernity, the "individual," highly valorized in modernism and modernity, becomes in postmodernity associated with hegemonic bourgeois formations.

11 Many works of political and cultural history, particularly in the wake of the thirtieth anniversary of May '68, have been written about the sixties, a number of them drawing on the extensive archival material available for such recent history (see bibliography, part 1 for an annotated list of the works on the sixties I have consulted in writing this book). I have undertaken a different kind of project here: again, neither a cultural nor a political history, for either of which original archival research would be necessary and invaluable, but rather a work of textual analysis, attempting to "locate," as Terry Eagleton says of his own project in the preface to his book *William Shakespeare*, "the relevant history in the very letter of the text" (Oxford: Blackwell, 1986, ix). Cultural history, and its attendant archival research, are of signal importance in current literary and cultural studies, retrieved from the oblivion of New Critical formalism, and conferring the sort of authority "doing theory" recently afforded. The archive is crucial to current critical interests in cultural-historical context, as well as in memory, witness, and buried trauma. For my project here, however, it seems most appropriate to understand the sixties' shift from the modern to the postmodern not through archives but rather by reading exemplary texts.

12 Raymond Williams, *Marxism and Literature* (Oxford: Oxford University Press, 1977). Future references to this edition will appear parenthetically in the text. Fredric Jameson's crucial formulation of postmodernism as the "cultural dominant of late capitalism" is indebted to Williams's work. Jameson also uses directly, in addition to the term "cultural dominant," Williams's "structure of feeling," as

well as his notions of "hegemony," as necessary periodizing concepts and termi-
nologies to discuss postmodernism as the cultural dominant of late capitalism. See
his introduction to *Postmodernism*, particularly xiv.

13 I discuss texts rather than authors. With the exceptions of the chapter on William
Burroughs, in which I discuss a group of his sixties texts, and the chapter on James
Baldwin, in which I discuss his major nonfiction sixties works, I make only cursory
reference to other works by the authors whose texts I analyze. I am aware that this
approach fails to account for changes over time in the ideas and aesthetics of each
author, and that other texts by the same author might require quite different
analyses. I have chosen this approach because each text I analyze is characteristic
of the sixties shift from modern to postmodern, in which the modern is dominant
and the postmodern is emergent. A consideration of the total oeuvre of each text's
author would necessarily reveal different sets of issues. Again, this is not a study of
the careers of major sixties authors, but rather a study of representative sixties
texts.

14 The question of works about, including criticism of, this vast array of cultural texts
arises here. Many of the books on postmodernism and on the sixties in the two
annotated bibliographies, the books that have been most influential in my arguments and analyses, are relevant to the kinds of cultural productions I discuss in
chapters 5 and 9. Beyond that, there are simply too many critical and cultural-
historical works on specific cultural producers and products to account for in any
meaningful, responsible way here. I have read and been influenced by hundreds of
these over the years; regretfully, and regrettably, I can only acknowledge them in
this general way.

15 In his (at best) ambivalence toward the postmodern and pain at the failures of the
sixties, Jameson also says that "utopian representation knew an extraordinary
revival in the 1960s; if postmodernism is the substitute for the sixties and the
compensation for their political failure, the question of Utopia would seem to be a
crucial test of what is left of our capacity to imagine change at all" (xvi). Jameson's
highly emotive language here is characteristic of the polemical nature of most
discussions of the sixties and of the postmodern. Again, I try to avoid these passionate, polemical positionings. Specifically, indebted as I am to Jameson, I nonetheless do not argue here that the postmodern is either a substitute for the sixties
or a compensation for its political failure; rather, I argue that the postmodern
emerged, with complex, undecidable implications for progressive agendas, from
the sixties conjuncture. However, I do agree with Jameson, as I have said, that the
status of the utopian is a key issue in this emergence and its significances.

1. Modern to Postmodern in Herbert Marcuse

1 *Critical Inquiry* 25.2 (winter 1999).

2 Herbert Marcuse, *One-Dimensional Man: Studies in the Ideology of Advanced
Industrial Society* (1964; rpt., with a new introduction by Douglas Kellner, Boston: Beacon Press, 1991). All future references to this volume will be included
parenthetically in the text. Max Horkheimer and Theodor W. Adorno, *Dialectic*

of Enlightenment (1944; rpt. trans. John Cummings, New York: Continuum, 1990). All future references to this volume will be included parenthetically in the text.

3   Most treatments of Marcuse are sympathetic. See, for example, Ben Agger, *The Discourse of Domination: From the Frankfurt School to Postmodernism* (Evanston: Northwestern University Press, 1992), which, interestingly in relation to my argument here, argues that Marcuse represents a pathway into the postmodern that retains the politically crucial notion of domination, repudiated by most postmodern thought; Joan Alway, *Critical Theory and Political Possibilities: Conceptions of Emancipatory Politics in the Works of Horkheimer, Adorno, Marcuse and Habermas* (Westport, Conn.: Greenwood Press, 1995), which, in a different register, sees Marcuse's theory of the genuinely liberated, rather than repressively desublimated, subject as having potential for a post-Marxist liberatory politics; John Bokiner and Timothy J. Lukes, eds., *Marcuse: From the New Left to the Next Left* (Lawrence: University Press of Kansas, 1994), another argument for Marcuse's relevance to the post-sixties, post-Marxist left, focused on questions of liberatory subjectivity; Paul Breines, ed., *Critical Interruptions: New Left Perspectives on Herbert Marcuse* (New York: Herder and Herder, 1970), a set of laudatory essays, supporting the elements of Marcuse's analyses consistent with New Left politics, contemporaneous with Marcuse's historical moment of great influence on the New Left; Morris Dickstein's tribute to Marcuse's crucial presence in and influence on the sixties, particularly in *Eros and Civilization*, *One-Dimensional Man*, and *An Essay on Liberation*, in *Gates of Eden: American Culture in the Sixties* (New York: Basic Books, 1977), chapter 3; Barry Katz, *Herbert Marcuse and the Art of Liberation* (London: Verso, 1982), focusing on the promise of Marcuse's liberatory aesthetics; Douglas Kellner, *Herbert Marcuse and the Crisis of Marxism* (Berkeley: University of California Press, 1984), another view of Marcuse as offering a pathway through cultural analysis out of determinist, economic base-superstructure analysis and therefore out of the postmodern crisis of Marxism; Peter Lind, *Marcuse and Freedom* (New York: St. Martin's Press, 1985), focusing again on Marcuse's liberatory emphases and potentialities; Robert B. Pippin, *Marcuse: Critical Theory and the Promise of Utopia* (South Hadley, Mass.: Bergin and Garvey, 1988), retrieving Marcuse's version of the utopian for a contemporary hopeful left politics; Charles Reitz, *Art, Alienation, and the Humanities* (Albany: SUNY Press, 2000), arguing that Marcuse's analysis of the aesthetic dimension has great relevance for the present cultural moment; Paul A. Robinson, *The Freudian Left* (New York: Harper and Row, 1969), an exposition of the Frankfurt School's leftist deployments of Freudian psychoanalysis; Morton Schoolman, *The Imaginary Witness: The Critical Theory of Herbert Marcuse* (New York: New York University Press, 1984), a responsible, detailed, thorough, sympathetic exposition of Marcuse's thought; Harold Washington, *The Philosophy of Herbert Marcuse* (Washington, D.C.: University Press of America, 1977), a lucid elaboration of Marcuse's major ideas; Joel Whitebook, *Perversion and Utopia* (Cambridge: MIT Press, 1995), focusing primarily on Adorno and Benjamin, but with interesting references to Marcuse's ideas about utopia. There are, however, a few unsym-

pathetic views: Paul Mattick, *Critique of Marcuse; One-Dimensional Man in Class Society* (London: Merlin Press, 1972), which critiques Marcuse from a tradi‑ tional Marxist perspective, as paying insufficient attention to the role of the pro‑ letariat in revolutionary politics, and Timothy Lukes, *The Flight into Inwardness: An Exposition and Critique of Herbert Marcuse's Theories of Liberative Aes‑ thetics* (London: Associated University Presses, 1985), which considers Marcuse's emphasis on aesthetic theory ultimately destructive to radical political motiva‑ tions. Judith Butler mentions briefly the centrality of the idea of sublimation in *Eros and Civilization* in *The Psychic Life of Power*, 58. Kevin Floyd discusses Marcuse's theories of reification in relation to the politics of sexuality in his article "Rethinking Reification: Marcuse, Psychoanalysis and Gay Liberation," *Social Text* 19.1 (spring 2001); David Savran also finds Marcuse useful for discussing sexuality and contemporary masculinity in *Taking It Like a Man: White Mas‑ culinity, Masochism, and U.S. Cultural Production* (Princeton: Princeton Univer‑ sity Press, 2000).

4   As Fredric Jameson says in *Postmodernism*, "This generalized 'end of ideology and of Utopia,' celebrated by the conservatives in the fifties, was also the burden of Marcuse's *One-Dimensional Man*, which deplored it from a radical perspec‑ tive. . . . If one inserts the sixties into this historical narrative [of utopian ide‑ ologies], everything changes: 'Marcuse' virtually becomes the name for a whole explosive renewal of Utopian thinking and imagination" (159–60).

5   See Susan Buck-Morss, *Dreamworld and Catastrophe*.

6   Michel de Certeau, *The Practice of Everyday Life*, trans. Steven F. Rendall (Berke‑ ley: University of California Press, 1984).

7   If one wanted to agree with Marcuse's analysis here, one could find confirmation in the current phenomenon of sold-out, mobbed blockbuster museum shows of sanc‑ tioned, canonized art, including what was once revolutionary modernist and avant-garde art, shows which culminate in every sense in the gift shop. Traveling around the world, or at least the West, to attend these shows has become an extremely popular mode of acquisition and display of cultural capital — of cultural consumerism in the classic Weberian mode.

8   See in particular pp. 135–36.

9   See particularly p. 158.

10   See particularly p. 151.

11   Andreas Huyssen's "Mapping the Postmodern," in *After the Great Divide: Mod‑ ernism, Mass Culture, Postmodernism*, 179–221, offers one of the most persuasive versions of this argument (that poststructuralist theory is modernist rather than postmodernist). I would also differentiate between the key writings of continental poststructuralist/psychoanalytic theory, most notably by Barthes, Cixous, Deleuze (and Guattari), Derrida, Foucault, Irigaray, Kristeva, Lacan, Lyotard, which are an endpoint of modernism in their difficulty, complexity, originality, and in their simultaneous search for great, unifying truths at the same time that they "de‑ construct" any such idea of a unifying truth or knowledge, and the postmodern academic phenomenon of "theory," particularly as it has operated in the American academy, which, through its simplification, systematization, and wide prolifera‑

tion of central ideas in the works of these great thinkers, has played an important role in the postmodern move toward accessibility and popularization both of arcane thought in general and also, in particular, of theorizations promoting the postmodern ideologies of egalitarian, diverse, antihierarchical, antiteleological, antidualistic flux, multiplicity, open-endedness, fragmentation, constructedness, shifting, non-self-identical subjectivity, hybridity, alterity, and indeterminacy. This pivot from the dominantly modern work of the continental psychoanalytical/poststructuralist theorists to the dominantly postmodern work of the many academics who have absorbed, systematized, rationalized, proliferated, and in some cases actually popularized this difficult work is another instance of the emergence of the postmodern from the dominant modernism/modernity of the sixties (a great deal of the work of the continental psychoanalytic/poststructuralist theorists was done during and at the end of the long sixties; they were greatly influenced by, and many participated in, the movements of the sixties).

2. *Popular Culture in* Mythologies

1 See especially Andreas Huyssen, *After the Great Divide: Modernism, Mass Culture, Postmodernism.*

2 On the imbrication of postmodernism with popular culture, see Angela McRobbie, *Postmodernism and Popular Culture*, also James Naremore and Patrick Brantlinger, eds., *Modernity and Mass Culture.*

3 Roland Barthes, *Mythologies* (1957; trans., New York: Hill and Wang, 1971). Subsequent quotations from this source will hereafter be cited parenthetically in the text by page number.

4 James Naremore and Patrick Brantlinger, in their introduction to *Modernity and Mass Culture*, say "the founding texts of cultural studies would certainly include Barthes's *Mythologies*" (1). See also, for example, Judith Williamson, *Decoding Advertisements: Ideology and Meaning in Advertising*; Dick Hebdige, *Subculture: The Meaning of Style*; Antony Easthope, *Literary into Cultural Studies* (London: Routledge, 1991); Simon During, ed., *The Cultural Studies Reader* (London: Routledge, 1993). Andrew Leak, in *Barthes, Mythologies* (London: Grand and Cutler, 1994), sees *Mythologies* as informed at the deepest level by a classical Marxist class analysis and claims that "admirers of a so-called postmodern Barthes tend to be less enamored" (7) of *Mythologies*. I assume he is referring here to admirers of the poststructuralist Barthes, but I think it is also true that some postmodern uses of this book are uneasy with its modern elements, most notably the Marxist tactic of unmasking bourgeois ideology in mass culture.

5 This is the term used by Andreas Huyssen in *After the Great Divide*, a text that has been crucial to the development of my analysis here.

6 Barthes seems to repudiate the notion of utopia in the closing essay of the anthology, "Myth Today": "Utopia is an impossible luxury for him ['the mythologist']: he greatly doubts that tomorrow's truths will be the exact reverse of today's lies" (157). The utopia he rejects here, however, is simply a naive, nondialectical reversal of the oppressions of contemporary society. The characteristic sixties utopian

ideology he in fact embraces is far more radical, encompassing utter destruction of
society and culture, to be replaced by what cannot yet be imagined: "history never
ensures the triumph pure and simple of something over its opposite: it unveils,
while making itself, unimaginable solutions, unforeseeable syntheses. . . . All the
values of his undertaking appear to him as acts of destruction: the latter accurately
cover the former, nothing protrudes . . . the future *is nothing but* the most profound apocalypse of the present" (157).

7   Barthes here shares Marcuse's view.

8   Relevant references are too numerous to list, but see, for example, Linda Hutcheon's discussion of "complicitous critique" in *A Poetics of Postmodernism: History, Theory, Fiction*. Complicitous critique is "operation margarine" rotated 180
degrees toward the postmodern.

9   I refer here to John Beverley's influential attack on the literary as hegemonic institution in *Against Literature* (Minneapolis: University of Minnesota Press, 1993).
Further discussion of cultural studies' postmodern suspicion of the literary will
follow.

10 Barthes has been extremely useful to a wide range of psychoanalytic/poststruc-
turalist feminist theorists, especially in his discourses on textual *jouissance*.

11 See especially Huyssen, "Mass Culture as Woman: Modernism's Other," in *After
the Great Divide*, 44–62, and Naomi Schor, *Reading in Detail: Aesthetics and the
Feminine* (New York: Methuen, 1987); Schor extensively acknowledges Barthes's
influence.

12 For a fascinating and useful history of the spread of plastics in the twentieth
century, see Eric Hobsbawm, *The Age of Extremes: A History of the World, 1914–
1991* (New York: Pantheon, 1994), 264.

3. Las Vegas Signs Taken for Wonders

1   See, for example, Mark Taylor's work on Las Vegas as an "economy of virtual
culture" in *About Religion: Economies of Faith in a Virtual Culture* (Chicago:
University of Chicago Press, 1999).

2   Tom Wolfe, *The Kandy-Kolored Tangerine-Flake Streamline Baby* (New York:
Farrar, Straus and Giroux, 1965), "Las Vegas (What?) Las Vegas (Can't Hear You!
Too Noisy) Las Vegas!!!!," originally published in *Esquire*, is the opening essay of
the collection. Future references to this volume will appear in parentheses in the
text.

3   Thompson was in fact influenced by and indebted to Wolfe, as were Venturi et al. I
will discuss the new journalism, with which Wolfe is so importantly associated,
and which links Wolfe and Thompson, in chapter 4 as well.

4   My colleague William Galperin has suggested, in conversation, a fascinating alternative reading of Wolfe's relation to popular culture. He considers Wolfe's style
nostalgic: characterized by an inherently belated cathexis onto a fantasized, superseded past. Wolfe's nostalgic style is an attempt (quoting Galperin directly) "to will
the popular into a canonizable aesthetic." The "only lexicon he has at his disposal"
for this canonization is the "vanguardist, elitist avant-garde aesthetic." Wolfe's

style is therefore a "wilful attempt to summon the earlier shock of the new." While I find this a powerful reading of Wolfe, in its understanding of the inextricable link in his work between the popular and the avant-garde, I do not of course think the avant-garde aesthetic is yet superseded in the sixties: the sixties was in fact, again, the site of a massive renaissance and resurgence of the avant-gardes. I do not see Wolfe's style as nostalgic; rather, it seems to me a characteristic, if sometimes exaggerated, sixties style of ironic excess and self-consciously passionate, even florid, overwriting, quite common in sixties texts, contributing to the fact that many of them are no longer read. The popular and the avant-garde were indeed seamlessly intermeshed in these sixties texts and in sixties cultural formations in general; only with the full entry into the postmodern did they become disjunct, even antithetical.

Wolfe's style, particularly in his sixties texts, literally cries out for critical attention, and critics have accounted for it over the years in divergent ways. It is often seen as representative of various contemporary ideologies. Richard A. Kallan, for example, argues that Wolfe's "message represents an oral, electronic rhetoric expressing itself, paradoxically, via the printed page. Primarily it is Wolfe's stylistic techniques that enable him to achieve this unique posture wherein form triumphs over content and the medium-transcends-message sermon of Marshall McLuhan becomes the speaker's guiding doctrine" ("Style and the New Journalism: Rhetorical Analysis of Tom Wolfe," *Communication Monographs* 46 [March 1979], rpt. in Harold Bloom, ed., *Tom Wolfe* [Philadelphia: Chelsea House, 2001], 71–83). See also, in general, Doug Shomette, ed., *The Critical Response to Tom Wolfe* (Westport, Conn.: Greenwood Press, 1992), and William McKeen, *Tom Wolfe* (New York: Twayne, 1995).

5 Sally Denton and Roger Morris's *The Money and the Power: The Making of Las Vegas and Its Hold on America, 1947–2000* (New York: Knopf, 2001) expands the sinister, Mob-controlled version of Vegas to make Vegas the locus, center, and motive of all the evils not just of contemporary global corporate capitalism but of the corruption of Kennedy, Johnson, Nixon, Reagan, and Clinton. This excessive view could be seen as in a sense absolving contemporary culture of the complexity of its phenomena by making Vegas its scapegoat. This reading of Vegas can also be seen as the obverse of the Venturian suppression of the presence of the Mob in Vegas, though that interpretation is somewhat glib.

6 William Galperin considers the "fetishization of old women" in this passage comparable to Wolfean style as reification of a superseded avant-garde aesthetic. This fetishization is "no more possible than the canonization of the popular" (conversation with William Galperin).

7 The Guggenheim-Hermitage in Las Vegas is housed in the Venetian Hotel, which is a facsimile of Venice in which the canals and gondolas are bathed in perpetual twilight, considered the most romantic and desirable lighting for the Venetian scene. The Bellagio Gallery of Fine Art in Las Vegas is stocked with canonical high-culture great art; the affiliated restaurant, the Picasso, which features paintings by the master, is highly successful.

8   In "Tom Wolfe in the 1960s," Thomas L. Hartshorne argues that, despite his consensual status and reputation as "a representative of the switched-on rebellious, anti-traditional culture of the 1960s" (85), Wolfe has always been a traditional moralist at heart, an adoptive New Yorker whose primary affiliation was always to his conservative southern roots: "he has certainly done his very best to play the role of the sophisticated New Yorker. Yet behind the sophistication and the flashy clothes and the flashy language there is a southern boy from Richmond, Virginia" (*Midwest Quarterly: A Journal of Contemporary Thought* 23.2 [winter 1982]; rpt. in Bloom, *Tom Wolfe*, 85–97; 96). It seems to me that this retroactive evaluation of Wolfe does not do justice to the evolution of his morally and stylistically traditionalist post-sixties work from his genuinely ambivalent, doubly positioned work of the sixties. As Barbara Lounsberry says in "Tom Wolfe's Negative Vision," "Readers simply have to explore the implications of a highly sophisticated narrative technique which bounces back and forth between elevation and damnation" (*South Dakota Review* 20.2 [summer 1982]; rpt. Bloom, *Tom Wolfe*, 99–112; 100). Lounsberry is discussing *The Electric Kool-Aid Acid Test* in particular, but this analysis applies equally well to Wolfe's other sixties work.

9   See Fredric Jameson's crucial *Postmodernism*, particularly his discussion of the difference between Vincent van Gogh's *A Pair of Boots* and Andy Warhol's *Diamond Dust Shoes*, 6–12, for a brilliant analysis of the contrast between modernist depth and postmodern flatness.

10 The Monte Carlo Hotel-Casino in Las Vegas trumps both Wolfe and Venturi et al., absorbing all class distinctions into postmodern commercial indifferentiation and simulacral culture.

4. Loathing and Learning in Las Vegas

1   Hunter S. Thompson, *Fear and Loathing in Las Vegas: A Savage Journey to the Heart of the American Dream* (New York: Popular Library, 1971). Future references will be included parenthetically in the text. For useful background, see the second of a projected three-volume edition of Thompson's letters, *Fear and Loathing in America: The Brutal Odyssey of an Outlaw Journalist, 1968–1976* (New York: Simon and Schuster, 2000), with an insightful introduction by the editor, Douglas Brinkley. The first volume, covering Thompson's association with the Beat movement, is *The Proud Highway: Saga of a Desperate Southern Gentleman, 1955–1967*, ed. Douglas Brinkley, foreword by William J. Kennedy (New York: Ballantine, 1997). Most secondary work on Thompson is biographical, including Paul Perry, *Fear and Loathing: The Strange and Terrible Saga of Hunter S. Thompson* (New York: Thunder's Mouth Press, 1992), and Peter D. Whitman, *When the Weird Get Going: The Twisted Life and Times of Hunter S. Thompson: A Very Unauthorized Biography* (New York: Hyperion, 1993). As these titles indicate, Thompson's biographers strain to imitate his style. William McKeon's *Hunter S. Thompson* (Boston: Twayne, 1991) is a useful, responsible overview of his work and his critical reception. As McKeon says, "Much has been said about the book as

302 NOTES TO CHAPTER 4

an epitaph for the 1960s" (61). Useful discussions of Thompson in general, and *Fear and Loathing* in particular, can also be found in Jerome Hellmann's book on the new journalism, *Fables of Fact* (Urbana: University of Illinois Press, 1981), and in Jerome Klinkowitz's crucial work on sixties fiction, *The Life of Fiction* (Urbana: University of Illinois Press, 1977). Thompson's other works, mostly collections of travel and political journalism, include: on Clinton and the 1992 election: *Better Than Sex: The Confessions of a Political Junkie* (New York: Random House, 1994); on Hawaii, with Ralph Steadman: *The Curse of Lono* (New York: Bantam Books, 1983); on the 1972 election: *Fear and Loathing on the Campaign Trail, 1972* (New York: Fawcett Popular Library, 1973); on the politics and culture of the Reagan era: *Generation of Swine: Tales of Shame and Degradation in the '80s* (New York: Summit Books, 1988); on the appeal of the Hell's Angels, as well as their disastrous role in the sixties, especially in Berkeley and Altamont: *Hell's Angels: A Strange and Terrible Saga* (New York: Ballantine, 1967); foreword (Jerry Garcia also wrote a foreword to this book) to Paul Perry, *On the Bus: The Complete Guide to the Legendary Trip of Ken Kesey and the Merry Pranksters and the Birth of the Counterculture*, ed. Michael Schwartz and Neil Ortenberg (New York: Thunder's Mouth Press, 1990); and a work of adventure fiction about Puerto Rico: *The Rum Diary: The Long Lost Novel* (New York: Simon and Schuster, 1998). As the array of top trade publishers of these authored works makes clear, Thompson has remained a highly viable writer. *Fear and Loathing* continues to sell widely, with its paperback cover image from the popular 1998 Terry Gilliam movie starring Johnny Depp as Duke and Benicio Del Toro as Gonzo. Hunter S. Thompson also appears in thousands of Web sites.

2 ". . . by June of '72 *we* (the Steadman-Thompson coverage, etc.) are very likely to be worth more than the sum of our parts. In other words, we can probably earn twice as much together than either one of us could earn separately" (*Fear and Loathing in America*, 458; December 16, 1971, letter to Ralph Steadman).

3 Thompson struggled, as part of the arduous process of producing this book, to integrate the two-part Las Vegas project with what began as a separate project on the end of the American Dream. See *Fear and Loathing in America*, especially 417–29.

4 As noted in the introduction, each text I discuss at length in this study stands in for hundreds of other similar texts, any of which could also, or alternately, have been used as exemplary. This book is not in any way a survey or overview of sixties texts, or an inclusive account of sixties cultural production, but rather an analysis, by means of detailed reading, of characteristic sixties texts, representative of the sixties as pivot from modern to postmodern, in which the modern was dominant and the postmodern emergent. In the case of works of new journalism, or journalism in general, including essays published in alternative, underground, mainstream, and intellectual publications, the potential field is enormous. Journalism was remarkably vibrant, innovative, influential, and generally brilliant in the sixties. Particularly, other works by Wolfe (especially *Electric Kool-Aid Acid Test*) and works by Norman Mailer (especially *Armies of the Night* and *Miami and the Siege of Chicago*), Joan Didion (especially the essays in *Slouching Towards Beth-*

lehem and *The White Album*), and Susan Sontag (especially the essays in *Against Interpretation* and *Styles of Radical Will*) were at once characteristic and extremely influential. Apologies to those readers already familiar with the significance of the new journalism in the sixties.

5   On shifts in masculinity in this period, see, for example, Lynne Segal, *Slow Motion: Changing Masculinities, Changing Men* (New Brunswick: Rutgers University Press, 1990), and *Is the Future Female?* (New York: Peter Bedrick Books, 1987); also Susan Jeffords, *The Remasculinization of America* (Bloomington: Indiana University Press, 1989).

6   Thompson has a chapter in John M. Macdonald, *Rape Offenders and Their Victims* (Springfield, Ill.: Thomas, 1971).

7   Robert Venturi, Denise Scott Brown, and Steven Inzenour, *Learning from Las Vegas* (Cambridge: MIT Press, 1972). Future references to this volume will appear parenthetically in the text. For analyses of Venturi's contribution to architecture, see *The Architecture of Robert Venturi: Essays by Vincent Scully, David Van Zanten, Neil Levine, Thomas Beeby, and Stephen Kieran*, ed. and with an introduction by Christopher Mead (Albuquerque: University of New Mexico Press, 1989). Venturi's other works include: on the Museum of Modern Art's architecture papers: *Complexity and Contradiction in Architecture*, introduction by Vincent Scully (New York: Museum of Modern Art Press; Boston: Distributed by New York Graphic Society, 1977); *Iconography and Electronics upon a Generic Architecture: A View from Robert Venturi* (Cambridge: MIT Press, 1996); *Mother's House: The Evolution of Vanna Venturi's House in Chestnut Hill*, ed. and with an introduction by Frederic Schwartz, preface by Aldo Rossi, with essays by Vincent Scully and Robert Venturi (New York: Rizzoli, 1992); *Venturi, Scott Brown and Associates on Housing* (London: Academy Editions; New York: St. Martin's Press, 1992); with Denise Scott Brown, *A View from the Campidoglio: Selected Essays 1953–84*, ed. Peter Arnell, Ted Bickford, Catherine Bergart (New York: Harper and Row, 1984).

8   Steven Izenour appeared briefly on ABC *World News Tonight with Peter Jennings*, March 14, 2001, in a segment called "Upping the Ante" by Judy Muller, which interestingly juxtaposes the quintessentially simulacral nature of Las Vegas—its Venice is lit in permanent sunset, for example, because that is its most appealing lighting—with the presence of "real" works of high art in its hotels and casinos, for example works by Picasso and Rauschenberg (though Rauschenberg is, of course, a great postmodernist). The segment also discusses the Vegas of the sixties and seventies, particularly the Strip on Fremont, as a quaint old style of neon environment, replaced now by what is known as the "tube of light"—an uninterrupted chute of neon, reminiscent of the new Times Square: Vegas has indeed spread everywhere. In a quintessential ironic postmodern gesture, Izenour calls for a casino to create a simulacrum of the "old" Vegas of thirty years ago.

9   For the defining analysis of postmodern hyperspace, see Fredric Jameson's discussion of the LA Portman Bonaventure in *Postmodernism*, 38–45.

10 In an ironic footnote (literally) to Venturi et al.'s project in this book, on a Charlie Rose show on PBS on December 17, 2001, Robert Venturi and Denise Scott Brown

said that their work has not ultimately appealed to the popular, commercial clients they had hoped to reach and in whose interests they developed their theories, particularly in *Learning from Las Vegas*. In fact, their clients are, and have been all along, almost exclusively elite Ivy League universities and prestigious cultural institutions. They say of those elusive commercial clients, "They think we're laughing at them but we're not." In support of this assertion, in a *New York Times* article by Guy Trebay on the real house used as the set for *The Sopranos* (August 12, 2002, A1 and A11), a house which the article describes as "nouveau riche" and a "McMansion," Venturi is quoted: "The Soprano house combines both modern and traditional elements and mixes them all up, . . . in a fashion that is 'rich with vitality' " (A 11). Apparently no one asks Venturi to build such houses, though, nor does he work for the average middle-class client he champions in *Learning*.

5. Endnotes I

1   See part 1.

2   Andreas Huyssen, *After the Great Divide*. Also, see bibliography, part I.

3   It has become fashionable in the new modernist studies to repudiate Huyssen altogether — he has become the same sort of scapegoat for popular-culture studies of modernism that "elitist" modernism itself used to be (and often still is) for popular-culture-oriented postmodernist studies and polemics. I find this repudiation a swing of the pendulum too far in the direction of recuperating modernism as enmeshed in popular culture. In the version of the modern and the postmodern I develop here, there is a meaningful difference between modernism's ambivalent deployments of and relations to the popular, including its negative view of "mass culture," and postmodernism's embrace of, dependence on, and integration into the popular.

4   For two important recent book-length works on sixties rock in America, see Greil Marcus, *Invisible Republic: Bob Dylan's Basement Tapes* (New York: Henry Holt, 1997), in which Marcus argues that Dylan's late-sixties collaboration with The Band in *The Basement Tapes* is rock's moment of greatest depth and profound American representativeness, and James Miller, *Flowers in the Dustbin: The Rise of Rock and Roll, 1947–1977* (New York: Simon and Schuster, 1999), a detailed, informative, eloquent, tendentious cultural history of American and British rock, tracing its rise through the fifties, particularly in the confluence of black and white popular music, to its climax in the sixties, most importantly with the Beatles, Stones, Dylan, and Dead, to its demise in late seventies and eighties violent self-indulgence. Miller's notes and discographies are invaluable sources not just for works on and of sixties rock, but also for biographical, autobiographical, critical, and cultural-historical accounts of the sixties counterculture's immersion in, dependence on, and inseparability from rock. For another analysis of the post-sixties demise of the greatness of American rock, see Martha Bayles, *Hole in Our Soul: The Loss of Beauty and Meaning in American Popular Music* (New York: Free Press, 1994).

5   Bob Dylan, "Stuck Inside of Mobile with the Memphis Blues Again," *Blonde on Blonde* (Dwarf Music, 1966), in *Lyrics 1962–1985* (New York: Knopf, 1985), 228. See also Bob Dylan, *Tarantula* (New York: Macmillan, 1966), a series of short pieces which begins with "Guns, the Falcon's Mouthbook & Gashcat Unpunished": "aretha/crystal jukebox queen of hymn & himdiffused in drunk transfusion wound would heed sweet soundwave cripple and cry salute to oh great particular el dorado reel & ye battered personal god but she cannot she the leader of whom when ye follow, she cannot she has no back she cannot." (1). See also John Lennon, *In His Own Write* (London: J. Cape, 1964), and *A Spaniard in the Works*, in *The Writings of John Lennon*, introduction by Paul McCartney (New York: Simon and Schuster, 1981), which also includes *In His Own Write*.

6   Jagger's willowy, long-haired grace, culturally marked as feminine and so unlike his current buff heartiness, is nowhere more apparent than in Albert and David Maysles's classic 1970 documentary of Altamont *Gimme Shelter*, as he sings "Sympathy for the Devil," "Street Fighting Man," and what is perhaps the most violently misogynistic song of the sixties, "Under My Thumb," surrounded by Hells Angels doing lethal violence to his adoring fans.

7   This argument is indebted to, and in agreement with, Susan Jeffords's argument in *The Remasculinization of America*. See bibliography, part II.

6. Participatory Democracy in Port Huron

1   Students for a Democratic Society (primarily Tom Hayden), *The Port Huron Statement* (1962; rpt. Chicago: Charles H. Kerr, 1990), hereinafter referred to as *PHS*. Future references to this volume will appear parenthetically in the text.

2   For the most useful, thorough, insightful discussion of *The Port Huron Statement* and its crucial role in the development of the American New Left, focusing particularly on the concept of participatory democracy, see James Miller, *"Democracy Is in the Streets": From Port Huron to the Siege of Chicago* (New York: Touchstone, 1987). Future references to this volume will appear parenthetically in the text.

3   Arthur Marwick, *The Sixties*, 54.

4   It is beyond the scope of this study to provide a meaningful historical account of the rise of the New Left. The left-wing activism that had its heyday in the thirties never died out in the forties and fifties. Many activists of the thirties continued their work in various forms during the dark years of McCarthy and the early cold war. SDS emerged from these movements but instituted significant changes in the directions of a more flexible, democratic Marxism dominated by youth movements, and, as this chapter discusses, an emphasis on participatory democracy. See Maurice Isserman, *If I Had a Hammer: The Death of the Old Left and the Birth of the New Left* (New York: Basic Books, 1987), for an excellent account of this history. See also Todd Gitlin, *The Sixties: Years of Hope, Days of Rage*, for a first-person account of a "red-diaper baby's" progression from the Old Left's youth movements, moribund by the early sixties, to the New Left and SDS, and Kirkpatrick Sale's comprehensive history of SDS (see bibliography, part II).

5   I assume in general a familiarity with the broad outline of the political and counter-
    cultural history of the sixties, beginning with the Beat and Civil Rights movements
    and third world liberation movements (most notably the Cuban revolution) in the
    mid- to late fifties; moving through the early, less radical phase of Civil Rights and
    the New Left, coincident with crucial Civil Rights gains in the South, with the
    escalation of the war in Vietnam, and with the waxing of the third world liberation
    struggle, the concomitant rise of the antiwar movement, and the beginnings of the
    counterculture in the rock and drug scenes, in the early- to mid-sixties, and the
    simultaneous proliferation, vast and fertile throughout the period, of counter-
    cultural, underground, avant-garde, and popular/avant-garde cultural produc-
    tion; to the mass antiwar movements, both pacifist and militant, the militantly
    separatist Black Power and Black Arts movements, the emergence of second-wave
    feminism and gay liberation, and the heyday of the counterculture as fully alterna-
    tive way of life, culminating in May '68 and the Prague Spring in Europe, and the
    enormous antiwar demonstrations and rock festivals of the late sixties in the
    United States and around the world; to the demise of the New Left and waning of
    Black Power, both through their own increasingly violent ideologies and tactics
    and, more importantly, through heavy infiltration and direct attacks from Nixon's
    FBI COINTELPRO and governments around the world, particularly the USSR in
    Czechoslovakia, along with the simultaneous waning and integration or coopta-
    tion of the counterculture avant-gardes into complicitously resistant postmodern-
    ism, and the massive diffusion of the "new social movements" (postcolonial, race-
    and ethnicity-based movements, gender- and sexuality-based movements) into
    broad, diverse, widespread, grassroots, socially transformative forces, in the early
    seventies. There are several useful chronologies of the history of the sixties in the
    books in bibliography, part II; see particularly Maurice Isserman and Michael
    Kazin, *America Divided: The Civil War of the 1960s.*

6   John Sayles uses this passage to great emotive effect in his excellent, underappreci-
    ated novel of the demise of the sixties, *Union Dues* (Harmondsworth: Penguin,
    1977), when the female protagonist quotes it to the damaged, naive male protago-
    nist to explain to him why she remains in such a betrayed, corrupted, vanquished
    movement (373).

7   The controversy surrounding these issues has been at the heart of the culture wars.
    See, for the right-wing position, Roger Kimball, *Tenured Radicals: How Politics
    Has Corrupted Higher Education* (New York: Harper and Row, 1990); on the
    other side of the controversy: Bruce Robbins, *Intellectuals: Aesthetics, Politics and
    Academics* (Minneapolis: University of Minnesota Press, 1990), and *Secular Voca-
    tions: Intellectuals, Professionalism, Culture* (London: Verso, 1993); also Cary
    Nelson, *Manifesto of a Tenured Radical* (New York: New York University Press,
    1997).

7. Paradise Then

1   For useful histories, descriptions, and critical analyses of the work of The Living
    Theatre, including the genesis and turbulent performance history of *Paradise*

Now, and also personal accounts by Julian Beck and Judith Malina, see Julian Beck, *The Life of the Theater: The Relationship of the Artist to the Struggle of the People*, foreword by Judith Malina (New York: Limelight, 1972; distributed by New York: Harper and Row: 1986); Pierre Biner, *The Living Theatre* (New York: Horizon Press, 1972); Robert Brustein, *Revolution as Theatre: Notes on the New Radical Style* (New York: Liveright, 1971); Judith Malina, *The Enormous Despair* (New York: Random House, 1972); Renfreu Neff, *The Living Theatre USA* (Indianapolis: Bobbs-Merrill, 1970); Aldo Rostagno with Julian Beck and Judith Malina, *We the Living Theatre* (New York: Ballantine Books, 1970); John Tytell, *The Living Theatre: Art, Exile and Outrage* (New York: Grove Press, 1995). For useful histories and critical analyses of American experimental theater focusing on the sixties, see Herbert Blau, *Take Up the Bodies: Theater at the Vanishing Point* (Urbana: University of Illinois Press, 1982); Herbert Blau, *The Eye of Prey: Subversions of the Postmodern* (Bloomington: Indiana University Press, 1987); Margaret Croydon, *Lunatics, Lovers and Poets: The Contemporary Experimental Theatre* (New York: McGraw-Hill, 1974); Christopher Innes, *Avant-Garde Theatre, 1892–1992* (London: Routledge, 1993); Michael Kirby, *A Formalist Theater* (Philadelphia: University of Pennsylvania Press, 1987); Richard Kostelanetz, *On Innovative Performance(s): Three Decades of Recollections on Alternative Theater* (Jefferson, N.C.: McFarland, 1994); Erik MacDonald, *Theater at the Margins: Text and the Post Structured Stage* (Ann Arbor: University of Michigan Press, 1993); James Roose-Evans, *Experimental Theatre: From Stanislavski to Peter Brook* (London: Routledge, 1989); Zoltán Szillassy, *American Theater of the 1960s* (Carbondale: Southern Illinois University Press, 1986). Group experimental theater, building on African American oral traditions, was also central to the Black Arts movement.

2   Judith Malina and Julian Beck, *Paradise Now* (New York: Vintage Books, 1971). Future references to this volume will appear parenthetically in the text. See Tytell, *The Living Theatre*, particularly, for a useful history of *Paradise Now*'s reception.

3   Allen Ginsberg, *HOWL and Other Poems* (San Francisco: City Lights Books, 1959). "Footnote to HOWL" opens:

> Holy ! Holy ! Holy ! Holy ! Holy ! Holy ! Holy ! Holy ! Holy ! Holy ! Holy !
>   Holy ! Holy ! Holy ! Holy !
> The World is holy ! The soul is holy ! The skin is holy ! The nose is holy ! The
>   tongue and cock and hand and asshole holy ! (21)

8. William Burroughs

1   "Throughout the 1960s, Burroughs' works were seen by attackers and defenders alike as somehow emblematic of the times" (Jennie Skerl and Robin Lydenberg, eds., *William S. Burroughs at the Front: Critical Reception, 1959–1989* [Carbondale: Southern Illinois University Press, 1991], 6). Also, the blatancy of self-contradiction in Burroughs's work and thought makes him an ideal marker of the dominant modern/emergent postmodern sixties that is my subject here. For a very

different view, which considers Burroughs "amodern" — neither modern nor post-modern, but in fact rejecting, and charting an alternative to, the modern/post-modern "dialectic" — see Timothy S. Murphy, *Wising Up the Marks: The Amod-ern William Burroughs* (Berkeley: University of California Press, 1997). Murphy's argument, with which, evidently, I disagree, is premised on the view of postmod-ernism as formalist and antipolitical with which I also disagree (see the introduc-tion). While Murphy provides a detailed, sympathetic, intelligent, useful, some-times passionately partisan overview of Burroughs's career, his assumption that postmodernism is strictly limited to writing that is formally self-reflexive and apolitical, that postmodern theory rejects the political in favor of language games, and that we must chart an "alternative," "amodern," politically engaged literary tradition, beginning with *Invisible Man* and moving through Heller, Vonnegut, Reed, Thompson, Pynchon, Morrison, Coover, Russ, Acker, and (Darius) James, seems unnecessary in light of the larger version of the politics of the postmodern developed by the theorists I draw on here (especially Haraway, Harvey, Hutcheon, Huyssen, Jameson, Owens). Murphy also makes the surprising claim that Deleuze, the theorist he engages most extensively, is, like Burroughs, "invisible" in contem-porary literary critical discourses. While I agree that Burroughs is undervalued, it seems to me that Deleuze, particularly in his collaborations with Guattari, has been central to many theorizations and treatments of the postmodern.

2 William Burroughs and Brion Gysin, *The Third Mind* (New York: Seaver Books, 1978), 3.

3 What I have called, in *A Different Language: Gertrude Stein's Experimental Writing* (Madison: University of Wisconsin Press, 1983), Gertrude Stein's "lively words" style — the radical experimental style of works such as *Tender Buttons*, written between 1911 and 1914 — is premised on precisely such unlikely, disjunc-tive but resonant, polysemous word juxtapositions. The term "heavy metal" that appears in *Nova Express* can be considered such a juxtaposition. The uncertain origination of this term has been attributed by some to Burroughs, though others dispute this attribution (thanks to Marcia Ian for this information). Most Bur-roughs critics consider *Naked Lunch* distinct from the three subsequent novels, designating those three a trilogy and *NL* a novel unto itself, because Burroughs used cut-up/fold-in only in the "trilogy" and not in *NL*. Nonetheless, all four novels were drawn from the same notes and occupy roughly a continuous imaginative universe, so I choose to consider the four works a tetralogy.

4 Burroughs adds the western to this repertoire in his later work — see David Glover, "Burroughs' Western," in Skerl and Lydenberg, *Burroughs at the Front*, 209–15.

5 William Burroughs, *Naked Lunch* (New York: Grove Press, 1959), 2. Future refer-ences to this volume will be included parenthetically in the text. The writing in the rest of the tetralogy, deploying Burroughs's cut-up/fold-in method, to be discussed later in this chapter, is far less conventional but frequently preserves the narrative tone and referential universe of hard-boiled detective fiction evident here.

6 William Burroughs, *Nova Express* (New York: Grove Press, 1964), 72. Future references to this volume will be included parenthetically in the text.

7   William Burroughs, *The Job*, interviews with William Burroughs by Daniel Odier (New York: Grove Press, 1974), 27. Future references to this volume will be included parenthetically in the text.

8   Anne Friedberg points to the Dada antecedents of cut-up/fold-in: "In one of the dadaist manifestos, Tristan Tzara commands: 'Take a newspaper / Take some scissors.' He then directs the making of a dadaist poem: A newspaper article is cut into its constituent words. The words are placed in a paper bag. The paper bag is shaken. The poem is 'constructed' by copying the words in the order they are pulled from the paper bag" ("'Cut-ups': A *Syn*ema of the Text," in Skerl and Lydenberg, *Burroughs at the Front*, 169).

9   McLuhan, of course, is a key luminary of the sixties transition to the postmodern. His work on the new media as the inception of the new era of cultural history, supplanting the "Gutenberg Galaxy," is at once profoundly accurate and also, characteristically of the sixties, profoundly utopian in its view of the egalitarian, participatory nature of the global community ("global village") the new media will enable.

10 As an undergraduate at the "Radcliffe Annex," star pupil of William James, Stein had participated in experiments concerning the relation of attention to writing; critics subsequently used this fact to characterize her experimental work as automatic writing. Stein always adamantly denied any such connection, nor did she associate herself in any way with Surrealist versions of this practice. Burroughs is aligning himself with Stein here.

11 Tony Tanner, in "Rub Out the Word," in Skerl and Lydenberg, *Burroughs at the Front*, 105–13, emphasizes Burroughs's "control over" the language of "ugliness" through "constantly regurgitating all the foul material" by means of the cut-up/fold-in method (111).

12 "Any appreciation of Burroughs has to answer the question: does he belong in a major literary tradition. I believe that the preceding analysis aligns Burroughs with novelists, such as Kafka and Beckett, whose major theme is ambivalence and indeterminacy" (Neal Oxenhandler, "Listening to Burroughs' Voice," in Skerl and Lydenberg, *Burroughs at the Front*, 145). Nicholas Zurbrugg, in "Beckett, Proust, and Burroughs and the Perils of 'Image Warfare'," (in Skerl and Lydenberg, 177–88), locates Burroughs alongside Beckett and Proust in their "diverging—and at times incompatible—approaches to the image of the self" (186).

13 Theodore Solotaroff, in "The Algebra of Need" (Skerl and Lydenberg, *Burroughs at the Front*, 85–89), revealing the formative power of the sixties modern/postmodern sensibility in his own critical analysis, compares Burroughs to both Lenny Bruce and T. S. Eliot; Lydenberg and Skerl, in their introduction, encapsulate this pivotal status, describing Burroughs as "the grand old man of the avant-garde and the pioneer of the space age" (8). They see his career as straddling modernism and postmodernism: "Many earlier critics had compared Burroughs either favorably or unfavorably to the high modernism of writers like Kafka or Joyce. In this decade [the eighties], instead of criticizing Burroughs as a failed modernist for his lack of continuity and organic wholeness, some critics celebrated his breakdown of con-

ventions, his dissolving of individual identity and voice, as a postmodern victory" (11). Burroughs moved fully into the postmodern in his later work.

14 William Burroughs, *The Ticket That Exploded* (Paris: Olympia Press, 1962), 53–54.

15 "Burroughs has, in recent years, modified the sort of provocatively misogynistic statement that characterized his early attacks on sexual dualism. He insists in response to a reviewer of *The Place of Dead Roads*, 'I have often said that it is not women *per se*, but the dualism of the male-female equation that I consider a mistake'" (Robin Lydenberg, *Word Cultures: Radical Theory and Practice in William Burroughs' Fiction* [Urbana: University of Illinois Press, 1987], 167).

16 Several critics have discussed Burroughs's masochism in terms of a desire to neutralize the terror of the pre-oedipal mother by assuming her position in relation to the infantile self: "The writer frees himself from the pre-oedipal mother by becoming his own mother and feeding himself with words. . . . Maintaining the self-sufficiency of the womb state, and at the same time transmuting passive reception of pain into active enjoyment of it, he feeds himself (and us) with poison words . . ." (Oxenhandler, "Listening to Burroughs' Voice," 140). Lydenberg makes a version of the link to feminist theory that I am suggesting here, pointing to Burroughs's attack on sexual dualism, though his move to do so through "eliminat[ing] women altogether from the arena of reproduction" makes this linkage, in Lydenberg's view, "perverse." She also sees Burroughs, in his repudiation of the maternal role as constructed by the patriarchal family, as occupying the vacated position of the mother: "I would stress that much of the violence against women in Burroughs' fiction can be best understood as part of this strategy of assimilation: to take the place of the mother Burroughs must first displace her. To take on the maternal role is to confuse both sexual dualism and family structure, to confound the power structures which limit and rule conventional reproduction. . . . The threatening matriarchal 'worde horde' which is terminated by the decapitation of the mother . . . finds itself cut loose from the mother's body to become a liberating flood. Anatomically, the 'sainted gash' [a mother-reference from NL] which indicates the mother's vagina is displaced to her slashed throat, where the flood of language may be most economically released. . . . In the 'Atrophied Preface' which concludes *Naked Lunch*, Burroughs claims for himself the 'word horde' he has associated with the ambivalently revered and despised maternal figure: 'Now I, William Seward, will unlock my word horde'" (*Word Cultures*, 168–70). David Savran argues, along similar lines, in *Taking It Like a Man: White Masculinity, Masochism, and U.S. Cultural Production* (Princeton: Princeton University Press, 1998), that in Burroughs's representative postwar white masculinity, characterized by a sadomasochistic, dually gendered self-division, the annihilated woman, represented for Burroughs by his wife Joan whom he accidentally shot and killed in 1951, becomes an identificatory figure for Burroughs the writer, introjected by Burroughs as male masochist: "as a subject, he is always split into a masculine — and sadistic — half that delights in displaying his prowess and his marksmanship, and a feminine — and masochistic — half that delights in being used as a target" (7). This split "plays itself out not in a static opposition but in a ceaseless and vertiginous oscillation between masculine and feminine positionalities" (84).

9. *Endnotes II*

1   I do not intend any disrespect either to these novelists or to the critics who champion them and see their work as defining postmodernism. I continue to value and admire most of these writers, and I think there is ample room in our general academic critical practice for divergent definitions of postmodernism, as well as for criticism of a wide variety of writers whose work largely avoids postmodern practices. In fact, because in the West we continue to live in the bourgeois society that produced the realist novel, many or perhaps most contemporary writers of fiction, both "literary" and popular, write primarily in conventional, realist modes (as has been the case throughout both the "modernist" and "postmodernist" periods) and would not be included in anyone's version of postmodernism (let Saul Bellow and Anne Tyler stand in, in a wholly symbolic rather than representative way, for this unbelievably long and diverse list of writers). I make these points here by way of making clear the implications for contemporary fiction of my view of postmodernism.

2   See Molly Hite, *The Other Side of the Story*, for a brilliant critique of McHale's and other masculinist versions of postmodernism.

10. *Politics of the Self*

1   Richard Poirier, *The Performing Self: Compositions and Decompositions in the Languages of Contemporary Life* (New York: Oxford University Press, 1971), vii. Future references to this volume will appear parenthetically in the text.

2   Many writers on sixties and post-sixties politics, most notably Todd Gitlin and Alice Echols, have lamented this shift from society-based to subjectivity-based politics as a loss or abandonment of the political itself. See bibliography, part I. I disagree with their analyses, and view this shift, again, as a relocation, rather than a renunciation, of the political.

3   For an excellent discussion of the meanings, both complementary and distinct, of these terms, see Elin Diamond's introduction to her edited volume *Performance and Cultural Politics* (New York: Routledge, 1996).

4   On the connection of avant-garde art and popular culture in sixties Britain in general, and a discussion of the Beatles' connection to the avant-garde in particular, including artist Peter Blake's album cover for *Sgt. Pepper*, see Simon Frith and Howard Home, *Art into Pop* (London: Methuen, 1987). For other works on the Beatles in the sixties, see James Miller, *Flowers in the Dustbin*. Needless to say, there are many such books and essays, and hundreds more on rock and counterculture in the sixties in general.

11. *Laing's Politics of the Self*

1   R. D. Laing, *The Politics of Experience* (New York: Pantheon Books, 1967), 23. Future references to this volume will be included parenthetically in the text.

2   Many, of course, situated at one end of this spectrum, repudiated the other end. I had many countercultural friends who would have nothing to do with radical

activism, considering it spiritually corrupt (remember the Beatles' "Revolution #9"), and many radical friends who scorned the counterculture as self-indulgent and politically quietist (hard-line radicals routinely derided the "carnival atmosphere" of countercultural participants in antiwar actions). This deep sixties divide permeated written and other expression at the time, but the sense of continuity between radical politics and the counterculture was, I would argue, more pervasive and characteristic than the sense of discontinuity.

3   This project may sound like postmodern inter- or trans- or cross- or multi-disciplinarity, of which African American studies, ethnic studies, women's studies, queer studies, and cultural studies, all initiated in the sixties, are prime instances, but in fact we have here another instance of sixties as dominant modern/emergent postmodern: this project did indeed represent the incipiently postmodern move toward breaking down the separation of distinct intellectual disciplines and areas of authority, but in the sixties the purpose of this move was a grand, unifying, integrating, metanarrative synthesis; in postmodernity, such a synthesis is rejected, and the new inter- or trans- or cross- or multi-disciplinary studies, like the "new social movements" out of which most of them emerged, are generally particularist, interested in partial, limited, temporary affiliations rather than unifying syntheses.

4   In a not unfamiliar stroke of postmodern irony, it is the right-wing survivalists and fundamentalists who have inherited both the apocalyptic vision and also the hyperventilated language of the sixties.

5   Some postmodern fiction deploys this tone, but ironically, self-mockingly, or at least self-consciously; for example, Paley, Roth, Rushdie.

6   I do not make use here of the corpus of psychoanalytic work on Laing, particularly on his original theories of schizophrenia, the unconventional therapeutic practices he derived from them, and his connections to British object relations theory, because it is not directly germane to the argument of this chapter. It would therefore constitute an empty gesture to list this substantial body of work in a note.

12. Tell Me Lies about Vietnam

1   Though the tormented, antiwar Vietnam movie genre seems to have petered out recently (the enraged, reactive Rambo genre ended with the Reagan era it marked), supplanted by the more heroic, morally simplistic, and jingoistically reassuring World War II movie, and, more recently still, by patriotic, propagandistic, promilitary, Pentagon-supported movies such as *Black Hawk Down* (the Mel Gibson movie *We Were Soldiers*, based on the nonfiction book by that title by Lt. Col. Hal Moore and Joseph L. Galloway, about the prophetically devastating 1965 battle of Ia Drang in which the authors fought, implicitly criticizes the war as doomed and fatally ill-advised, but, in the current mood, celebrates its heroic soldiers), these continue to be Vietnam books, one of the most recent of which is Robert Mann's ambitious *A Grand Delusion: America's Descent Into Vietnam* (New York: Basic Books, 2001)—this title clearly indicates the author's point of view. *Dispatches* (1977; New York: Vintage, 1991), Michael Herr's great, scathing, deeply antiwar

new-journalistic book of Vietnam reporting, is designated, on its back cover, "Military History / Vietnam." Evidently, powerfully damning critiques of the war - of the military command structure as well as of politicians — like Herr's (though he is also appreciative of the "grunts," despite their terrifying murderousness, which he also reports fully, and is caught up in reporting what he insists on calling the "glamor" of the war as well as its horror), are now taught as military history: the failures and mistakes of this "doomstruck" (to use Hunter Thompson's word) war are now assimilated to a dominant military strategy governed by avoiding at all costs (one hopes — even this certainty is now eroding) any future Vietnam-like "quagmire."

2   As Terry H. Anderson says in the introduction to his fifteen-page select bibliography in his 1995 book *The Movement and the Sixties* (see bibliography, part II), "Enough to fill a library has been written on the era from the 1950s to the 1970s. Just on the Vietnam War, Richard Dean Burns and Milton Leitenberg's 1984 bibliographic guide, *The Wars in Vietnam, Cambodia, and Laos, 1945–1982*, is 300 pages" (457). Rather than attempt to reproduce or even remotely summarize, or make a gesture, necessarily perfunctory, toward summarizing this enormous body of work, I will just stipulate here that, while my overall understanding of the war, and of the antiwar movement, is indebted to the many works on Vietnam I have read over the years, the specific argument of this chapter concerning the pivotal dominant modern/emergent postmodern structure of *Fire in the Lake* is not.

3   Frances FitzGerald, *Fire in the Lake: The Vietnamese and the Americans in Vietnam* (New York: Random House, 1972); "the national bestseller, winner of the Pulitzer Prize, winner of the National Book Award, winner of the Bancroft Prize for History," as the front cover of the 1973 paperback proclaims. All future references to this volume will be included parenthetically in the text.

4   One thinks immediately of a cultural production such as Oliver Stone's 1986 Academy Award–winning *Platoon*, which is organized around the Charlie Sheen character's moral struggle between allegiance to the sergeant played by Tom Berenger, who is a grotesque killer, and the other sergeant, played by Willem Dafoe, who is a noble, pure martyr, and ends with the Sheen voice-over assertion that the real Vietnam War was fought not against the Vietnamese but by Americans against ourselves.

5   Michael Herr's *Dispatches* makes this crucial fact of the American military-psychic relation to the Vietnamese vividly clear.

6   "Monicagate" is exemplary of this shaded, nuanced, relativistic complexity.

13. Fire Next Time *or Rainbow Sign*

1   Malcolm X with Alex Haley, *The Autobiography of Malcolm X* (New York: Ballantine, 1965), 377–78. In this chapter, as in chapters 12 and 14, I can only refer to the existence of scores of important, sometimes crucial works on Civil Rights, Black Power, the Black Arts movement, African American culture in and since the sixties, and in relation to the Black Atlantic and the global African diaspora; on the Vietnam War, the international protests against it, and its mas-

sively variegated cultural manifestations; on second-wave feminism and its similarly massive and diverse theories and political, social, and cultural impacts and expressions. Again, hundreds of these works, read over the years, have informed this book.

2 According to Andrew Young (*Charlie Rose*, February 27, 2002), Malcolm X said to Martin Luther King Jr., shortly before Malcolm's assassination, that he did not oppose King's program, that they were both working toward the same general goals, and that he (Malcolm X) could draw the fire away from King and thereby enable King's movement to succeed.

3 Martin Luther King Jr., *I Have A Dream: Writings and Speeches that Changed the World* (1986; rpt. San Francisco: HarperSanFrancisco, 1992), 85. Future references to this volume will appear parenthetically in the text. This quote — "Injustice anywhere is a threat to justice everywhere" — appeared on a beautiful, enormous banner that was a permanent decoration on one wall of the auditorium of the Brooklyn, New York, public elementary school my children attended. It is on its way toward, or perhaps is already in, the tablets of American democracy's guiding principles that include "Ask not what your country can do for you . . . " and "All men are created equal."

4 Eldridge Cleaver, *Soul on Ice* (New York: Dell, 1967), 72. Future references to this volume will appear parenthetically in the text.

5 Angela Y. Davis, "Reflections on the Black Woman's Role in the Community of Slaves," 1971, in *The Angela Y. Davis Reader*, ed. Joy James (Oxford: Blackwell, 1998), 116. Future references to this volume will appear parenthetically in the text.

6 Frantz Fanon, *The Wretched of the Earth* 1961; rpt. trans. Constance Farrington (New York: Grove Press, 1963). Future references to this volume will appear parenthetically in the text. Frantz Fanon, *Black Skin, White Masks* 1952; trans. Charles Lam Markmann (New York: Grove Press, 1967).

7 There is a long, important, rich history of debate concerning the nature and political significations of identity politics, just as there is a complex history of various modes of identity politics. There is no such thing as "identity politics" with a singular, consensual meaning or history. It has become a favorite scapegoat for various modes of liberal, Marxist, and right-wing positions in the culture wars. I am using the term here without reference to those histories and debates. Rather, I am using it in its most neutral descriptive sense, as referring to political ideas and movements based on notions, either constructed or essentialist, of a group identity based on shared race, gender, sexuality, ethnicity, geographical location, age, abledness, and other axes of identification/difference.

8 James Baldwin, *Collected Essays*, selected by Toni Morrison, including *Notes of a Native Son, Nobody Knows My Name, The Fire Next Time, No Name in the Street, The Devil Finds Work*, and other essays (New York: Library of America, 1998). Future references to this volume will appear parenthetically in the text. *No Name in the Street*, 1972, and *The Devil Finds Work*, 1976, as well as the dozens of other essays, written throughout Baldwin's career and published in a wide

variety of distinguished venues, which are included in the *Library of America* volume, are on a par with the earlier essays in brilliance and complexity, but not, I would argue, in influence — it is the first three volumes that were most influential and widely read.

9   Eldridge Cleaver notoriously launched an extremely homophobic attack on Baldwin in *Soul on Ice*, considering Baldwin insufficiently black because insufficiently masculine. The analyses of race and queer sexuality that recently have dominated studies of Baldwin, and still do, are crucial but otherwise only tangentially germane to my argument here. See, for example, Marcellus Blount and George P. Cunningham, eds., *Representing Black Men* (New York: Routledge, 1996), in which several essays, informed by the intersections of queer studies and African American studies, discuss Baldwin and homosexuality; Dwight A. McBride, ed., *James Baldwin Now* (New York: New York University Press, 1999), which has a section titled "Baldwin and Sexuality"; several essays in the other four sections also address issues of sexuality. Michelle M. Wright's " 'Alas, Poor Richard!': Transatlantic Baldwin, the Politics of Forgetting, and the Project of Modernity," in *James Baldwin Now*, 208–232, which situates Baldwin in relation to the postmodern, postcolonial project, specifically Paul Gilroy's crucial development of the idea of the Black Atlantic, is very useful in relation to my argument here. For other generally useful works on Baldwin, see Harold Bloom, ed., *James Baldwin: Modern Critical Views* (New York: Chelsea House, 1986), for a range of essays, mostly focusing on Baldwin's literary writing, including Stephen Adams, "*Giovanni's Room*: The Homosexual as Hero" (131–39); David Leeming, *James Baldwin* (New York: Knopf, 1994), a thorough, highly useful biography; Horace A. Porter, *Stealing the Fire: The Art and Protest of James Baldwin* (Middletown: Wesleyan University Press, 1989), organizing Baldwin's oeuvre primarily around major influences, specifically Harriet Beecher Stowe, Richard Wright, and Henry James, but with a chapter on *Notes of a Native Son* (21–27) very useful and germane to my argument here, in which Porter argues that the title essay is precisely at once particularly autobiographical in a familiar African American protest mode and also universal in its liberatory agenda; Fred L. Standley and Louis H. Pratt, eds., *Conversations with James Baldwin* (Jackson: University Press of Mississippi, 1989), including wonderful interviews with Baldwin, organized chronologically, beginning with Studs Terkel in 1961 and ending with Quincy Troupe's posthumously published interview (1988) with Baldwin just before his death in 1987; Carolyn Wedin Sylvander, *James Baldwin* (New York: Frederick Ungar, 1980), a detailed, insightful, chronologically-generically organized critical overview of Baldwin's oeuvre.

10   See Porter, *Stealing the Fire*, on this essay.

11   For a brilliant discussion of this passage in particular, and Baldwin's work in general, in relation to feminist, queer, and critical race studies, see Cora Kaplan, " 'A Cavern Opened in My Mind': The Poetics of Homosexuality and the Politics of Masculinity in James Baldwin," in Blount and Cunningham, *Representing Black Men*, 27–54.

12 Black racial self-hatred is also, of course, the central issue in Toni Morrison's first novel, *The Bluest Eye*, published in 1970 but begun in 1962; written, therefore, entirely as a production of the sixties.

13 Yoshinobu Hakutani, in "*No Name in the Street*: James Baldwin's Image of the American Sixties," argues that Baldwin is "one of the most gifted essayists America has produced," and that, though "later readers, even after *No Name in the Street* had appeared, were more impressed by this manner [his brilliant style] than his matter," in fact "it is doubtful that his expression can generate such power without substance" (*James Baldwin Now*, 277). I emphatically agree with this assessment. Hakutani also argues that the progression toward increasing political radicalism in Baldwin's essays is a reflection of the growing militancy of the time. Hakutani believes that Baldwin's position on race, particularly in the earlier works, "reflects the attitude of the liberals of the time. Similarly, *The Fire Next Time* (1963) . . . reflects public sentiment on the subject at the time" (278). *No Name in the Street* represents a further move toward militancy. I agree with Hakutani about the progression in Baldwin's views reflecting the progression toward radicalism in the course of the sixties, but I would argue that it is only in retrospect that Baldwin's views can seem to "reflect public sentiment." Baldwin's views were by no means held by a majority of the population, even in the early sixties, when Martin Luther King Jr. was still a troubling, fearsome figure to most whites, in the North as well as the South, and Civil Rights activism appeared for the most part dangerous and threatening. Baldwin was, of course, considered insufficiently militant and too middle-of-the-road, even accommodationist, by many black radicals — see, particularly, Cleaver's attack in *Soul on Ice*.

14. Personal and Political

1 See for example Jane Flax, Donna Haraway, Meaghan Morris, Linda Nicholson, Jennifer Wicke, Andreas Huyssen, Craig Owen, and David Harvey, in bibliography, part I.

2 While it would take far too long to acknowledge all the great feminist writings of the past forty years, and stretching behind them back to Mary Wollstonecraft, on which the arguments of this chapter are founded and which they assume, I do want to acknowledge here some very important recent works on the second wave, which have been extremely useful to me in writing this chapter: Rosalyn Baxandall and Linda Gordon, eds., *Dear Sisters: Dispatches from the Women's Liberation Movement* (New York: Basic Books, 2001); Susan Brownmiller, *In Our Time: Memoir of a Revolution* (New York: Dial, 1999); Rachel Blau DuPlessis and Ann Snitow, eds., *The Feminist Memoir Project: Voices from Women's Liberation* (New York: Three Rivers Press, 1998); Alice Echols, *Daring to Be Bad: Radical Feminism in America, 1967–1975* (Minneapolis: University of Minnesota Press, 1989); Sara Evans, *Personal Politics: The Roots of Women's Liberation in the Civil Rights Movement and the New Left* (New York: Vintage Books, 1980); Ruth Rosen, *The World Split Open: How the Modern Women's Movement Changed America* (New York: Viking, 2000); Miriam Schneir, ed., *Feminism in Our Time: The Essential*

Writings, World War II to the Present (New York: Vintage, 1994); Lynne Segal, *Is the Future Female? Troubled Thoughts on Contemporary Feminism* (New York: Peter Bedrick Books, 1987); and Segal, *Straight Sex: Rethinking the Politics of Pleasure* (Berkeley: University of California Press, 1994).

3   "Redstockings Manifesto," in Schneir, *Feminism in Our Time*, 127. Future references to this volume will be included parenthetically in the text.

4   Robin Morgan, ed., *Sisterhood Is Powerful: An Anthology of Writings from the Women's Liberation Movement* (New York: Vintage, 1970). Future references to this volume will appear parenthetically in the text.

5   Redstockings of the Women's Liberation Movement, *Feminist Revolution* (New York: Random House, 1975). Shulamith Firestone, *The Dialectic of Sex: The Case for Feminist Revolution* (New York: William Morrow, 1970). Future references to this volume will appear parenthetically in the text.

6   Naomi Weisstein, quoted in Schneir, *Feminism in Our Time*, p. 108.

7   I am strategically collapsing these very diverse works together, because they are in fact united in their reconfiguration of feminism away from that essentialist white Western bourgeois "woman" and toward multiplicities of differential specificity. As with the wide range of feminist work informing this chapter in general, it would be impossible to annotate these crucial works here.

8   See the introduction and chapter 1 for expansions of this argument.

9   Joan W. Scott, *Only Paradoxes to Offer: French Feminists and the Rights of Man* (Cambridge: Harvard University Press, 1996). Future references to this volume will appear parenthetically in the text.

10   Ann Snitow, "A Gender Diary," in Marianne Hirsch and Evelyn Fox Keller, eds., *Conflicts in Feminism* (New York: Routledge, 1990). Snitow is currently working on a book project based on this essay.

11   Hatred of the oppressor, coupled with the conviction of their pernicious uselessness, and the concomitant desire to eliminate them from the face of the earth, is characteristic of many radical and revolutionary movements throughout history (thanks to Bonnie Smith for reminding me of this fact). It is the location of this feminist sentiment within the problematics of categorizations of subjectivity and their attendant politics, emerging in the sixties as a shift to postmodernity, that strikes me as particularly significant here. Despite the rage evident in Morgan's writing, again, there is a dispassionate assessment of progressive and retrograde potentialities of gendered categories of subjectivity that is characteristic of the emergence of postmodern subject politics.

12   See Marilyn Boxer, *When Women Ask the Questions: Creating Women's Studies in America* (Baltimore: Johns Hopkins University Press, 1998), especially pp. 117–22, for a balanced, nuanced, informative recent analysis of the question of a link between identity politics and depoliticization.

13   Barbara Johnson, *The Feminist Difference* (Cambridge: Harvard University Press, 1998), 2; Mary Childers and bell hooks, "A Conversation about Race and Class," in Hirsch and Keller, *Conflicts in Feminism*, 70 (also quoted by Johnson in her introduction).

14   See Rita Felski, *Beyond Feminist Aesthetics: Feminist Literature and Social Change*

(Cambridge: Harvard University Press, 1989), for an excellent, highly influential analysis of this phenomenon.

15 Florence Howe, ed., *No More Masks!* (1973; rpt. New York: HarperCollins, 1993).

16 The hybrid styles of postmodern fiction often include elements of modernist form. Of the white male American fiction writers who move successfully from sixties avant-garde into postmodern writing, E. L. Doctorow — who will be discussed in chapter 15 — along with Pynchon and DeLillo, is one of the most important (see chapter 9).

15. Utopia Limited

1 For an argument that the United States has been more influenced by utopianism than other societies because of its founding revolutionary, Enlightenment commitments to liberty and equality, see Barbara Goodwin and Keith Taylor, eds., *The Politics of Utopia* (New York: St. Martin's Press, 1982), 183–84. For an argument that postmodernism, as a definitive break with modernism, is quintessentially North American, see Huyssen, "Mapping the Postmodern," in *After the Great Divide*. My understanding and deployment of the term "utopian" is influenced by a number of utopian discourses, most notably those of Karl Mannheim, especially *Ideology and Utopia* (New York: Harcourt, Brace and World, 1936); Ernst Bloch, especially *A Philosophy of the Future* (New York: Herder and Herder, 1970); and Herbert Marcuse, especially *The Aesthetic Dimension: Toward a Critique of Marxist Aesthetics* (Boston: Beacon Press, 1978), and *An Essay on Liberation* (Boston: Beacon Press, 1969).

2 I refer to Linda Hutcheon's term, "historiographic metafiction." She uses this term, in *The Poetics of Postmodernism* (New York: Routledge, 1998), to designate postmodern fiction that "is both metafictionally self-reflexive and yet speaking to us powerfully about real political and historical realities" (5).

3 For a thorough, highly informative discussion of the importance of feminism in Owenite socialist utopianism in England and the United States, see Barbara Taylor, *Eve and the New Jerusalem* (1983; rpt. Cambridge: Harvard University Press, 1993).

4 For a classic and highly influential discussion of the Freedmen's Bureau and its demise, see W. E. B. Du Bois, *The Souls of Black Folk* (1903; rpt. New York: Bantam Books, 1989), chapter 2, "Of the Dawn of Freedom," 10–29.

5 On the continuities of 1960s countercultural communes with nineteenth-century American utopian communities, see, for example, James Gilbert, "New Left: Old America," in Sohnya Sayres, Anders Stephanson, Stanley Aronowitz, and Fredric Jameson, eds., *The 60s without Apology* (Minneapolis: University of Minnesota Press, 1984), 244–47.

6 See Paul Starr, "The Phantom Community," in John Case and Rosemary C. R. Taylor, eds., *Co-ops, Communes and Collectives: Experiments in Social Change in the 1960s and 1970s* (New York: Pantheon, 1979), 245–73. He also discusses the antagonism between hippies and New Left radicals.

7   For an extended discussion of the centrality of the concept of participatory democracy to the *Port Huron Statement* and to the New Left in general, see chapter 6, and also James Miller, *"Democracy Is in the Streets": Port Huron to the Siege of Chicago*.

8   For one analysis of postmodernism as post-utopian, see Fredric Jameson, "Secondary Elaborations (Conclusion)," in *Postmodernism or, the Cultural Logic of Late Capitalism*, 297–418, especially 334–40 and 401–06. See also Angelika Bammer, *Partial Visions: Feminism and Utopianism in the 1970s* (New York: Routledge, 1991).

9   See, perhaps most notably, Jean-François Lyotard, *The Postmodern Condition: A Report on Knowledge*. In his foreword, for example, Lyotard claims that "this is the sense in which high modernism can be definitively certified as dead and as a thing of the past: its Utopian ambitions were unrealizable and its formal innovations exhausted" (xvii).

10 E. L. Doctorow, *The Waterworks* (New York: Random House, 1994); Toni Morrison, *Beloved* (New York: Knopf, 1987). Subsequent references to these works will appear parenthetically in the text.

11 See Linda Hutcheon, *The Poetics of Postmodernism*; also Hutcheon, *A Politics of Postmodernism*. I take this aggregation of high-literary and popular narrative modes, resulting from the breakdown of the modernist "great divide" between art and popular culture, to be the most important characteristic of postmodernist fictional form (see Huyssen, *After the Great Divide*, and chapter 9). Unlike modernism, which draws heavily on popular sources but assimilates them to its radically innovative, oppositional, high-art aesthetic practices, postmodernism leaves popular modes more or less intact (see the introduction and bibliography, part I). For an interesting recent discussion of *Beloved* as postmodern fiction, which in part addresses the issue of its composite form, see Rafael Perez-Torres, "Knitting and Knotting the Narrative Thread — *Beloved* as Postmodern Novel," in Nancy J. Peterson, ed., *Toni Morrison: Critical and Theoretical Approaches* (Baltimore: Johns Hopkins University Press, 1997), 91–109.

12 Morrison also centrally deploys the African American genres of the slave narrative, the folk tale, storytelling, and oral tradition in general.

13 See Ann duCille, *The Coupling Convention: Sex, Text and Tradition in Black Women's Fiction* (New York: Oxford University Press, 1993), especially pp. 143–45.

14 For discussions of modernist form as utopian, see, for example, Fredric Jameson, *The Political Unconscious: Narrative as a Socially Symbolic Act*; Bloch, *A Philosophy of the Future*; Marcuse, *The Aesthetic Dimension*; and Marianne DeKoven, *Rich and Strange: Gender, History, Modernism* (Princeton: Princeton University Press, 1991). Again, I disagree with characterizations of postmodernism, such as those of Ihab Hassan or Jean-François Lyotard, as primarily or typically formally experimentalist. I agree with Linda Hutcheon that postmodernism is oppositional from a position within literary or other aesthetic conventions, in contradistinction to modernism, which defines itself as a negation of and alternative to convention.

15 See Jewell Parker Rhodes, "Toni Morrison's *Beloved*: Ironies of a 'Sweet Home'

Utopia in a Dystopian Slave Society," *Utopian Studies* 1 (1990): 77–92. See also the blues song "Sweet Home Chicago": the Great Migration brought real hope and promise as well as bitter disappointment for African Americans leaving the Black Belt South for the urban North throughout the first half of the twentieth century.

16 "This girl Beloved, homeless and without people, beat all, though he [Paul D] couldn't say exactly why, considering the coloredpeople he had run into during the last twenty years. During, before and after the War he had seen Negroes so stunned, or hungry, or tired or bereft it was a wonder they recalled or said anything. Who, like him, stole from pigs; who, like him, slept in trees in the day and walked by night; who, like him, had buried themselves in slop and jumped in wells to avoid regulators, raiders, paterollers, veterans, hill men, posses and merrymakers. Once he met a Negro about fourteen years old who lived by himself in the woods and said he couldn't remember living anywhere else. He saw a witless coloredwoman jailed and hanged for stealing ducks she believed were her own babies" (66).

"Eighteen seventy-four and whitefolks were still on the loose. Whole towns wiped clean of Negroes; eighty-seven lynchings in one year alone in Kentucky; four colored schools burned to the ground; grown men whipped like children; children whipped like adults; black women raped by the crew; property taken, necks broken. He [Stamp Paid] smelled skin, skin and hot blood. The skin was one thing, but human blood cooked in a lynch fire was a whole other thing. . . . It was the ribbon. Tying his flatbed up on the bank of the Licking River, . . . he caught sight of something red on its bottom. . . . [it] was a red ribbon knotted around a curl of wet woolly hair, clinging still to its bit of scalp. . . . 'What *are* these people? You tell me, Jesus. What *are* they?' " (180).

17 See Perez-Torres, "Knitting and Knotting the Narrative Thread," for another discussion of this passage.

18 The one exception is Amy Denver, a young destitute girl, escaping indenture and therefore at the bottom of the white power structure. Like Sethe, she is abused and on the run; also like Sethe, she is almost superhumanly strong and resourceful. She delivers Denver, who is therefore named for her, and saves Sethe's life.

19 A great deal of feminist psychoanalytic maternalist criticism has been written on this novel. For a useful bibliography of articles on *Beloved*, including many in the above category, see Debbie Mix, "Toni Morrison: A Selected Bibliography," in Peterson, ed., *Toni Morrison*, 812–17. My reading emphasizes the deformations of history rather than the problems of the absolute pre-Oedipal maternal bond as analyzed from within a nonhistorically inflected psychoanalysis. For an argument with an emphasis on writing and constructions of maternity in African American women's fiction, see Carol Boyce Davies, "Mother Right/Write Revisited: *Beloved* and *Dessa Rose* and the Construction of Motherhood in Black Women's Fiction," in Brenda O. Daly and Maureen T. Reddy, eds., *Narrative Mothers: Theorizing Maternal Subjectivities* (Knoxville: University of Tennessee Press, 1991), 44–57. Mae Henderson's "Toni Morrison's *Beloved*: Re-Membering the Body as Historical Text," in Hortense Spillers, ed., *Comparative American Identities: Race, Sex,*

and Nationality in the Modern Text (New York. Routledge, 1991), 62–86, is another article that has been very important to my understanding of *Beloved*.

20 Compare, for example, this passage from Cixous, "Sorties," in Cixous and Catherine Clément, *The Newly Born Woman*, trans. Betsy Wing (Minneapolis: University of Minnesota Press, 1986): "in woman there is always, more or less, something of 'the mother' repairing and feeding, resisting separation. . . . Text, my body: traversed by lilting flows; listen to me . . . it is the rhyth-me that laughs you; the one intimately addressed who makes all metaphors . . . the part of you that puts space between yourself and pushes you to inscribe your woman's style in language. Voice: milk that could go on forever. Found again. The lost mother/bitter-lost. Eternity: is voice mixed with milk" (93).

21 There is an uncanny, and probably deliberate, echo here of Eliot's "The Love Song of J. Alfred Prufrock": "In the room the women come and go."

22 For discussions of Doctorow's use of the 1870s to evoke contemporary New York, see, for example, Luc Sante, "The Cabinet of Dr. Sartorius," *New York Review of Books* (June 23, 1994), 10–12, and Ted Solotaroff, "Of Melville, Poe and Doctorow," *The Nation* (June 6, 1994), 784–790.

23 Doctorow incorporates many ellipses into the text of *The Waterworks*. Those ellipses which are mine will be placed in brackets.

24 Unlike Morrison, Doctorow does not close with this apocalyptic passage. He adds one more sentence, which ominously but ambiguously relocates us in historical time and place: "And let me leave you with that illusion [the illusion of ice-encased New York lifted by God out of time] . . . though in reality we would soon be driving ourselves up Broadway in the new Year of Our Lord, 1872" (253). This metafictional moment leaves us in the year of the defeat of the Freedmen's Bureau.

25 "A friend from Prague," quoted in Erazim V. Kohak, "Requiem for Utopia," in Nicolaus Mills, ed., *Legacy of Dissent: Forty Years of Writing from Dissent Magazine* (New York: Simon and Schuster, 1994), 389–401.

26 "Incorporated" both in the sense of subsumed by late-capitalist consumer culture and also in the sense of Gilbert and Sullivan's *Utopia, Limited*: literally becoming a corporation.

27 See Jameson, *Postmodernism*, chapter 6, "Utopianism after the End of Utopia" (155–80), on utopian impulses in certain modes of contemporary visual art, deployed around various manifestations of postmodern spatiality.

Conclusion

1 August 20, 2000, "Arts and Leisure," 1, 18–19.

2 See Andreas Huyssen, "Memories of Utopia," in *Twilight Memories: Marking Time in a Culture of Amnesia* (New York: Routledge, 1995), 85–101, for an argument that utopian possibilities and desires persist within, and in spite of, postmodernity's repudiation of utopia, in contemporary art's turn toward memory and history: "a shift from anticipation to remembrance" (88). Utopian possibility, still a hope or desire for the future, is now located in the search for the past: "In this

search for history, the exploration of the no-places, the exclusions, the blind spots on the maps of the past is often invested with utopian energies very much oriented toward the future" (88). See also Drucilla Cornell, *At the Heart of Freedom: Feminism, Sex and Equality* (Princeton: Princeton University Press, 1998), chapter 7, "Feminism, Utopianism, and the Ideal," for a useful discussion of feminist utopianism as existing within what she calls the "imaginary domain": "A good definition of *utopian* is that what is possible cannot be known in advance of social transformation. This is the sense of *utopian* I have consistently defended because of the pride of place given to the imagination, including its function as fundamental to reason" (185).

SELECTED ANNOTATED BIBLIOGRAPHY

I. The Postmodern

Anderson, Perry. *The Origins of Postmodernity*. London: Verso, 1998. Essentially a sympathetic tribute to Fredric Jameson's crucial, definitive work on postmodernity and postmodernism, but also a brilliant, invaluable history of the key theorizations of postmodernity and postmodernism, and of the emergence of postmodernity itself, in relation to questions of politics and culture, by one of the most important left intellectuals of our time.

Arac, Jonathan, ed. *Postmodernism and Politics*. Minneapolis: University of Minnesota Press, 1986. A very important early anthology, assessing in complex and relatively dispassionate terms various aspects and dimensions of the political situation of postmodernity. The collection includes essays by major voices in the field: Paul A. Bové, Mary Louise Pratt, Dana Polan, Andrew Parker, Rainer Nägele, John Higgins, Cornel West, Bruce Robbins.

Baudrillard, Jean. *Selected Writings*. Ed. Mark Poster. Cambridge: Polity Press, 1988. Baudrillard, with his notion of the dominance of the simulacrum, his jeremiads against the depthless, nonreal, commodified culture of images and consumerist America as prime location of postmodern culture, is one of the most important critical theorists of (against) postmodernity and postmodernism.

Bauman, Zygmunt. *Postmodernity and Its Discontents*. New York: New York University Press, 1997. Bauman echoes here the great Freudian title, as does E. Ann Kaplan's 1988 collection. In a complex, highly suggestive set of philosophical inquiries, Bauman contemplates the postmodern discontents arising from an excess of individual freedom, or license, as opposed to modernity's discontents, arising, as analyzed by Freud, from an excess of order.

Bertens, Hans, and Douwe Fokkema, eds. *International Postmodernism: Theory and Literary Practice*. Amsterdam: John Benjamin Publishing Company, 1996. An encyclopedic, eclectic, inclusive survey, refusing to exclude any viable strains, locations, definitions, or theorizations of postmodernism in theory, the arts, various modes of writing, and of varieties of postmodernism in particular national cultures.

Blau, Herbert. *The Eye of Prey: Subversions of the Postmodern*. Bloomington: Indiana University Press, 1987. A powerful, complex set of meditations on theory, theater, writers (particularly Beckett), performance, and postmodern culture in general. The first essay, "(Re)sublimating the Sixties," rigorously avoids nostalgia and acknowledges the excesses of the sixties while at the same time insisting on the power of its liberatory outrage. Blau argues that Marcusean desublimated eros has been resublimated into theory, as an erotics of discourse. Blau is one of the most important theorists and critics of contemporary, particularly experimental, theater. His 1964 *The Impossible Theater* stands with works by Peter Brooks, Joseph Chaikin, Jerzy Grotowski, and Richard Schechner in defining and theorizing the sixties renaissance of experimental theater (see chapter 7).

Bourdieu, Pierre. *Distinction*. Trans. R. Nice. London: Routledge, 1984. Though Bourdieu does not discuss the question of postmodernism directly, his analysis of cultural capital as owned by the hegemonic bourgeoisie has been crucial to postmodern critiques of modernist elitism.

Calinescu, Matei. *Faces of Modernity: Avant-garde, Decadence, Kitsch*. Bloomington: Indiana University Press, 1977. Calinescu develops a powerful critique of the avant-garde in decline (into "decadence and kitsch") in late modernity.

———. *Five Faces of Modernity: Modernism, Avant-garde, Decadence, Kitsch, Postmodernism*. Durham: Duke University Press, 1987. Calinescu expands his analysis here to include a more explicit critique focusing on the decadence and kitsch he sees as inherent in postmodern cultural production.

Chow, Rey. "Rereading Mandarin Ducks and Butterflies: A Response to the 'Postmodern' Condition." *Cultural Critique* 5 (1986): 69–93. In this balanced essay, crucial to postcolonial, feminist postmodern literary studies, Chow raises the question of the "unpresentable" in third world cultural traditions as occluded by the notion of postmodernism as a set of language games, at the same time that she finds useful the understanding of power relations in the constructedness of cultural formations espoused by postmodern ideologies.

Connor, Steven. *Postmodernist Culture: An Introduction to Theories of the Contemporary*. Oxford: Blackwell, 1990. A useful, balanced, penetrating analysis and overview of key postmodern cultural thought and movements.

Debord, Guy. *Comments on the Society of the Spectacle*. London: Verso, 1990. Debord's notion of the "society of the spectacle" (originally published in French in 1968 as the theoretical manifesto and underpinning of the radical avant-garde Situationist movement, a characteristic sixties political/cultural group), is, like Baudrillard's of the simulacrum, a key critical theorization of postmodern culture.

de Certeau, Michel. *The Practice of Everyday Life.* Trans. S. Rendell. Berkeley: University of California Press, 1984. This text has been crucial to postmodern cultural analysis of the subversive potential of popular culture, lodged in the "refunctioning" practices of appropriation inhering in everyday "tactics" of reception.

Deleuze, Gilles, and Félix Guattari. *A Thousand Plateaus.* Trans. Brian Massumi. Minneapolis: University of Minnesota Press, 1987. This book, along with but even more than Deleuze and Guattari's *Anti-Oedipus*, provides a key theoretical foundation for postmodern thought, particularly in the articulation of antiteleological, antihierarchical, branching, "rhizomatic" structures, rejecting, and providing an alternative to, modernist narratives of hierarchy and progress.

Docherty, Thomas, ed. *Postmodernism: A Reader.* New York: Columbia University Press, 1993. An extremely useful pedagogical tool. Docherty's introductions to the eight parts of this collection are lucid and informative; he includes essays by most of the major theorists of postmodernism and postmodernity. He also includes a wonderfully comprehensive bibliography of books and articles, through the early nineties (covering therefore the heyday of work on postmodernism), relevant to a range of issues in postmodern thought.

DuPlessis, Rachel Blau. *The Pink Guitar: Writing as Feminist Practice.* New York: Routledge, 1990. A wide-ranging, brilliantly written collection of essays on postmodern feminist theoretical, literary, and critical practices, containing the groundbreaking essay "For the Etruscans," which argues for an experimental postmodern writing practice as a crucial lever or opening for feminist analysis and cultural work.

Durham, Scott. *Phantom Communities: The Simulacrum and the Limits of Postmodernism.* Stanford: Stanford University Press, 1998. Durham investigates the complexities and multiplicities of the notion of the simulacrum in postmodern culture, particularly as elaborated by (a surprising trio) Jean Genet, J. G. Ballard, and Pierre Klossowski. Durham's analysis of the elusive, "phantom" but nonetheless crucial promise of the utopian in the cultures of the postmodern simulacrum he elaborates through his work on these writers is of particular value to this study.

Eagleton, Terry. "Capitalism, Modernism and Postmodernism," *New Left Review* 152 (July/August 1985): 60–73. In this highly influential essay, a favorite target of advocates of postmodernism, Eagleton condemns postmodernism as the defeat of the left and the triumph of a debased, retrograde capitalist consumerism.

———. *The Illusions of Postmodernism.* Oxford: Blackwell, 1996. Eagleton both expands and moves on from the theses of his 1985 essay here, retaining his attack on postmodern consumerism but acknowledging the emergence into visibility, audibility, and agency of subaltern minorities in postmodernity, and also acknowledging the subversive force of postmodern theories of the subject, power, desire, and the body.

Flax, Jane. *Thinking Fragments: Psychoanalysis, Feminism, and Postmodernism in the Contemporary West.* Berkeley: University of California Press, 1990. Flax develops a complex, thoughtful analysis, making a powerful case for a postmodern feminism by linking the three terms of her subtitle around feminist object relations theory in order to argue that the positivist, empiricist feminism she associates with pre-postmodern feminist thought is hampered by an inadequate account of the subject as unified individual, but that Lacanian thought, while it establishes the non-self-identical subject, is also hampered by its masculinism. Object relations theory provides an adequate basis for a postmodern feminism that avoids both these pitfalls.

Fokkema, Douwe, and Hans Bertens, eds. *Approaching Postmodernism*. Amsterdam: John Benjamins Publishing Company, 1986. An important collection of excellent, largely sympathetic work on postmodern culture, whose admirable purpose is to establish the meaning of the term more clearly. It contains general theoretical essays on postmodernism in relation to modernism and essays on postmodernism in a variety of arts, genres, and national locations.

Foster, Hal, ed. *The Anti-Aesthetic: Essays on Postmodern Culture*. Port Townsend, Wa.: Bay Press, 1983. One of the most important early collections in the field. Hal Foster's sympathetic account of an "oppositional postmodernism," informed by the radical elements of modernism and the avant-gardes but "exceeding" them in relevance to the cultural present, was highly influential, as was Craig Owens's link of postmodernism to feminism in "The Discourse of Others: Feminists and Postmodernism." This collection contains Fredric Jameson's crucial, widely reprinted attack on postmodernism as the "cultural dominant" of a triumphant consumerist late capitalism, "Postmodernism and Consumer Society," as well as Jürgen Habermas's equally crucial and widely reprinted attack on postmodernism, "Modernity—An Incomplete Project," arguing that we still exist in modernity and that postmodernity or postmodernism is an empty invention (Habermas's debate with Lyotard on this issue was a staple of postmodern analysis). This collection also contains essays largely sympathetic to postmodernism by some of its key exponents: Kenneth Frampton (architecture was of course a crucial field in the rise of postmodernism); Rosalind Krauss on sculpture; Douglas Krimp on the bankruptcy of the museum; Gregory L. Ulmer on the shift in the notion of the object of criticism as stable and external to the critic; Jean Baudrillard, a key exponent of the notion of the postmodern as culture of the "simulacrum," on "The Ecstasy of Communication"; and Edward W. Said on the interestedness of cultural analysis.

Foucault, Michel. *The Order of Things: An Archaeology of the Human Sciences*. 1966 (*Les Mots et les choses*); 1970. New York: Vintage, 1973. A crucial early intervention by Foucault in the development of what would become a key theorization of the postmodern, but his entire oeuvre could be included here. No one has been more influential than Foucault in the development of postmodern thought, particularly in his notions of capillary power flows, of the substitution of incomplete hegemony always accompanied by resistance or subversion for massive dualisms of domination and revolution. Because I consider poststructuralist theory, with which Foucault is also associated, more a manifestation of endpoint modernism than of postmodernism (see chapter 1), I do not include in this appendix the great works by Barthes, Cixous, Derrida, Irigaray, Kristeva, Lacan, and other continental theorists often associated with postmodernism.

Graff, Gerald. *Literature against Itself: Literary Ideas in Modern Society*. Chicago: University of Chicago Press, 1979. Graff's critique of the notion of a "postmodern breakthrough" has been influential for those who deny the emergence of the postmodern as a distinct cultural mode.

Habermas, Jürgen. "Modernity — An Incomplete Project." In Hal Foster, ed., *The Anti-Aesthetic*.

———. *The Philosophical Discourse of Modernity*. Trans. F. G. Lawrence. Cambridge: MIT Press, 1987. Contains the full development of Habermas's theories of justice and democracy as the incomplete projects of modernity. Habermas's debates with Lyotard concerning the nature and political, cultural implications of postmodernity and modernity were at the heart of the emergence of postmodern studies in the eighties.

Haraway, Donna. *Simians, Cyborgs, and Women: The Reinvention of Nature*. New York: Routledge, 1991. This book contains, along with many other crucial essays on the constructedness of nature and the interestedness and narrativity of knowledge (key concepts in the syncretic version of postmodernism/postmodernity I develop here), the crucial essays "A Cyborg Manifesto: Science, Technology, and Socialist-Feminism in the Late Twentieth Century" and "Situated Knowledges: The Science Question in Feminism and the Privilege of Partial Perspective." The notion that all knowledge is "situated" — marked, located, local, embodied, partial, historical — is crucial to my view of the postmodern, as is Haraway's commitment to egalitarian, diverse, progressive political agendas, her notion of the boundary-crossing, hybrid, minoritarian (in Linda Hutcheon's key term) cyborg as a model for feminist subjectivity, and her view of the postmodern, particularly of its global cybertechnologies and their attendant gendered economies and politics, as simultaneously destructive and liberatory. Donna Haraway is one of the few most important theorists of a progressive feminist postmodernism/postmodernity.

———. *Modest_Witness@Second_Millennium*. New York: Routledge, 1997. Haraway continues her brilliant investigations of the social-political constructions of gender, nature, science, and technology in postmodernity, with particular attention to simultaneously terrifying and potentially liberatory recent developments in biotechnologies.

Hardt, Michael, and Antonio Negri. *Empire*. Cambridge: Harvard University Press, 2000. In this groundbreaking, enormously influential study of contemporary politics, economics, and culture, Hardt and Negri identify U.S. global capitalism as "empire," or the next stage beyond imperialism. Hardt and Negri's empire is a postmodern global system based on flows of communication and capital, in which the nation-state is indeed undermined, but which is nonetheless controlled primarily by the interests and power of the United States. In their view of this all-embracing global system, and in their simultaneous, positive view of multiple global sites of continual, inventive resistance to it, Hardt and Negri provide one of the best accounts available of the current situation of postmodernity assumed in this study.

Harvey, David. *The Condition of Postmodernity*. Cambridge, Mass.: Blackwell, 1989. One of the few most important books on the shift from modern to postmodern, extremely useful to me in this project, written from a Marxist perspective linking the emergence of postmodernity, as Jameson does, to a shift in capitalism, which Harvey, like Soja, defines as characterized by more flexible modes of capital accumulation, and to simultaneous, related shifts in "space-time compression." Harvey's first chapter provides an extremely useful overview of the emergence of the postmodern from the modern.

Hassan, Ihab. *Paracriticisms: Seven Speculation of the Times*. Urbana: University of Illinois Press, 1975. Hassan was perhaps the most important, influential early theorist of postmodernism, and this book was one of the earliest articulations of the notion of postmodernism in literary/cultural production, aligning it fully with the avant-garde experimentalist tradition of the twentieth century. Hassan subsequently wrote a number of important books and articles developing these analyses, including most notably *The Dismemberment of Orpheus: Toward a Postmodern Literature* (Madison: University of Wisconsin Press, 1982). Many, many subsequent works, by a wide range of critics and theorists, of literary analysis of postmodernism, or postmodern literary analysis, or analysis of postmodern literature, generally written from a sympathetic point of view, defining postmodernism primarily in terms of formal experimentalism, and viewing it as a culturally, politically progressive aesthetic development — far too many to credit here — have also informed my work in this book. Most notable among these, working primarily in the early years of postmodern literary study but also continuing to the present, are Max Apple, *Free Agents* (New York: Harper and Row, 1984); Charles Caramello, *Silverless Mirrors: Book, Self and Postmodern American Fiction* (Tallahassee: University of Florida, 1983); Raymond Federman, ed., *Surfiction: Fiction Now and Tomorrow* (Chicago: Swallow Press, 1975); Molly Hite, *Ideas of Order in the Novels of Thomas Pynchon* (Columbus: Ohio State University Press, 1983); Jerome Klinkowitz, *Literary Disruptions: The Making of a Post-Contemporary American Fiction* (Urbana: University of Illinois Press, 1975, rpt. 1980); Richard Kostelanetz, *The Old Fictions and the New* (Jefferson, N.C.: McFarland, 1987); David Lodge, *The Modes of Modern Writing: Metaphor, Metonymy and the Typology of Modern Literature* (Ithaca: Cornell University Press, 1977); Larry McCaffrey, *The Metafictional Muse* (Pittsburgh: University of Pittsburgh Press, 1982); Charles Newman, *The Post-Modern Aura: The Act of Fiction in an Age of Inflation* (Evanston: Northwestern University Press, 1985); Patrick O'Donnell, *Passionate Doubts: Designs of Interpretation in Contemporary American Fiction* (Iowa City: University of Iowa Press, 1986); Charles Russell, *Poets, Prophets and Revolutionaries: The Literary Avant-Garde from Rimbaud through Postmodernism* (New York: Oxford University Press, 1985); Robert Scholes, *Fabulation and Metafiction* (Urbana: University of Illinois Press, 1979); Tony Tanner, *City of Words: American Fiction, 1950–1970* (New York: Harper and Row, 1971); Alan Wilde, *Horizons of Assent: Modernism, Postmodernism and the Ironic Imagination* (Baltimore: Johns Hopkins University Press, 1981).

Hebdige, Dick. *Subculture: The Meaning of Style*. London: Methuen, 1979. A very influential work on the politically subversive capabilities of postmodern cultural practices, particularly those of minority and other youth subcultures.

Hite, Molly. *The Other Side of the Story: Structures and Strategies of Contemporary Feminist Narrative*. Ithaca: Cornell University Press, 1989. A crucial juxtaposition of feminist narrative analysis with postmodernist theory and aesthetic practice, arguing that "postmodernism" as it had been defined up to that point in the literary academy was almost exclusively male and masculinist, omitting not only women writers but formal, intellectual, political, and cultural concerns and practices that define a broader, more complex and inclusive, politically inflected view of the postmodern.

Hutcheon, Linda. *A Poetics of Postmodernism*. New York: Routledge, 1988. A crucial intervention in the field of postmodernist studies. Hutcheon and Donna Haraway, David Harvey, Andreas Huyssen, and Fredric Jameson are the theorists of the postmodern who have had the greatest influence on the understanding of postmodernism and postmodernity that informs this study. Hutcheon develops here her notions of "complicitous critique," "resistance from within," the "minoritarian and ex-centric," and "historiographic metafiction," all of which have been of signal importance. She concentrates on the ironic self-reflexivity and constructed narrativity of postmodern cultural ideology and production, on its simultaneously appropriated and subversive "complicitous critique" and "resistance from within," and on the emergence in postmodern cultural production of heretofore relatively silenced "minoritarian" racial, ethnic, sexual, gendered, located voices.

——. *The Politics of Postmodernism*. London: Routledge, 1989. Hutcheon here extends the insights of the *Poetics*, focusing more explicitly on the political implications of irony in minoritarian discourses, particularly, in the last section, those of feminism. The first chapter of this book, like that of David Harvey's *The Condition of Postmodernity* and like Docherty's introduction to *Postmodernism: A Reader*, provides a very useful summary of the modernism/postmodernism debates, oriented, of course, toward Hutcheon's own concerns with the potentialities of postmodernism for "complicitous critique" and "resistance from within."

Huyssen, Andreas. *After the Great Divide: Modernism, Mass Culture, Postmodernism*. Bloomington: Indiana University Press, 1986. One of the few most important books on postmodernism. Huyssen's development of the thesis of the breakdown in postmodernism of the "great divide" between high and low culture that characterized modernism has been extremely influential, for me as for many others as well. Huyssen, along with Craig Owens, was one of the first to connect postmodernism with women and feminism through their common association with mass and consumer culture. This book's chapter "Mapping the Postmodern," the clearest development of these ideas, has been widely reprinted and incorporated, often foundationally, into many other analyses of the postmodern.

Jameson, Fredric. *Postmodernism, or, The Cultural Logic of Late Capitalism*. Durham: Duke University Press, 1991. This is the book that has been most influential in my understanding of postmodernism and postmodernity as "cultural dominant," in Jameson's term, of late (consumer) capitalism, though I do not share

Jameson's pervasive condemnation of the phenomena he observes or his predominant pessimism concerning postmodern cultural production. The omission of the role of feminism and the other new social movements in the emergence of postmodernism limits the reach of Jameson's conclusions, but the substance of his analyses of postmodern culture, particularly in his formulations of postmodern consumer culture's construction as surface, spatiality, hyperspace, and free-floating affect, and of the complex fate of utopia in postmodernity, apart from the gloom of his overall tone, is profoundly illuminating and crucial to any understanding of postmodernity.

———. *The Seeds of Time*. New York: Columbia University Press, 1994. These are Jameson's 1991 Wellek Library Lectures at the University of California, Irvine. In these essays he develops his notion, crucial for my arguments here, of postmodern "antinomy," in which the classical dialectic breaks apart into incommensurable, multiple differences.

Jencks, Christopher. *What Is Postmodernism?* London: Academy Editions, 1987. Jencks is one of the most important theorists and advocates, here and in an array of other publications, of postmodern architecture, the field in which postmodernism emerged most definitively. Jencks sees postmodern architecture as responding to the contemporary society and culture of fragmentation, pluralism, and dissonance.

Kaplan, E. Ann, ed. *Postmodernism and Its Discontents: Theories, Practices*. London: Verso, 1988. An important collection published in the heyday of interest in postmodernism, containing a very useful introduction by Kaplan, outlining the debates around postmodernism as they stood at the time, focusing primarily on what was then considered the central division between a "utopian," Derridean postmodernism (which I would now call poststructuralism rather than postmodernism, precisely because it is still enmeshed in utopian modernity) and a "co-opted," Baudrillardean postmodernism of the simulacrum, the primary or most influential exponent of which is Fredric Jameson. Jameson's crucial "Postmodernism and Consumer Society," later revised and incorporated in *Postmodernism*, appears in this collection (as in others), in part 1, "The Postmodernism Debate," as do essays by Kaplan on MTV, and essays, largely either sympathetic to postmodern modes of cultural production or skeptical about large claims concerning postmodernism as a cultural dominant, and therefore antagonistic to Jameson's views, by Dana Polan, Fred Pfeil, Mike Davis, and Warren Montag. Part 2, "Postmodernism, Feminism and Popular Cultural Theory," contains useful essays by Linda Williams, Robert Stam, William Galperin, and David E. James developing the suggestive links among those terms.

Krauss, Rosalind. *The Originality of the Avant-Garde and Other Modernist Myths*. Cambridge: MIT Press, 1985. Krauss finds postmodern aesthetic practices in early-twentieth-century avant-gardes.

Kroker, Arthur, and David Cook. *The Postmodern Scene: Excremental Culture and Hyper-Aesthetics*. London: Macmillan, 1988. A highly negative assessment of the "panic" culture of postmodernity as an ecstasy of horror. The authors hope to force this nihilistic culture of the simulacrum to implode by means of the "hyper-intensity" of their theorization.

Laclau, Ernesto, and Chantal Mouffe. *Hegemony and Socialist Strategy: Towards a Radical Democratic Politics*. London: Verso, 1985. Laclau and Mouffe provide one of the most useful, profound theorizations of a postmodern democracy of affiliation, moving beyond modernity's totalizing metanarrative and its discredited and oppressive hegemonies, but insisting on retaining the emancipatory legacy of modernity in democracy's unique, egalitarian progressive potentialities. Evidently, this theorization is extremely useful in relation to my interest in postmodern egalitarianism.

Lefèbvre, Henri. *The Production of Space*. Trans. Donald Nicholson-Smith. Oxford: Blackwell, 1991. A brilliant analysis of the shifts in spatiality and conceptualizations/constructions of spatiality in modernity and postmodernity. Lefèbvre agrees with Jameson and the other Marxist geographers that in postmodernity, modernization has reached its endpoint, eliminating all nonmodernized territories. His most powerful particular contribution to this discourse involves his notion of the overlapping, simultaneous layering of disjunct historical moments within postmodern locations, particularly in those preeminently constructed urban environments.

Lyotard, Jean-François. *The Postmodern Condition: A Report on Knowledge*. 1974. Trans. Geoff Bennington and Brian Massumi. Minneapolis: University of Minnesota Press, 1984. One of the few most important books on postmodernism, in which Lyotard makes his crucially influential argument, essentially linking postmodernism with poststructuralist theory, that postmodernism is a direct descendent of the twentieth-century avant-gardes and is constructed as and through language games, polysemy, limitless, shifting possibility, and free play.

McGowan, John. *Postmodernism and Its Critics*. Ithaca: Cornell University Press, 1991. Like Bauman, McGowan is interested in the political, oppositional possibilities and problematics of freedom opened up in postmodernity.

McHale, Brian. *Postmodernist Fiction*. 1987. London: Routledge, 1989. McHale's analysis of modernism as characterized by an "epistemological dominant" and postmodernism by an "ontological dominant" has been very influential and useful (I include McHale here, despite my stricture concerning lack of space in which to give credit to the myriad works on literature and postmodernism that have informed this book, because of the large theoretical provenance of his work.) McHale's version of postmodern fiction, here and in his later book *Constructing Postmodernism*, is defined by an earlier version of postmodernism that I consider late modernist, avant-garde experimentalism, written almost exclusively by white men.

———. *Constructing Postmodernism*. London: Routledge, 1992. McHale expands his earlier analyses here, including a more extensive discussion of Pynchon, an overview of narratives of postmodernism, and a discussion of cyberpunk.

McRobbie, Angela. *Postmodernism and Popular Culture*. London: Routledge, 1994. An extremely useful and interesting study of the oppositional politics of a range of postmodern theory and popular cultural practices, focusing particularly on feminism and youth culture.

Morris, Meaghan. *The Pirate's Fiancée*. London: Verso, 1988. Morris's book is a major contribution to the articulation of feminism with postmodernism, particularly through the dynamics of film and reading practices. The first chapter of this book, titled "Feminism, Reading, Postmodernism," has been most influential, particularly in its pointed critique, similar to Molly Hite's, of postmodern masculinism, and its articulation of feminist postmodernism as a multiple, diffuse, open-ended, but marked, located, and embodied reading practice, in the most general sense of that term: a practice for reading not just cultural productions but culture itself, society itself.

Naremore, James, and Patrick Brantlinger, eds. *Modernity and Mass Culture.* Bloomington: Indiana University Press, 1991. "Modernity" also encompasses postmodernity in this important collection, with essays treating various aspects, from a progressive point of view, of the politics of popular culture.

Nicholson, Linda J., ed. *Feminism/Postmodernism.* New York: Routledge, 1990. This collection makes a case for a progressive postmodernist feminism (with a few demurrals, notably by Nancy Hartsock), including a strong introduction by Nicholson, arguing for postmodernism as a corrective to the intellectual and political limitations of liberal feminism, and essays from many of the most important feminist scholars working in this field, including Nancy Fraser, Jane Flax, Christine di Stefano, Sandra Harding, Seyla Benhabib, Susan Bordo, Nancy Hartsock, Elspeth Probyn, Donna Haraway, Andreas Huyssen, Anna Yeatman, Iris Marion Young, Judith Butler (though Butler does not write directly about postmodernism, her work on queer theory is a crucial aspect of a broader reach of postmodern feminist theory). Many other feminist theorists could be included in this bibliography, theorists whose work, similarly relevant to a broader definition of the question of intersections of feminism and postmodernism, informed my work in this project in general and in particular the discussion in chapter 14 in innumerable ways, but, as with works on literary postmodernism, the list would simply be too long.

——. *The Play of Reason: From the Modern to the Postmodern.* Ithaca: Cornell University Press, 1999. Nicholson expands her important work on postmodern feminism in this book, arguing that the emancipatory legacies of modernity, specifically the egalitarianism and commitment to social justice of Marxism and of classical liberalism, can be retained in a postmodern feminism liberated from modernity's totalizing structures of domination.

——, and Steven Seidman, eds. *Social Postmodernism: Beyond Identity Politics.* New York: Cambridge University Press, 1995. This rich collection of essays, focused on a wide variety of approaches to social, political, and cultural questions inflected by/ toward varieties of postmodern theory, assumes that the "social postmodernism" associated with the new social movements, when tempered by careful, critical awareness of its limitations in relation to postcolonial, queer, and other subaltern subjectivities, can be extremely useful in reimagining democratic politics. Contributors of this collection include many of the most influential current voices in this field, including Nicholson herself.

O'Donnell, Patrick. *Latent Destinies: Cultural Paranoia and Contemporary U.S. Narrative.* Durham: Duke University Press, 2000. O'Donnell powerfully analyzes

paranoid postmodern subjectivity in a wide range of contemporary texts,
organized around issues of nation, gender, and criminality, addressing film and
television as well as fiction, using a combination of Jameson's crucial analysis of
postmodernism as the cultural dominant of late capitalism, entailing a universal
commodification and a repression of historical temporality, with theories of
postmodern subjectivity as fluid, multiple, "rhizomatic" (Deleuze). In this complex
analysis of contemporary "cultural paranoia," the commodified self is actually,
paradoxically, rigidified in its fluidity and multiplicity through a paranoia of
exclusion.

Portoghesi, Paolo. *Postmodern: The Architecture of the Postindustrial Society*. Trans.
E. Shapiro. New York: Rizzoli, 1983. Portoghesi is skeptical about relatively
uncritical accounts and overly eclectic practices of postmodern architecture and
argues for a more politically astute and focused development of "the small city."

Rorty, Richard. *Consequences of Pragmatism*. Minneapolis: University of Minnesota
Press, 1982. Rorty's is one of the central contributions to a philosophy of
postmodernism as ethically responsible without recourse to moral metanarratives.

Ross, Andrew, ed. *Universal Abandon?* Edinburgh: Edinburgh University Press, 1988.
An important collection of essays focusing on the cultural politics of
postmodernism, written largely from a sympathetic point of view. Chantal
Mouffe's essay in this collection, "Radical Democracy, Modern or Postmodern?," is
particularly useful.

Soja, Edward. *Postmodern Geographies*. London: Verso, 1990. Soja has been very
important in conceptualizing postmodernity as an order of spatiality rather than
temporality, revealing simultaneities and lateral mappings that undo "carceral
historicism." Los Angeles, the most visible location of the flexible capitalist
accumulation that defines postmodernity for Soja, is his quintessential postmodern
space. See also Harvey, Jameson, and Lefèbvre.

Trachtenberg, Stanley, ed. *The Postmodern Moment: A Handbook of Contemporary
Innovation in the Arts*. Westport, Conn.: Greenwood Press, 1985. A useful
collection of studies that defines postmodernism in terms of experimentalism and
aesthetic innovation in a range of artistic practices.

Waugh, Patricia. *Feminine Fictions: Revisiting the Postmodern*. London: Routledge,
1989. Waugh rethinks the masculine postmodern in relation to the postmodern
characteristics of the traditionally feminine romance subgenre.

Wicke, Jennifer, and Margaret Ferguson, eds. *Feminism and Postmodernism (A
Boundary 2 Book)*. Durham: Duke University Press, 1994. A strong set of essays
emphasizing the mutual theoretical imbrications of feminism and postmodernism,
and the empowerment of women through postmodern popular cultures of
consumerism.

Williamson, Judith. *Decoding Advertisements: Ideology and Meaning in Advertising*.
London: Marion Boyars, 1978. Though she does not discuss postmodernism or
postmodernity directly, Williamson develops a brilliant analysis here of the
complex, mixed political significances (both oppressive and potentially liberatory)
of advertising, one of its key cultural manifestations.

Ziarek, Ewa Płonowska. *An Ethics of Dissensus: Postmodernity, Feminism, and the*

Politics of Radical Democracy. Stanford: Stanford University Press, 2001. Ziarek argues for a fusion of democratic politics in general, and feminist politics in particular, with postmodern ethics, opposing the view that postmodern ethical ideologies of responsibility and freedom, derived from the highly influential theories of Emmanuel Lévinas, support either a conservative privatized discourse, or militate against possibilities of political activism through an "anarchic obligation" (Lévinas) to the Other. The "ethics of dissensus" focuses on embodiment, a key postmodern trope and source of both intellectual and cultural postmodern practices, as entry to positive feminist political uses of postmodern ethics.

Zurbrugg, Nicholas. *Critical Vices: The Myths of Postmodern Theory*. Amsterdam: Overseas Publishers Association, 2000. A collection of many, very short essays on postmodern artists and theorists. Zurbrugg celebrates the vitality of postmodern avant-garde creativity (he is a particular admirer of William Burroughs) and repudiates the attacks on postmodernism and postmodernity by Marxist and other left theorists.

———. *The Parameters of Postmodernism*. Carbondale: Southern Illinois University Press, 1993. Zurbrugg continues his celebratory analysis of avant-garde postmodern writers and artists, and his polemic against anti-postmodern theory, particularly the Marxist work of Fredric Jameson and Terry Eagleton.

II. The Sixties

Adelson, Alan. *SDS: A Profile*. New York: Scribner's, 1972. An SDS member's sympathetic history of the late-sixties radical heyday of the movement, beginning with the Columbia University occupation in 1968; less well known and also less critical of SDS than Kirkpatrick Sale's *SDS*, which is considered the definitive history of the organization. Adelson, writing in 1971, assumes that SDS will regroup and prevail as a less violent, more worker-oriented organization. This book reflects the optimism of some surviving remnants of SDS in the very early seventies.

Albert, Judith Clavir, and Stew Albert, eds. *The Sixties Papers*. New York: Praeger, 1985. A useful collection of original New Left and countercultural documents.

Anderson, Terry H. *The Movement and the Sixties: Protest in America from Greensboro to Wounded Knee*. New York: Oxford University Press, 1995. A balanced, detailed, responsible account, incorporating a great deal of important archival material, of the major events and people of the sixties radical movements, from the Civil Rights lunchroom sit-ins starting in Greensboro, North Carolina, in 1960, to the siege of Wounded Knee in 1973. Anderson's narrative, though admirably complex in its understanding of how the history of the sixties unfolded through the chronological impact of specific historical events, follows the usual structure of hopeful rise followed by cataclysmic fall. Despite the nascent politics of subjectivity crucial to the Civil Rights and Black Power movements and to feminism, Anderson insists that his defining term, "activist," is "free," as he puts it, of race and gender.

Banes, Sally. *Greenwich Village 1963: Avant-Garde Performance and the Effervescent Body*. Durham: Duke University Press, 1993. An important, persuasive case for the crucial impact of the early-sixties Greenwich Village avant-garde renaissance (rather than the Beats, as Russell Jacoby argues in *The Last Intellectuals*) on the subsequent formation of the counterculture. Covering a wide range of what we now call performance art, Banes also argues that this avant-garde, which she dates from 1963, had a historical significance comparable to the Civil Rights march on Washington of the same year. The crucial link between the two is democratization, which itself gives the avant-garde direct political significance and ramifications. Banes also argues that the avant-garde's primary commitment to democracy made it postmodern rather than modernist, and in fact itself marked the end of the modernist avant-gardes and the inception of postmodernism.

Bayles, Martha. *Hole in Our Soul: The Loss of Beauty and Meaning in American Popular Music*. New York: Free Press, 1994. As its title indicates, this book views sixties rock music as the pinnacle of the genre, and post-sixties popular music as not just a decline from, but a totally vitiating destruction and selling-out of, rock and roll.

Bates, Tom. *Rads: A True Story of the End of the Sixties*. New York: HarperCollins, 1992. Bates narrates, primarily through the story of the bomber Karl Armstrong, a detailed history of the bombing of the Army Mathematics Research Center at the University of Wisconsin, Madison, in 1970 as characteristic of the violent culmination and demise of sixties radicalism. Despite its sympathy for earlier, less violent phases of the movement, this narrative focuses primarily on the deluded destructiveness of the movement's final violent phase.

Berman, Paul. *A Tale of Two Utopias: The Political Journey of the Generation of 1968*. New York: Norton, 1996. A fairly optimistic reading of sixties utopianism (which Berman sees as a convergence of cultural, spiritual, and political movements) as reemerging in the more liberal-democratic "utopianism" (I would call it progressive rather than utopian) anticommunist revolutions of 1989.

Braunstein, Peter, and Michael William Doyle, eds. *Imagine Nation: The American Counterculture of the 1960s and '70s*. New York: Routledge, 2002. An excellent anthology, emphasizing the complex, pervasive interrelations of the sixties countercultures with radical politics. Topics include the connection of the drug culture with radical defiance of oppressive laws; the connection between the "consciousness expansion" of the drug culture and the "consciousness raising" of feminism; the two-pronged "assault on the culture" represented by the counterculture and radical politics; identity politics across countercultural and radical political movements; countercultural art practices as self-consciously politically radical; communalism and environmentalism as simultaneously countercultural and radical political movements.

Breines, Wini. *Community and Organization in the New Left, 1962–1968: The Great Refusal*. 1982. New Brunswick: Rutgers University Press, 1989. Breines uses Marcuse's crucial formulation of the "Great Refusal" to make a powerful, detailed argument contrasting the anarchic, antihierarchical, communal, participatory-democratic, diverse, inclusive, utopian structure of local community organizations in the New Left, which she considers largely successful, with the centralized, bureaucratic, hierarchical, white male organization of national SDS, which, as she sees it, ultimately doomed the movement to failure.

Burner, David. *Making Peace with the 60s*. Princeton: Princeton University Press, 1996. Burner attributes the failure of the sixties political and cultural movements to unnecessary conflict between groups with similar goals, groups that might have formed productive alliances and achieved progressive agendas. Instead, the Civil Rights movement was split against itself into integrationist and Black Power factions, left liberalism was drowned out by the radical left, and peaceful, nonviolent antiwar groups were at cross-purposes with an increasingly radical, violent Marxist-Leninism (evidently, Burner prefers Civil Rights, left liberalism and nonviolent antiwar groups).

Buzzanco, Robert. *Vietnam and the Transformation of American Life*. Oxford: Blackwell, 1998. A clear, straightforward account both of the history of the Vietnam War and the crucial role of the antiwar movement in generating a wide range of radical transformations in American politics and culture.

Carmichael, Stokeley, and Charles V. Hamilton. *Black Power: The Politics of Liberation in America*. New York: Vintage, 1967. An influential polemic for the Black Power movement by one of its most charismatic and visible advocates.

Collier, Peter, and David Horowitz, eds. *Destructive Generation: Second Thoughts about the Sixties*. New York: Summit Books, 1989. This collection, which includes pieces by Todd Gitlin and Kirkpatrick Sale as well as by the editors, attacks what it sees as the self-destructive, self-deluded megalomania and violence of sixties radicals and theorists, and the fall into post-sixties cultural and identity politics. It is characteristic of the widespread current backlash against the sixties and repudiation of sixties politics by many former activists. See also Gitlin's *The Twilight of Common Dreams*.

Dark Star, ed. *Beneath the Paving Stones: Situationists and the Beach, May 1968*. Oakland, Calif.: AK Press, 2001. A collection of key Situationist writings, such as "On the Poverty of Student Life" by Mustapha Khayati, a broadside that played a key role in May '68, and "The Totality for Kids" by Raoul Vaneigem, a précis of world history, from hunter-gatherer culture to the coming revolution of 1968, premised not just on repudiation of the society of the spectacle but also on the new social movements, particularly feminism, Black Power, and third world liberation movements, as well as workers' movements.

Dickstein, Morris. *Gates of Eden: American Culture in the Sixties*. 1977. Cambridge: Harvard University Press, 1997. A definitive, classic text, still unsurpassed in the breadth, subtlety, detail, and penetration of its analyses of the counterculture, beginning with the Beats and the eruption out of fifties complacency, and moving through the absurdist humor of the early sixties, to the new journalism, the Black Arts movement, rock music, and experimental fiction. Dickstein sees the sixties cultural movements as participating in the great American utopian tradition (hence the title), become secular, Romantic, modernist and avant-garde in its particular origins, and eclectic in its sixties manifestations (his emphasis on sixties utopianism is obviously crucial here) He also argues that the great Romantic socialism of the sixties was destroyed by militant violence by the end of the decade

——. *Leopards in the Temple: The Transformation of American Fiction, 1945–1970.* Cambridge: Harvard University Press, 2002. Here Dickstein, focusing especially on the horrors of the war as motive for resistance against fifties conformism, on black-influenced fifties rock and roll, on the influence of existentialism, on the Beats, on black, Jewish, and gay writers, and on Norman Mailer, argues for the importance of subversive, oppositional postwar works of the late forties and the fifties in preparing the ground for the radical cultural and political changes of the sixties.

Diggins, John Patrick. *The Rise and Fall of the American Left.* 1973. New York: Norton, 1992. A useful, judicious introductory overview of the history of the American left in the twentieth century. Diggins's analysis of the demise of the New Left focuses on its failure to connect with the potential radicalism of the working class, a failure that he considers characteristic of the repeated failures of left radical movements in the twentieth century.

Echols, Alice. *Shaky Ground: The Sixties and Its Aftershocks.* New York: Columbia University Press, 2002. A collection of essays by the author of the groundbreaking history of the myriad groups and ideologies that made up early second-wave radical feminism, *Daring to Be Bad.* Echols sustains her advocacy of the radical force of popular cultural practices in this collection, attributing genuine transformative power to (generally American) countercultural movements, particularly in rock music. Echols champions postmodern developments in popular culture that she sees emerging from elements of the sixties counterculture.

Farber, David. *The Age of Great Dreams: America in the 1960s.* New York: Hill and Wang, 1994. Farber is one of the most influential, important recent historians of the sixties. His argument here—presented in a highly readable, historically responsible narrative—as the title indicates, is that the sixties represented the culmination of American power and prosperity, based on capitalism's unceasing "creative destruction" of the old and invention of the new. Nonetheless, the history of the sixties is ultimately tragic, because the great dreams were defeated, both by the self-destructive violence of the radicals and also by the crushing forces of the right: Nixon, the FBI, COINTELPRO, the backlash in general. Yet, politics and culture changed for the better, overall, as a result of the sixties movements.

——, ed. *The Sixties: From Memory to History.* Chapel Hill: University of North Carolina Press, 1994. This useful collection of essays by major writers on the sixties, including Alice Echols, one of the most important historians of second-wave feminism; Terry H. Anderson, author of *The Movement and the Sixties*; George Lipsitz, who has written extensively about popular culture; and Farber himself, among others, covers a wide range of key sixties movements, issues, and events: liberalism, Vietnam, race and ethnicity, feminism, the counterculture, the sexual revolution, the changes in business (capitalism, as I would describe it), and the right-wing reaction. In his introduction, Farber presents the thesis he develops in *Age of Great Dreams*: that the sixties transformed the nature and criteria of "cultural authority and political legitimacy" (1), and that the period was dominated by progressive liberalism but was also a "seedbed" (4) for right-wing reaction.

Fink, Carole, Philipp Gassert, and Detlef Junker, eds. *1968: The World Transformed.* Cambridge: Cambridge University Press, 1998. A thoughtful, sophisticated collection of scholarly essays, mostly on the West German left in the late sixties (with 1968 as the paradigmatic, emblematic, as well as literally crucial year for European radicals), but also on sixties radicalism in a range of other countries, including the United States, Czechoslovakia, China, Poland, France, Italy, East Germany, Spain, and Israel. These essays focus on international political networks and formations, emphasizing the concertedly global nature of sixties political radicalism.

Frank, Thomas. *The Conquest of Cool: Business Culture, Counterculture, and the Rise of Hip Consumerism.* Chicago: University of Chicago Press, 1997. Frank sees the rapid absorption of hippie styles, and of the counterculture in general, into American consumerism, business practices, and particularly advertising culture not as cooptation but rather as sympathetic rebellion on the part of like-minded, flexible, freewheeling businessmen, mostly of the same generation as the counterculture itself. This argument does not appeal to postmodern theory but is congruent with certain postmodern arguments about the subversion-from-within that characterizes the critical postmodern relation to consumer culture.

———. *One Market under God.* New York: Doubleday, 2000. In this more recent book, Frank is much more critical of, and pessimistic about, post-sixties entrepreneurial capitalism than he was in *The Conquest of Cool.* He sees ex-hippie entrepreneurs, in the name of antigovernmental populism (for example, in the celebration of the unregulated Internet), betraying and vitiating liberal values of active government.

Fukuyama, Francis. *The Great Disruption: Human Nature and the Reconstitution of Social Order.* New York: Free Press, 1999. This conservative theorist sees the radical and countercultural movements and events of the sixties, as is evident in his title, in an entirely negative light, as a "great disruption" of American moral fiber and civic and family values. However, Fukuyama believes that since human beings are genetically hardwired to restore order, we will recover completely from this great disruption, and the order of capitalist culture and the patriarchal nuclear family will be restored.

Gitlin, Todd. *The Sixties: Years of Hope, Days of Rage.* New York: Bantam Books, 1987. Gitlin's are among the best, most influential books on the sixties. Like so many other comprehensive works on the sixties, this book narrates a trajectory of the powerful emergence of a new American left, which destroyed itself — "imploded," in Gitlin's term — in the late sixties, defeated by its own violence and the contradictions of its communal and individualistic agendas. Gitlin's work is eloquent, penetrating, intelligent, deeply insightful; it gives a vivid, accurate account of the experience of sixties radicalism.

———. *The Twilight of Common Dreams: Why America Is Wracked by the Culture Wars.* New York: Henry Holt, 1995. Here Gitlin, now almost entirely disenchanted with the sixties, attacks the excesses of the radical left and counterculture, blaming them for the defeat of the American left, for the backlash, and for the destructive, virulent divisions of the culture wars.

————. *The Whole World Is Watching.* Berkeley: University of California Press, 1980. A brilliant, highly influential book on the role of the mass media in the construction of the radical New Left in the sixties. Gitlin gives a nuanced, complex account of the ways in which mass media vied with and, by the mid-sixties, largely displaced the underground media of the New Left, which represented activism from its own point of view. Mass media both manipulated the left and created its own version of it, focusing on, and therefore empowering, militant, flamboyant, white male celebrities.

Hall, James C. *Mercy, Mercy Me: African-American Culture and the American Sixties.* Oxford: Oxford University Press, 2001. Hall characterizes the most significant attribute of black cultural production in the sixties (the "Second Black Renaissance") as what he calls its "antimodernism." By this he means not postmodernism but rather a critique of and skepticism toward liberal narratives of American progress. He assembles an eclectic group of cultural producers to make this argument, including W. E. B. Du Bois, Robert Hayden, Paule Marshall, William Demby, John Coltrane, and Romare Bearden.

Hobsbawm, Eric. *The Age of Extremes: A History of the World, 1914–1991.* New York: Pantheon Books, 1994. A brilliant and highly useful short history of the post–World War I twentieth century, which presents the sixties as both the culmination of the "golden age" of mid-twentieth-century prosperity and progress, and also as its downfall, through strains on, and generated by, global capitalist development and revolutions of rising expectation.

Hersch, Charles. *Democratic Artworks: Politics and the Arts from Trilling to Dylan.* Albany: State University of New York Press, 1998. Hersch analyzes the often complex, subtle democratizing impact of characteristic cultural productions of the sixties, arguing against conservative cultural critics, notably those most closely associated with the culture wars, such as Allan Bloom and Hilton Kramer, who attack sixties cultural production as either anarchic or solipsistic.

Howard, Gerald, ed. *The Sixties: The Art, Attitudes, Politics and Media of Our Most Explosive Decade.* New York: Marlowe, 1995. A collection of excerpts from major sixties writings, both political and cultural, useful as an introduction to the sixties for a new generation totally unfamiliar with it. The selection of texts is apt, including, among others, excerpts from Paul Goodman, C. Wright Mills, Herbert Marcuse, Michael Harrington, James Baldwin, Eldridge Cleaver, Norman Mailer, Tom Wolfe, Norman O. Brown, R. D. Laing. Howard also includes a selection from Morris Dickstein's classic work on the sixties, *Gates of Eden.*

Isserman, Maurice, and Michael Kazin. *America Divided: The Civil War of the 1960s.* New York: Oxford University Press, 2000. Isserman, author as well of the excellent history of the left leading up to the sixties, *If I Had a Hammer: The Death of the Old Left and the Birth of the New Left,* is one of the most important historians of the radical American tradition; Kazin is a distinguished historian of populism and earlier labor movements. *America Divided* is one of the best recent books on the sixties. Narrating the cultural as well as the political history of the period, with both rich detail and a powerful overview, Isserman and Kazin emphasize the right-wing forces continually at war with radicalism and the counterculture, not just in the wake of the sixties but throughout the period. This is a crucial, insufficiently emphasized fact of the complex political and cultural dynamics of the sixties. Isserman and Kazin also include a useful chronology and bibliographical essay.

Jacoby, Russell. *The End of Utopia: Politics and Culture in an Age of Apathy*. New York: Basic Books, 1999. Continuing the attack on the bankruptcy of contemporary intellectual and cultural life he undertook in *The Last Intellectuals* (New York: Basic Books, 1982), Jacoby laments the demise of utopia as the demise of political activism and engagement.

Jeffords, Susan. *The Remasculinization of America: Gender and the Vietnam War*. Bloomington: Indiana University Press, 1989. In this extremely useful, important, intelligent book, with which I agree entirely, Jeffords argues that the violent defeats of the Vietnam War, encompassing the necessity for masculine bonding and the abjection of defeat as feminized, "remasculinized" American masculinity, away from the gentler, androgynous, nonviolent styles promulgated by the counter-culture, and toward the hypermasculine machismo prevalent in post-sixties American culture.

Kaiser, Charles. *1968 in America: Music, Politics, Chaos, Counterculture, and the Shaping of a Generation*. New York: Grove Press, 1988. A celebratory, fairly nostalgic twentieth-anniversary book, reminding us of the triumphs of the sixties counterculture, most notably those of rock music, focusing particularly, appropriately enough, on the Beatles, the Rolling Stones, and Bob Dylan.

Kimball, Roger. *The Long March: How the Cultural Revolution of the 1960s Changed America*. New York: Encounter Books, 2000. Quite simply, the conservative Kimball believes that sixties radical politics and countercultures completely and irreparably destroyed every facet of American political, social, and cultural life.

Macedo, Stephen, ed. *Reassessing the Sixties: Debating the Political and Cultural Legacy*. New York: Norton, 1997. Despite an attempt at balance, and despite the presence in it of some arguments at least partly sympathetic to the legacies of the sixties, notably by Todd Gitlin, Martha Nussbaum, and Cass Sunstein, this volume, with a foreword by George F. Will and essays by a number of right-wing writers, most notably Alan Wolfe, comes down heavily on the anti-sixties side of the culture wars.

Marcus, Greil. *Invisible Republic: Bob Dylan's Basement Tapes*. New York: Henry Holt, 1997. Although this book focuses on one sixties figure, Bob Dylan, and one crucial rock group, The Band, it qualifies as a general book on the sixties because Marcus makes a very large claim for *The Basement Tapes*, recorded by Dylan and The Band in 1967 (and released in 1975, though much bootlegged in the intervening years) as a quintessential production of the sixties as high point of American populist culture.

Marwick, Arthur. *The Sixties: Cultural Revolution in Britain, France, Italy, and the United States, c. 1958–c.1974*. Oxford: Oxford University Press, 1998. Marwick's enormous (nearly 900 pages) book provides a useful, detailed comparative analysis of sixties politics and culture in four major national locations; the majority of books on the sixties focus primarily on the United States or on other single countries. Marwick has a strong bias against both political and cultural radicals. His thesis is that utopian radicalism came to a destructive, self-destructive dead end, but that sixties "moderates" had an enormous impact, mostly for the good, on post-sixties culture and politics. He uses the odd term of opprobrium "Marxisant" to denounce the political left, while praising establishment moderates, particularly entrepreneurs, who incorporated sixties changes into a more flexible, tolerant, open, diverse democratic capitalism. Marwick's analysis casts in a favorable light what analysts on the left consider the cooptation and neutralization of sixties cultural and political radicalism by a triumphant consumer capitalism.

Mension, Jean-Michel. *The Tribe*. San Francisco: City Lights, 2001. A collection of interviews with Mension, who was closely involved with the Situationist International, a characteristic radical political-countercultural sixties group in France, including extensive documentation of Situationist writings, advocating revolution through total withdrawal from and revision of the capitalist culture of the "society of the spectacle," as well as photos of actions and of Guy Debord, the leader of the group (Debord's *Society of the Spectacle* was its inspiration and key manifesto). This book is most useful as documentation of the activities of the Situationists, rather than as analysis of its ideologies or impact.

Miller, James. *"Democracy Is in the Streets": From Port Huron to the Siege of Chicago*. New York: Touchstone, 1987. One of the most important, intelligent, useful histories of the New Left, filled with enlightening interviews and careful investigation of historical archival materials. SDS's 1962 *Port Huron Statement* is at the heart of Miller's argument. He begins with *Port Huron*, the hopeful, promising articulation of participatory democracy as a revitalized ideology for a new democratic American left, and moves through the increasing radicalism of the New Left to its violent demise. Miller argues that the New Left undervalued *The Port Huron Statement*, and participatory democracy in general; as a result, the movement was destroyed by the violence of the hard-line Marxist-Leninists.

——. *Flowers in the Dustbin: The Rise of Rock and Roll, 1947–1977*. New York: Simon and Schuster, 1999. Primarily a narrative of the rise and triumph of rock and roll, but also a narrative of its rise and fall, tracing its early blossoming, through black music conjoined with white rebels and businessmen, through its great heyday in the sixties, again conjoining white rebels with mass-marketing geniuses, focusing primarily on Elvis Presley, the Beatles, the Rolling Stones, Bob Dylan, and the Grateful Dead, to its destruction in the late seventies by the bland manipulations and packaging of the mass market and by the destructive triumph of the *ressentiment* of the violent adolescent. Miller's notes contain extremely useful references to particular works on the central figures of rock he discusses, their discographies, as well as references to some general works on rock, drugs, and the counterculture in the American and British sixties; of the latter, as Miller says (I generally agree), Tom Wolfe's 1968 *Electric Kool-Aid Acid Test*, his brilliant narrative of Ken Kesey and the Merry Pranksters on their bus, and of their involvement, featuring Jerry Garcia and the Grateful Dead, in the drug and rock counterculture in its San Francisco heyday (the loss of which Hunter Thompson laments in *Fear and Loathing*), "remains one of the great pieces of Sixties reportage" and "is a tour de force of subtle moral commentary" (385).

Miller, Stephen Paul. *The Seventies Now: Culture as Surveillance*. Durham: Duke University Press, 1999. Miller locates the defeat of the idealistic, broad-based, grassroots, egalitarian democratic goals associated with sixties activism in the seventies turn inward, which he associates particularly with the current culture of total surveillance, both external and internal, through a variety of governmental and cultural institutions, including the pervasive self-scrutiny enforced by dominant consumer culture.

Patterson, James T. *Grand Expectations: The United States, 1945–1974*. New York: Oxford University Press, 1996. One of the most important and useful recent histories of post–World War II America, focusing on the rising, and unprecedentedly fulfilled, expectations that enabled and largely produced the utopian radical movements of the sixties. In nearly 800 pages, with a wealth of detail and incisive analysis, Patterson moves steadily toward the defeat of the sixties movements, particularly Civil Rights and the antiwar movements, by the backlashes they generated.

Powers, Thomas. *The War at Home: Vietnam and the American People, 1964–1968*. New York: Grossman Publishers, 1973. One of the most important of the early books on the antiwar movement, still impressive in its argument and documentation (as I note in chapter 12, it would be impossible to credit the hundreds and hundreds of books and essays on Vietnam; Powers's work stands out for me as one of the most effective and cogent of these, eloquent in its immediacy). Powers's thesis is that the antiwar movement was successful in ending America's involvement in the war, despite radicals' feelings of defeat and futility during the period Powers covers.

Reich, Charles A. *The Greening of America*. 1970. New York: Crown Publishers, 1995. One of the most influential popularizations of New Left and countercultural ideologies, particularly the hippie ideology of a "new consciousness," for the mass market of mainstream culture, marking the transition to the postmodernity into which these ideologies were absorbed.

Ross, Kristin. *May '68 and Its Afterlives*. Chicago: University of Chicago Press, 2002. Focusing on the conservative eighties revisionism of sixties radicalism in France, a radicalism which, as Ross emphasizes, was unique in its genuine unification of students and workers, and therefore in its genuine potential for revolutionary transformation, Ross argues that this genuine radical potential has been subsequently rewritten as an Americanized, or "Anglo-Saxonized," coopted, cultural liberation, a liberation primarily of depoliticized countercultural practices and consumerist desire, that suppresses not only the political radicalism of May '68 but also its true international dimension: the worldwide resistance to imperialism instantiated by resistance to the Vietnam War.

Rossinow, Douglas. *The Politics of Authenticity: Liberalism, Christianity and the New Left in America*. New York: Columbia University Press, 1998. Like Breines, Rossinow provides a wealth of material on grassroots New Left organizations, contrasting them to violent, flamboyant national organizations like SDS. But, unlike Breines, Rossinow is interested in nonviolent, moderate New Left organizations, committed to reform rather than revolution.

Roszak, Theodore. *The Making of a Counter Culture: Reflections on the Technocratic Society and Its Youthful Opposition.* 1969. Berkeley: University of California Press, 1995. Like Reich's *Greening of America*, Roszak's book popularized hippie and radical ideas for a mass-market, incipiently mainstream postmodern culture. Roszak's "counter culture" took hold and subsequently became the defining term uniting the various strands of hippie ideologies and practices.

Rowbotham, Sheila. *Promise of a Dream: Remembering the Sixties.* New York: Verso, 2001. In this avowedly, unashamedly pro-sixties memoir of her prefeminist life as a sixties radical in Britain, one of the most important founders, theorists, and historians of socialist second-wave feminism writes an encomium of sixties radicalism that tries to be urgent rather than merely nostalgic, insisting that sixties utopian visions were not naive, deluded, or self-indulgent but rather embodied a powerful dream that still holds promise for the future. Rowbotham provides a useful bibliography of sixties memoirs.

Sale, Kirkpatrick. *SDS.* New York: Random House, 1973. Considered the definitive history of SDS, Sale's book starts at the beginning, in 1960, and ends with the cataclysmic bombings and other Weatherman violence of 1970. Sale produces a gripping drama of the hopeful rise of a revitalized, democratic American left, followed by the tragic fall of an increasingly violent, deluded, narcissistic, pseudorevolutionary movement plunging into self-destruction. The book is filled with useful, informative, detailed information on every aspect of the organization.

Sayre, Nora. *Sixties Going on Seventies.* 1973. New Brunswick: Rutgers University Press, 1996. This wonderful collection of Nora Sayre's journalism from the sixties is largely sympathetic to the wide range of political and countercultural events she covers (she also does careful justice to the right-wing opposition). Each essay uses a particular event to reflect thoughtfully on the general issues raised by the politics and cultures of the sixties. The revised edition includes a new introduction and afterword. Despite her clear-eyed acknowledgment of the defeats and failures of the sixties movements, and the power of the right-wing opposition, Sayre generally finds the broad positive impact of cultural change wrought by the sixties more significant than its debacles.

Sayres, Sohnya, Anders Stephanson, Stanley Aronowitz, Fredric Jameson, eds. *The 60s without Apology.* Minneapolis: University of Minnesota Press, 1984. As its title indicates, this excellent, important collection, by a range of the most visible, influential American left cultural and political analysts, many of them, including the editors, associated with the journal *Social Text*, is written against the conservative backlashes of the eighties and is sympathetic to the political and cultural movements of the sixties and their legacies. The essays are not simplistically celebratory, however; they are carefully balanced in analyzing the strengths and weaknesses of sixties movements and are focused on historical specificity rather than polemics. A deep sense of the tragedy of the defeat of the sixties coexists with an analysis of the breadth and significance of its transformative impact and the extent to which sixties values and agendas survive into the present in altered forms.

Schulman, Bruce J. *The Seventies: The Great Shift in American Culture, Society, and Politics*. New York: Free Press, 2001. Schulman argues that the seventies marked the shift from democratic activism aimed at realizing a broad, public political vision toward a market-dominated, introverted individualism. Schulman locates in the seventies the critique of the decline of sixties activism common among many analysts who see the defeat of sixties political goals as aligned with consumer culture's cooptation of many countercultural "lifestyles," the individualist turn inward, and/or the rise of "identity politics."

Sullivan, James D. *On the Walls and in the Streets: American Poetry Broadsides from the 1960s*. Champaign: University of Illinois Press, 1997. Sullivan documents, through the extensive use of archives, the pervasiveness, impact, and importance of the cultural work done by ephemeral poetry broadsides in a range of sixties activism. Sullivan then traces the historical trajectory of these broadsides from the "street" to the archive, where they have become increasingly inaccessible to all but the wealthy collector and the academic cultural historian.

Swerdlow, Amy. *Women Strike for Peace: Traditional Motherhood and Radical Politics in the 1960s*. Chicago: University of Chicago Press, 1993. A powerful historical account of a previously disregarded, nearly buried precursor of second-wave feminism — a sixties antiwar group, the organization Women Strike for Peace, active against war in general and the Vietnam War in particular throughout the sixties. Swerdlow focuses particularly on the way WSP used traditional maternalist feminine rhetoric to enable housewives to become active in this radical antiwar movement.

Unger, Irwin, and Debi Unger, eds. *The Times Were a Changin': The Sixties Reader*. New York: Three Rivers Press, 1998. A thoughtful, useful anthology, ideal as a college text, of excerpts from a wide range of sixties writings, mostly political but also cultural, on the right as well as the left, divided into broad, important categories, with helpful, intelligent editorial introductions to each.

Whalen, Jack, and Richard Flacks. *Beyond the Barricades: The Sixties Generation Grows Up*. Philadelphia: Temple University Press, 1989. A very useful collection of interviews with former activists from the University of California at Santa Barbara. For the most part, at the time of the interviews (in the eighties) they still identified in some form with their sixties political beliefs and commitments.

Wyatt, David. *Out of the Sixties: Storytelling and the Vietnam Generation*. Cambridge: Cambridge University Press, 1993. Wyatt emphasizes the way in which each major cultural producer he discusses forged a unique individual subjectivity in the crucible of the Vietnam War. Wyatt covers many genres, tellingly refusing to differentiate between literary and popular culture, or between major and minor figures. He organizes two pairs and two groups of three artists in persuasive, sometimes surprising ways, around broad thematic categories: "Nostalgia" includes George Lucas and Bruce Springsteen; "Celebrity" includes Sam Shepard and Ann Beattie; "Family Romance" includes Sue Miller, Ethan Mordden, and Alice Walker; "Survival" includes Gregory Orr, Louise Glück, and Michael Herr.

Marianne DeKoven is a professor of English at Rutgers University. Her previous books include *Rich and Strange: Gender, History, Modernism; A Different Language: Gertrude Stein's Experimental Writing;* and the edited collection *Feminist Locations: Global and Local, Theory and Practice.*

Library of Congress Cataloging-in-Publication Data
DeKoven, Marianne.
Utopia limited : the sixties and the emergence
of the postmodern / Marianne DeKoven.
p. cm. — (Post-contemporary interventions)
Includes bibliographical references and index.
ISBN 0-8223-3280-9 (cloth : alk. paper)
ISBN 0-8223-3269-8 (pbk. : alk. paper)
1. Postmodernism — Social aspects. 2. Civilization, Modern —
1950– 3. Nineteen sixties. 4. Radicalism. 5. Counterculture.
6. Popular culture. I. Title. II. Series.
HM449.D39 2004   306 — dc22   2003022707